Torture and Peacebuilding in Indonesia

State-sponsored torture and peacebuilding encapsulate the essence of many of the current conflicts in Indonesia. Papua in particular provides a thought-provoking example of the intricacy and complexity of building peace amidst enduring conflict and violence.

This book examines the complex power relations that have constructed the gruesome picture of the fifty-year practice of torture in Papua, as well as the ongoing Papuan peacebuilding movements that resist the domineering power of the Indonesian state over Papuans. Conceptualising 'theatres of torture and peace', the book argues that torture in Papua is performed in public by the Indonesian state in order to communicate its policy of terror towards Papuans – it is not meant for extracting information, gaining confessions or exacting punishment. A Torture Dataset is provided, codifying evidence from a broad range of cases, collected through sensitive interviews. In examining the data, the author crafts a new, more holistic framework for analysing cases of torture and employs an interdisciplinary approach integrating three different theories: Foucault's theory of governmentality and sovereignty, Kristeva's theory of abjection and Metz's theory of *memoria passionis* (the memory of suffering).

The book successfully establishes a new understanding of torture as 'public theatre' and offers a new perspective of strengthening the existing Papuan peacebuilding framework of Papua Land of Peace. It will be of interest to academics working on Southeast Asian Studies, Peace and Conflict Studies, Transitional Justice, Peacebuilding, Human Rights and Anthropology of Violence.

Budi Hernawan is Lecturer at *Driyarkara* School of Philosophy in Jakarta, Indonesia. Prior to his academic career, the author worked as a human rights activist in the conflict area of Papua, Indonesia (1997–2009).

Routledge Contemporary Southeast Asia Series

80 **Religious Violence and Conciliation in Indonesia**
Christians and Muslims in the Moluccas
Sumanto Al Qurtuby

81 **Identity Politics and Elections in Malaysia and Indonesia**
Ethnic Engineering in Borneo
Karolina Prasad

82 **Rethinking Power Relations in Indonesia**
Transforming the Margins
Edited by Michaela Haug, Martin Rössler and Anna-Teresa Grumblies

83 **Indonesia and the Politics of Disaster**
Power and Representation in Indonesia's Mud Volcano
Phillip Drake

84 **Nation-Building and National Identity in Timor-Leste**
Michael Leach

85 **Visual Media in Indonesia**
Video Vanguard
Edwin Jurriëns

86 **Maritime Security and Indonesia**
Cooperation, Interests and Strategies
Senia Febrica

87 **The King and the Making of Modern Thailand**
Antonio L. Rappa

88 **Society in Contemporary Laos**
Capitalism, Habitus and Belief
Boike Rehbein

89 **Migrant Workers and ASEAN**
A Two Level State and Regional Analysis
Anisa Santoso

90 **The Political Economy of the Agri-Food system in Thailand**
Hegemony, Counter-Hegemony, and Co-Optation of Oppositions
Prapimphan Chiengkul

91 **Transforming Society**
Strategies for Social Development from Singapore, Asia and Around the World
Edited by Ngoh Tiong Tan

92 **Torture and Peacebuilding in Indonesia**
The Case of Papua
Budi Hernawan

Torture and Peacebuilding in Indonesia
The Case of Papua

Budi Hernawan

LONDON AND NEW YORK

First published 2018
by Routledge
2 Park Square, Milton Park, Abingdon, Oxon OX14 4RN

and by Routledge
711 Third Avenue, New York, NY 10017

Routledge is an imprint of the Taylor & Francis Group, an informa business

© 2018 Budi Hernawan

The right of Budi Hernawan to be identified as author of this work has been asserted by him in accordance with sections 77 and 78 of the Copyright, Designs and Patents Act 1988.

All rights reserved. No part of this book may be reprinted or reproduced or utilised in any form or by any electronic, mechanical, or other means, now known or hereafter invented, including photocopying and recording, or in any information storage or retrieval system, without permission in writing from the publishers.

Trademark notice: Product or corporate names may be trademarks or registered trademarks, and are used only for identification and explanation without intent to infringe.

British Library Cataloguing-in-Publication Data
A catalogue record for this book is available from the British Library

Library of Congress Cataloging-in-Publication Data
Names: Budi Hernawan, J., author.
Title: Torture and peacebuilding in Indonesia: the case of Papua / Budi Hernawan.
Description: New York: Routledge, 2017. | Series: Routledge contemporary Southeast Asia series; 92 | Includes bibliographical references and index.
Identifiers: LCCN 2017025251 | ISBN 9781138184961 (hbk) | ISBN 9781315644820 (ebk)
Subjects: LCSH: Torture–Indonesia–Papua.
Peace-building–Indonesia–Papua. | Papua (Indonesia)–Politics and government.
Classification: LCC HV8599.I5 B833 2017 | DDC 364.6/7099516–dc23
LC record available at https://lccn.loc.gov/2017025251

ISBN: 978-1-138-18496-1 (hbk)
ISBN: 978-1-315-64482-0 (ebk)

Typeset in Times New Roman
by Wearset Ltd, Boldon, Tyne and Wear

Printed and bound in Great Britain by
TJ International Ltd, Padstow, Cornwall

For my beloved Meylani Yo and Octo Mote

Contents

	List of illustrations	viii
	Acknowledgements	x
	List of abbreviations	xii
1	Locating torture in Papua	1
2	Reconstructing torture: sovereign power, abjection and *memoria passionis*	22
3	A genealogy of torture	49
4	The anatomy of torture	90
5	Theatre of torture	134
6	Theatre of peace: reimagining 'Papua Land of Peace'	177
7	Lenses on torture and peacebuilding	214
	Index	227

Illustrations

Figures

3.1	One of the dormitories used to intern DMP in Merauke left abandoned in 2010	59
3.2	A scar on the female body caused by a bombing in the Wamena area in 1977	62
3.3	The Morning Star flag raised side by side with the Indonesian national flag in Jayapura in 2000	69
3.4	The demonstration to 'hand back' *Otsus* at Papuan parliament house in July 2010	74
4.1	Survivors based on occupation	94
4.2	Survivors based on residence	95
4.3	Prosecution of torture survivors	96
4.4	Survivors based on ethnicity	98
4.5	Survivors based on gender	101
4.6	Torture against women	101
4.7	Torture against male survivors	102
4.8	Description of the torturers	107
4.9	Reasons for torture	112
4.10	Bruised Papuan students	113
4.11	The suspects were being held in a parade	113
4.12	Participants of the Third Papuan Congress rounded up by the Indonesian State Security Services	114
4.13	Regimes and torture	115
4.14	Locations of torture	118
4.15	Prosecution for the torturers	119
4.16	Who exposed torture in Papua?	121
5.1	Theatre of torture model	137
6.1	The architecture of Papua Land of Peace	178
6.2	Theatre of peacebuilding	192
6.3	A model of transformation from the theatre of torture to the theatre of peacebuilding	193
6.4	Pyramid of accountability	205

Illustrations   ix

Map

Map of Papua   xiv

Tables

4.1	List of Papuan highlander survivors	97
4.2	List of Papuan coastal survivors	98
4.3	Physical methods of torture	108
4.4	Psychological methods of torture	108
4.5	Deprivation of basic needs	108

Acknowledgements

Torture is not my favourite subject. It became part of my focus when I personally and professionally worked with torture victims in Papua and their caregivers to address this long-term practice. It is not an easy job to deal with this confronting subject but not an impossible mission either. Rather, it is always part of the ongoing struggle of Papuan civic movements in fighting for justice and dignity vis-à-vis the cycle of impunity, from which the movements have formulated the philosophical concept of 'Papua as a Land of Peace'. This slogan makes up the second element of the book.

Papuans are not alone. They work very closely with all kinds of interested parties who are committed to contributing to their cause, including lawyers, journalists, NGO activists, academics, Church leaders, politicians, foreign diplomats and international observers. As a result they are not voiceless, as many would call them. On the contrary, the Papuans have been outspoken in challenging the status quo at both national and international fora.

The book is deeply inspired by this joint struggle. It would not have existed had I not been part of the Papuan struggle for more than a decade. Therefore, this is only a modest recollection of a larger mosaic of what I call '*memoria passionis*' or the memory of suffering of Papuans. Many more stories have remained unknown for us until today.

I have been humbled to have been given unique opportunities to listen and learn a great deal from so many personal stories, not only from Papuans but also from Indonesian government officials, Papuan Church leaders and NGO workers, as well as national and international observers. Because of confidentiality agreements with them, I cannot name any of them in this book. But without them, this book would never have been written.

During the process of producing this manuscript, I owe so much to the vibrant and supportive environment of the School of Regulatory Institutions Network at the Australian National University where I completed the majority of this book as my doctoral thesis in 2013. The School generously granted me with a short fellowship in 2015 to turn the thesis into a book. Along the way, a number of colleagues and friends have continued to encourage me to finalise the manuscript, especially my former PhD supervisor John Braithwaite, Hilary Charlesworth, Martin Krygier, Jaap Timmer, Frank Brennan, Ulrich Dornberg,

Ahmad Suaedy, Indria Fernida, Mike Cookson, Chris Ballard, Belinda Lopez, Irwan Firdaus, Benny Giay and many others whom I cannot name one by one. In particular I thank the anonymous reviewers and Richard Chauvel for giving so much of his busy time to look into my manuscript and give me invaluable feedback. Last but not least, all mistakes are solely my responsibility.

Abbreviations

ALDP	*Aliansi Demokrasi untuk Papua* (Democratic Alliance for Papua)
AMP	*Aliansi Mahasiswa Papua* (Papua Students Alliance)
BIA	*Badan Intelijen ABRI* (Indonesian Military Intelligence)
BIN	*Badan Intelijen Nasional* (Indonesian National Intelligence Agency)
BPUPKI	*Badan Penyelidik Usaha-Usaha Persiapan Kemerdekaan Indonesia* (Preparatory Body for Indonesian Independence)
Brimob	*Korps Brigade Mobil* (Indonesian Police Mobile Brigade)
CAT	Convention Against Torture, and Other Cruel, Inhuman or Degrading Treatment or Punishment
CDA	Critical Discourse Analysis
DAP	*Dewan Adat Papua* (Papuan Customary Council)
DMP	*Dewan Musyawarah Pepera* (Consultative Council for Popular Consultation)
Elsham Papua	Institute for Human Rights Study and Advocacy (*Lembaga Studi dan Advokasi HAM*)
FOKER LSM Papua	*Forum Kerjasama LSM Papua* (an umbrella organisation of Papua NGOs)
GPK	groups that cause security threats (*Gerombolan Pengacau Keamanan*)
ICC	International Criminal Court
ICTR	International Criminal Tribunal for Rwanda
ICTY	International Criminal Tribunal for the Former Yugoslavia
KNPB	*Komite Nasional Papua Barat* (West Papua National Committee)
Kodam	*Komando Daerah Militer* (Regional Military Command)
Kodim	*Komando Distrik Militer* (District Command)
Komnas HAM	*Komisi Nasional Hak Asasi Manusia* (Indonesia's National Commission on Human Rights)

Abbreviations xiii

KontraS	*Komisi untuk Orang Hilang dan Tindak Kekerasan* (The Commission for the Disappeared and Victims of Violence)
Kopassus	*Komando Pasukan Khusus* (Army Special Forces)
Koramil	*Komando Rayon Militer* (Sub-district Command)
LIPI	*Lembaga Ilmu Pengetahuan Indonesia* (Indonesian Institute of Science)
merdeka	'independence', the terminology that encapsulates Papuan political aspirations for independence
MPR	*Majelis Permusyawaratan Rakyat* (People's Consultative Assembly)
MRP	*Majelis Rakyat Papua* (Papuan People's Council)
NKRI	*Negara Kesatuan Republik Indonesia* (Indonesian State Ideology of Territorial Integrity)
OPM	*Organisasi Papua Merdeka* (Papuan Freedom Movement)
Otsus	*Otonomi Khusus* (Special Autonomy for Papua)
PDP	*Presidium Dewan Papua* (Papuan Presidium Council)
Pepera	*Penentuan Pendapat Rakyat* (Popular Consultation)
PGGP	*Persekutuan Gereja-gereja di Papua* (Papuan Ecumenical Council of Churches)
Polri	*Polisi Republik Indonesia* (Indonesian Police)
PTSD	post-traumatic stress disorder
RPKAD	*Resimen Para Komando Angkatan Darat* (Army Para Commando Regiment)
SAL	Special Autonomy Law
SKP	*Sekretariat Keadilan dan Perdamaian* (Office for Justice and Peace of the Catholic Church in Papua)
TNI	*Tentara Nasional Indonesia* (Indonesian Military)
TPN	*Tentara Pembebasan Nasional* (The Armed Wing of Free Papua Organisation)
TPNG	Territory of Papua New Guinea
TRC	Truth and Reconciliation Commission
TRCP	Truth and Reconciliation Commission for Papua
ULMWP	United Liberation Movement for West Papua
UNHCR	United Nations High Commission for Refugees
UNTEA	United Nations Temporary Executive Administration

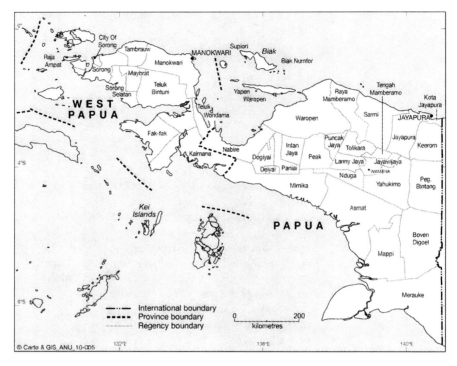

Map of Papua.
Source: The Australian National University, College of Asia and the Pacific, CartoGIS.

1 Locating torture in Papua

Confronting disturbing phenomena

In early 1998 during the first six months of my residence as a member of the Pastoral Team of St Joseph's Parish in Enarotali in the highlands of Paniai, Papua,[1] I confronted marks of torture presented to me by the locals. During private conversations with torture survivors, who were mostly our parishioners, I witnessed marks of torture left by the Indonesian military (*Tentara Nasional Indonesia*/TNI) on the bodies of Papuans in the highlands of Paniai. The survivors narrated their stories in whispering voices while showing swollen legs and hands, bruised eyes, or red scars all over their bodies. Although none of them were bleeding, it was obvious that they could not hide their pain, with terrified faces and tears in their eyes. In confidence, one by one they voluntarily told their experiences of being almost drowned in freezing water in a ditch, beaten up with a piece of wood or a rifle butt, humiliated in front of their family, or being forced to give some cash to the Indonesian soldiers in exchange for promises of protection from further harassment. All of this mistreatment happened because the TNI accused them of supporting a Free Papua Movement (*Organisasi Papua Merdeka*/OPM) based in Paniai led by the late TPN-OPM leader Tadeus Yogi by providing supplies and logistics.

I had carefully documented some ninety victims' stories before I found similar incidents in the neighbouring villages, especially around the Waghete area. When I put all the jigsaw pieces together, I found that patterns of mistreatment of the TNI against the Papuans were no coincidence. They indicated a high degree of intentionality and regularity. All incidences were reported by the three main Church leaders of Papua (Catholic, GKI and KINGMI) to the Commander of the Army in Jayapura in July 1998 under the title '*Hak-Hak Azasi Manusia di Wilayah Paniai dan Tigi, Irian Jaya*' (The Human Rights Situation in Paniai and Tigi, Irian Jaya). The Churches' report had an impact on the ground as the TNI groups were replaced by new ones which were reportedly more restrained. However, we never heard of any criminal investigation over the incidents and thus we cannot assume that the soldiers were ever held accountable, although by then Indonesia's *reformasi* was on the move.

My confrontation with torture incidents in Papua did not stop there. In 2010, torture footage from Papua was leaked on YouTube and grabbed international

2 Locating torture in Papua

attention (Hernawan 2016). The footage contains graphic images of two Papuan highlanders being tormented by a group of TNI in front of their community. As I will fully discuss this particular incident in Chapter 3, it will suffice to say at this stage that the event was not uncommon but the distribution of the footage through the internet was entirely novel. The setting of the incident was very much similar to that in Paniai. It targeted villagers/highlanders who were located in the remote area of Papua with limited access to public scrutiny. The way of responding to the incident and exposing the crime was entirely different from what the Papuan Church leaders did in 1998. The human rights activists called on the international public to act, which eventually led to prosecution of the perpetrators.

Finally, another confronting phenomenon occurred on 2 May 2016. At least 2,190 Papuans, men and women, members of *Komite Nasional Papua Barat* (*KNPB*/West Papua National Committee) were arrested by the Indonesian police in seven Indonesian cities, including Jayapura, Sorong, Merauke, Wamena, Semarang, Makassar and Manokwari.[2] They took to the street to protest what they called the beginning of Indonesian's occupation over then West New Guinea back in 1 May 1963. This was the day when the United Nations Temporary Executive Authority transferred the administration of West New Guinea to Indonesia's hands. The protesters believed that 1 May 1963 was when the Indonesian oppression against indigenous Papuans began by violating Papuan rights to self-determination. Therefore, they demanded a new referendum for Papuans to be held again today.

The incident constituted the largest police arrests in a single day throughout the history of Papua. The Indonesian police forced people to strip their clothes, including women, to half-naked. Most of them were beaten and left bare under the scorching sunlight in the front yard of the Mobile Police (BRIMOB) headquarters in Kotaraja. In the downtown Provincial Capital of Jayapura, the police harassed a journalist from a local online publication, *Suara Papua*, and denied access to other journalists to cover the event. Nevertheless, the police publicly demonstrated that they had no hesitation in deploying large state resources to suppress the demonstration, even if the public closely watched their action across eight locations in Indonesia. The police actions were captured by amateurs who instantly distributed images and videos through both the mainstream[3] and social media.

The KNPB demand was also a signpost for another related event held in London on the following day (3 May 2016). A group of concerned lawyers and parliamentarians under the name of International Parliamentarians for West Papua (IPWP) expressed their calls for reviewing the so-called Act of Free Choice, which had been held nearly fifty years ago in 1969 under the UN auspices (see Chapter 3), as it was considered legally flawed. Although the event received little attention from the British public, it drew various reactions from the Indonesian audience and Indonesian authorities, including a visit from the Indonesian Coordinating Minister for Security, Legal and Political Affairs, Luhut Panjaitan.

Locating torture in Papua 3

If we juxtapose the three cases, we will find that the victims experience the impact of torture in different ways. In the first two instances, although they were exposed by national and international media, torture broke the spirit of the victim villagers as they became traumatised, paralysed and silenced. On the contrary, the young Papuans became more resilient in pursuing their campaign for their agenda for a referendum. They continue expressing their political aspirations in public both inside and outside Papua. In the three settings, apart from victims and perpetrators, we should not forget the role of caregivers who work closely with victims, such as the Papuan churches, human rights organisations and the media. Caregivers play a central role in exposing the disturbing phenomenon of torture.

The dynamics of the three torture incidents encapsulate the essence of this book. That is, torture in Papua is a theatre. The acts of torture are not hidden in a secret chamber. Rather, they have been displayed in public by the Indonesian security apparatus to infuse terror into the Papuan society. In the last fifty years, the practice of public torture in Papua has become an integral part of how the Indonesian state governs Papua with complete impunity, and hence it constitutes what Foucault (1991) calls a symbolic torture. These stories, however, are only the tip of the iceberg of state-sponsored torture in Papua, as recorded in the Torture Dataset which I generated from the available archives in Papua.

But we might ask: why have the Papuans experienced the long-term practice of state-sponsored torture, so that this book only deals with Papua? I found at least three answers for this. First is the question of sovereignty. Papua is the only region in Indonesia that was incorporated into the Indonesian state through a lengthy post-colonial dispute over sovereignty. This historical background has consolidated a legacy of political resistance in Papua which began when President Sukarno launched *Trikora* (the Three Peoples' Commands) to date (see Chapter 3).

Second, Papua is the only region in Indonesia that confronts the issue of separatism. Following Indonesia's *reformasi* in 1998, Papua was one of the three areas, including Aceh and East Timor, to be granted greater autonomy to govern their own regional governments. These three regions experienced high levels of state violence, which have followed different paths towards resolution. East Timor was granted an opportunity by President B.J. Habibie to exercise the right to self-determination, in which the people of Timor-Leste eventually opted for independence in 1999. Aceh, in contrast, embarked upon peace negotiations that resulted in a peace accord, internationally known as MOU Helsinki, in 2005. Apart from the question of justice and accountability, which remains unresolved, the two regions have experienced considerable peace and reconciliation at the interpersonal and communal levels. Such a situation does not apply in Papua. It continues to confront the issue of separatism, which has met with an oppressive response from the Indonesian state.

The level of oppression becomes the final reason to select this location. As a consequence of ongoing resistance, Papua has become the most violent area of Indonesia that has experienced a high level of militarisation since it was administered by Indonesia in 1962. While militarisation was a common phenomenon

4   *Locating torture in Papua*

across Indonesia during Sukarno and Suharto's regimes, Papua's experiences with the intensity and duration of Indonesian militarisation seem incomparable with any other regions in Indonesia. The impact of long-term oppression with almost complete isolation from any attention from the outside world can be observed from the spread of many Papuan refugees not only in the Pacific, such as in PNG, Australia and Vanuatu, but even across continents such as in the US, the UK, the Netherlands and Sweden, although their numbers are actually not very high in international comparative terms.

Therefore, I ask four questions to examine this disturbing phenomenon:

a   *What are the* raison d'être *and structure of the politics of torture in Papua?*

This question is examined through the Torture Dataset to identify key patterns of torture and their dynamics that have constructed the politics of torture in Papua.

b   *What is the underlying logic that underpins this politics?*

This question will lead the investigation into the discussion of webs of powers to explicate the mechanisms and governing principles that construct, maintain and reproduce torture in the Papua setting.

c   *What are the differences between the ways in which the politics of torture is understood by perpetrators, torture survivors and spectators?*

This question aims at understanding internal and interpersonal dynamics of actors involved in torture. This investigation will analyse similar, different and contradicting arguments among different actors to explicate their motivations, justifications, postures and mindsets in relation to torture conceptualised as a 'theatre of torture'.

d   *What kind of peacebuilding will adequately come to grips with these logics and practices?*

Having identified the nature and underlying principles of torture in Papua, this investigation will analyse existing peacebuilding frameworks to integrate new elements identified from the Torture Dataset. This integration may help strengthen the existing frameworks, particularly the Papua Land of Peace framework, as a 'theatre of peacebuilding'.

Inspired by the hope of generating a new theory from a case study as advocated by some scholars (Flyvbjerg 2004; George and Bennett 2004), this book reflects upon a detailed examination of a complex case study of torture in a specific context to generate a 'paradigmatic case'. This term refers to 'cases that highlight more general characteristics of the societies in question' such as the Panopticon and European prisons for Foucault, the 'deep play' and the Balinese cockfight for Geertz as identified by Flyvbjerg (2004: 427).

Risks and challenges

I found that researching a politically sensitive topic, like torture, in a vulnerable society, like Papua, is a risky and challenging business. I confronted a number of challenges in collecting data. First, keeping records in Papua and across Indonesia remains a big issue. Very few government offices, NGO archives or university libraries in Papua keep records in an organised manner. I managed to access sixteen sources of data, twelve of which are public archives, whereas only four sources are personal archives. Moreover, only 17 per cent of the total cases come from the private archives. This means 83 per cent of the Torture Dataset does not come from secret reports, but has become public knowledge in Papua, Indonesia and even the international community, because it has been presented to relevant authorities and placed in the public domain.

Second, as written public documents, the torture files are not raw materials but they have been subjected to three different levels of scrutiny: first, by the reporting organisations and individual researchers that wrote those reports; second, by the Indonesian authorities that received the reports; and finally, by the public.

The challenge, however, is that the 'torture files' do not record all stories of Papuan oral traditions. For example, many recorded events post-1990 and very limited records on the events of 1960–1980 are publicly available, whereas other historical materials, including Indonesian military history (Cholil 1971; Osborne 1985; Pusat Sejarah dan Tradisi TNI 2000; TAPOL 1983), explain that Papua witnessed various intensive military operations during these periods. Such events might have resulted in a significant number of casualties, disappearances and torture victims as in any war and conflict situation. This links to another reality: that human rights NGOs did not exist in Papua at the time and the role of Papuan churches in monitoring and documenting cases of torture and other human rights cases was limited. In relation to the role of the Catholic Church in Papua, Steenbrink (2015) notes that the Catholic Church put social justice and human rights among its main agendas only at the end of the 1990s.

The issue of reliability also influenced my interviews. The long familiarity with the *habitus* of Papua has helped minimise erroneous judgements. Similarly, the difference discovery method I used has also helped me to examine layers of information and identities of participants. However, being absolutely certain that an oral history captures a truth remains problematic. This issue goes back to the previous point of 'truth in the making'.

Third, there is the issue of balanced representation. The focus on the narratives of victimhood is problematic. All sources place victim narratives at the centre of their reports. Narratives of perpetrators are only in the margin and very minimal voices of spectators are represented. The sources depict the characteristics of victims in great detail, not only name, ethnicity, sex, address and sometimes religious affiliation, but also their personal views. Such portrayals signify a clear perspective of many sources to advocate for the voice of victims because by definition, the reporting organisations are, with one exception, non-state

6 Locating torture in Papua

actors and thus represent non-state actors' voices. They have vigorously attempted to rewrite Papuan history from the perspective of the victims to reclaim the history that has been dominated by the Indonesian state narrative. Therefore, the narrative of survival plays a central role in researching indigenous people, as Linda Tuhiwai Smith (1999), a Maori researcher, argues.

Surprisingly, most reports do not record the age of the victims so this constitutes a weakness.

Although only Komnas HAM reports include an explanation of their methodology, none of them explains why they failed to codify age in their reports. As the reports focus on the narratives of victimhood, most of them do not record extensive details of legal representation either for the victims or for the perpetrators. Based on my previous engagement with Papua, such a reality may have resulted from the limited capacity among these organisations to document the events, and also from logistical issues that frequently impaired these organisations. The general information available from the reports is limited to basic identification of the perpetrators such as their institutional affiliations, and sometimes names or ranks. Similarly, the voices of spectators are less recorded. Often NGOs do not present their own interpretation in the reports so as to avoid any bias or conflicts of interest that may have jeopardised the credibility of their reports.

Fourth, is it really torture? The Indonesian equivalent of the word 'torture' is '*penyiksaan*'. Just as in the English vernacular context, the word '*penyiksaan*' is commonly used to refer to a wide range of painful practices and feelings. That is why in examining the torture files, different and often opposing interpretations of torture among survivors, perpetrators and spectators were often discovered. However, this common phenomenon poses a methodological question of selection criteria of torture cases that meet the working definition of torture in Chapter 1. While the torture files will identify general patterns of torture in Papua (see Chapter 4), any cases which do not exactly match the general patterns will not be eliminated. Instead, these cases will be juxtaposed and contrasted to the general patterns to refine the patterns.

Fifth, there is the issue of truth in the making. During my fieldwork, some respondents confessed that they did commit torture in Papua in the 1960s and in the 1980s but none of them related to any specific cases in the torture files. Moreover, there is no other material available to corroborate their stories. While their confessions confirm the long-term practice of torture in Papua, methodologically it is unlikely we will be able to triangulate these cases.

Similarly, in a number of places in Papua, many informants invited me to visit the graveyards of those who were remembered as victims of torture and killing by the Indonesian security forces. The informants and their communities keep their stories among themselves and very selectively share their memories with outsiders. This oral history signifies the vivid *memoria passionis* which I highly respect. However, it remains problematic to meet the rules of evidence. There is no other material, such as written documents or stories from the other side of this phenomenon, that might corroborate the story. To establish truth out of this evidence, one may have to undertake a forensic investigation which obviously goes beyond the scope and the capacity of this book. However, this information remains invaluable to be kept so that at any given time, when the Indonesian authority or any political willingness decides to come to terms with the past of Papua, these dots might be joined as a single storyline. In other words, the truth that can be best constructed is truth that is still in the making.

Finally, my identity is an issue. Although I spent more than a decade of working in Papua in the area of human rights, this long experience does not give a full guarantee of full access to any victim communities and Indonesian authorities. As Papua is heavily militarised, Indonesian military surveillance is inevitable. It closely monitored my research activities. The appointments with the high-ranking military and police officers help minimise these suspicions.

The suspicion, however, not only comes from the government side but also the Papuan side. I was expelled from the Iowara refugee camp in Papua New Guinea by a group of Papuan refugees since they believed I was working as an *intel* of the Indonesian security forces when I visited the camp on 13 July 2011. Other groups of Papuan refugees protected me and escorted me to a safe place in Kiunga.

Torture Dataset

In analysing my data collection, I use the triangulation method to unpack identifiable elements of the practice of torture in Papua to codify them into a Torture Dataset. By 'triangulation' I mean the combination of different methodologies to explain the same phenomenon (Denzin 1970: 26–7; Martyn 2008; Silverman 1985: 105–6). Further, Jick (1979) argues that this method aims at capturing a 'more complete, *holistic*, and contextual portrayal of the unit(s) under study'. Various methods, including archival methods, comparative methods, snowball techniques to secure interviews, difference discovery methods (see Burgess 1984; Minichiello *et al.* 1995) and ethnographic methods, have all been deployed in this book to investigate all the identifiable elements that have constructed torture as a formidable phenomenon in Papua.

Using triangulation, I analyse two major sources of my data: an aggregate of a large and rather disparate set of written documents and interviews, which I coded as 'the Torture Dataset'. These contain 431 codified cases of torture that have been collected from fifteen different sources covering the period of 1963–2010 as well as 214 face-to-face individual interviews and dozens of group interviews conducted during the research period of 2010, 2014 and 2015 inside Indonesia (Papua and Jakarta) as well as outside Indonesia, such as Australia, Papua New Guinea, the Netherlands, the United Kingdom and the United States. These periods, however, were grounded in my existing professional and personal experience of working as a Church worker and human rights defender for twelve years (1997–2009).

8 *Locating torture in Papua*

Written documents

The written documents are classified into two categories based on their origins: public and private sources. Private archives are not available in the public domain and I obtained permission from their owners to use these materials for this research. The public sources, on the other hand, are publicly available and have been submitted to the relevant authorities by the respective organisations on the list.

Archival methods have been deployed to select relevant materials from archives kept in NGO offices in Papua, the office of Komnas HAM, government offices in Papua, various human rights NGOs in Jakarta and the Institute of Dutch History in The Hague. They include historical archives and Indonesian government documents that contain policies on politics, security and society in Papua and Indonesia in general. These archives help provide the broader context of the Torture Dataset. In this context, a large aggregate of written documents has been selected including relevant government materials, internal documents of the Indonesian military and police force, national and international NGO reports, police statements, court decisions, OPM statements and documents, as well as foreign government records. All of these materials play an instrumental role in reconstructing the long-term practice of torture in Papua within the historical and political context of Indonesia. In this sense, Papua has been positioned in the framework of Indonesia rather than in isolation, to exhibit the power networks that have structured and underpinned the relations in which the practice of torture is located.

In alphabetical order the written sources are listed below.

The private sources:

1   Benny Giay's private archives
2   Budi Hernawan's private archives
3   Chris Ballard's private archives
4   Dirk Vlasblom's private archives.

The public sources are as follows:

1   Aliansi Demokrasi Papua (ALDP)
2   Elsham Papua
3   Jaringan Advokasi and Penegakan Hukum dan HAM
4   Justice, Peace and the Integrity of Creation (JPIC) of the GKI Synod of Papua
5   Komnas HAM
6   *Lembaga Bantuan Hukum* (LBH Papua/Legal Aid Papua)
7   *Lembaga Penelitian, Pengajian, dan Pengembangan Bantuan Hukum* (LP3BH/Institute of Research, Analysis and Development for Legal Aid) Manokwari
8   Papua NGOs coalition

Locating torture in Papua 9

9 *Sekretariat Keadilan dan Perdamaian* (SKP/Justice and Peace Office) Jayapura
10 *Sekretariat Keadilan dan Perdamaian* (SKP/Justice and Peace Office) Merauke
11 *Sekretariat Keadilan dan Perdamaian* (SKP/Justice and Peace Office) Timika
12 Dirk Vlasblom's report (2004).

The materials have been coded following four clusters of patterns, namely patterns of identity, description of torture, types of legal and non-legal response to torture, and types of political regime. This coding aims at identifying typologies that will be the basis for an analysis and interpretation in the following chapters. First, informed by the Kristevan notion of abjection, the patterns of identity, which include their name, age, gender, occupation, religious affiliation, ethnicity and residence, have been constructed to portray three main types of actors involved in the torture setting, namely survivors, perpetrators and spectators. Second, influenced by Rejali's (2007) analysis of the technology of torture to identify its nature, the description of torture identifies methods of torture used, locations of torture to determine whether a case was committed in a private or public space, place and time of torture, reasons of torture to determine rationalities of torture, and an element of detention to assess whether torture is part of a criminal investigation or simply a form of 'shock on-the-spot' punishment. Third, types of legal and non-legal response describe whether there is prosecution of the alleged torture perpetrator to measure the level of impunity involved in the torture practice; the extent of stigmatisation of survivors whenever they are prosecuted; or the responses from spectators who exposed the torture case. Finally, the coding covers the regime of political power to measure whether and how the torture practice has any association with the respective regime. The common assumption is that the more authoritarian a regime, the more likely it is that various forms of brutality are committed. This lens will be used to explore data from Papua to identify any correlations between different Indonesian political regimes and the intensity of the practice of torture.

While the coding maps the patterns of the torture phenomenon, it also helps identify gaps of information that are still missing. Fieldwork plays an instrumental role in filling gaps as much as possible.

Clarifying concepts of torture and peacebuilding

Torture signifies a wide range of painful feelings. In this book, torture, however, has a specific meaning. It broadly involves state authorities inflicting pain on the body for a particular purpose. While deliberate intention to inflict pain constitutes a central element in any definition of torture, scholars differ in drawing the boundaries of the phenomenon. Some scholars (Herman 1992; Scarry 1985) underscore the notion of inflicting pain that destroys personality and the world of meaning of the tortured. Others (Dershowitz 2002; Greenberg 2005; Nowak

10 Locating torture in Papua

2008; Rejali 2007) focus more on the purpose of torture as part of policing, including obtaining confessions and extracting intelligence. Others are more concerned with structural explanations that underpin torture such as state ideology (Maran 1989; Stanley 2008) and social policy (Crelinsten 2003; Foucault 1991; Green and Ward 2004; Kelman 2005), whereas others argue that torture derives from the paradigm of evil[4] as commonly applicable to genocide discourse (Card 2010).

Despite a wide variety of perspectives on torture, Kenny (2010: 10–18) identifies key elements that distinguish between torture and other forms of abuse. These include:

1 *pain*, which suggests an act of inflicting an injury on the body
2 *intentionality*, which underlines the notion of a deliberate act to inflict pain
3 *instrumentality*, which signifies that inflicting pain is not an end in itself but is a medium to achieve a purpose
4 *control*, which encapsulates asymmetric power relations between powerful torturers and the defenceless tortured. This approach is not explicit in underscoring the role of the state authorities, however, which is commonplace in the history of torture throughout the ages.

Scott (1940) has investigated the ways in which ancient Western civilisation invented crucifixion as the most sophisticated technology at the time. It was designed to inflict excruciating pain in a calculable and incremental way and to humiliate a culprit in front of the public until the culprit is ultimately destroyed physically, mentally and socially. However, such a method only applied to 'foreigners' and 'slaves' and did not apply to the category of 'citizens' of ancient Athens or the Roman Empire.

This discrimination is not only a legal technical matter but rather derives from a philosophical foundation. Scholarly analyses (DuBois 1991; Gagarin 1996; Mirhady 1996; Rejali 2007) of torture by the Ancient Greeks reveal that the concept of the citizenry correlates with human dignity in a sense that only citizens of Athens can possess the status of human dignity because they have *logos*, reason. This quality enables Athenian citizens to comply with the code of conduct of citizenship. This is the fundamental element for qualification as a citizen. In contrast, foreigners and slaves are unable to achieve the status of human beings simply because they do not have *logos*. Aristotle argued explicitly in his *Politics* that slaves are not fully human because they do not possess *logos*. Therefore, during any court hearings, when a master was under examination and refused to give a confession, his slave would be tortured to secure the truth. In this sense, torture is believed to be the only possible way to elicit the truth embedded in slaves' bodies which otherwise will not be discovered. This paradigm becomes the justification of the use of torture in the ancient Greek judicial system, which had significant influence on Western legal and philosophical systems until the eighteenth century. However, Roman philosophers, such as Seneca, Cicero and Tertullian, had already challenged any justification for

Locating torture in Papua 11

torture on the basis of arguments of justice and also of the futility of torture in establishing truth (Scott 1940: 134).

Over many centuries, Western civilisation used torture for a variety of reasons. The justification ranged from religious arguments such as that applied during the Church Inquisition in the thirteenth century (Maycock 1969) to judicial arguments that were common in continental Europe until the early nineteenth century (Langbein 1977; Spierenburg 1984). As opposed to Foucault, who assumes that the abolition of judicial torture was a contingent historical process, scholars (Garland 1990; Langbein 1977; Scott 1940; Spierenburg 1984) provide evidence that this was not a teleological development. They contend that the abolition of torture in Europe derived from a convergence of various factors. First, there was a shift of the rule of evidence in which confession of a suspect was no longer required to judge him or her. Rather, free judicial evaluation became the main rule of the game. It required the application of legal science and legal practice (Langbein 1977: 11). Second, in the eighteenth century in Europe, the shift from public execution to discipline occurred not as a spontaneous process, but was brought about by strong opposition to the practice and the changing mentality across continental Europe that forced monarchs to end the public display of expiring bodies. As a result, the monarchs found public execution no longer effective as the public increasingly and deliberately ignored it. Spierenburg describes this as 'a change in sensibilities' (Spierenburg 1984). Third, the emergence of the notion of humanity in the nineteenth century and eventually the emergence of universal human rights after World War II were important. The latter laid the ground for further formulation of an international legal instrument dealing with torture.

It took thirty-nine years after the UN Charter before seventy-eight UN member-states signed the UN Convention Against Torture and Other Cruel, Inhuman or Degrading Treatment or Punishment (CAT) on 10 December 1984. This document marked a new international commitment to eradicate the torture that had caused so much suffering across the globe. Article 1 of the 1984 UN Convention Against Torture defines torture as follows:

> The term 'torture' means any act by which severe pain or suffering, whether physical or mental, is intentionally inflicted on a person for such purposes as obtaining from him or a third person information or a confession, punishing him for an act he or a third person has committed or is suspected of having committed, or intimidating or coercing him or a third person, or for any reason based on discrimination of any kind, when such pain or suffering is inflicted by or at the instigation of or with the consent or acquiescence of a public official or other person acting in an official capacity. It does not include pain or suffering arising only from, inherent in or incidental to lawful sanctions.

Based on their personal involvement in formulating the CAT, Burgers and Danelius (1988) provide a compelling account revealing that this formulation is

12   Locating torture in Papua

a compromise of various interests which is not uncommon in an international diplomatic forum. Despite the adoption of a new international treaty, torture has not disappeared from state practices and policies in the twenty-first century, notwithstanding the fact that many autocracies have collapsed. On the contrary, states are more able to develop technologies and legal and moral justifications for torture. This reality poses a more intriguing question about how torture exists in democracies given that this type of regime assumes the rule of law and compliance with human rights standards as the basis of its architecture of power.

Despite the now near universal commitment[5] of UN member-states to eradicate torture, Rejali's study (2007) on the relationship between torture and democracy provides historical and empirical grounds to argue that the more democratic a society is, the more hidden and invisible torture technologies are. In this sense, torture does not disappear even though states have declared it legally and morally prohibited in absolute terms. Rejali identifies three chief arguments that explain this phenomenon: the National Security model, the Juridical model and the Civil Discipline model. In the first model, torture enters democracy through the argument of national security as the basis to target anyone, either citizens or foreigners, because of their political activities. In this context, national security overrides legal and moral constraints because it uses exceptionalism to justify its action.

For instance, the French war in Algeria was based on the premise that fighting those labelled 'terrorists' justified all means, including illegal and immoral ones. Today torture gains a new momentum driven by terrorist attacks on the US presence in various places around the world. This phenomenon has also encouraged scholars to debate the subject following the revelation of a systematic deployment of torture under the US war on terror (e.g. Levinson 2004; Schulz 2007; Wisnewski and Emerick 2009).

The second model, Rejali argues, explains the ways in which torture enters democracy through the legal system, which puts a high emphasis on the need for confession of the accused. While this approach was common from the European Middle Ages until the era leading to the formulation of the UN Convention Against Torture, we can still find this practice in many contexts today.

Finally, the third model explains the fact that torture links to democracy in that the public demands a civic order, which the state applying the rule of law is unable or unwilling to provide. Therefore, state security services resort to torture as disciplinary measures targeting those believed to be undermining public order. Just as Ancient Greeks' torture targeted non-citizens, modern torture targets quasi citizens, such as street children, illegal immigrants and vagrants, simply because they enjoy less legal protection from the state. Rejali concludes: 'What drives torture in these cases is neither war nor a permissive legal environment, but informal arrangements among police, residents, and businesses to shape the urban landscape' (Rejali 2007: 60).

While historians (Langbein 1977; Scott 1940) have examined the ancient roots of this technology, many justifications can be traced back to Jeremy Bentham's utilitarian argument for the use of torture in the eighteenth century

Locating torture in Papua 13

(Twining and Twining 1973). He argues that on the basis of protecting public interests, torture can be used to elicit intelligence information from a suspect. Inspired by Bentham's line of argument, Alan Dershowitz (2002: 142–3) has become one of the most prominent contemporary scholars who advocate the 'ticking bomb' argument. The argument is based on speculation of an emergency situation where a bomb timer is ticking and state authorities have a suspect at hand who refuses to give any information to locate the bomb. In such a situation, Dershowitz argues that torture warrants should be issued to authorise the use of torture by law enforcers to extract information from specific suspects who are believed to retain intelligence information that will save lives which otherwise will not be obtained.

Whereas this utilitarian perspective provides a useful analytical tool to examine the current torture phenomenon in the United States, it may not explain the whole reality of torture in Papua. The Papua Torture Dataset (analysed in Chapter 4) leads in a different direction of investigation where a utilitarian argument is not the main motif. This pattern needs a different set of analytical tools. Papua's experience will be revealed by the data in this book to suggest torture occurs as a public event in which anybody can watch it, experience it, hear it and sometimes even participate in it. In this setting, intelligence information or confession is not the ultimate goal of torture. It suggests state-sponsored action beyond utilitarian goals as the state communicates its unrestrained power through the body of the condemned. If this is the case, another school of thought on torture, particularly a Foucauldian approach, may be helpful in explaining the phenomenon of torture in Papua that is largely committed by the Indonesian security services in the public arena over a period of fifty years with almost complete impunity.

In his *Discipline and Punish*, Michel Foucault reflects on the phenomenon of the public execution of the regicide Robert Damiens in 1757 in front of the Parisian public. Foucault conceives torture as 'a policy of terror: to make everyone aware, through the body of the criminal, of the unrestrained presence of the sovereign. The public execution did not re-establish justice; it reactivated power' (Foucault 1991: 49). In Foucault's view, torture equals terror. It does not have anything to do with extracting information from a suspect or with obtaining a confession as we saw in the ticking bomb argument. Rather, the purpose is to demonstrate how powerful the sovereign is and how pervasive its influence is. Therefore, this type of torture has to meet three fundamental criteria: being (1) gradually painful, (2) scarring and (3) spectacular (Foucault 1991: 33–4).

The third element has a central role in ensuring that torture is performed as a public event and thus reaches the maximum terrifying impact on the social body. This is the ultimate goal of the public display of the injured body. It is not only to inflict agonising pain and suffering upon the individual, but more importantly to ensure also that the whole social body witnesses the power of the sovereign as inscribed over the body of the condemned. This message has to be very clear to the public to complete the torture ritual and to minimise any misinterpretation (Foucault 1991). Here we have a stark contrast to Bentham's school of thought: the Foucauldian view focuses more on the source of power and the ways in

14   *Locating torture in Papua*

which that power communicates to an audience. The body of the condemned itself is not the centre of attention. Rather, it is a medium necessary to convey a message from the holder of power. Therefore, the audience should not be distracted from the main goal of the torture ritual by only focusing on the atrocity being committed in front of their eyes; rather, they should fix on the shock and awe generated by the power being exhibited.

Drawing on this analytical framework, scholars have, for example, examined experiences of torture in Latin America during the dictatorship era of the 1970s–1980s, underscoring the elements of visibility, public display, conveying messages to the public and the 'power of gaze' (Graziano 1992; Rothenberg 2003). This Foucauldian term refers to the Panopticon, a system that exerts control over prisoners by infusing consciousness into their minds that they are being constantly watched by invisible eyes. All of these elements suggest the logic of communication. In the Papua situation, both types of torture – utilitarian and symbolic – overlap. This book seeks to assess which school of thought best explains the long-term experience of torture in Papua.

Peacebuilding

This book adopts a broad definition of 'peacebuilding'. The term was internationally consolidated by then-UN Secretary-General Boutros Boutros-Ghali (1992) when he presented *An Agenda for Peace*. In this document, he outlined how the United Nations and the international community could embark upon a new role in dealing with conflicts that takes several steps of engagement: *preventive diplomacy* as actions to confine conflict and prevent it from further escalation, *peacemaking* as actions to bring hostile parties to agreement, *peacekeeping* as the deployment of a UN security presence in the field and post-conflict *peacebuilding* as 'the construction of a new environment'. Under this framework, peacebuilding is conceived as a later stage after conflict is terminated.

Scholars disagree, however, on drawing the boundaries of peacebuilding so narrowly. Jeong (2005), for instance, understands peacebuilding as a 'rehabilitation process' and summarises a variety of scholarly work that holds a similar view. Other schools of thought conceive peacebuilding in a broader sense (Braithwaite, Charlesworth *et al.* 2010; Galtung 1969; Galtung, Jacobsen and Brand-Jacobsen 2002; Lederach 1997; Philpott and Powers 2010). In his *Building Peace*, John Paul Lederach, for instance, argues that while he concurs with the Secretary-General's proposal, he would not limit 'peacebuilding' strictly to a post-conflict stage. Instead he holds the view that

> Peacebuilding is understood as a comprehensive concept that encompasses, generates, and sustains the full array of processes, approaches, and stages needed to transform conflict toward more sustainable, peaceful relationships. The term thus involves a peace accord. Metaphorically, peace is seen not merely as a stage in time or a condition. It is a dynamic social construct.
>
> (Lederach 1997: 20)

Locating torture in Papua 15

Lederach understands peacebuilding as a *process*. It requires investments, materials, architectural design and coordination of labour to lay a solid foundation and detailed finish work as well as continuing maintenance. In a similar fashion, Braithwaite adopts a broad concept of peacebuilding in his *peacebuilding compared* project. He underscores Boutros-Ghali's term 'creation of a new environment' conducive for peace in his book on peacebuilding in Bouganville (Braithwaite *et al.* 2010: 3).

In this sense, the 'Papua Land of Peace' concept resembles Lederach's understanding of peacebuilding. Papua Land of Peace is a social construct that derived from the long process of reflection and engagement of Papua community leaders on negative realities that confront them, including violence, poverty, environmental degradation and discrimination, as well as their vision of building a new Papua that is characterised by justice, peace and reconciliation. The term Papua Land of Peace was first introduced in 2000 in Biak during the meeting of the Evangelical Christian Church in Papua (MacLeod 2015; Tebay 2009). This meeting was to come to terms with the 1998 tragedy of the 'Morning Star' flag raising in Biak. On 1 July 1998, a group of Biakers led by Filep Karma raised the 'Morning Star' flag, the long-banned Papuan symbol, on top of a water tank in the city of Biak. This action immediately drew serious attention not only from his own people, who immediately gathered around him, but also from the regent of Biak as well as the military. After negotiations with Karma and his supporters failed, the military launched a coordinated action against the protesters. ELSHAM (1999), a prominent local NGO, reported that many people disappeared, were arbitrarily detained, tortured and killed, and their bodies were dumped in the Pacific Ocean. Hundreds of people were marched to the harbour and forced to lay down on the wharf. Then, while they were forced to stare at the sun, they were beaten up, stomped on and stabbed with bayonets. Those who tried to flee the scene were shot dead. Others were taken to Indonesian navy ships and never returned (Elsham Irian Jaya 1999). Instead of subjugating Papuans under the reign of terror, this incident has fuelled the resurgence of the Papuan spirit of resistance. The shock and awe of the inscription of pain on the bodies of victims only galvanised the commitment to Papua Land of Peace.

However, it took time before Papua Land of Peace was formulated into a more substantial framework during a communal gathering organised by *Sekretariat Keadilan dan Perdamaian* in Jayapura in 2002 (Hernawan 2005; MacLeod 2012). While Chapter 7 will fully elaborate this discussion, this section aims at clarifying the genealogy of this term. Today Papua Land of Peace is not only the common denominator of a wide variety of peacebuilding movements in Papua; it has also become a common rallying concept that is widely used and sometimes overused. Some actors apply the term to projects of passive compliance in a way that peace can be narrowly interpreted as surrender, no opposition or no critical thinking. Other actors, such as the Papua Peace Network, have developed the Papua Land of Peace framework into a platform to consolidate a wide range of actors and ideologies among Papuans under a shared commitment to transformative 'dialogue' (Jaringan Damai Papua 2010; MacLeod 2012; Tebay 2009).

16 *Locating torture in Papua*

Caution about engagement with peacebuilding is not unique to Papua but is a common phenomenon across Indonesia. The analysis of Braithwaite and his companions explains that this phenomenon stems from the empirical experience of negative peace over a long period of time. Papua never experienced positive peace or 'commitment to peace and justice'. Braithwaite and his companions argue that

> positive peace requires the motivational posture of commitment among combatants, not just capitulation. It is enabled by a whole web of institutions that support positive peace: the rule of law, respect for human rights and social justice, reconciliation and market institutions that distribute opportunities widely.
>
> (Braithwaite, Braithwaite *et al.* 2010: 141)

This study suggests that Papua suffers from a long-term negative peace. That is, the war-like situation – composed of such things as killing, isolated fighting or kidnapping – never escapes Papua. It may undermine the capacity and trust of some key actors in the peacebuilding framework such as Papua Land of Peace. In the broader context of Indonesia, these scholars refer to 'anomie' as the context of this inability to build positive peace. Anomie signifies 'a breakdown of the regulatory order that secured institutional order (the rules of the game)' (Braithwaite, Braithwaite *et al.* 2010: 1). Anomie is one way of understanding scepticism over the effectiveness of the peacebuilding and non-violence approach. And Papua Land of Peace in this book is conceived as seeking to lay a foundation for transcending anomie and acquiescence in negative peace.

To deal with this doubt, Chenoweth and Stephan's quantitative study on the subject may shed new light (Chenoweth and Stephan 2011). Based on 323 case studies worldwide from 1900 to 2006, their research shows non-violent resistance was successful in 53 per cent of cases in comparison to only 26 per cent of armed struggles in achieving the objectives of a resistance movement. The core factors in the success of non-violent methods lie in their ability to cause the defection of state security forces to take the side of non-violent movements and to mobilise broad participation from a general public. In the Papuan context, however, causing the defection of the TNI to the Papuan cause would be very difficult. Another part of their argument is that non-violence attracts more sympathy and support from the international community than violence.

Chapter outline

The rest of the book is divided into six semi-autonomous chapters with different emphases to serve readers' different interests. This design allows us to pick any chapter that would interest us most and explore it in itself. Chapter 2 is heavily theoretical. It discusses a theoretical framework that provides tools to analyse and interpret the Dataset. It draws on Foucault's model of power and Kristeva's theory of abjection, and highlights some specific elements,

Locating torture in Papua 17

particularly subjectivity, agency, abjection and resistance. Further, it is inspired by Metz's theory of *memoria passionis* that explores the role of collective memory as a source of change and solidarity, and the role of narrative as a vehicle to mobilise support for change.

On the contrary, Chapter 3 is entirely descriptive and historical. It investigates the genealogy of torture within the history of Indonesia. It explores the evolution of the deployment of torture by the Indonesian security services to eradicate the Papuan resistance movement. Further, it reflects on how torture becomes a mode of governance deployed by the Indonesian state to govern Papua. It suggests that torture is not merely a technology of inflicting pain to gain confession or to collect intelligence from torture survivors. Rather, it represents broader and more structural mechanisms of coercive power.

Chapters 4 and 5 unpack findings from the field. Chapter 4 presents us with a quantitative analysis organised as the Torture Dataset. We will explore the patterns and logics of governmentality of torture that underpin the five-decade practice of state-sponsored brutality. Further, ten patterns of torture are identified, which lead to the conclusion that torture operates as a spectacle that functions as a mode of governance. It is concluded that torture in Papua constitutes the core tenet of the web of power relations in Papua that have constructed and governed Papua and Papuans as abject.

Using the model of 'theatre', as a qualitative analysis, Chapter 5 interprets stories collected from the fieldwork and structures them into three main themes, but also mixed themes and exceptions according to the sources of narratives. *Domination* is the organising theme of the narratives of perpetrators. *Suffering* is the predominant theme among torture survivors although it contains sub-themes of victim, warrior, agent and secondary victim. Finally, the narrative of *witnessing* by spectators varies in degrees of witness engagement. It ranges from caregivers as the most engaged third party, 'beneficiaries' as engaging but for their own benefit, observers who engage with a clear distance and finally bystanders who disengage. The chapter, therefore, explores the correlations and interdependence of all these types of actors and their internal dynamics that construct and reproduce the politics of torture in Papua.

Having analysed the nature and structure of the politics of torture throughout Chapters 3 to 5, Chapter 6 proposes a policy analysis that will address the problems of torture as a spectacle. Rooted in *memoria passionis*, we will explore the metamorphosis of the negative past beyond a tipping point to a positive future, from the theatre of torture to a theatre of peacebuilding. The discussion will outline the trajectory of *memoria passionis* that plays a decisive role in transcending the trinity of *domination-suffering-witnessing* into an alternative trinity of *revolt-healing-solidarity*. This is a path for strengthening the Papua Land of Peace framework, as one of the most comprehensive peacebuilding frameworks in Papua, by providing institutional grounds for it through a permanent truth and reconciliation commission for Papua (TRCP). It includes institutionalising *memoria passionis*, belief systems and social networks to strengthen the architecture of peacebuilding in a conflict and post-conflict situation.

18 *Locating torture in Papua*

Chapter 7 is the concluding chapter. It does not only summarise key findings and draw theoretical and practical implications of this research. Rather, it also reconnects us with a broader literature on torture that has constituted a resurgence of scholars' interest today. Further, this chapter will engage in policy-making discourse to contribute to practical paths to combat torture and thereby contribute to peacebuilding in the long run in Papua.

Notes

1 In the current daily life in Papua, Papuans call the Western part of New Guinea Island 'Papua', not 'West Papua' as is common in Western debates (e.g. Kirksey 2012; MacLeod 2012; Rutherford 2012; Webb-Gannon 2011). This reference may ignore the fact of the administrative divisions between the Province of Papua and the Province of West Papua. While 'Papua' refers to a geographical reference to the Western half of New Guinea Island, in this book Papua is conceived as an 'imagined community' (Anderson 2006) that shares a collective identity and memory, which are distinct from other nations. The current literature on Papua (Chauvel 2005; Cookson 2008; Drooglever 2009) investigates how Papuans developed their identity by being exposed to the formation of Indonesian nationalism. In the Dutch colonial era, Papua was a world of its own, inhabited by a wide variation of tribes living apart with a minimal sense of collective identity in comparison to the current social and political context under Indonesia (Drooglever 2009). Today, 'Papua' denotes a political identity that consolidates indigenous Papuans to assert their cultural boundaries in relation to other ethnicities (Chauvel 2005; Timmer 2005).
2 See 'Report of the Unlawful Arrests of 1,930 West Papuans Between 25 April and 3 May 2016' by the Jakarta Legal Institute.
3 Some international coverage includes www.aljazeera.com/news/2016/05/mass-arrests-reported-indonesia-restive-papua-160503085332325.html, accessed on 15 February 2017; http://eveningreport.nz/2016/05/02/hundreds-of-papuans-arrested-in-mass-indonesian-crackdown-say-reports, accessed on 15 February 2017.
4 It is Hannah Arendt who introduces the concept of evil from theology into social science to explain the unfathomable reality of the Holocaust. Further, Bernstein (2002) develops this framework under the term 'radical evil'. This has become a central unit of analysis in genocide studies.
5 To date, 161 member-states are parties of the UN Convention Against Torture, and Other Cruel, Inhuman or Degrading Treatment or Punishment (CAT). (https://treaties. un.org/doc/Publication/MTDSG/Volume%20I/Chapter%20IV/IV-9.en.pdf, accessed on 15 February 2017).

References

Anderson, B. 2006, *Imagined Communities: Reflections on the Origin and Spread of Nationalism*, Verso, London and New York.

Aristotle 2000, *The Politics*, Penguin, London.

Bernstein, R.J. 2002, *Radical Evil: A Philosophical Interrogation*, Polity Press, Cambridge.

Boutros-Ghali, B. 1992, *An Agenda for Peace: Preventive Diplomacy, Peacemaking and Peace-keeping*, United Nations, New York.

Braithwaite, J., Braithwaite, V., Cookson, M. and Dunn, L. 2010, *Anomie and Violence: Non-Truth and Reconciliation in Indonesian Peacebuilding*, ANU Press, Canberra.

Braithwaite, J., Charlesworth, H., Reddy, P. and Dunn, L. 2010, *Reconciliation and Architectures of Commitment: Sequencing Peace in Bougainville*, ANU E-Press, Canberra, A.C.T.

Burgers, J.H. and Danelius, H. 1988, *The United Nations Convention against Torture: A Handbook on The convention against Torture and Other Cruel, Inhuman or Degrading Treatment or Punishment*, Martinus Nijhoff Publishers, Dordrecht, Boston, London.

Burgess, R.G. 1984, *In the Field: An Introduction to Field Research*, Contemporary Social Research Series, George Allen & Unwin, London, Boston, Sydney.

Card, C. 2010, *Confronting Evils: Terrorism, Torture, Genocide*, Cambridge University Press, Cambridge.

Chauvel, R. 2005, *Constructing Papuan Nationalism: History, Ethnicity, and Adaptation*, vol. 14, East-West Center Policy Studies East-West Center, Washington, DC.

Chenoweth, E. and Stephan, M.J. 2011, *Why Civil Resistance Works: The Strategic Logic of Nonviolent Conflict*, Columbia University Press, New York.

Cholil, M. 1971, *Sedjarah Operasi: Pembebasan Irian Barat*, Pusat Sejarah ABRI, Jakarta.

Cookson, M.B. 2008, 'Batik Irian: Imprints of Indonesia Papua', PhD thesis, Australian National University.

Crelinsten, R.D. 2003, 'The World of Torture: A Constructed Reality', *Theoretical Criminology*, vol. 7, no. 3, pp. 293–318.

Denzin, N.K. 1970, *Research Act in Sociology: A Theoretical Introduction to Sociological Methods*, Butterworths, London.

Dershowitz, A.M. 2002, *Why Terrorism Works: Understanding the Threat, Responding to the Challenge*, Yale University Press, New Haven, CT and London.

Drooglever, P. 2009, *An Act of Free Choice, Decolonization and the Right to Self-Determination in West Papua*, One Word, Oxford.

DuBois, P. 1991, *Torture and Truth*, Routledge, New York.

Elsham Irian Jaya 1999, *Nama Tanpa Pusara, Pusara Tanpa Nama: Laporan Pelanggaran HAM di Biak, Irian Jaya*, Elsham Irian Jaya, Jayapura.

Flyvbjerg, B. 2004, 'Five misunderstandings about case-study research', in C. Seale, G. Gobo, J.F. Gubrium and D. Silverman (eds), *Qualitative Research Practice*, Sage, London and Thousand Oaks, CA, pp. 420–34.

Foucault, M. 1991, *Discipline and Punish: The Birth of Prison*, Penguin Books Ltd, London.

Gagarin, M. 1996, 'The Torture of Slaves in Athenian Law', *Classical Philology*, vol. 91, no. 1, pp. 1–18.

Galtung, J. 1969, 'Violence, Peace, and Peace Research', *Journal of Peace Research*, vol. 6, pp. 167–91.

Galtung, J., Jacobsen, C.G. and Brand-Jacobsen, K.F. 2002, *Searching for Peace: The Road to TRANSCEND*, Pluto Press, London and Sterling, VA.

Garland, D. 1990, *Punishment and Modern Society*, University of Chicago Press and Oxford University Press, Chicago, IL and Oxford.

George, A.L. and Bennett, A. 2004, *Case Studies and Theory Development in the Social Sciences*, MIT Press, Cambridge, MA and London.

Graziano, F. 1992, *Divine Violence, Spectacle, Psychosexuality, and Radical Christianity in the Argentine 'Dirty War'*, Westview Press, Boulder, CO, San Francisco, CA, Oxford.

Green, P. and Ward, T. 2004, *State Crime: Governments, Violence and Corruption*, Pluto Press, London and Sterling, VA.

20 *Locating torture in Papua*

Greenberg, K.J. and Joshua L. Dratel (ed.) 2005, *The Torture Papers: The Road to Abu Ghraib*, Cambridge University Press, New York.

Herman, J.L. 1992, *Trauma and Recovery*, Basic Books, New York.

Hernawan, B. (ed.) 2005, *Papua, Land of Peace: Addressing Conflict, Building Peace in West Papua* Office for Justice and Peace, Catholic Diocese of Jayapura, Jayapura.

Hernawan, B. (ed.) 2016, 'Torture as Theatre in Papua', *International Journal of Conflict and Violence*, vol. 10, no. 1, pp. 77–92.

Jaringan Damai Papua 2010, *Tawaran Konsep Dialog Jakarta-Papua*, Jaringan Damai Papua, Jayapura.

Jeong, H.-W. 2005, *Peacebuilding in Postconflict Societies: Strategies and Process*, Lynne Rienner Publishers, Boulder, CO and London.

Jick, T.D. 1979, 'Mixing Qualitative and Quantitative Methods: Triangulation in Action', *Administrative Science Quarterly*, vol. 24, no. 4, pp. 602–11.

Kelman, H.C. 2005, 'The Policy Context of Torture: A Social-Psychological Analysis', *International Review of the Red Cross*, vol. 87, no. 587, pp. 123–34.

Kenny, P.D. 2010, 'What is Torture?', *Polity*, vol. 42, no. 2, pp. 131–55.

Kirksey, S.E. 2012, *Freedom in Entangled Worlds: West Papua and the Architecture of Global Power*, Duke University Press, Durham, NC and London.

Langbein, J. 1977, *Torture and the Law of Proof, Europe and England in Ancien Régime*, University of Chicago Press, Chicago, IL and London.

Lederach, J.P. 1997, *Building Peace: Sustainable Reconciliation in Divided Societies*, United States Institute of Peace, Washington, DC.

Levinson, S. (ed.) 2004, *Torture: A Collection*, Oxford University Press, Oxford.

MacLeod, J. 2012, 'Civil Resistance in West Papua (Perlawanan tanpa kekerasan di Tanah Papua)', PhD thesis, University of Queensland.

MacLeod, J. 2015, *Merdeka and The Morning Star: Civil Resistance in West Papua*, University of Queensland Press, St Lucia, Queensland.

Maran, R. 1989, *Torture: The Role of Ideology in the French-Algerian War*, Praeger, New York.

Martyn, H. 2008, 'Troubles with Triangulation', in M.M. Bergman (ed.), *Advances in Mixed Methods Research*, Sage, London, vol. 22–36.

Maycock, A.L. 1969, *The Inquisition from its Establishment to the Great Schism: An Introductory Study, with an Introd. by Ronald Knox*, Reprint of the 1927 London ed. Bibliographical footnotes edn, Harper & Row, New York.

Minichiello, V., Aroni, R., Timewell, E. and Alexander, L. 1995, *In-Depth Interviewing: Principles, Techniques, Analysis*, 2nd edn, Longman, Sydney.

Mirhady, D.C. 1996, 'Torture and Rhetoric in Athens', *The Journal of Hellenic Studies*, vol. 116, pp. 119–31.

Nowak, M. 2008, *The United Nations Convention Against Torture: A Commentary*, Oxford University Press, Oxford and New York.

Osborne, R. 1985, *Indonesia's Secret War*, Allen & Unwin, Sydney, London, Boston.

Philpott, D. and Powers, G.F. (eds) 2010, *Strategies of Peace: Transforming Conflict in a Violent World*, Oxford University Press, Oxford.

Pusat Sejarah dan Tradisi TNI 2000, *Sejarah TNI Jilid I (1945–1949)*, vol. 1, 5 vols, Sejarah TNI, Markas Besar Tentara Nasional Indonesia Pusat Sejarah dan Tradisi TNI, Jakarta.

Rejali, D. 2007, *Torture and Democracy*, Princeton University Press, Princeton, NJ and Oxford.

Rothenberg, D. 2003, '"What We Have Seen Has Been Terrible": Public Presentational Torture and the Communicative Logic of State Terror', *Albany Law Review*, vol. 67, no. 2, pp. 465–99.

Rutherford, D. 2012, *Laughing at Leviathan: Sovereignty and Audience in West Papua*, University of Chicago Press, Chicago, IL and London.

Scarry, E. 1985, *The Body in Pain: The Making and Unmaking of the World*, Oxford University Press, New York, Oxford.

Schulz, W.F. (ed.) 2007, *The Phenomenon of Torture*, University of Pennsylvania Press, Philadelphia, PA.

Scott, G.R. 1940, *The History of Torture throughout the Ages*, Kegan Paul, London and New York.

Silverman, D. 1985, *Qualitative Methodology and Sociology: Describing the Social World*, Gower Pub. Co., Aldershot, Hampshire, Brookfield, VT.

Smith, L.T. 1999, *Decolonizing Methodologies, Research and Indigenous Peoples*, Zed Books Ltd. and University of Otago Press, London, New York, Dunedin.

Spierenburg, P.C. 1984, *The Spectacle of Suffering: Executions and the Evolution of Repression: From a Preindustrial Metropolis to the European Experience*, Cambridge University Press, Cambridge, New York.

Stanley, E. 2008, *Torture, Truth and Justice: The Case of Timor-Leste*, Routledge, London and New York.

Steenbrink, K. 2015, *Catholics in Independent Indonesia, 1945–2010*, Brill, Leiden.

TAPOL 1983, *West Papua: The Obliteration of a People*, Tapol, London.

Tebay, N. 2009, *Dialog Jakarta-Papua: Sebuah Perspektif Papua*, 1st edn, Sekretariat Keadilan dan Perdamaian, Keuskupan Jayapura, Jayapura.

Timmer, J. 2005, 'Decentralisation and Elite Politics in Papua', *SSGM Discussion Paper Series*, vol. 2005/2006.

Twining, W.L. and Twining, P.E. 1973, 'Bentham on Torture', *Northern Ireland Legal Quarterly*, vol. 24, no. 3, pp. 305–56.

Vlasblom, D. 2004, *Papoea: een Geschiedenis*, Mets & Schilt, Uitgevers.

Webb-Gannon, C. 2011, 'Birds of a Feather: Conflict and Unity within West Papua's Independence Movement ', PhD thesis, University of Sydney.

Wisnewski, J.J. and Emerick, R.D. 2009, *The Ethics of Torture*, Continuum, London/New York.

2 Reconstructing torture
Sovereign power, abjection and *memoria passionis*

Introduction

One perspective on torture introduced in Chapter 1 suggests it has a symbolic role: about ways of exercising and displaying the sovereign power of the Indonesian state over Papuans. Hence the practice indicates some degree of governance. This chapter builds on this discussion through introducing three different theories that will help explain the dynamics of torture in Papua: the idea of sovereign power as developed by Michel Foucault, the theory of abjection as coined by Julia Kristeva and the theory of *memoria passionis* (collective memory of suffering) developed by Johann Baptist Metz. The purpose of using these different lenses is that all three provide useful insights into parts of the picture we need to unveil. This also means that a single perspective is too limited to reveal all layers of the governance at work in the practice of torture in Papua. By piecing them together I hope to develop a more holistic view on the governance of torture in Papua. However, as this book does not address the three theories as its main preoccupation, it will not discuss their every detail. Rather, it will selectively employ insights from each theory to explore the empirical findings of torture in Papua. Further, the findings (see Chapters 4 and 5) will eventually illuminate the validity claims of the three theories to further clarify their contribution and limits for the book.

Below I will highlight governance mechanisms at the macro (society and polity) as well as the micro (psychic and individual) levels. The value of bringing together these levels will be illustrated in the following chapters in which I will examine the historical context and contemporary practices of torture in Papua. The groundwork for the analytical framework will be laid in this chapter. I will specifically discuss key elements of the theories that facilitate the development of a theoretical framework.

The chapter begins with a discussion of the historical context, which provides us with a background to the three theories before moving on to a discussion of Foucault's theory of power. This theory is a useful tool for examining the power relations revealed by the practice of Papuan torture. Imagined as a network, these power relations can be conceptualised as a form a 'government', defined as 'any more or less calculated and rational activity, undertaken by a multiplicity of

Reconstructing torture 23

authorities and agencies' (Dean 2010: 18). This discussion will illuminate three key elements in the governance of Papua over the last half-century: sovereign power, resistance and torture.

The ideas of Foucault are useful for examining torture in the context of power relations between macro-structural and micro-individual levels. However, torture is also a form of violence with deep impacts on the internal psychological functions of an individual. In this sense, Foucault's theory is limited since it only focuses on the dynamics of power at both macro and micro levels without scrutinising the psychological processes of individuals as a result of torture. Thus, this chapter will introduce the ideas of Kristeva who explores how torture affects the level of individuals' psyches. Encapsulated in the notion of 'abjection', Kristeva's theory helps us understand the contradictory characterisation of Papuans – and Papua as a collective – within and by the Indonesian state. While on the one hand, Papuans have been excluded and marginalised from the nation-state of Indonesia, they have been claimed and colonised to constitute Indonesia as a post-colonial state. The effect of these notions of ambiguity and ambivalence on the Papuan psyche will be further explored in relation to Kristeva's concept of 'revolt'. By discussing revolt, Kristeva manages to outline the idea of social transformation by which she means the renewal of all aspects of a society, not only the political aspect.

Still missing in our holistic picture is the level of society, and particularly spiritual solidarity in societies, featuring in between the individual level and the levels of governance outlined by Foucault. Metz's theory of *memoria passionis* will fill this gap. Given the term *memoria passionis* has become vernacular[1] in the Papuan context (Giay 2000; Glazebrook 2008; Hernawan and van den Broek 1999), his theory will be discussed to explore the convergence of the social recollection of Papuans – the oppressed – about their suffering as the source of emancipatory energy for Papuans to craft a new future that is free from oppression.

Confronting the networked governance of autocrats and resistance

Although they represent different scholarly fields and have developed along varying intellectual paths, Foucault (1926–1984), Kristeva (born in 1941) and Metz (born in 1929) were contemporaries who shared a common concern. Their work reflected on spectres of tyranny that haunted Europe in the first half of the twentieth century. While Foucault and Kristeva were strongly influenced by resistance movements in Europe, they reflected on the foregoing phenomena of Fascism, Stalinism and Nazism through the 1960s French intellectual revolution (Foucault 1982: 779; McAfee 2004: 5–6). Metz's thoughts, on the other hand, are rooted in the German intellectual tradition and grappled with the catastrophic reality of Auschwitz (Schuster and Boschert-Kimming 1999: 14–15).

The three theorists were all preoccupied with questions regarding subject formation and power in human history. In stark contrast with the Cartesian subject,[2] which assumes autonomy and authority over the objective world, these theorists

24 *Reconstructing torture*

characterise the subject as more ambiguous and fluid in relation to power. Foucault and Kristeva, in particular, share a common approach in that they explore the bodily visible impacts of power relations on the human body, not merely their symbolic and abstract significance. However, their starting points for reflection, their methods of analysis and their analytical foci diverge when it comes to the subject in history and their understandings of the nature of power. In contrast to Foucault and Kristeva, Metz is more preoccupied with the catastrophic impacts of totalitarian power, such as its capacity to destroy human lives, as well as its limits. In examining the role of collective memory by which humanity recovers and rebuilds its history, Metz discovers the subject's capacity to resist totalitarianism. To relate to these distinctions in the holistic model necessary for understanding torture in Papua, the relations between the three theorists will be discussed first. This will be followed by an explanation of how the ideas of Foucault, Kristeva and Metz can be combined into a new theoretical framework for understanding the dynamics of torture in Papua.

First of all, it is necessary to determine in which part of the holistic model the three theories fit and what their contribution means in terms of power, agency and social transformation. In relation to power, Foucault is more concerned with the question of *how* power works rather than of *who* wields it. For Foucault, the practices, techniques and strategies of power are considered much more important for an understanding of modern politics than the identity of the rulers. Hence, he uses the term 'art of government' to encapsulate his argument that power governs – and in turn, produces – a subject, rather than the other way around (Foucault 1982: 778). In interpreting Foucault's notion of governmentality, Mitchell Dean highlights the core element as 'different rationalities' or different ways of reasoning. Governmentality constitutes an interaction between 'different types of agency and authority and different types of thought' (Dean 2010: 27). Therefore, in Dean's interpretation, the analysis of governmentality centres on the interplay between thought and its manifestations in practice.

Independently from Foucault, Metz also focuses on the question of power and its concrete, tangible, visible and particularly catastrophic impacts on humanity. His work centres on subjectivity and agency operating within a society and polity. He alleged that German – specifically German Christian – society and its Christian faith and theology were silent on the issue of Auschwitz (Metz 1998: 7). While Foucault remains indecisive on whether resistance can eventually change or transform any power relations, Metz reveals the ways a society can explore its social memory to resist totalitarianism. In this sense, Metz's analysis is beneficial as he emphasises the role of agency in generating change. His direct contact with Auschwitz survivors provides him with an empirical grounding for this view. Metz was inspired by those who sacrificed their lives inside and those who survived Auschwitz. Both the martyrdom of Dietrich Bonhoeffer, a Protestant German theologian, who was hanged in the Flossenbürg concentration camp, and the testimony of Elie Wiesel,[3] a prominent Jewish writer and a Nobel peace laureate, who survived the Holocaust, influenced Metz's theology.

Reconstructing torture 25

Freudian and Lacanian psychoanalysis, on the other hand, inspired Kristeva. Her focus is on the construction of the subject that emerges from an act of disavowing Mother. During the creation of the subject in the Mother's womb, Kristeva argues, the subject generates its subjectivity by separating and disavowing Mother. Hence drawing clear boundaries between the subject and Mother marks the emergence of the subject. By this framing, Kristeva locates the question of the subject at the micro level, the psyche, and at the earliest stage of human development. In parallel to Foucault's view that the subject is constructed by power relations, Kristeva also writes, in *Desire in Language* (Oliver 2002a), of the notion of the 'subject-in-process', meaning that the identity of the subject is always in the making, open to change and intervention. These features of the subject – its mutability and openness to intervention – signify its fragility as well as its ambiguity. In contrast to the Cartesian notion of an autonomous subject, Iris Young (1986: 11) interprets Kristeva to be implying that 'the subject is not a unity'. Rather, it is 'always in a constant process of oscillation between instability and stability or negativity and stasis. The subject is continually being constituted within this oscillation between conscious and unconscious as an open system, subject to analysis' (Oliver 2002a: 18). Like Foucault and Metz, Kristeva reveals the vulnerability of the subject, although the context in which she does so is completely different. While Foucault's analysis deals with the macrostructural level, Kristeva examines the subject at the micro-individual level.

This background provides a context in which we can situate the three theories in a historical perspective. More importantly, if we juxtapose European tyranny and Papuan torture, the theories will aid in making sense of the interplay between the kind of networked governance of repression and resistance that characterises the context of torture in Papua. The following sections will further elaborate the most relevant elements of the three theories to disclose the nature of torture in Papua as a mode of governance.

Foucault's model of power

Foucault claimed to build his philosophy as an antinomy to grand theories, particularly Marxism and critical theory, in that he refused any claim to universalism and systematic theory (Poster 1984). In *Power/Knowledge* (1980), he expressed his aim, 'to invert it [theory], to give due weight ... to the fact of domination, to expose both its latent nature and its brutality' and 'the multiple forms of subjugation' (Foucault 1980: 95–6). Mark Poster argues that the major accomplishment of Foucault's project to overcome Marxism lies in the fact that he did not need metaphysical baggage to explain mechanisms of domination. In contrast to Marxism, which believes in 'universal emancipation' and 'the proletarian social revolution' as metaphysical objectives, Foucault's analysis of domination focuses on prisons and sexuality as historical phenomena (Poster 1984: 159).

Although Foucault was at odds with much of the critical theory of the time,[4] Hindess argues that he shared a similar obsession with two closely related issues: 'one concerning processes of rationalization in Western societies during the

26 *Reconstructing torture*

modern period, and the other concerning the ideal of the person as an autonomous moral agent' (Hindess 1996: 147). Whereas much Western thought elevated the idea of progress embedded in modernisation, Foucault was suspicious of this. For him, the promise of modernity encapsulated in the term 'civilisation' generates madness or insanity at the macro-structural level. Power relations have led to social exclusion and confinement of those who are considered insane by society (Dreyfus and Rabinow 1982).[5] Foucault believes that even in a liberal democracy these forms of power relations are not entirely immune from authoritarianism. Rather, an element of authoritarianism remains embedded in a liberal democracy in the forms of racism and war (Dean 2002).

In a similar fashion, Foucault and much of Western thought proffer nearly oppositional understandings of the status of the subject (see McCarthy 1990). Many members of the Frankfurt School, for instance, believe that persons can be autonomous and free subjects and thus assume full control over their will (e.g. Marcuse, Habermas etc.). So consent becomes crucial, as the exercise of power depends on whether a subject gives or withholds consent. Once the power gains consent, it assumes obedience from individuals to policies that the power formulates. That is why emancipation has become a key idea to liberate society and individuals from the negative effects of power and domination. In contrast, Foucault's framing does not embrace this kind of consent, a conscious will to surrender to power or to resist power. In Foucault's view, a subject is situated in a web of power relations which are part of the human conditions and social dynamics. These relations include the relationship to the sovereign. Foucault believes power is everywhere in the form of domination. By domination, he refers to multiple forms of relations of subjugation, not just one person, and those forms are 'perpetually asymmetrical and allow an extremely limited margin of freedom' (Foucault 2003a: 35). In this framework, consent becomes irrelevant, because power is exercised regardless.

In discussing domination, Foucault acknowledges agency exists, and more importantly, is capable of confronting domination by way of resistance. Foucault recognises agency, but not autonomy. That is to say, a person can resist domination notwithstanding that she can never act independently, autonomously, from its effect. Agency is more important for Foucault than the subject. Unlike the subject which is entangled in a web of domination, agency refers to the capacity to resist and evade technologies of power. The ethic of care for the self is thus very important, because it provides us with types of resistance that can sustain 'liberation'. Foucault believes that 'a person who took proper care of himself would, by the same token, be able to conduct himself in relation to others and for others' (Foucault 2003a: 30). Kevin Thompson interprets the notion of Foucault's ethics in the framework of self-control and self-management rather than external relations of the self with the world. The ethics is meant 'to refuse the given, to uncover what is possible, and to have the courage to master one's own life' (Thompson 2003: 133). As will be discussed in more detail later in the chapter, Foucault's emphasis on agency rather than the subject finds parallels in Kristeva's notion of revolt and Metz's concept of *memoria passionis*.

Reconstructing torture 27

The theme of resistance requires analysis here as it provides a useful means to expose Papuan agency through the capacity to resist. In his later work, Foucault emphasised that the exercise of power assumes some degree of freedom on the part of subjects (Foucault 1982: 790). This freedom suggests that power and resistance as well as evasion are inescapable, as they are part of human nature (Hindess 1996: 150). Consequently, there is no contradiction between the ubiquity of power and the care of the self, because subjects have some degree of freedom that allows room for them to look after themselves. Thus the subject is the result of power, which operates through the body. With this insight in mind, we will interrogate the extent to which Papuans are able to experience agency given the domination of the Indonesian state over the last half-century. This raises the question of how Papuans can escape from the technology of power in the form of torture.[6]

The discussion of power and agency already outlines the point of departure of Foucault's theory of power. In contrast to the then-mainstream Western thought about power as capacity and 'rights' (e.g. natural or legal), Foucault defines power in terms of technologies and strategies. He further specifies and develops his notion of power in many of his key works, sometimes in seemingly conflicting ways.

Power relations, for Foucault, are not dependent upon the subject's agency (Taylor 1992: 83). Rather, it is about what he refers to as 'conduct of conducts' [sic] (Dreyfus and Rabinow 1982: 220–1) that generates the subject. That is to say, power operates independently as a network that governs and even controls 'conducts' [sic] of agency. The term 'governmentality' encapsulates the dynamics between technologies of power and various forms of rationalities that underpin the technologies of governing behaviours of multiple actors and authorities simultaneously. The complex interactions of multiple actors, plural actions and heterogeneous authorities characterise the model of power relations advocated by Foucault (Foucault 2003b). He explains that governmentality consists of three interrelated elements: (1) assemblages of institutions, procedures and strategies to exercise power which target populations, (2) the tendency of power to generate a specific governmental apparatus and knowledge and (3) the transformation of the old state model of the Middle Ages into the administrative state and eventually the governmentalised state (Foucault 2003b: 244). These three elements illustrate that in Foucault's view, governmentality is not only dynamic in nature but more importantly, purposive and transformative. It targets populations, develops and establishes technologies of control, and transforms a society.

Dean breaks down Foucault's explanation of governmentality. He identifies four key questions that the concept of governmentality raises for our analyses: (1) '*what* we seek to govern' which examines the purpose of governing, (2) '*how* we govern' which analyses technologies and strategies of government, (3) '*who* we are when we are governed' which deals with the question of identity of the governed, and finally, (4) '*why* we govern' which delves into the rationale of government (Dean 2010: 26–7). In contrast to historians and social thinkers who pursue theoretical dimensions of thought, Dean concludes, 'studies of

28 *Reconstructing torture*

governmentality are more concerned with how thought operates within our organized ways of doing things, our *regimes of practices [sic]*, and with its ambitions and effects' (Dean 2010: 27). This way of thinking offers a useful framework to analyse the Papuan experience of torture because it goes beyond a single unit of analysis. The framework prompts us to consider (1) the purpose of the practice of torture as a mode of governance, (2) the technologies and strategies of torture, (3) the identity of Papuans as a result of the long-term practice of torture and (4) the rationality that underpins, cultivates and justifies the practice of torture. The genealogical investigation presented in this book will highlight and seek to explain these four elements in the historical context of Papua (see Chapter 3). The aim is to reveal the specific characteristics (see Chapter 4) as well as the dynamic governance of torture in this region (see Chapter 5).

However, governmentality is not the only form of power relation examined by Foucault. As Dean identifies, governmentality is just one of three forms of power relation he analysed. The others are sovereignty and discipline. Dean argues that these three forms of power relations do not operate on a continuum but instead as three elements of a triangle which simultaneously target the human population (Dean 2010: 122). In *History of Sexuality Vol. 1* (1978), Foucault elucidates two ways in which power relations target human bodies: discipline and bio-power. The two forms of power relations have the same target, namely human life. However, they differ in the scale of human life targeted. Discipline targets the physical body of individuals whereas 'bio-power' or 'bio-politics' targets the human population. Discipline renders the human body as a machine to be tamed whereas bio-power generates 'an explosion of numerous and diverse techniques for achieving the subjugation of bodies and the control of populations', such as birth rate, public health, housing and migration (Foucault 1978: 139–40). Further, *Discipline and Punish* (1991), which best encapsulates Foucault's discussion on the evolution of punishment from public execution to the prison system, explains the goal of both discipline and bio-power as being the creation of a docile body. This term refers to both the individual and social body that has become an object of domination for a calculated manipulation. The body, Foucault argues, is converted into a 'capacity', which can be increased or decreased in accordance with the dynamics of power.

Targeting the human body to keep it alive and docile constitutes a stark contrast with the aim of sovereignty. In Foucault's view, sovereignty targets human life to limit, control and eventually destroy it. Foucault defined sovereignty as 'symbolic power' which relies on the imagery of blood, sword and crown (Dean 2010: 25). In his posthumously published work, *Society Must be Defended* (2003c), Foucault further develops his notion of sovereignty, describing the sovereign's assumption of the rights of life and death as a 'strange right'. He states that

> The very essence of the right to life and death is actually the right to kill: it is at the moment when the sovereign can kill that he exercises his right over life. It is essentially the right of the sword.
>
> (Foucault 2003c: 240)

The emphasis on the right to kill underlines the stark contrast with the previous models of power, discipline and bio-power, which focus on life and ways to regulate life through various techniques and mechanisms to control it. While Foucault suggests possible transformation of power from sovereign power to bio-power, he does not expect it all to occur at once. In fact, he believes that domination and control remain embedded in all forms of power relations. Foucault's emphasis on omnipresent forms of domination and control will pose a stark contrast with the model of transformation that Metz's theory offers later in this chapter.

Sovereign power and torture ritual

The first part of *Discipline and Punish* summarises Foucault's conceptualisation of sovereignty. It describes the horrifying ritual of the public execution of Robert Damiens, who had attempted regicide, in front of the Parisian crowd in 1757. The king demonstrated his unrestrained power by inscribing it through the punishment of Damiens' body. The aim was for the public to witness the awesomeness of the king's power and feel overwhelmed by it. The main focus of the torture ritual was not the body of the condemned but rather the message from the king transmitted to the public who witnessed the execution. Hence, Foucault interprets this ritual as showing that torture constitutes 'a policy of terror: to make everyone aware, through the body of the criminal, of the unrestrained presence of the sovereign. The public execution did not re-establish justice; it reactivated power' (Foucault 1991: 49). At the end of the analysis of the book this definition will turn out in some important ways to be a more serviceable one than the one we started with in Chapter 1. It is clear that in Foucault's view, torture equals terror. To achieve its terrifying effects, torture has to meet three necessary conditions: being (1) gradually painful, (2) scarring and (3) spectacular (Foucault 1991: 33–4).[7]

The first and second criteria suggest that Foucault recognises that torture can be used in a utilitarian way as was a common practice of the European judiciary in the eighteenth century under a hidden setting. However, the third criterion illustrates that inflicting pain on the body is only a means to achieve an objective beyond the pain itself. That objective is communicating the power of the king. Foucault further elucidates the ritual of torture which clarifies the notion of 'spectacularity'. The ritual consists of four consecutive stages by which the truth of crime rendered by Damiens' body is revealed:

1   *Self-proclamation of guilt* in that the condemned is the one who has to announce his/her guilt to the public using his or her own body as a sign of guilt. For example, Damiens was forced to carry a placard explaining his charges. This stage highlights the intervention of the king into the body of the condemned by converting the body into a sign of guilt. Foucault summarises this step by stating that '[i]t [public punishment] made the guilty man the herald of his own condemnation' (Foucault 1991: 43). The element of visibility begins from this stage.

30   *Reconstructing torture*

2   *Self-confession of truth* in that the condemned was forced to tell the truth to the public who witnessed the execution. The king constructed the public execution as a semblance of Christian confession in which Christians told their sins to a priest in private. However, instead of delivering confession voluntarily and privately, Damiens was coerced to acknowledge the truth as produced by the king. The element of producing truth is obvious to Foucault when he states 'the function of the public torture and execution was to reveal the truth' (Foucault 1991: 44).

3   *Inscribing a crime scene on the body of the condemned* in that the public execution was designed not only to reenact the crime scene but most importantly to punish the particular part of the body that had been used to commit crimes. Damiens, for instance, had to hold the dagger he had used to commit the crime and arm and dagger were smeared with sulphur and burnt together. Foucault illustrates this stage by referring to examples: 'the tongues of blasphemers were pierced, the impure were burnt, the right hand of murderers was cut off; sometimes the condemned man was made to carry the instrument of his crime' (Foucault 1991: 45). In his view, inscribing a crime on the body of the condemned signifies the 'symbolic torture'. It is meant to make a visible reference between the forms of execution and the nature of the crimes. Therefore, this principle dictates the way in which punishment has to be performed not only at a re-enacted crime scene but accurately on the body that committed the actual crime.

4   *Producing agonising death as a proof of guilt.* In Foucault's view, this final stage of the ritual of torture was designed to generate a slow, agonising death. He states: '[T]he slowness of the process of torture and execution, its sudden dramatic moments, the cries and sufferings of the condemned man serve as an ultimate proof at the end of the judicial ritual' (Foucault 1991: 45). The end of the ritual has to be a moment of truth, as was experienced by the Parisian spectators when they eventually witnessed how Damiens' body was torn into pieces. His death was portrayed as evidence that God did not save him. Rather, God let him die. Moreover, Damiens' death not only proved him guilty of regicide, a crime against the king, the one who received his legitimacy from God, it also precisely communicated the king's policy of terror to the Parisians.

Once all these rituals are completed, the body becomes 'a synthesis of the reality of the deeds and the truth of the investigation, of the documents of the case and the statements of the criminal, of the crime and the punishment' (Foucault 1991: 47). Further, Foucault underscores the meaning of the public execution as not only a punitive ritual but also, and more importantly, a political one through which power is manifested (Foucault 1991: 47). Damiens' body was presented through torture as a sign that revealed the truth about the awesomeness of the king and thus became the product on the sovereign power of the king. This ritual became an effective means to convey the awesomeness of the king to the Parisian public to tame the Parisian social body.

The Foucauldian notion of symbolic torture provides an effective tool to capture the logic of communicating power through the body of the condemned, which otherwise remains unexplored. The effectiveness of this model is the way in which it reveals that torture is not merely a technique of inflicting excruciating pain on the body. Rather, it shows that torture is a mode of governance or a 'policy of terror'. This consists of technologies and strategies of sovereign power that render the body as either visible (Feldman 1991; Rothenberg 2003; Taylor 1997) or invisible (Graziano 1992), underpinned by the logic of spectacularity. Building on this insight, further scrutiny will enable us to better understand how power/knowledge practices communicate their spectacular qualities or veil them. The study of the governmentality of torture exposes the inseparability of power relations and knowledge, in which the sovereign power not only targets the body of individuals but also the social body or the whole population.[8] Moreover, as Dean suggests in his abovementioned four key questions, the study of governmentality also identifies the identities of individuals and/or population constructed by the governance of torture. The discussion of identity leads us to Kristeva's examination of the abject as a form of identity formation.

Kristeva's theory of abjection

The study of governmentality reveals the nexus between domination of the body and the targeting of the population. However, governmentality fails to explore the impacts of power on internal processes of individuals that can lead to the production of the subject. Julia Kristeva fills this gap with her study of abjection. She focuses on the mechanisms of the psyche of individuals and how these mechanisms engender the subject. Kristeva describes this as 'the subject in process', meaning an open-ended process of constructing an individual. Her commentators (Harrington 1998; McAfee 1993, 2004; Oliver 1991) argue that the theory of the abject has a central role in Kristeva's theory of subjectivity. It also aids in understanding her approach to the notions of foreignness and exile, issues that preoccupy her. The following discussion will focus only on the ideas of 'abjection', 'foreignness' and 'revolt', given their relevance to this book.

The abject

Abjection means expulsion, exclusion or casting away. Kristeva's theory of abjection builds on Freudian psychoanalysis relating to the genesis of individuals as social beings. McClintock (1995) argues that Freud was the first to suggest that a civilisation is built on expulsion of all things that are considered impure by society, such as incest or the Oedipus complex. Following Freud, in her dense analysis *Powers of Horror: An Essay on Abjection* (1982), Kristeva explains that the abject emerges from the subject's expulsion of its ties with the Mother to become a full and autonomous being. Hence, the act of rejection marks the main characteristic of the process of abjection. With the term 'abject' Kristeva

32   Reconstructing torture

illustrates the construct of nonperson, an entity between subject and object, which is rejected both by subject and object. The abject equals non-existence.

> The abject is not an object facing me, which I name or imagine ... What is abject is not my correlative, which, providing me with someone or something else as support, would allow me to be more or less detached and autonomous. The abject has only one quality of the object – that of being opposed to *I*.
>
> (Kristeva 1982: 1)

Nöelle McAfee, one of the most important commentators on Kristeva's theory, summarises the process of abjection as

> the process by which an infant emerges from the undifferentiated union it has with its mother and surroundings. It does this by expelling, physically and mentally, what is not part of its clean and proper self. In this way, it begins to develop a sense of a discrete 'I' even before the mirror stage of development and before learning language. But what the child abjects is not gone once and for all. The abject continues to *haunt* the subject's consciousness, remaining on the periphery of awareness.
>
> (McAfee 2004: 49; my emphasis)

As a process, abjection is part of the construction of identity of a subject. The abject also underscores the notion of ambiguity of the subject. On the one hand, the subject disavows the abject, but on the other, the subject claims the existence of the abject to sustain its own existence. That is why McAfee underlines the element of *haunting* that illustrates the desire of the abject to penetrate the boundaries between the subject and the abject. Further, McAfee illustrates the relationship between the subject and the abject:

> The subject finds the abject both repellent and seductive and thus his or her borders of self are, paradoxically, continuously threatened and maintained. They are threatened because the abject is alluring enough to crumble the borders of self; they are maintained because the fear of such a collapse keeps the subject vigilant.
>
> (McAfee 1993: 50)

McAfee explains that the relationship between the subject and the abject is characterised by suspicion and tension, but also by seduction. The abject is not entirely controllable, nor is it powerless. That is why Kristeva locates the abject in between subject and object in her *Powers of Horror*. In McClintock's view, the abject is 'everything that the subject seeks to expunge in order to become social' (McClintock 1995: 71). The subject has to expel all that is considered impure by a society including food disgust, waste and the signs of sexual difference (Grosz 1990).[9] However, Kristeva differs from Freud who believes that

Reconstructing torture   33

impure elements can be permanently suppressed to the subconscious level of the self. She asserts that the impure elements can never be fully suppressed. Instead, they remain haunting at the edge of the self (see McAfee 1993).[10] The abject is 'waste, excluded from our culture and yet haunting it through the need for ritualistic purifications' (Sjöholm 2005: 98). Hence, for Kristeva, 'The abject has only one quality of the object – that of being opposed to *I*' (Kristeva 1982: 1). *I*, in this case, refers to the subject. In other words, the abject is always oppositional to the subject.

With the concept of abjection, Kristeva captures the most extreme form of disgust. In front of the subject, the abject is decomposed, stripped of its essence and rendered beyond the comprehension of the subject. The subject then deliberately erects boundaries, both psychological and cultural, in the form of taboos that prevent an abject from being reintegrated with the subject. The abject becomes a kind of black hole that absorbs any meaning. Anything that belongs to the abject will lose its value and meaning. The reality of horror and suffering belongs to the abject and thus lies beyond human comprehension because its qualities are 'immoral, sinister, scheming and shady' (Kristeva 1982: (4). However, despite this total rejection, the subject continues to retain the abject at the edge of its identity. The subject disavows the abject, but to mark its existence, the subject has to claim and retain the abject at the same time just across the boundaries of its existence. Ambivalence and ambiguity, in Kristeva's view, become two key characteristics that mark the subject's relationship to the abject.

Drawing on the notion of abjection, McClintock's study on colonialism, *Imperial Leather*, examines 'the paradox of abjection, as a formative aspect of modern industrial imperialism' (McClintock 1995: 72). McClintock argues that under imperialism, certain groups, such as those of the slum, the ghetto, the brothel and other undesirables, are expelled and forced to live outside the margins, but at the same time they are claimed by modernity to mark the boundaries of modernity and the sovereign as the symbol of modernity. This assertion helps reconcile the notion of abjection with Foucault's concept of the sovereign. McClintock richly clarifies different types of abject and thus broadens the notion of abjection to identify how nations construct abjection at various levels. These abject objects and positions cover a wide range, including

> abject *objects* (the clitoris, domestic dirt, menstrual blood), abject *states* (bulimia, the masturbatory imagination, hysteria), abject *zones* (the Israeli Occupied Territory, prisons, battered women's shelters), socially appointed *agents* of the abject (soldiers, domestic workers, nurses), abjected *groups* (prostitutes, Palestinians, lesbians), *psychic* processes of abjection (fetishism, disavowal, the uncanny), and *political* processes of abjection (ethnic genocide, mass removals, prostitute 'clean ups').
>
> (McClintock 1995: 72)

This discussion allows us to bridge the psychic and the social in that the abject is not isolated in the domain of the psyche. Furthermore, McClintock has critically

34 Reconstructing torture

addressed the questions of social boundaries and identities, drawing on the notion of abjection to identify abjected zones, groups and agents as a result of colonialism.

Indirectly, McClintock's study offers an answer to Nancy Fraser's critiques of Kristeva and bridges the abject and sovereign power. Fraser argues that Kristeva's framework fails to build a bridge between the psychic and the social because the framework only focuses on internal psychological processes within an individual and does not address the relationship between individuals. Therefore, in Fraser's view, the gap between the psychic and the social remains unresolved (Ziarek 1995: para 1). Like McClintock's work, this study will explore how the notion of abjection can explain the contradictory nature of power relations between the Indonesian state, imagined as the subject, and Papuans, imagined as the abject. On the one hand, Indonesia exiles Papua to the edge of the nation-state through the long-term practice of torture, but, on the other hand, this post-colonial state retains and constitutes Papua to maintain the existence of the Indonesian state.

Despite criticisms that refer to the gap between the psychic and the social, Kristeva (1991), in her later work, explores the notion of the abject as a critique of nationalism. In particular, she responds to the rise of militant nationalism and militant ethnicity in Europe in which foreigners and strangers are treated not only as alien to a non-native society but even as a threat (Goodnow 2010: 64). Norma Moruzzi compares Kristeva's theory of abjection to the formation of the nation-state. She states: 'Historically, the nation-state establishes itself through the convulsions of a body politic which rejects those parts of itself, defined as other or excess, whose rejected alterity then engenders the consolidation of a national identity' (Moruzzi 1993: 143). As an imagined subject, the nation-state denies but, at the same time, claims the foreigners as imagined abjects. The nation-state does not suppress foreigners. It simply draws clear boundaries that prevent foreigners from being integrated into the nation-state.

In Kristeva's view, the foreigner is not exterior to the self. On the contrary, 'the foreigner lives within us: he is the hidden face of our identity, the space that wrecks our abode, the time, in which understanding and affinity founder' (Oliver 2002b: 264). Given that this element contains an 'uncanny strangeness', foreigners have been construed as 'frightening', a notion which has been repressed but managed to be unleashed and has come to light (Oliver 2002b: 283). It is precisely the penetration of uncanny strangeness from the unconscious to conscious level that poses a threat to nationalism. In this context, drawing on a Freudian approach to uncanniness, Kristeva proposes a strategy to address this threat by analysing and recognising the uncanny as an integral part of ourselves (Oliver 2002b: 290). While this approach is consistent with her notion of heterogeneity of the subject, Kristeva's suggestion tends to reduce politics to psychoanalysis. Critics of reductionist approaches blame Kristeva for her 'romanticisation of transgression' (Sjöholm 2005: 100). However, for the purpose of this book, the notion of foreignness is beneficial to bridge the psychic, as encapsulated in the concept of abjection, and the social, as represented in the concept of nationalism.

The concept of foreignness further justifies the conceptualisation of Papuans as the abject in relation to the Indonesian state imagined as the subject. This conceptualisation illustrates how Kristevan abjection is not limited to the psychic. Rather, this framework can be beneficial to explore power relations in a setting like Papua where a group of people is oppressed by the state.

In *Revolt, She Said* (2002), Kristeva explores the notion of resistance. She defines 'revolt' in its literary sense and then frames it in a psychoanalytic sense. She outlines her argument on 'revolt' as distinct from 'revolution':[1]

> I work from its etymology, meaning return, returning, discovering, uncovering, and renovating. There is a necessary repetition when you cover all that ground, but beyond that, I emphasize its potential for making gaps, rupturing, renewing. Rebellion is a condition necessary for the life of the mind and society.
>
> (Kristeva 2002: 85)

Similar to Foucault's notion of resistance, Kristeva underlines revolt as something productive and creative. She underscores the necessity of revolt to renew 'the life of the mind and society'. 'Revolt', she states, 'is a very deep movement of discontent, anxiety, and anguish' (Kristeva 2002: 99), encompassing an area broader than politics. She emphasises,

> Social protest should not be a purpose in itself. It should be an integral part of a larger process of general anxiety, which is simultaneously psychic, cultural, religious anxiety, etc.
>
> (Kristeva 2002: 103)

In comparison to Foucault's notion of resistance (and, as I discuss in the next section, Metz's notion of memory), Kristeva's 'revolt' shares a similar element of creative production that generates change. Taken together Foucault, Kristeva and Metz do not limit their notion of resistance to merely a sense of opposition. Rather, they perceive it in a more positive way. However, whereas Foucault avoids the questions of subject, Kristeva and Metz explicitly argue that the subject can take the lead in generating change.

What is the relevance of Kristeva's model of abjection to the question of torture in Papua? In confronting the protracted reality of torture in Papua, Kristeva's concept of the abject helps to capture the gravity and logic of the ways this atrocity operates in contradictory ways. On the one hand, the governance of torture is designed to cast away many Papuans from the mindset of the Indonesian state and treat them as 'foreigners'. But on the other hand, it continues to claim and constitute Papua at the edge of this state to maintain the post-colonial state of Indonesia. The theory of the abject is crucial to assess how Papuan torture survivors embody these relations. The level of abjection is not limited to their relations to the Indonesian state, but frequently applies to their social networks as well. Further, the Papuan experience will demonstrate that Indonesian

36 *Reconstructing torture*

repression does not entirely silence Papuans. On the contrary, abjected Papuans continue to pose a threat to Indonesia in the form of the Papuan resistance movement. In sum, the model of the abject helps in deconstructing the rendering of Papuan subjectivity as non-existence and how the abject challenges the identity of the subject through resistance movements. Furthermore, the concept of revolt provides a useful tool to assess the extent of the ability of the Papuan resistance to renew all dimensions of Papuan society.

Metz's theory of *memoria passionis*

Foucault's and Kristeva's theories have contributed to this study by outlining the production of subject/abject and the dynamics of resistance. However, these theories are not specific enough to identify which part of human capacity allows the abject to reclaim its agency. Metz's theory of *memoria passionis*, which derives from what Metz calls a 'new political theology',[12] can fill the gap. Rooted in and developed from the cohort of German theologians[13] that resisted the National Socialist Regime, this theology is a critique of the silence of German society and Christian faith and theology in dealing with the catastrophic reality of the Holocaust. Metz posits that this silence derived from the fact of suppression of the phenomenal atrocity in the German public consciousness because any public awareness of the Holocaust was considered dangerous by the Nazi and post-Nazi regimes.

Metz's criticisms focus on two major problems: secularisation[14] and privatisation of religion. Matthew J. Ashley, an English translator of Metz's main works, argues that the novelty of Metz's political theology lies in four elements, namely (1) the advocacy of a creative engagement with modernity, (2) a willingness to embrace images and ideas from the Christian tradition to counter modernity, (3) incorporating memories of history's catastrophes into theology and Christian faith, and finally, (4) a defence of hope, a theology that has to 'include unconditional solidarity with and action on behalf of those who suffer, those whose hope is most endangered' (Ashley 2004: 245). Metz's theology takes the suffering and memories of victims as the centre of its reflection, marking a stark contrast with other political theologians, such as Carl Schmitt, who serve the interests of the state.

Metz's political theology was developed in parallel with Gustavo Gutierrez's liberation theology in Peru. Both have become highly influential in Catholic circles not because of their novel ideas but primarily because 'they were the first fruits of the Second Vatican Council' (Aguilar 2007: 25). Steven T. Ostovich (1990) identifies two major camps of criticism of Metz's approach, describing them as 'disappointment' and 'fear'. The disappointment camp comes from more radical groups, including revolutionists and liberation theologians, who contend that Metz's theology is not radical enough. It does not provide clear guidance on how to engage in political activism. The fear camp, which represents a more conservative line of thought, takes the opposite view. They accuse Metz's theology of being a threat to the role of the Church because it suggests integration

Reconstructing torture 37

with 'the world'. They contend that if this happens the distinctive nature of the Church will be eliminated and thus becomes meaningless.

As opposed to both schools of thought, Ostovich argues that they have misunderstood the notion of politics in Metz's political theology. Metz does not endorse 'a politicisation of faith' or a 'clericalisation of politics' (Ostovich 1990: 37). Rather, he advocates for an engagement with social justice issues and policy and not a retreat from them. 'The world' in Metz's view is a history, record or product of human activity. Inspired by his theologian contemporaries, Metz focuses his attention on the engagement of Christian faith and theology with the reality of suffering in the world as a continuous dialectic. That is the reason why he always emphatically refers to Auschwitz, to exemplify what he means about suffering and why theology is confronted with an enormous task to rethink its reflection on Christian faith and the historical world (Metz 1981). 'For me Auschwitz signaled horror that transcends all familiar theologies, a horror that makes every noncontextual talk about God appear empty and blind' (Metz 1994: 611).

In analysing Metz's political theology, scholars (Ashley 1998; Colombo 1990; Matthiesen 1986) identify three central categories – memory, narrative and solidarity – which will be discussed in the following sections. I later consider how these categories will help in the analysis of the Papuan experience of torture (see Chapter 5).

Memoria passionis

The term 'memory' here refers to a philosophical rather than a physiological or psychological realm (Ostovich 2005). *Memoria passionis* is the Latin equivalent of 'memory of suffering'. Metz coined this term by developing it from two German philosophers: first, Walter Benjamin, whose philosophy underlines the importance of memories and stories that contain energy for emancipation of the subject from technical rationality; and second, Ernst Bloch who interrogated the status quo of the present and sought change through the power of suffering towards a utopian future (Ashley 2004: 244).

In *Faith in History and Society* (1980), Metz distinguishes 'memory of suffering' from other memories. He identifies two types of memories: the memory of the 'good old days' and 'memory of transfiguration'. The former is defined as a memory that treats the past as a paradise without danger or an escape from our present reality. The latter is the opposite, where the past is defined as a dangerous, oppressive and demanding, but also as vanished. There is no need to remember. Metz, using a metaphor of an old soldier telling his war story, contends that this latter type of memory loses its connection with the future. He emphasises that such a memory 'can easily become a "false consciousness" of our past and an opiate for our present' (Metz 1980: 109).

In contrast to the previous types of memory, Metz introduces his 'memory of suffering', *memoria passionis*, rooted in *memoria passionis, mortis and resurrectionis Iesu Christi* (the memory of the suffering, death and resurrection

38 *Reconstructing torture*

of Jesus Christ). This becomes the source of action for Christian faith. In other words, Metz argues that Christianity is founded in the memory of the suffering of Jesus. For Christians, this memory should be the basis for engagement with suffering. It should provide an impetus to change society and the polity, and to be in solidarity with the poor and those who are oppressed by totalitarian regimes. Memory in this sense clearly does not relate to the 'good old days' or the transfiguration, but rather it is a source of energy for change for the better. The notion of change and bringing the forgotten into public consciousness resonates with his previous criticism of the Christian faith in the German context which privatises faith and separates it from history. In Metz's words, *memoria passionis* is characterised as 'dangerous memories':

> There are memories in which earlier experiences break through to the centre-point of our lives and reveal new and dangerous insights for the present. They illuminate for a few moments and with a harsh steady light the questionable nature of things we have apparently come to terms with, and show up the banality of our supposed 'realism'. They break through the canon of the prevailing structures of plausibility and have certain subversive features. Such memories are like dangerous and incalculable visitations from the past. They are memories that we have to take into account, memories, as it were, with a future content.
>
> (Metz 1980: 109–10)

The notion 'dangerous' and 'subversive' entails the notion of interruption. *Memoria passionis* interrupts the status quo of the present and discloses 'the banality' of reality that we tend to take for granted. Further, the dangerous memory seeks to identify new ways of seeing. In this sense, this memory has a subversive quality which is able to destabilise the status quo. Moreover, in parallel to Foucault's and Kristeva's analysis of modernity, this critique highlights the pathology of modernity that suppresses the reality of 'human misery, dependence, past suffering, the voiceless dead' (Matthiesen 1986: 48). The centrality of memory in Metz's theory can also be observed through his emphasis on its pivotal role in human history: 'the enslavement of men begins when their memories of the past are taken away' (Metz 1980: 110). The logic of memory is at odds with the logics of technology and pragmatic reason that characterise modernity. This logic of modernity treats memory as 'superstitious' and thus falls under the realm of private individuals. 'The memory of human suffering forces us to look at the public *theatrum mundi* [the theatre of the world] not merely from the standpoint of the successful and the established, but from that of the conquered and the victims' (Metz 1980: 105).

Metz's treatment of the memory of suffering as a critique of modernity suggests that his political theology is not limited to religious discourse. In reality, he was in intensive dialogue with other contemporary thinkers. For instance, while he engaged with the work of Herbert Marcuse and Walter Benjamin, two social philosophers of the Frankfurt School who examined memory, he eventually split

Reconstructing torture 39

with them. From Marcuse, Metz draws on the notion of remembrance and 'dangerous insight' of the past, and from Benjamin he develops the notion of hope for the future deriving from 'the awakening of the dead'. However, he splits with these social philosophers on their interpretations of a dialectic of emancipation as a way to address the problem of suffering. Metz criticises Marcuse and Benjamin because they failed to take history seriously. In his view, Marcuse's and Benjamin's interpretations only ended up in abstract concepts; they became ideological (Ashley 1998: 119) and thus failed to address the reality of human suffering, for example Auschwitz (Ostovich 1990: 60–2). At the end of *Faith in History and Society*, Metz summarises his concept of memory:

> Memory should not be regarded as a concept of resignation or tradition in contrast to that of hope. It should above all, in the sense of a dangerous memory, be thought of as the expression of eschatological hope, elaborated in its social and historical mediation.
>
> (Metz 1980: 184)

It is clear that he underlines the dynamics and interconnections between the past as preserved in memory, the future hope and the social and historical context of the present. Instead of drawing a clear line between different time frames in a linear fashion, Metz suggests time is something integral and interconnected. He emphasises the notions of change and struggle towards the future. The orientation towards the future is not left undefined. Instead, Metz equates memory of suffering as 'memory of freedom' because it 'acts as an orientation for action that is related to freedom' (Metz 1980: 195). So memory of suffering here is defined as being not only about the past but also about the agenda for future actions that 'resist being identified, either openly or in secret, with a praxis that is expressed as a progressive control of nature' (Metz 1980: 195).

Narrative

For Metz, memory and narrative are inseparable.[15] To allow narrative to embody memory, Metz turns upside down the supremacy of theory and argument in theology over narrative.[16] This approach helps this study to explore the role of Papuan narratives in reclaiming subjectivity. Metz believes that narrative is a more effective, concrete and natural way of transmitting and communicating religious meaning and experience (Colombo 1990; Ostovich 1990). Metz further elucidates broader aspects of narratives which include performative and practical, pastoral and social, as well as theological aspects. For the purposes of this book, however, the performative and practical aspects of narrative are more relevant to exploring Papuan oral histories of torture. 'Performative' entails a notion of a sign, 'a linguistic action in which the unity of the story as an effective word and as practical effect is expressed in the same process' (Metz 1980: 208). Metz makes a link between narrative and action to underline that narrative is not constrained by words but paves the way towards action. This resonates with

40 *Reconstructing torture*

Metz's endorsement of engagement with the world. The 'practical' element, on the other hand, suggests the notion of the self-explanatory value of narrative. 'It [narrative] verifies or falsifies itself and does not simply leave this to discussion about the story which lies outside the narrative process' (Metz 1980: 208). This assertion underscores the internal logics of narrative which rely on its internal mechanisms to measure truth and meaning in transmitting and communicating messages.

Solidarity

Metz defines solidarity, the last category of the trinity of his political theology, as follows: 'Solidarity is above all a category of help, support and togetherness, by which the subject, suffering acutely and threatened, can be raised up' (Metz 1980: 229). Solidarity is an action towards those who suffer and are threatened that enables them to regain their agency. Consistent with his political theology, Metz reiterates the notion of practicality, action, engagement and his preferential option for those who suffer. This engagement aims at restoring the dignity of the subject so that it can be 'raised up'. In this sense, Metz's notion of solidarity underscores the dynamics of agency that resonates with the Foucauldian notion of resistance and the Kristevan concept of revolt.

Derived from Metz's orientation towards change of the status quo, his concept of solidarity cannot be separated from images of the church of his time. He identifies three models of the church: 'a pre-bourgeois paternalistic church, a bourgeois supply or services church, and a post-bourgeois initiative taking church' (Metz 1981). The first image represents a rejection of the Enlightenment and prefers to go back to the past. This type of church embraces rigidity of rules and believes that people need to be protected from the world by upholding meticulous rules. Therefore, this model often closes its door to the modern world. The second image, in contrast, endorses an approach that Christianity should serve the interests of bourgeois values of progress and the autonomous subject and thus ignore and even suppress the reality of suffering in the history of humankind, as symbolised by Auschwitz.

As an alternative to these two church images, Metz proposes the third model: a post-bourgeois church. This church is characterised by a 'new subjectivity' and solidarity. The new subjectivity is precisely marked by solidarity and not by bourgeois individualism. Solidarity, however, does not mean elimination of individuality. On the contrary, it is based on decisions of autonomous individuals to engage with a world characterised by suffering, fragility and even catastrophic events. However, Metz contends that this model does not exist in the German Church of his time (Metz 1981: 87). While solidarity resonates with the dynamics of agency that Foucault and Kristeva identified, it also underlines some kind of mission embedded in agency. Metz believes that the mission of agency is to engage with suffering to liberate it. The notion of liberation again finds a parallel in Foucault's concept of resistance and Kristeva's notion of revolt.

Reconstructing torture 41

Colombo (1990) argues that Metz's concept of solidarity contains two inseparable aspects: mystical and political. They are inseparable because they constitute the 'checks and balances' of solidarity. On the one hand, without the mystical element, solidarity becomes purely political, 'repressive, and totalitarian'. On the other hand, without the political element, solidarity becomes purely 'interiorised and spiritualised' (Metz 1980: 196).

> In a practical fundamental theology, the essentially twofold structure of solidarity is preserved. In other words, solidarity is seen on the one hand as mystical and universal and on the other hand as political and particular. This double structure protects the universal aspect of solidarity from apathy and its partisan nature from hatred and forgetfulness. It raises again and again the question: With whom should there be solidarity? What form should solidarity take?
>
> (Metz 1980: 232)

In conjunction with memory and narrative, solidarity becomes a vehicle to release the dangerous memory of suffering and the narrative of liberation. While memory of suffering is the energy for change, the narrative is the expression for change. The following section further explores these elements.

Towards a 'theology of revolt'

Memoria passionis, narrative and solidarity provide a rich source for theological resistance necessary to interpret the Papuan capacity to resist the practice of torture in Papua. The absence of theological resistance, in Metz's view, constituted not only a big gap in Christian theology but a failure to respond to Auschwitz. Therefore, Metz radically challenges Christians to listen to the Jewish voices today and to learn from them, particularly the experience with Auschwitz (Metz 1981: 17–32). The non-resistance response, however, has not ended in futility. Rather, it has generated a theological resistance response such as Metz promoted, a political theology that deliberately puts human suffering at the centre of its theological reflection.[17] Informed by the three theorists, this study may lead to a 'theology of revolt' which calls not only for the subject to listen to Papuans as the abject but also, more radically, to recognise the abject's humanity and incorporate it into the subject.

In the Papuan context, drawing on Metz's notion of '*memoria passionis*', Theo van den Broek and I (1999) made sense of the first official expression of '*merdeka*' of Papuan leaders to the then-President Habibie and his cabinet on 26 February 1999. This was an historic moment. For the first time 100 Papuan leaders had the opportunity to express their will without an immediate risk of suppression. This marked the moment when Papuans began to reclaim their subjectivity. Although the message turned out to be highly unexpected by President Habibie and his cabinet, it broke ground for and gave momentum to the diplomatic battle for Papuan independence. Prior to that moment, it had been hidden

42 *Reconstructing torture*

in the jungle and represented by traditional Melanesian warfare. Papuan pro-independence aspirations had been represented as abject because they could only pose a threat from the margin of the nation-state of Indonesia. In this context, *memoria passionis* can be conceived thus:

> *Memoria passionis* is like magma. It is hidden from ordinary eyes but retains latent powerful energy which is ready to turn the status quo upside down.[18]

The term 'memoria passionis' has not only entered the vernacular for the Papuan public, but has also been developed by Papuan theologians incorporating local content. In *Menuju Papua Baru* (*Towards the New Papua*) (2000), Benny Giay, a prominent Papuan theologian, for instance, develops the notion of the memory of suffering to outline his road map for rewriting Papuan history to incorporate local narratives, particularly those of abjected voices. Just as in Metz's political theology, so too is Giay's discussion of change not limited to social and political change but is cast more broadly. It embraces the social, political, cultural and theological domains. In light of Metz's political theology, a theology of revolt will be further tested to explore the Papuan experience in confronting the long-term practice of state-sponsored torture.

Concluding remarks

The three theories help conceptualise torture as a mode of governance in Papua. The governmentality framework is fundamental to building a holistic approach. This approach consists of three analytical lenses: sovereign power, abjection and *memoria passionis*. The Foucauldian model of power offers the triangle of governmentality, sovereign power and discipline as multiple analytical lenses to examine the experience of torture in Papua at the macro-structural level. While the Foucauldian framework outlines the ubiquitous nature of domination, it also allows for agency to resist domination. This becomes, nevertheless, a limit of Foucault's theory because it fails to explain the dynamics of agency and domination at the micro and individual levels. These dynamics are best encapsulated by Kristevan abjection, which captures the impacts of the most extreme form of domination on individual psyches. At the social and political level, abjection helps with pondering the question of the identity formation of those who are oppressed. This concept may be beneficial to characterise the ambiguous and ambivalent relationships between the nation-state of Indonesia and Papua. Just as Foucault recognises agency and resistance, so Kristeva introduces the term 'revolt' to cover a broader area than politics. Although these two theories suggest a politics of hope, they are not specific enough to give it flesh. Metz fills the gap. It is Metz who provides us with the clearest example of how agency not only cannot be defeated and constructed permanently as abjection but also, more importantly, is inherently capable of renewal. The memory of suffering is at the core of the human capacity to resist. Deploying narratives as a vehicle, *memoria passionis* of the abject is capable of mobilising solidarity among abjects to

Reconstructing torture   43

generate change in the long run. In this sense, Metz contradicts both Kristeva and Foucault. But perhaps, in doing so, Metz solves the problems of Kristeva's ambiguity and Foucault's elusive subject. However, as a revolt, the call of the abject goes beyond Metz's assertion of engaging the abject. The abject demands recognition and re-integration into humanity. The call will be explored in the following chapter which discusses the genealogy of torture in Papua. The governmentality framework is therefore not only beneficial for explaining power structures of domination in Papua but also instructive for analysing the politics of hope of Papua Land of Peace. Grounded in the historical context and empirical evidence of contemporary practices of torture in Papua, the following chapters will further explore the effectiveness and limits of my governmentality framework revised with the insights of Metz and Kristeva in explaining the long-term practice of torture and in reimagining peacebuilding in Papua.

Notes

1 The Office for Justice and Peace of the Catholic Diocese of Jayapura, a Catholic organisation as part of the Catholic Church, uses the term '*memoria passionis*' to name its series of human rights documentations.
2 Drawing on Descartes' philosophy that puts reason as the determinant of the subject, the Cartesian subject means autonomous rational subject that assumes control over the world. The subject is positioned

> at the center of the epistemic and moral universes, and not only for theoretical reasons: It undergirds the egocentric, domineering, and possessive individualism that has so disfigured modern Western rationalism and driven it to exclude, dominate, or repress whatever is different.
>
> (McCarthy 1990: 438)

3 See Matthiesen (1986) for a further discussion on a comparative study between Metz and Wissel.
4 In his comparative study of the critical theory of the Frankfurt School and Foucault, Thomas McCarthy (1990) identifies how the two share similar intellectual endeavours which at the same time have become points of departure. These include: (1) seeking transformation and radicalisation of the Kantian critique of reason, (2) rejecting the Cartesian concept of an autonomous and rational subject that assumes control to conquer the world, (3) upholding the primacy of practical reason, (4) appreciating philosophical hermeneutics, (5) identifying the need of critical analysis of the established human sciences of the time and (6) focusing on the nexus between critique and praxis as an open-ended journey rather than as closed theoretical systems.
5 In *Madness and Civilisation*, Foucault explains madness not in terms of psychoanalysis but of the sociology of power represented by the figure of the doctor. He is the one who holds authority over confinement based on a juridical and moral guarantee rather than on his medical skills (Foucault 1988: 270). In contrast to mainstream Western thought of his time, Foucault explains madness as a form of Otherness which reason and science are not able to grasp (Dreyfus and Rabinow 1982: 11).
6 Chapter 3 will deal with these questions more fully through a close examination of the power relations at play in Papua.
7 Drawing on the Foucauldian notion of symbolic torture, scholars such as Diana Taylor (1997) and Frank Graziano (1992) ponder the notion of spectacularity in relation to Argentina's Dirty War. Both examine the paradox of state practices of disappearance because this act renders a public secret. On the one hand, the public has knowledge

44 *Reconstructing torture*

about it but on the other, it has to suppress the knowledge at the same time. Taylor centres her inquiry on 'the politics of looking' at the state-sponsored disappearances, construed as female bodies, which prevent the audience from seeing them. Her objective is 'to make visible again, not the invisible of the imagined, but that which is there but not allowed to be seen' (Taylor 1997: 27). This precisely underscores the notion of spectacularity in a sense that the spectacle is there but suppressed. Graziano, on the other hand, explores the notion of 'the abstract spectacle' as a means of the *junta* to communicate a policy of terror. In this setting, he argues that this sort of spectacle was produced by demonstrating excessive power to an '*implied audience*' rather than to direct witnesses. This audience was the Argentine population which had some knowledge of the 'dirty war' even though this knowledge may have been denied, suppressed or ignored (Graziano 1992: 78).

8 See Mitchell Dean (2010) and Nikolas Rose *et al.* (2006) for further discussion on governmentality.

9 An earlier analysis by Mary Douglas, *Purity and Danger* (1969), examined concepts of pollution and taboo in different cultures and religions as bases for rituals of purification.

10 In Freud's framework, the subject's desires have to be denied and repressed into the unconscious for subjectivity and civilisation to develop. This argument assumes that repression of desire is entirely successful and thus a subject develops its identity.

11 Kristeva investigates the original Latin meaning of 'revolt' from '*revolvere*' and criticises the reduction of revolt into 'revolution', merely a domain of social-political protest. Moreover, she criticises the idea that a revolt tends not to have a 'self-critique' or be a vehicle for 'questioning new ideas'. For instance, in the French Revolution, the Third Republic turned to the guillotine. The Russian Revolution established a totalitarian regime as the final development of the idea of the 'proletariat'. These are examples where revolts turned to tyranny.

12 Scholars traced back the term 'political theology' as far as Stoic philosophy in the ancient Roman Empire (Colombo 1990; Fiorenza 2005; Ostovich 1990). In essence, political theology was developed in Roman civil religion. In modern history, political theology entails a critique of modernity in which 'the diverse impulses of modernity (democracy, rights, and pluralism) need to be examined' (Fiorenza 2005: 87). Fiorenza further categorises political theology into three camps: critique of the Enlightenment and French Revolution, critique of liberal democracies by scholars such as Carl Schmitt who advocates exceptionalism and critique of privatisation of religion, to which Metz refers.

13 Werner G. Jeanrond reviewed the response of German theologians in confronting the reality of Nazism. Their initial response emerged in 1934 with the Barmen Declaration in which the Confession Church opposed the Nazi-supported German Christian movement which campaigned for anti-Semitism and extreme nationalism. Karl Barth, the spiritual father of the declaration, came to the fore to attack the Nazi regime. Another prominent German theologian, pastor and martyr, Dietrich Bonhoeffer, exemplifies the resistance of German theologians. His life was sacrificed in a concentration camp. However, Jeanrond argues that this theological response was not highly coordinated because 'there was no solid theological foundation available upon which a theology of resistance could have been constructed' (Jeanrond 1992: S187).

14 Colombo (1990: 158) argues that the term 'secularisation' is for Metz broader than its use in social science discourse. For Metz, secularisation means the emergence of 'modernity' which is characterised by the collapsing of boundaries between the state and the church.

15 It should be noted, however, that the idea of the inseparability of memory and narrative is not unique to Metz but is commonly found in the literature of memory. Edward S. Casey (1987), James Fentress and Chris Wickham (1992) are only a few of

Reconstructing torture 45

the scholars who specifically examine the anatomy of memory and explore the relationships between memory, narrative and oral history. Memory has become a central theme in the historical justice and transitional justice literatures.

16 Situated in the German theology of his time, which put much emphasis on argument and theory, Metz was deeply concerned that Christianity faced the risk of being reduced to theory. He contends:

> Christianity is not only a community engaged in interpretation and argument, but also a community of practical intention of memory and narrative. The verbal content of Christianity should therefore be seen primarily as a major narrative which contains argumentative structures and elements and produces such structures.
>
> (Metz 1980: 216)

Drawing on the Old Testament where stories play a pivotal role in transmitting and exchanging messages between God and his prophets, his critique aims at restoring the role of narrative as the main vehicle of 'the transmission of religion and the formation of the identity of the subject' without necessarily eliminating all arguments and theory from faith and theology (Colombo 1990: 192).

17 In this sense, Metz's work resonates with similar theological resistance movements in Latin America, as represented by Gustavo Gutierrez and Jon Sobrino, to name two. Despite his praise to Metz and acknowledgement of German society and polity that might constrain Metz's theology, Gutierrez (1973: 223–4) criticises Metz for not being concrete in recovering the political dimension of Christianity and for not sufficiently tackling the issue of secularisation from theology. Deriving from Latin American experience, Gutierrez underscores the danger to theology not only because of privatisation and marginalisation of religion but also from collaboration between the state and the church.

18 The original text reads: 'Memoria Passionis *itu bagaikan magma yang tersembunyi dari pandangan mata biasa tetapi menyimpan energi laten yang dahsyat dan siap menjungkirbalikkan segala status quo yang ada*' (Hernawan and van den Broek 1999).

References

Aguilar, M.I. 2007, *The History and Politics of Latin America Theology*, SCM Press, London.

Ashley, J.M. 1998, *Interruptions: Mysticism, Politics, and Theology in the Work of Johann Baptist Metz*, University of Notre Dame Press, Notre Dame, IN.

Ashley, J.M. 2004, 'Johann Baptist Metz', in P. Scott and W.T. Cavanaugh (eds), *The Blackwell Companion to Political Theology*, Blackwell Publishing Ltd, Malden, MA, Oxford, Carlton, pp. 241–55.

Casey, E. 1987, *Remembering: A Phenomenological Study*, Indiana University Press, Bloomington and Indianapolis.

Colombo, J.A. 1990, *An Essay on Theology and History: Studies in Pannenberg, Metz, and the Frankfurt School*, Scholars Press, Atlanta, GA.

Dean, M. 2002, 'Liberal Government and Authoritarianism', *Economy and Society*, vol. 31, no. 1, pp. 37–61.

Dean, M. 2010, *Governmentality: Power and Rule in Modern Society*, 2nd edn, Sage, London.

Douglas, M. 1969, *Purity and Danger: An Analysis of Concepts of Pollution and Taboo*, Routledge and Kegan Paul, London.

46 *Reconstructing torture*

Dreyfus, H.L. and Rabinow, P. 1982, *Michel Foucault: Beyond Structuralism and Hermeneutics With an Afterword by Michel Foucault*, University of Chicago Press, Chicago, IL.

Feldman, A. 1991, *Formation of Violence: The Narratives of the Body and Political Terror in Northern Ireland*, University of Chicago Press, Chicago, IL.

Fentress, J. and Wickham, C. 1992, *Social Memory*, Blackwell, Oxford and Cambridge, MA.

Fiorenza, F.S. 2005, 'Political Theology and the Critique of Modernity: Facing the Challenges of the Present', *Distinktion: Scandinavian Journal of Social Theory*, vol. 6, no. 1, pp. 87–105.

Foucault, M. 1978, *The History of Sexuality, Volume I: An Introduction*, Pantheon Books, New York.

Foucault, M. 1980, *Power/Knowledge Selected Interviews and Other Writings 1972–1977*, The Harvester Press, Sussex.

Foucault, M. 1982, 'The Subject and Power', *Critical Inquiry*, vol. 8, no. 4, pp. 777–95.

Foucault, M. 1988, *Madness and Civilization, A History of Insanity in the Age of Reason*, Vintage Books, New York.

Foucault, M. 1991, *Discipline and Punish: The Birth of Prison*, Penguin Books Ltd, London.

Foucault, M. 2003a, 'The Ethics of the Concern of the Self as a Practice of Freedom', in P. Rabinow and N. Rose (eds), *The Essential Foucault: Selections from The Essential Works of Foucault 1954–1984*, The New Press, New York and London.

Foucault, M. 2003b, 'Governmentality', in P. Rabinow and N. Rose (eds), *The Essential Foucault: Selections from Essential Works of Foucault, 1954–1984*, The New Press, New York and London.

Foucault, M. 2003c, *'Society Must Be Defended': Lectures at the College de France*, Picador, New York.

Giay, B. 2000, *Menuju Papua Baru: Beberapa Pokok Pikiran Sekitar Emansipasi Orang Papua*, Deiyai/Elsham Papua, Jayapura.

Glazebrook, D. 2008, *Permissive Residents: West Papuan Refugees Living in Papua New Guinea*, ANU E-Press, Canberra, A.C.T.

Goodnow, K.J. 2010, *Kristeva in Focus: From Theory to Film Analysis*, Berghahn Books, New York and Oxford.

Graziano, F. 1992, *Divine Violence, Spectacle, Psychosexuality, and Radical Christianity in the Argentine 'Dirty War'*, Westview Press, Boulder, CO, San Francisco, CA, Oxford.

Grosz, E. 1990, 'The Body of Signification', in J. Fletcher and A. Benjamin (eds), *Abjection, Melancholia, and Love: The Work of Julia Kristeva*, Routledge, London and New York, pp. 80–103.

Gutierrez, G. 1973, *A Theology of Liberation: History, Politics and Salvation*, SCM Press Ltd., New York.

Harrington, T. 1998, 'The Speaking Abject in Kristeva's "Powers of Horror"', *Hypatia*, vol. 13, no. 1, pp. 138–57.

Hernawan, B. and van den Broek, T. 1999, 'Dialog Nasional Papua, Sebuah Kisah "Memoria Passionis" (Kisah Ingatan Penderitaan Sebangsa)', *TIFA Irian*, March, no. 12.

Hindess, B. 1996, *Discourses of Power: From Hobbes to Foucault*, Blackwell Publishers, Oxford.

Reconstructing torture 47

Jeanrond, W.G. 1992, 'From Resistance to Liberation Theology: German Theologians and the Non-Resistance to the National Socialist Regime', *The Journal of Modern History*, vol. 64, Supplement: Resistance Against the Third Reich, pp. S187–S203.

Kristeva, J. 1982, *Powers of Horror: An Essay on Abjection*, Columbia University Press, New York.

Kristeva, J. 1991, *Strangers to Ourselves*, Harvester Wheatsheaf, New York and London.

Kristeva, J. 2002, *Revolt, She Said*, MIT Press, Cambridge, MA and London.

Matthiesen, M.M. 1986, 'Narrative of Suffering: Complementary Reflections of Theological Anthropology in Johann Metz and Elie Wiesel', *Religion & Literature*, vol. 18, no. 2, pp. 47–63.

McAfee, N. 1993, 'Abject Strangers: Toward an Ethics of Respect', in K Oliver (ed.), *Ethics, Politics, and Difference in Julia Kristeva's Writing*, Routledge, New York and London, pp. 116–34.

McAfee, N. 2004, *Julia Kristeva*, Routledge, New York and London.

McCarthy, T. 1990, 'The Critique of Impure Reason: Foucault and the Frankfurt School', *Political Theory*, vol. 18, no. 3, pp. 437–69.

McClintock, A. 1995, *Imperial Leather*, Routledge, New York and London.

Metz, J.B. 1980, *Faith in History and Society Toward a Practical Fundamental Theology*, Burns & Oates, London.

Metz, J.B. 1981, *The Emergent Church: The Future of Christianity in a Postbourgeois Society*, SCM Press Ltd, London.

Metz, J.B. 1994, 'Suffering unto God', *Critical Inquiry*, vol. 20, no. 4, pp. 611–22.

Metz, J.B. 1998, *A Passion for God: The Mystical-Political Dimension of Christianity*, Paulist Press, New York and Mahwah, NJ.

Moruzzi, N.C. 1993, 'National Abjects: Julia Kristeva on the Process of Political Self-Identification', in K Oliver (ed.), *Ethics, Politics, and Difference in Julia Kristeva's Writing*, Routledge, New York and London, pp. 135–49.

Oliver, K. 1991, 'Julia Kristeva, Powers of Horror', *Diacritics*, vol. 21, no. 2/3, p. 43.

Oliver, K. 2002a, 'Introduction', in K Oliver (ed.), *The Portable Kristeva*, Updated edn, Columbia University Press, New York.

Oliver, K. (ed.) 2002b, *The Portable Kristeva*, Columbia University Press, New York.

Ostovich, S.T. 1990, *Reason in History: Theology and Science as Community Activities*, Scholars Press, Atlanta, GA.

Ostovich, S.T. 2005, 'Dangerous Memories and Reason in History', *KronoScope*, vol. 5, no. 1, pp. 41–57.

Poster, M. 1984, *Foucault, Marxism, and History: Mode of Production versus Mode of Information*, Polity Press; B. Blackwell, Cambridge, UK, New York.

Rose, N., O'Malley, P. and Valverde, M. 2006, 'Governmentality', *Annual Review of Law and Social Science*, vol. 2, pp. 83–104.

Rothenberg, D. 2003, '"What We have Seen has been Terrible": Public Presentational Torture and the Communicative Logic of State Terror', *Albany Law Review*, vol. 67, no. 2, pp. 465–99.

Schuster, E. and Boschert-Kimming, R. 1999, *Hope Against Hope*, Paulist Press, New York.

Sjöholm, C. 2005, *Kristeva and the Political*, Routledge, London and New York.

Taylor, C. 1992, 'Foucault on Freedom and Truth', in D.C. Hoy (ed.), *Foucault: A Critical Reader*, 5th edn, Basil Blackwell, Oxford and Cambridge, MA.

Taylor, D. 1997, *Disappearing Acts: Spectacles of Gender and Nationalism in Argentina's 'Dirty War'*, Duke University Press, Durham, NC and London.

48 *Reconstructing torture*

Thompson, K. 2003, 'Forms of Resistance: Foucault on Tactical Reversal and Self-Formation', *Continental Philosophy Review*, vol. 36, pp. 113–38.

Young, I. 1986, 'The Ideal of Community and the Politics of Difference', *Social Theory and Practice*, vol. 12, no. 1, pp. 1–26.

Ziarek, E. 1995, 'The Uncanny Style of Kristeva's Critique of Nationalism', *Postmodern Culture*, vol. 5, no. 2.

3 A genealogy of torture

The genealogical project

Equipped with theoretical lenses, in this chapter we will investigate the genealogy of torture that means the genesis, development, institutionalisation and perpetuation of torture in Papua. We will interrogate how in the Papuan context, torture as a form of governmentality has produced and reproduced both Indonesia as the imagined subject, and the disavowed Papuans as the abject. Inspired by Foucault (1984), the term 'genealogy' does not focus on tracing back historical development as a linear and singular process to find origins, the essence of things. Rather, it will help us ponder the development of multiple processes of power relations that have produced an object as it is. 'A genealogy should be seen as a kind of attempt to emancipate historical knowledges from that subjection, to render them, that is, capable of opposition and of struggle against the coercion of a theoretical, unitary, formal and scientific discourse' (Foucault 1980: 85). This 'capability of opposition' of a genealogical method refers to the Foucauldian notion of resistance as a capacity to creatively generate something new, or even to the Kristevan notion of revolt to renew 'the life of the mind and society' (Kristeva 2002: 85).

In five stages, we will dismantle all layers of power relations that generate the co-production of the imagined subject, the abject, the dynamics of the Papuan *memoria passionis*, the revolt and the ways in which all these elements render an opportunity for change. First, we will explore the ways the Dutch colonial power produced and colonised the space by inscribing sovereignty over the Papuan space. Then, we will analyse torture as a mode of governance in Papua during Sukarno's regime. Third, the analysis will be followed by an examination of the proliferation and institutionalisation of torture during Suharto's New Order. Fourth, we will explore ambiguous and ambivalent relationships between the imagined subject of Indonesia with the abject of Papua during the *reformasi* era. Finally, we will identify why the networked governance of torture continues during the Special Autonomy (*Otsus*) period in the present day despite an opportunity for change towards the better as offered by the Papua Land of Peace framework.

50 *A genealogy of torture*

The Dutch period: producing and colonising the Papuan space

During the era of colonial empire in the eighteenth century European powers carved up among themselves the so-called unknown territories, including New Guinea (now Papua). Three British travellers, John Crawfurd, George Windsor Earl and Alfred Russel Wallace, described the inhabitants of New Guinea as 'Oceanic Negro' (Ballard 2013: 169) as opposed to Malay to emphasise their racial marks of 'dark skin and frizzy hair'. This racial representation has profoundly influenced Western representations of Papua and Malay even up to today (Ballard 2013: 187).

Under the 1824 Treaty of London the Dutch and the British settled their disputes by exchanging their colonies in Asia. The Dutch obtained the whole territory of East Indies and New Guinea from the British, which gave up its colonies in East Indies. In return, the Dutch left the Malay Peninsula and the Indian subcontinent. As a result, the 141st meridian became the astronomical border for the Dutch who renamed the area 'Netherlands New Guinea'. The inhabitants of the land of New Guinea lived as many separate peoples and had minimal contact, if any, that could constitute a form of proto-nationalism. Therefore, what the Dutch produced and colonised at the same time was not only the space of Papua. They also colonised identities like the Dani and the Marind, which were real at that time when Papua was not a real identity. Colonisation did not produce a Papuan space that possessed agency. However, the Dutch were not the only producers of the Papuan space at the time. The Dutch Historian Pieter Drooglever describes the colonisation of Papua as 'done rather smoothly' between the Dutch on the Western side and Germany and England on the Eastern side to agree on the division of the Island of New Guinea (Drooglever 2009: 11–12). Therefore the imperial powers of the time collaboratively created the territory of Papua, marking it out as a new territory on imperial maps.

The Treaty of London did not necessarily benefit the local people even if the latter had some degree of agency. Historical records of the first contact between the Dutch and indigenous Papuans suggest contact was not always consensual (Drooglever 2009; Souter 1963). A number of violent incidents occurred during the first contacts. This signifies the level of hostility from both sides. For example, a clash occurred between the Dutch and locals in Triton Bay (Souter 1963: 22) when the colonial power wished to step into the so-called Bird's Head area in 1828.[1] Similarly, when the Dutch sought to open a post in 1892 in the Southern New Guinea close to the 141st meridian to mark their presence in this border area, they were severely attacked by the Marind and the detachment had to leave (Drooglever 2009: 14). After this incident, the Netherlands New Guinea government put stronger efforts into inscribing its power over this territory. However, there is no record to suggest that torture was used by the colonial power against locals.

Drooglever's account elucidates how the Dutch government asserted sovereignty over the western half of New Guinea. Various expeditions were carried

A genealogy of torture   51

out to map most of the territory and to establish government posts. At the same time missionaries introduced Christianity partly through their work supporting schooling, agricultural projects and health care. All of these left deep marks in the relationship between Papuans and outsiders. The following passage illustrates the Dutch administration's views about this territory:

> Most of them [the Dutch civil servants] regarded being stationed at New Guinea as a punishment. Wherever possible, they left after a couple of years. They always lived there without their families or the comforts of good housing, roads, cars and all the other things that made life on Java so pleasurable. And, of course, let us not forget malaria, for which absolutely no cure at all existed in those days.
>
> (Drooglever 2009: 51)

This passage precisely encapsulates the Dutch view that Papua was an unpleasant, uncanny, dangerous, savage and even deadly place because of incurable malaria. Therefore Dutch civil servants viewed a post in Papua as 'punishment' and something to be avoided as much as possible. These conditions prevailed at least until World War II. Based on this description, the Dutch arguably constructed Papua as an abject in this period. It was portrayed as the antonym of the positive subject, the 'modern' Dutch colonial power. The latter rarely allowed the abject to cross boundaries and integrate with the subject. Papua was disavowed but at the same time, claimed. It was denied but simultaneously colonised. Similarly, the network of colonial powers at the time did not recognise the existence of Papua and the only representation that could penetrate public consciousness at the time was the notion of 'the unknown, savagery and primitiveness' (Drooglever 2009: 51).[2] This ambiguous relationship between the coloniser and colonised essentially marked the very existence of the space[3] of then New Guinea.

If New Guinea was not recognised by the colonial powers of the time, what was the nature of relationship between New Guinea and Netherlands East Indies which is now Indonesia? Historians found little evidence that Papua had much to do with the Netherlands East Indies during the Dutch time from the seventeenth until the early nineteenth century (Drooglever 2009; Widjojo 2009). Drooglever (2009: 3–13) demonstrates that the only regular contact recorded since ancient times was between the western coast of Papua and Biak with Maluku, particularly Tidore and Ternate in the forms of slavery and piracy (Gerrit 2010; Lapian 2009: 127–31). The Sultan of Tidore in particular asserted his power and collected tax from Papua through *hongi* expeditions. The *hongi* fleet was essentially a violent and terrifying way to collect tax because Papuans were robbed, murdered or taken off as slaves. Even though under an agreement between the Dutch and the Tidorese in 1859 the *hongi* were forbidden and other forms of slavery were addressed, this traumatic experience marked relationships between the Tidorese and Papuans from then on.

Despite the limited ties among Papuan inhabitants, this historical evidence suggests that Papua had been treated as the abject by the Dutch colonial power

52 *A genealogy of torture*

and neighbouring local powers. Historical evidence suggests that Papua was of little importance for the Dutch although at a later date, the colonial power had knowledge about the world's largest gold deposit in Grassberg (now Tembagapura) (see Poulgrain 2015). Dutch rule was limited to a few cities in the North such as Manokwari, Fak-fak and Merauke while the vast majority of the area, particularly the central highlands, was left abandoned and underdeveloped. In a similar vein, neighbours only came to Papua to recruit slaves. However, in contrast to Kristeva's notion of abjection, according to which the abject is unable to fully cross the boundaries between itself and the subject, groups of Papuans were capable of fighting against the Dutch such as in Triton Bay in 1828 (Souter 1963: 22) or much later, in Obano, Paniai in 1956 (Giay 2011). This situation would gradually change after World War II, when Papua witnessed a new development that eventually led to the creation of a new social and political landscape.

Sukarno's period: introducing governmentality of torture

Drooglever (2009: 64–70) describes the Papuan experience with World War II as shocking but also revealing. The shocking element relates to Papuan encounters with the Japanese. This was at the same time revealing, as they were exposed to the assertive role of African American soldiers. Papuans were exposed to everyday harsh measures from the Japanese, including corporal punishment, raids, requisition and forced labour (Drooglever 2009: 64). Second, they also witnessed how the Dutch, the white men, were humiliated and brought to their knees. Third, they experienced a resurgence of messianic movements that had been abandoned for some time. Finally, they were deeply impressed with the black Americans in the military who gave orders to white fellow soldiers. Papuans made sense of this experience through the lens of the *koreri*, a messianic belief that interprets the reversal of world power as the sign of victory for Papuans (Osborne 1985: 12). However, the Japanese occupation was short.

Following the conclusion of World War II, colonisation came to an end in most parts of the world and decolonisation began. New nation-states emerged all over the world and this included Indonesia which proclaimed its independence from the Dutch on 17 August 1945. This new post-colonial state claimed the territory of the former Netherlands East Indies after the proclamation of Indonesian independence on 17 August 1945 by Sukarno and Mohammad Hatta. Having confronted the shocking experiences of war, Papuans increasingly became aware of the rapid changes around their territory and also of the window of opportunity to assert an identity, although as Drooglever argues, the Indonesian proclamation had little impact on them (2009: 82). This new awareness became evident during the Malino conference in South Sulawesi organised by Van Mook in 1946 where the territory of Indonesia was negotiated between the Dutch and Indonesia. During the conference Frans Kaisiepo, the only Papuan representative, drew the line between Papua and the eastern part of Indonesia by introducing the term 'Irian' and explicitly opposing the word 'Papua' as it reminded Papuans in the

A genealogy of torture 53

Tidoran language of 'slave' (Drooglever 2009: 89). In other words, thanks to *memoria passionis*, the brutality and humiliation of the *hongi* fleet by the Tidorese was still fresh in the minds of the Papuans at the time and thus led the Papuan representative to a decision to dissociate themselves from Eastern Indonesia.

This was not the case on the Indonesian side. Since the meetings of the preparatory committee for Indonesia's independence (*Badan Penyelidik Usaha-usaha Persiapan Kemerdekaan Indonesia*/BPUPKI), a number of founding fathers, such as Mohammad Yamin, Sukarno and Muzakir, insisted on incorporating Papua into Indonesia's territory while others, such as Mohammad Hatta, constantly opposed this proposal on the ground of race (Bahar, Sinaga and Kusuma 1992). In the following years, during the negotiations between Indonesia and the Netherlands, Papua was increasingly becoming a protracted subject of negotiation with the Netherlands, the former colonial power. During the Linggajati Agreement on 25 March 1947, there were two main points of negotiation, namely (1) the transfer and recognition of the sovereignty of Indonesia as a new nation and (2) the territory of Indonesia, which was claimed as the former Netherlands East Indies (Budiarjo 1992). During this negotiation, Budiarjo (1992) argues, the wisdom of accepting Papua as part of Indonesia was raised by the Dutch for the first time. However, the two main points about sovereignty and territory (except Papua) were deemed much more urgent to be addressed thoroughly by both parties and thus the issue of Papua was pushed aside from the negotiations altogether. The latter was postponed for the next round of Indonesia–Netherlands negotiations. The main preoccupation of the negotiation was the issue of federation as the format proposed by the Netherlands for the new state of Indonesia and the formation of a broader Union between the Netherlands and the sovereign Indonesian state.

Although the agreement managed to accommodate the word 'sovereignty' as Sukarno insisted, the implementation was torn to pieces when the Dutch launched military attacks on Yogyakarta, as the national capital of the Republic of Indonesia, in 1947 and 1949.[4] The question of Papua reappeared in the next negotiations, the 1949 Round Table Conference in The Hague, which led to the recognition of the sovereignty and territory of Indonesia by the Netherlands on 27 December 1949 (Drooglever 2009: 159). This agreement marked the emergence of Indonesia as a new nation-state, a new imagined subject. However, this agreement delayed the question of incorporating Papua territory without achieving any meaningful solution to it because the Netherlands continued to retain Papua. The Dutch became more determined to prepare Papua for self-determination by developing a cohort of Papuan public servants to govern the area (see Visser 2012). Further, the Dutch spent a significant amount of money to develop infrastructure, agriculture, health and education. One of the key steps undertaken by the Dutch was to establish the New Guinea Council on 1 December 1961. All these efforts signalled the clear intention of the Dutch government to retain its sovereign rights over Papua's territory regardless of Papuan and Indonesian consent.

54 *A genealogy of torture*

As a response, Indonesia asserted its claim over Papua in equally forceful ways.[5] First, to assert his authority, President Sukarno founded a still fully provisional government of *Provinsi Irian Barat* (Province of West Papua) in Soasiu, Tidore, on 17 August 1956, and appointed Zainal Abidin Syah as the governor (Pusat Sejarah dan Tradisi TNI 2000a: 112). Second, he declared *Trikora*, three people's commands, on 19 December 1961 in Yogyakarta[6] calling for: (1) preventing the establishment of the puppet state of Papua, a product of the Dutch colonial power, (2) raising the Red and White flag in West Irian, the motherland of Indonesia and (3) preparing general mobilisation to defend the independence and the integrity of the motherland and nation of Indonesia. Third, he established *Komando Mandala*, the central strategic command based in Makassar with Major General Suharto as the commander (Pusat Sejarah dan Tradisi ABRI 1995; Ridhani 2009) to prepare a massive coordinated military attack on the Dutch involving the Indonesian army, navy, air force and even police force, namely *Operasi Djajawijaya* (Djajawijaya Operation). These three grand strategies signified the Indonesian military's ambition of conquest.

The interplay of Indonesia's military visions of conquest and the haunting spectre of Communism sent a worrying signal to world power relations under the Cold War since Indonesia sought financial and military support from the Soviet Union (Poulgrain 2015). The action was interpreted by the West as the Indonesian move towards the Communist bloc. This signal successfully mobilised international support for the New York Agreement on 15 August 1962 as the legal basis for the transfer of Papua's territory into the hands of Indonesia. The role of the Kennedy Administration was instrumental in ensuring this agreement was signed by both parties. This also demonstrated how Cold War techniques of power had a strong influence to prevent Indonesia to fall into the Communist bloc. Under this provision, the Dutch transferred the territory to the United Nations Temporary Executive Authority (UNTEA), which governed it for a year from 1 May 1962. Chauvel (2005), Drooglever (2009), Saltford (2003) and Vlasblom (2004) note that this agreement indicated victory in the diplomatic battle for Indonesia as the provision explicitly stipulated the transfer of Papua to Indonesia by 1 May 1963.

Once Indonesia assumed full administrative control over the territory in 1963, the policy of President Sukarno leaned towards ignoring his responsibility to conduct a plebiscite of Papuans as he had previously stated to the US President Kennedy on 24 April 1961.[7] He decided to discontinue the country's membership of the United Nations on 20 January 1965. This action isolated Indonesia from the outside world and consequently Papua became much more invisible. The establishment of an army territorial command *Kodam Tjenderawasih* in 1963 was only a logical consequence of the existing military strategies of taking back Papua's territory. Although it was not unique to Papua, this military structure played an instrumental role not only in introducing coercive methods, notably torture, as a means to tame the Papuan social body but also to colonise the Papuan space by installing excessive Indonesian military representation across Papua from the provincial down to village level. The military has largely contributed to the production and maintenance of the governance of torture since then. A rare testimony of a former member of the special unit of the Indonesian army who was deployed as part of a grand strategy to eradicate the Free Papua Movement in the 1960s verifies this analysis. He confessed:

> My job at the time was in charge of combat intelligence unit and had to be in disguise. The training I had to take was really really heavy: trained to steal documents like a pick pocket without being spotted and all sorts of other training. In Papua, my job was to arrest members of the OPM and take them to KODAM. So I invited him to take a walk with me around here and then disappeared. Another unit took him. This applied to the hardliners but for those who were more approachable, we provided vocational training on agriculture.[8]

Although he did not specifically mention torture, he revealed not only the existence of state-sponsored violence targeting Papuan resistance movements but more importantly, coordinated strategies to eliminate the so-called 'hardliners'. Albeit patchy documentation, Dirk Vlasblom (2004) complements this evidence with narratives of torture survivors. As early as 1963, two university students were arrested, detained and tortured in different locations in Manokwari by Indonesian security services because they expressed their dissenting opinions to Indonesian authorities. They demanded the Act of Free Choice was implemented through casting ballots of all adult men and women, not by a group of representatives selected by the Indonesian military. Although the reported cases were minimal due to the circumstances discussed in Chapter 1, these cases are instructive. They indicate that the rule of law was not the method the Indonesian state relied upon to govern Papua from the beginning. Instead, the Indonesian state apparatus did not hesitate to deploy coercive methods against Papuans who expressed their opinions in a peaceful way.

As a response to the arrival of a repressive regime, a group of ex-PVK (the Papuan Volunteer Corps) led by Ferry Awom took a stand. In conjunction with the Arfak leaders, Lodewijk and Barend Mandatjan and Meidudga, he launched the first attack on an Indonesian army station in July 1965 (Djopari 1993: 168; Drooglever 2009: 642; Ondawame 2010: 64; Saltford 2003: 78–80; Vlasblom 2004). It was some months before the Indonesian army commander in Sukarnopura (now Jayapura) issued an order to launch a counter attack, but even then it did not result in a great success (Pusat Sejarah dan Tradisi TNI 2000b: 126). Although Awom's attack ultimately did not succeed militarily, this incident is important for our analysis here for three reasons: (1) it clearly reveals an element of opposition within the power relations in Papua, (2) it may contradict a widespread belief of the might of the Indonesian military always prevailing easily as recorded in official military histories and (3) it has been well recorded in Papuan oral history in the form of a popular lyric that inspires resistance movements.

This historical period shows us the introduction of a mode of governance of torture into the Papuan space. It derived from a convergence of military

56 *A genealogy of torture*

strategies of conquest, juridical strategies to secure a legal ground to incorporate Papua into Indonesia and political strategies to win international support at the UN level. These strategies were intertwined with a rationality of decolonisation in which Indonesia as a former Dutch colonised territory reclaimed its territory exactly as the lands the former coloniser had occupied. The decolonisation dispute did not leave much space for the abjected Papuans to participate. Instead, they were entangled in the power struggle between the Dutch and Indonesians. Once Indonesia secured its claim over Papua, its grip on Papua acquired an ambiguous character. On the one hand, it tightly retained, controlled and did not tolerate opposition, but on the other hand, the Indonesian state showed minimal gestures to fully recognise Papuans as free subjects by guaranteeing their freedoms and developing their well-being. Torture had a prominent place. The introduction of torture as a technology of domination exemplifies the notion of subjugation. Papua was important as long as it supported the formation of the nation-state of Indonesia. This analysis resonates with the Kristevan notion of abjection in which the imagined subject 'Indonesia' was created by forcefully excluding the abjected Papua. The latter was not suppressed into the subconscious level. Rather, it was constituted and located at the margins of the nation-state to sustain the core character and existence of Indonesia. The period that followed witnessed an intensification of this trend.

The Suharto period: proliferation and institutionalisation of torture

Although during Sukarno's regime torture was introduced, this regime did not survive the 1960s. Following the failed army coup, *Gerakan 30 September*,[9] marked by one of the bloodiest state-sponsored massacres in Indonesian modern history, Sukarno fell from power. Then Major General Suharto came to power and developed his totalitarian regime, the New Order.[10] One of the important elements of this architecture was the establishment of *Kopkamtib*, the Operational Command for the Restoration of Security and Order, in 1965. In its official brochure, this new intelligence agency did not hide its sources of authority and power. The authority derived from the MPR, the supreme legislative body in Indonesia; the intelligence officers had the power to arrest, detain and access all government and non-government offices at all levels across the country. The only limits were 'the provisions of the 1945 Constitution and the Law as well as the principle of PANCA SILA' (KOPKAMTIB 1977: 6). In other words, it was very broad and vague and open to abuse. Richard Tanter (1990) argues the power of this new architecture of surveillance was not only almost absolute but more importantly, operated through all sorts of government agencies and structures at all levels. Hence, *Kopkamtib* encapsulated the sophisticated techniques of power of the Indonesian state to intimidate civilians on the pretext of restoring order and by exploiting the notion of the haunting spectre of Communism. Under this framework, Papua was specifically targeted by this structure under the name of *Operasi Khusus* (Special Operation) as it was classified under the

A genealogy of torture 57

category of 'the separatist armed band OPM/GPL (namely the separatist movement of the so-called Papua Freedom Movement)' (KOPKAMTIB 1977: 4).

Suharto introduced a different approach to Papua. As opposed to Sukarno's policy, the new regime resumed its commitment to cooperate with the international community, particularly with Western countries and the UN, and to abide by the New York Agreement, specifically in holding a plebiscite for the Papuans. In 1966, the Indonesian Foreign Minister, Adam Malik, went to the UN headquarters in New York to discuss the rejoining of Indonesia to the UN as well as the necessary preparation towards the implementation of the Act of Free Choice (Saltford 2003: 89).

As a result of Malik's visit to the UN, on 1 April 1968 Ortiz Sanz was appointed as the representative of the UN Secretary-General for the implementation of the Act of Free Choice as stipulated by article 18 of the New York Agreement. The plebiscite was his main focus and increasingly he was confronted with serious challenges from different elements within the Indonesian government, including President Suharto himself. The letter of the Agreement itself was ambiguous since both 'one man, one vote' and *musyawarah* (deliberation) options were equally accepted (Drooglever 2009: 675). The latter denotes a method of discussion to reach consensus. Ortiz Sanz tirelessly argued with Jakarta proposing a mixed method before he accepted the fact that Jakarta was more than determined to use the *musyawarah* method to conduct the Act of Free Choice (Saltford 2003: 114).

During his period, the UN administration received 156 complaints[11] from various elements of Papuan society. Thirty-five letters specifically mentioned 'political prisoners, killing, repression of freedom of expression, torture' and even 'bombing' committed by the Indonesian military. The quantum of complaints suggests that the political atmosphere was not peaceful and free. In response to these complaints Ortiz Sanz openly discussed them with the Head of the Indonesian Government Representative in Papua Sujarwo Tjondronegoro, who generally issued reports arguing that the matter was somewhat exaggerated. The UN, however, did not take any further action so the complaints only ended up in the UN archives. In contrast to Tjondronegoro's statement, the history book of the Indonesian military tells a different story. It is clear that several military operations were carried out to eradicate the resistance movement to secure the implementation of the Act of Free Choice (Pusat Sejarah dan Tradisi TNI 2000b: 197–204). Given the reputation of the Indonesian military operations in Papua, such operations most likely resulted in mistreatment of locals. Furthermore, the reports of the British Embassy in Jakarta refer to the use of bombardment in 1967 resulting in many casualties (Saltford 2003: 78–9).

The impact of military oppression was also reflected from the increasing number of Papuan refugees to the Territory of Papua New Guinea (TPNG) from 1963 (Saltford 2003: 86–9). In the first three months of 1967 the TPNG administration listed 527 persons crossing its border and asked for refugee status in PNG.[12] This situation remained the same following the Act of Free Choice in 1969.[13] One of the Papuan refugees from this time testified that he joined a

58   A genealogy of torture

group of young Papuans at the Indonesia-TPNG border and waited for the implementation of the Act of Free Choice. Once the result was in favour of Indonesia, he crossed the border and joined the Matias Wenda-led OPM group in Bewani, outside Vanimo.[14] The pattern of 'border crossing' to PNG territory has become common for Papuans whenever they felt threatened in their homeland since then.

As Jakarta had clearly signalled, the Act of Free Choice was implemented through *musyawarah*. Therefore, 1,025 Papuan representatives were selected by the Indonesian authority to join the *Dewan Musyawarah Penentuan Pendapat Rakyat* (DMP) in eight cities: Merauke, Wamena, Nabire, Fak-fak, Sorong, Manokwari, Biak and Jayapura. Those who were selected were put in special internment and isolated from any contact with the outside world, even with their own families (see Figure 3.1). They were guarded by the army and had to go through rigorous drills to learn by heart their wishes to integrate with Indonesia (Drooglever 2009: 721). One of the survivors provided her testimony confirming the historical account as follows:

> We were interned for about a month. Not much happened inside the dorm. Every night, I had to practice reading out loud with Mr Laurens, the commander of RPKAD [the Indonesian Army Special Forces]. 'You can't make any mistakes', they told us. We were from Asmat, Mappi, Marind Dek, Biau and the city of Merauke. The government and *Opsus* had chosen us. Some of us were teachers, others were illiterate. I walked in and read the text. I pledged to join Indonesia. I was so emotional because it felt like a total surrender. I could feel a burning fire inside me. The truth was I had no intention of submitting to Indonesia. But such a feeling could not be expressed. It had to be suppressed. Those who spoke out were sent to *Kodim* and many of them died because of the electric shocks they received.[15]

Internment exemplifies a deliberate intention to brainwash people and arguably constitutes a form of psychological torture. The survivor quoted above also stated that there were electric shocks as well. The members of DMP were being disciplined, drilled and suppressed to conform to the Indonesian state narrative that they would choose to integrate with Indonesia. The role of RPKAD (the Indonesian Army Special Forces) is also prominent here in preventing the members of DMP from opting for anything other than being united with Indonesia. This non-consensual method was effective in securing the intended outcome. The DMP was unanimously in favour of joining the Republic of Indonesia.

The role of the army was highly influential in manipulating the members of DMP. The latest book on the history of the Indonesian military (Pusat Sejarah dan Tradisi TNI 2000b: 204) confirms an active role of the army in securing the outcome as follows:

> the efforts undertaken by Kodam XVII/Cenderawasih to fulfill the Act of Free Choice were implemented in accordance with the New York Agreement.

A genealogy of torture 59

Figure 3.1 One of the dormitories used to intern DMP in Merauke left abandoned in 2010.
Source: Hernawan's private collection.

> The result was the people of West Irian decided to remain united within the territory of the Republic of Indonesia.[16]

In his mission report, Ortiz Sanz reported his conclusions, which were subsequently approved by the United Nations General Assembly on 19 November 1969. This decision put to an end the conflict over the sovereignty of the territory of Papua as well as the chapter of Indonesia's decolonisation (Saltford 2003: 175). By then Papua was fully and officially integrated into Indonesia despite fierce criticisms from the Papuan leaders about the way the Act was conducted. This fact resonates with Frank Graziano's (1992) assertion in his analysis of torture in Argentina's Dirty War how torture is so spectacular but at the same time, the knowledge of the audience of the existence of this technology was suppressed and silenced so they were not even able to mention an open secret of torture. This notion is helpful to explore the meaning of the Act of Free Choice.

The Act of Free Choice is instructive for this book in revealing a distinct element of the notion of sovereignty: 'space' or 'territory'. All actors involved in the Act of Free Choice interpreted sovereignty not in terms of 'capacity' or 'right' over life and death as Foucault suggests, but rather, in relation to 'territory'. By securing the declaration of Papuan integration into Indonesia, the Indonesian state exercised its power to generate a Papuan territory distinct from

60 *A genealogy of torture*

that which the Dutch had created in the early nineteenth century when it signed the agreement with the British. The Act of Free Choice becomes a cornerstone of architecture of domination in that it exemplifies a sophisticated governance of torture which is paradoxical in nature. On the one hand, the architecture of torture was so spectacular, an open secret, that anyone could watch and feel its shock and awe but on the other hand, the knowledge of this spectacularity was suppressed and thus rendered invisible.

Internment of Act of Free Choice delegates occurred at eight different locations in eight cities of Papua. Various Indonesian state agencies were involved in drilling the targeted Papuan representatives to recite a script prescribed by the Indonesian state apparatus. In highly calculated measures, the representatives were confined in highly controlled facilities, interned and stripped of their freedoms of expression and movement. Under extreme pressure, and fearing torture, they were forced to declare that they wanted to integrate into Indonesian territory. As Papuan public space had been colonised, Indonesian security services found little difficulty to colonise the body and the soul of the Papuan representatives. Further, this governmentality managed to secure approval from the international community despite official complaints received by the UN representative at the time. This is only the foundation. We will further investigate the whole architecture of torture erected on this basis in the next section.

The internment constituted a small element of the larger machinery of torture during Suharto's regime produced in the Papuan social body including colonising public space, war, hidden torture chambers, prison systems and integration methods. The first is colonising public space. From the City of Sentani, about 40 km from the provincial capital Jayapura, locals have documented through oral history a collective memory of a military operation around 1972 in this area that resulted in disappearances, arbitrary arrest and detention, and killing. Five families[17] provided me with information on their disappeared family members. They never received any answers or explanations from the authorities concerning the fates of their loved ones. One of the chiefs[18] in this area specifically mentioned a particular location around Lake Sentani, where the Indonesian army dumped the bodies that had been executed in Ifar Gunung, the main training ground for the army. Another chief confirmed this and even mentioned a song[19] that was composed by survivors of the detention centre in memory of Ifar Gunung.

Second is the technology of war. In contrast to Sentani which experienced hidden and asymmetric war, Wamena in the Central Highlands of Papua was a battle front in which both sides sought to assert domination over one another in the most spectacular way. On the battlefield the Indonesian security forces and the Papuan freedom fighters exchanged coercive force and violent techniques. Matias Wenda started his fight in Pyramid, a village outside the city of Wamena in early 1977. One of the few surviving eyewitnesses provides a description of the situation as follows:

> In 1977 the 'influence'[20] from Jayapura penetrated us and the people erected *honay* in the whole Pyramid valley. The people were not able to move

A genealogy of torture 61

freely. The guard posts '*Papua Merdeka*' were erected and they dealt with communal disputes. Those who were found guilty were punished with corporal punishment. If somebody reported to the police or the army, his/her property would be confiscated. Inside the post guard compound they organised military training, such as crawling.

All people here were united and attacked the army guard post. Then the army retaliated and hunted the attackers. As a result, the people fled to the jungle until Kobakma. Between Kimbim and Pyramid lied the battlefield for a year. The army together with the people from Kimbim hunted the people in the jungle around Makki.[21]

Although Wamena is not the only battlefield in Papua,[22] it probably became the longest battleground in Papuan history. Papuan oral history has recorded devastating impacts on the lives of the Papuans in their *memoria passionis*. The locals were caught up between the freedom fighters and the Indonesian army. Many Papuans were internally displaced. Unaccounted numbers died as refugees; many young men joined the Matias Wenda-led OPM movement (Ondawame 2010: 101) and their livelihoods were destroyed. One of the female survivors told her story of being shot during an Indonesian airstrike on her *kampong* outside the city of Wamena (see Figure 3.2):

In 1977 at night around six to seven pm, I was about to fetch some water before leaving my *honay* to take refuge to another village. I was shocked because all of the sudden an airplane was coming and dropped bombs. I was so panicked and ran away back to the *honay*. First I didn't feel anything wrong but suddenly felt numb because the wound on my back was so deep. The wound forced me to remain isolated because it was not treated properly and smelt horrible. So whenever we had meals in *honay*, I was told to stay away from the group because they could not stand with me. I chose to sit outside then.[23]

This story reveals a different kind of experience with terror, the very foreign, unfamiliar idea of terror and awesome power inflicted from the skies. It is highly visible, very powerful but also leaves visible scars on bodies, cityscapes and landscapes. Such a terrifying experience can only be found in a war zone like the bombing of Dresden in World War II or the bombing of Afghanistan after 9/11 as a terror tactic. For Melanesians, for whom the landscape embodies their mothers, their clans, bombing means inscribing power not only on physical bodies, but also on the bodies of ancestors. Those who are marked with the inscription of terror might further suffer from marginalisation and isolation from their communities such as this woman. Therefore the technology of war has profound impacts on every aspect of Papuan society: physical bodies, social body, cityscapes and landscapes.

Although the Indonesian state narrative does not record the details of the ways the Indonesian security forces conducted the operation, it explicitly records

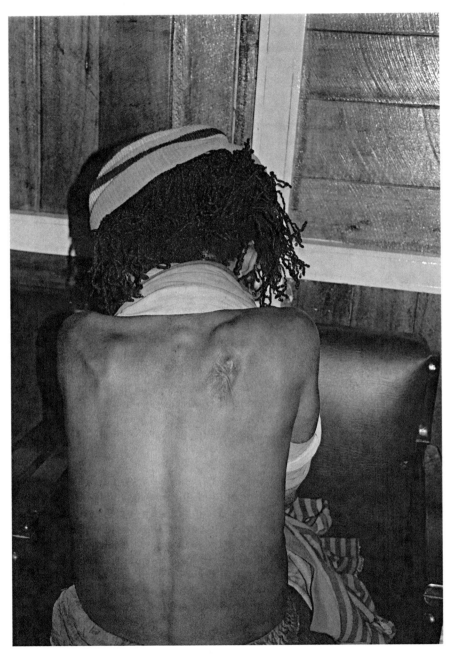

Figure 3.2 A scar on the female body caused by a bombing in the Wamena area in 1977.
Source: Hernawan's private collection.

A genealogy of torture   63

this incident under the category of military operations to eradicate the separatist movement in Papua (Pusat Sejarah dan Tradisi TNI 2000b: 130). While this record confirms the existence of the operation, it also signifies the deliberate intention of Indonesian state policy to construct Papuans as the abject. Papuans were perceived as posing a threat to the territorial integrity of Indonesia and thus deserved 'perpetual war' (Kirsch 2010: 5–8)[24] to ensure that the abject remained under Indonesia state control and did not break the boundaries of the Indonesian nation-state. This pattern confirms a paradox of excluding and claiming the abject.

The third was establishing hidden locations of torture. The following is an example collected from Jayapura. This type of technology was common until the 1990s. One of the Papuan combatants who was captured, detained and tortured in the early 1980s but managed to escape recalled that a number of military commands in Jayapura were designated to detain, torture and kill those who were labelled 'OPM'. He shared his story of how he was arrested, detained and tortured to confess his connection with the OPM while he was a student at the University of Cenderawasih.

> We were brought to Angkasa II [Jayapura], the Kopassus[25] headquarters and were being interrogated. They threatened me with death by putting a pistol on my head twice as if they wanted to blow my head off ... they swore at me, beat me, and all sorts of things. They forced me to confess that I had connections with people of the bush. But because I was silent, they sliced my hands with a cutter. They often didn't give us food. That was the suffering I experienced. There were five of us. But because we were students then they wanted to use us to collect information. We were put in the house arrest. I thought they used me for a while until they felt enough and would get rid of me. So it's better to escape while I could.[26]

The fourth element was the Indonesian national prison system. In the late 1980s one of the non-combatant Papuan leaders experienced a typical form of mistreatment meted out against those who were considered 'a Papuan leader':

> After I gave a speech to the crowd gathered in UNCEN, I had been targeted. I felt not safe so I ran to the PNG consulate in Dok VIII Atas [in Jayapura] to take refuge. On 28 December 1988, I was arrested and detained in the military detention in Waena. Then I was transferred to Polda, KODAM and back again to Waena before eventually transferred to Biak and Ujung Pandang prisons. During interrogations, they used electric shocks on me. On 23 February 1995 I was again transferred to Kalisosok prison in Surabaya and in July at the year, they sent me to Tangerang prison in West Java. Here they put me into an isolation cell in a kind of a tower for almost two years. I was cramped because the cell was so small. I could not stand up so I had to crawl. I was not allowed to go out so they sent meals with a rope to my cell. This went on until Reverend Anthony who visited us regularly raised this

64 *A genealogy of torture*

> case to the U.S. In November 1997 I was again transferred to Cipinang prison, where I spent time with Xanana Gusmao [from Timor-Leste], and after *reformasi*, my status was changed into a city prisoner until 2007.[27]

This narrative indicates not only a chain of specific locations that were designed to torture Papuan leaders inside Papua but more importantly, a national system designed to torture Papuan political prisoners across Indonesia. Technologies, procedures and strategies of torture were not limited to the space of Papua but more broadly involved the Indonesian national prison systems, such as Kalisosok Surabaya and all relevant government agencies. Prison symbolises an ambivalent notion of visibility. On the one hand, the infrastructure is visible and to some extent accessible for outsiders to visit prisoners, but on the other hand, the exact details of its daily life and its oppressive-mystique quality to a large extent remain hidden from public knowledge. Prison also gives a clear message that incarceration is meant to exclude, not rehabilitate. Further, the above story also illustrates how the rule of law collapsed as we did not see any due process. On the contrary, we can only follow the line of arbitrary arrest and detention, imprisonment without trial and eventually solitary confinement for a prolonged period of time. All these suggest a sophisticated and calculated technology of torture targeting the Papuan leadership.

The fearsome mystique of the prison building exemplifies an open secret of institutionalised torture. The Papuan public was made aware that behind the prison walls, torture had been committed but the public was prevented from witnessing actual events of torture. This technology, however, does not entirely fit a Foucauldian notion of torture because as Graziano suggests, it represented more an imagination of torture, not an actual event of torture itself. The actual event is always suppressed from public knowledge. Therefore, the spectacularity of this type of torture lies in its invisibility that embodies the haunting panoptic gaze of the prison. However, the quoted story also indicates that imprisonment cannot be seen in isolation. Rather it is only a chain of commands that works as a system.

The fifth element has been the deployment of the integration method. Although this method uses persuasion, which is the complete opposite of torture, this option has been generally used as a first attempt before shifting into coercion. So it should be seen as a continuum. Samsudin's account provides one of the best descriptions of the method. It details an operation to release a group of hostages held by an OPM leader, Martin Tabu, in the border area between Indonesia and PNG in 1978 (Ondawame 2010: 94–5; Samsudin 1995). In comparison to other hostage accounts, which are generally based on an oral history of non-state actors, Samsudin provides a revealing account because it is based on a story of a state actor who played a central role. This incident drew major attention from the Indonesian army because among the hostages there were a number of public figures, such as the commander of the army unit, a Catholic priest and an important local government official. Through prolonged negotiations, Martin Tabu agreed to release the hostages without any casualties and more importantly, no military action took place. Moreover, Martin Tabu was then admitted into the

A genealogy of torture 65

Indonesian armed forces. Colonel Samsudin called this operation *Operasi Senyum* (the Smiling Operation). His candid autobiographical account not only captures the complexity of decision-making processes within the Indonesian military organisation but also illustrates his and his organisation's ambiguous attitude towards Papuan combatants, in particular, and Papuans in general. We can observe this attitude from the aftermath of the hostage release. Martin was admitted to the Indonesian army but neither Samsudin nor the Indonesian army was totally convinced. He and his organisation failed to come to terms with the notion of the uncanniness of Papuans and Tabu in that their relationships were characterised by suspicion, strangeness and ambivalence. Papuans remained deceitful in the eyes of Samsudin's colleagues (Samsudin 1995: 411). This unsettled feeling resulted in an attempt to poison Tabu but it was cancelled at the last minute because of Samsudin's commitment to befriend Tabu (Samsudin 1995: 363–5). This rarely candid account of a middle officer precisely captures the notion of abjection in that Tabu was needed, recruited and even given a decent military position, but at the same time denied, undermined and nearly assassinated.

The five accounts illustrate how torture was institutionalised through different types of technologies of governance. While it perpetuated the logic of decolonisation established by the previous regime, it illustrates a broader network involving assemblage of institutions, procedures, personnel, training for personnel, funding, equipment, calculations and tactics, and rationalities of torture. All these elements were much less developed in the previous stage. These elements resonate with Foucauldian notions of governmentality in the sense that torture is not merely a singular and independent technique of causing great pain. Rather, it is a prominent part of a mix of technologies of power covering a vast variety of components. Further it generated 'a whole series of specific governmental apparatuses' (Foucault 2003: 244) such as *Kopkamtib*, prison systems, public space, the battle front and the integration method. All of these technologies were produced based on the rationality of domination which aims at incorporating the territory of Papua into Indonesia.

What was the impact of technologies of domination during this period? Apart from continuing to foment a violent response, resistance creatively generated a space of freedom. There were three new forms of opposition that emerged during this period, including refugees, NGOs and human rights narratives. First are Papuan refugees. In 1984, the world recorded an exodus of some 10,000 people from the Southern part of Papua to Papua New Guinea (PNG). It caused a diplomatic incident between Indonesia and Papua New Guinea involving the United Nations High Commissioner for Refugees (UNHCR). As both countries were not parties of the 1950 UN Convention on Refugees, both agreed to not give these people refugee status. Instead, they invented the ambiguous term 'border crossers', which had serious legal, political and social impact because these people were not entitled to any protection. They could be repatriated to the country of origin. They were not entitled to public services in Papua New Guinea because they were not PNG citizens. The identity 'border crossers' forced them

66 *A genealogy of torture*

to reconstruct their liminal identity (Glazebrook 2004, 2008; Smith 1991; Zocca 1995, 2008). In Kristeva's view, by giving a stateless status, both countries effectively constructed Papuan refugees as an abject that only provoked disgust, certainly distancing and rejection, from both countries and put them beyond their responsibility to protect. In other words, Papuan are 'foreigners'.

Second, although the power of surveillance and coercion was omnipresent, the 1980s also witnessed the birth of NGOs with strong support from the Catholic Church and the Evangelical Christian Church (GKI). The Legal Aid Foundation (LBH), YPMD and YPKHM were among the important pioneer organisations dealing with the issues of land rights, rural development and litigation. In art, Arnold Ap and his musician group 'mambesak' initiated a cultural project that collected and produced traditional songs across Papua as an attempt to have cultural representation for Papua within Indonesia (see Glazebrook 2008). All these can be interpreted as manifestations of non-violent resistance that took form in art and community building.

Third, by the 1990s, human rights narratives entered Papuan discourses. These built bridges with international discourses of human rights. One of the most revealing incidents that paved the way for the international community to get involved was the human rights abuses committed by the Indonesian army inside Freeport Mining company's operation site. The then-Catholic Bishop of Jayapura, Herman Münninghoff OFM (ACFOA 1995; Münninghoff 1995), exposed this incident by submitting the first Catholic Church report on the human rights situation to the authorities. The report details how nine security guards, who were active members of the Indonesian security forces, shot dead innocent Amungme people just after they finished their Christmas celebration in 1994 simply because of suspicions that these people were Kelly Kwalik-led OPM members. For the same reason, other Amungme people were tortured and detained in a Freeport container, which was full of human faeces and freezing cold. This report was crucial in a number of ways. First, it constituted a landmark of the Catholic Church involvement in advocating human rights for Papuans. Second, this report became a milestone towards beginning to unravel the entanglement of the state authorities with foreign investment companies that would not hesitate to deploy torture to protect their interests. Third, it suggests a failure of Komnas HAM, the official national human rights body, to penetrate the network of military power that controlled the crime scene. Nevertheless, four soldiers were punished with minor jail terms (Ballard 2001: 26; Leith 2003: 198). Since then Freeport continues to be a site of death and impunity (Ballard 2002b; Kirksey and Harsono 2008). In sum, these three examples suggest various forms of resistance which in Foucault's view has a broader meaning than the term 'opposition'. While the variety of resistance underscores the importance of agency, it also reveals the notion of creativity and productivity, not merely confronting the dominating power in a violent way.

This violent method continues, however. A group of scientists, foreign and Indonesian nationals, was taken hostage by OPM for three months in 1996. Every effort to negotiate fell apart and left the government to conclude that its only option was for a military operation by Indonesian Army Special Forces. Major General Prabowo Subianto led the operation and released all the hostages. Unfortunately, the cost was significantly high. Two members of the team were reportedly killed by the OPM. Adinda Saraswati (1997) and Daniel Start (1997), two eyewitnesses, recorded their dramatic survival and provided vivid accounts in their separate publications. While both were appalled with violent tactics[28] of the OPM by kidnapping them, Start seemed more understanding whereas Saraswati tended to rely on state narratives to interpret the story *inter alia* by using the term '*Gerombolan Pengacau Keamanan*-OPM'[29] to refer to her kidnappers. It took a few years before the world discovered the dark side of the military operation to release the hostages when local NGOs and Church leaders[30] submitted a report (Indonesian Evangelical Church, Catholic Church and Evangelical Christian Church 1999) to the authorities in Jakarta detailing the human rights violations committed by the Indonesian armed forces. The report not only documented killings, torture, rape and burning of houses by the Indonesian security forces but also found disturbing information of involvement of ICRC (International Committee of Red Cross) personnel[31] and foreign mercenaries in the operation. Both the Indonesian authorities and ICRC headquarters denied the allegations. Nonetheless, ICRC closed its office in Jayapura not long after the report was published. The incident[32] captured an interplay of highly complex power relations in that the sovereign power of the state, the human rights narrative, opposition and humanitarian discourses converged.

Reformasi period: ambiguity of change

Following looming economic crises, pressure from the IMF and pro-democracy protests organised by university students in Jakarta, President Suharto decided to resign in May 1998. His authoritarian regime came to an end and he passed his mandate to his vice president, B.J. Habibie. Indonesia entered the era of *reformasi* (reform) and was overwhelmed with the euphoria of democracy after being oppressed for more than thirty years under Suharto's New Order. Major reforms took place such as the amendment of the 1945 constitution to include provisions on human rights. The UN Convention Against Torture was ratified and became Indonesian Law no. 5/1998; the police force was separated from the Indonesian armed forces; the structure of the legislature (DPR and MPR) was reformed to eliminate the appointed quota for the police and the armed forces. The spirit of *reformasi* was to hold state actors accountable, particularly the military and the executive, and to reinstate the rule of law and human rights as guiding principles of democracy. In a similar vein, decentralisation, a theme that has been one major focus of contemporary Indonesian scholarship (Aspinall and Fealy 2003), was introduced to implement power sharing between the centre and periphery. *Reformasi* resonates with the Kristevan notion of revolt in that it renewed every aspect of individual life and society.

The spirit of *reformasi* was extended across Indonesia, including Papua. Although this openness allowed Papuans to regenerate a sense of agency, there

68 *A genealogy of torture*

were at least five incidents that suggest ambiguity in the change. First was the Biak massacre that exemplified the technology of war as already discussed in Chapter 1. This harsh response from the Indonesian security forces towards the peace protest signified the reality that the spirit of *reformasi* did not fully penetrate Papua. Calling for *merdeka* (independence) and raising the Morning Star were probably considered beyond the limits of the *reformasi* framework by the Indonesian security apparatus (Kirksey 2012).

This incident did not stand alone. The 'Morning Star' flag was also raised in Jayapura and Wamena in the same month but resulted in no casualties or harsh action. However, the second deployment of the technology of war occurred when the university students of the University of Cenderawasih organised a demonstration to call for dialogue and Steven Suripatty,[33] a student activist of Ambonese background, was shot dead. A non-Papuan witness described this incident as 'very cruel'.[34] Scholars interpreted the flag raising as a clear example of reemergence of Papuan nationalism (Chauvel 2005; van den Broek and Szalay 2001), but in regard to Biak, Rutherford also saw this as connected to the revival of millenarianism (Rutherford 1999). In contrast to the Biak massacre, in this incident there was also targeting of non-Papuans who joined the Papuan opposition to the Indonesian government. It is instructive to highlight this pattern because Suripati's killing suggests that the sovereign power of Indonesia will not only tolerate the Papuan opposition but also anyone who supports it. Suripati's body becomes a medium to convey a message to the audience: those who support the abject will become the abject themselves and punishable by death. However, ethno-nationalist Papuans currently tend to ignore this element that might potentially mobilise broader solidarity inside and outside Papua.

Following these bloody incidents, the third indicator of ambiguity arose, namely negotiation. A delegation of DPR-RI came to Jayapura to discuss the situation with local leaders seeking a solution. The main recommendation was to hold a dialogue with the President himself. FORERI (Forum of Reconciliation of the Irianese) emerged as a mediator that led to the meeting between the Papuan representatives and the President. This marked a milestone towards holding a national dialogue, which was then held on 26 February 1999 at the Presidential Palace in Jakarta. Tom Beanal led the '100 team' of Papuan leaders to meet with President Habibie and his cabinet. Unexpectedly, drawing on Papuan *memoria passionis* (Hernawan and van den Broek 1999), Tom Beanal conveyed the message that Papua wanted independence, separate from Indonesia. The president was stunned and could only ask the team to go home and reflect. Chauvel (2005: 14) argues that Beanal's assertion marked a decisive moment of Papuan nationalism by stating that Papua had gained independence in 1961 and Indonesia came to annex the territory in 1963. Once the team landed in Jayapura, the Papuans welcomed them as heroes.

Meanwhile, in national politics, a new leadership came to power: the new President was Abdurahman Wahid, a well-known progressive Moslem cleric. He allowed the Papuan flag to fly side by side with the Indonesian national flag as long as it was raised lower (see Figure 3.3). This marked the only moment in

Figure 3.3 The Morning Star flag raised side by side with the Indonesian national flag in Jayapura in 2000.
Source: Hernawan's private collection.

Indonesian history that the Papuan flag could be raised without any blood being spilt.

By the end of 1999, the President renamed Irian Jaya, Papua. This was the beginning of the recognition of Papuan identity. The Papuan spring began. To mark the first anniversary of 'the national dialogue', the 100 team convened a *Musyawarah Besar* (*Mubes*/a great deliberation) in Sentani, which managed to establish the Papuan leadership in a collegial form called *Presidium Dewan Papua* (PDP/Papuan Presidium Council). PDP had the mandate to convene a Papuan Congress. With the full support of President Wahid, the 2nd Papuan Congress was held in Jayapura from 29 May–June 2000. All of these events constituted the fourth indicator of ambiguity in which Papuans were given a greater space to redefine their agency. This proliferation of freedom allowed Papuans to express their *memoria passionis* explicitly during this extraordinary period. *Musyawarah Besar* and the Congress become the culmination of Papuan narratives to consolidate the abjects and to mobilise solidarity intra and extra the abjected Papuans.

Following the Congress, a shift of power took place within the Indonesian web of power. President Wahid was impeached and Megawati Sukarnoputri, his former vice president, came to power with a completely different attitude

70 A genealogy of torture

towards Papua. The crackdown began.[35] This marked the fifth indicator: regression to technologies of war. In October 2000 in Wamena, the security apparatus clashed with *Satgas Papua*[36] (the Papuan Task Force). Many were killed and there was an exodus of the migrants out of Wamena (Tim Kemanusiaan Wamena 2001). Some people were then blamed, tried and sentenced heavily. Not long afterwards in December 2000, an unidentified group attacked a police station of the city of Abepura and killed three police officers. This attack immediately sparked police retaliation targeting student dormitories around Abepura. Hundreds of people, mostly Papuan highlanders and students, were arrested, detained and tortured, in some cases in public. Two students died in Jayapura police custody and one was shot and severely injured. NGOs and Papuan Church leaders reported this serious incident to Komnas HAM, calling for an independent and thorough investigation. In its concluding report, Komnas HAM stated that the police committed crimes against humanity, a serious crime under Law no. 26/2000 on the Human Right Court which had recently been passed by the Indonesian parliament (Komnas HAM 2001).[37] Komnas HAM recommended twenty-five police officers be prosecuted. The Attorney General only tried two police commanders. Eventually, both were acquitted when the court found insufficient evidence against them (Christianty, Kasim and Dewi 2007).

Finally, in June 2001, the technology of war in support of investment reappeared in Wasior, a small village in Wondama Bay where a national timber company operated. Following the killing of six members of *Brimob* (paramilitary police) and stealing their weapons by an allegedly OPM group, it did not take long before the police dispatched another *Brimob* unit to restore public order and find the stolen weapons. This mission turned Wasior into a battleground. The Papuan NGOs and the local Christian Church (ALDP 2002; Elsham Papua 2002; LP3BH 2001; Manuaron 2001) claimed that the police committed crimes against humanity, including torture, extrajudicial killings and destroying the houses and livelihoods of the Wasior people. Such brutal action, including public torture, prompted an influx of refugees to neighbouring cities, particularly Manokwari and Nabire. Maintaining his innocence, one of the torture survivors described his lingering anger and desperation seven years after the actual incident (see Box 3.1), stating:

> Give me my rights. They have to pay back my blood. I'm innocent. I'm still shocked with what happened to me. Revenge is still within me. If I see the scar on my face through the mirror, the intention to take revenge comes back. I cannot accept this. Please tell everyone. Please convey the aspirations of the Papuans.[38]

He not only lost his dignity but also his property because Brimob bulldozed and burnt his house to the ground. The two-and-a-half-year sentence, however, seems extremely light and thus incompatible with the verdict of committing a serious crime, like murder. Moreover, Kirksey's account reveals that the real killers were persons under the pseudonyms 'Daniel Awom and Barnabas

A genealogy of torture 71

Box 3.1 A scaffold of the sovereign power

In the rain that night, I was about to go home from work [at the timber company] when four Brimob members stopped me and pointed their guns on me. So I was confused and asked, 'What's going on?' but they answered me with punching. I was under gun point so I surrendered to them. I saw many people were already arrested and gathered at the bay, including the head of the village. I didn't recognise these Brimob as they wore plain clothes and their pant uniform with bands in their heads. They beat me and beat me until I was bleeding and fainted.

They separated workers from villagers and told us to go in to a tug boat. In front of the body, they did an interrogation and asked who did this. 'I don't know,' I said. But they responded, 'You want get shot?' I was then tied up in pole like a crucifix on the tug boat while they kept punching me with their rifle. They ground hot chilies and forced me to eat. I was terrified so I followed whatever they told. They brought us to Manokwari.

Arriving there, the head of criminal investigation unit put me into the quarantine cell. I was detained for 40 days in Manokwari police station.

When they were doing interrogation, they put me under the gun point and forced me to give answers according to their will. Sixteen people were detained but they only prosecuted me. I was no longer in control of myself. Every time a police officer came to the room, I shed my blood. So I just followed whatever they wanted.

Antonius, a detective, dragged me out of the room to the police yard. He collected pebbles in a can. Every time I could not answer his question, I was forced to grind a pebble. O God! I had no choice so I did it and I broke all my teeth. See! [he showed me his broken teeth]. He also beat me with a wooden bar (5×5 cm) on the back of my head so I fell down and had seizures. My ears were deafened. Bahrun, another police, stabbed my left nostril through my mouth with his bayonet.

I saw a human rights lawyer come in to provide legal aid for me. But they slapped him in his face and kicked him out. I didn't know him at the time.

I was forced to crawl under a table and they stepped on my toes while pressing questions. I didn't dare to say no. So I followed whatever they wanted which I never did.

During the court hearing, when the prosecutor asked whether I was involved in the killing or not, I answered I made the police statement under extreme pressure. A police officer who was in the court room would have shot me, if the judge had not expelled him from the room. But at the end I was sentenced to 2.5 year in jail for murder.

Mawen' (Kirksey 2012: 128–9). This punishment suggests that short incarceration was a form of shock therapy for a broader audience who witnessed and knew the ritual of torture had been performed against this man. It also sent a message that the sovereign power of the Indonesian state had the power to penetrate and use the justice system to punish those who wanted to trifle with the sovereign. Therefore, the justice system is not about upholding the rule of law but rather performing the power of the sovereign.

72 *A genealogy of torture*

This genealogical investigation identifies ambiguity on the part of Indonesian state authorities towards Papua. On the one hand, Indonesia entered the era of democracy that upheld the rule of law and human rights, but on the other hand, its liberalism balked at the question of sovereignty over Papua. Four of the six examples just discussed illustrate the Indonesian nation-state remains intolerant when it comes to the question of sovereignty that symbolises the effort of abjected Papuans to transgress against the boundaries of the nation-state. Indonesia is not hesitant to deploy networked governance of torture consisting of technologies of war, public display of bodies and colonisation of public space to communicate its message to the Papuan social body and all supporters to maintain its control. The sphere of *reformasi* was apparently confined to any question but sovereignty. That is why Papuans remained subjected to the architecture of coercion and surveillance as they questioned the legitimacy of the sovereign power of the Indonesian state. This resonates with Foucault's analysis of the sovereign power of 'the King', who would not tolerate any challenge or even slight criticism. Just as the King held the monopoly of the right to death and life, the Indonesian nation-state exercised its sovereign right in the form of broken bodies publicly displayed in Biak, Abepura, Wamena, Wasior and other places. When this happens, the space of negotiation within the boundaries of the rule of law collapses. In this context, even the judicial power, fed cases by Komnas HAM, and the executive power, such as the Wahid government, obviously were found incapable of penetrating the sovereign power of the Indonesian state. If in the reform era, Papuans were treated as the abject, does this condition continue today? Let us now turn to the last stage of this investigation.

Otsus period: continuity of networked governance of torture

During *reformasi* a special autonomy status was granted to Papua and Aceh in 1998 by the *Majelis Permusyawaratan Rakyat*, the Consultative People's Assembly, the highest legislative body in Indonesia. This political decision was not translated into law until 2001 when the Indonesian National Parliament passed Law 21/2001 on Special Autonomy for Papua (*Otsus/Otonomi Khusus*).[39] When then-President Megawati delivered this new regulation to Papuans during Christmas celebrations in Jayapura in 2001, the occasion was deeply overshadowed by the grief of the assassination of Theys Eluay, the Chairman of PDP, by members of a Kopassus unit stationed in Hamadi, Jayapura. On the way home after attending dinner with the Kopassus commander to commemorate National Heroes Day, he was kidnapped. On the following day the police found his body with clear marks of torture and his car left abandoned at the outskirts of Jayapura. His driver, Aristoteles Masoka, remains missing to this day (Ramandey and Keagop 2007). Court martial hearings convicted Lieutenant Col. Hartomo and his six subordinates for murder and sentenced them between three and three and a half years.[40]

This case is instructive because it exemplifies both notions of visibility and invisibility in the production of the abject by the Indonesian security services. In contrast to Eluay's body, which was publicly displayed by *Kopassus* in the vicinity of Jayapura, Masoka's body was made invisible, suppressed and even the court was not able to recover it from the perpetrators. However, the effect is the same. These (in)visible bodies effectively revived the message of terror to the Papuan audience which had greatly reduced during reformasi. The reinstatement in the Papuan imagination of a tortured body of a leader they loved asserted the sovereign power of the Indonesian state to reclaim its boundaries with the abjected Papuans. The boundaries of the nation-state of Indonesia, which had been compromised under *reformasi* and particularly Wahid's government, were now reinforced to convey the clearest message to the audience that toleration for separatist Papuans was no longer applicable.

While *Otsus* was designed to rebuild trust between Jakarta and Papua, it turned into a new technology to control Papuans. President Megawati, who had personally signed the law, issued a Presidential Decree no. 1/2003 to divide Papua into three new provinces. This decision sparked anger and confusion not only for the general public but also for local governments because such provisions contradicted the letter and the spirit of Special Autonomy. It was seen as a divide-and-rule tactic to assert central sovereignty. The ongoing dispute on the implementation of *Otsus* remained unresolved, particularly the promise to protect the existence of the indigenous Papuans and uplift the welfare standard of Papuans as fundamental principles of *Otsus*. First, there is very little evidence that justice has been done for the victims of human rights abuses. Second, land acquisition (Ballard 1995, 2002a) continues to undermine the livelihood of Papuans who mostly live in subsistence economies. In this regard investment has played an important role in perpetuating extractive industries with little benefit to the local population. Freeport in particular continues to inscribe 'the signature of terror' (Ballard 2002b) over the landscape of the land of the Amungme through unresolved killings (Kirksey and Harsono 2008).

Third, the Papuan calls for a review of this legal framework have met with little attention from the relevant actors, including MRP, the provincial parliament (DPRP), the provincial governments of West Papua and Papua, the central government and the national parliament (DPR-RI). While these actors have been caught up in a power struggle, the rapidly growing new district (*kabupaten*) governments with poor quality to deliver public services have exacerbated the existing low-level capacity of local governance (McWilliam 2011). Fourth, despite the dramatic increase of funding available for the province, infrastructure has little improved and thus the high-cost economy in the rural and remote areas remains impenetrable. Fifth, there is the problem of mounting corruption and greediness among Papuan leaders (Timmer 2008). Aspirations to tackle all these challenges converged into a demonstration to 'hand back' *Otsus* in July 2010 (see Figure 3.4) (Hernawan 2011).

This unfinished business of *Otsus* not only generated confusion but also encouraged further Papuan opposition. The legacy of an ambiguous attitude towards change was further contested. First a revival of a war strategy was seen. On 14 April 2003, a group of people broke into the Kodim arsenal in Wamena and stole some weapons and ammunition. Almost immediately the army

Figure 3.4 The demonstration to 'hand back' *Otsus* at Papuan parliament house in July 2010.

Source: Hernawan's private collection.

deployed additional special troops directly from Java to hunt down the burglars. This operation turned Wamena and its surrounding areas into a war zone. A number of civilians were killed and many were arbitrarily arrested, detained and publicly tortured (Koalisi LSM untuk Perlindungan dan Penegakan HAM di Papua 2003; Komnas HAM 2004). The state brutality was extreme. In its report, Komnas HAM found evidence that members of TNI committed crimes against humanity and filed the dossier to the Attorney General for prosecution. However, it has been delayed since 2004 because prosecutors keep demanding additional materials before they can lay a charge.[41] Hence, the cases have gone nowhere while the victims' longing for justice remains unresolved.

In a similar fashion, the police reacted brutally in 2006 when five Brimob members were stoned to death during a student protest demanding the closure of the Freeport Mining operation. Brimob raided student dormitories around Abepura, a similar action to their raid of December 2000, looking for suspects. This violent incident forced Jakarta to send a very high delegation of government officials to address the situation, including the Coordinating Minister of Security Affairs and the Chief Commander of the Military. Nonetheless, twenty-three young Papuans were arrested, detained, tortured and charged with treason. Despite the fact that these suspects were forced under torture to confess as perpetrators, the court convicted and sentenced all of them. By this verdict, the popular demand to close Freeport mine and hold its managers accountable for

A genealogy of torture 75

the allegation of human rights abuses was completely diverted. In their report submitted to Komnas HAM, Papuan NGOs and the Churches (PGGP 2006) requested an independent investigation by Komnas HAM to review the whole case and court proceedings. This never happened.

These two separate incidents sent a clear message to the Papuan audience that the sovereign power of the state is not something to trifle with. The Indonesian state revealed its capacity to turn daily life into a war zone instantly wherein the rule of law collapses and the state of exception reigns (Schmitt 1985). The shock and awe of the state became a dominant message when the army arsenal in Wamena was attacked and Brimob members were killed in Wasior. Assuming that the army and the police embody the sovereign power of the Indonesian state, these institutions interpret these attacks as a threat to the sovereign itself and thus punishable by death. The charge of treason confirms this assertion and ordinary legal instruments like Komnas HAM could do little against the extraordinary power of the military under the state of exception.

The second strategy that leaked to the surface is public display of torture. A graphic video on torture was distributed through YouTube in October 2010.[42] The video depicts two Papuan men being tortured by a group of Indonesian soldiers to reveal the location of OPM weaponry. While seven soldiers were convicted and sentenced to between six and twelve months in jail, none of them was sentenced for torture. All were punished for disobedience and the court martials only used the word 'assault'.[43] This only confirms an analysis of some respondents who work for the military and the police force that '[t]he hardest part to change the military and the police institution is to change their culture. The culture of violence is so intact and deeply entrenched in these institutions'.[44]

This is not the first or the last case reported by civil society organisations, but this is among the few that gained major attention from the wider public. This ritual resonates with the ritual of the execution of Damiens at the front of the Parisian crowd (see Chapter 2) in which theatrical brutality was deliberately presented to the public. It exemplifies the way torture functions as a method of colonisation of public space by communicating the message of the absolute power of the sovereign. The colonisation, however, is not limited to this single incident. A study done by a Jakarta-based NGO, *Imparsial* (Araf *et al.* 2011), suggests a correlation between the excessive presence of the Indonesian army and human rights violations in Papua. The study also provides evidence of how the oppressive structures of the Indonesian military increased, not decreased, despite *Otsus* provisions that regulate the military presence.

How do Papuans react to the continuation of the networked governance of torture? In strategic moves, Papuans use international relations and human rights narratives to reclaim their subjectivity by mobilising international solidarity. Papuans rocked the boat of bilateral relations between Indonesia and Australia when forty-three Papuans were granted asylum[45] by the Howard government after risking their lives on a boat journey from the Merauke area to the Torres Strait in early 2006. On the one hand, this decision terminated all efforts of the Susilo Bambang Yudhoyono (SBY) government to return them to Indonesia but

76 *A genealogy of torture*

on the other hand, it opened up long and complicated negotiations between Indonesia and Australia involving the highest level of government from both sides. President Yudhoyono and Prime Minister Howard discussed this issue in Batam in June 2006, followed by ministerial meetings on separate occasions. All of these negotiations were formulated in the so-called Lombok Treaty.[46] The document explicitly emphasises the issues of 'sovereignty' and 'territorial integrity', two sacrosanct elements, in this bilateral relation, particularly for Indonesia. While Papua is never mentioned in the letter of the document and both countries publicly denied that the treaty had anything to do with Papua, Papua has inscribed its signature of the abject onto the bilateral relations of the neighbouring countries. Papua was considered to pose a latent threat to the boundaries of the subjectivity of 'Indonesia' and 'Australia'. Today, Herman Wanggai, the group leader, has become one of the leading new generation of Papuan activists in the diaspora that promotes Papua's cause in international fora.

In a similar fashion, Papuans use human rights narratives to mobilise support at the UN level. Towards the end of 2007, two UN Special Rapporteurs visited Papua:[47] Hina Jilani for human rights defenders issues and Manfred Nowak for torture issues. They came on separate occasions and managed to meet with Papuan civil society. These visits were not out of the blue. Rather, they were the result of long-term Papua lobby networking that engaged with UN human rights mechanisms and other international fora. This network was the continuation of the East Timor international lobby focusing on human rights issues but distancing itself from political agenda such as self-determination. As the members are located in strategic places in Europe and the US with strong connections with the grassroots, this network effectively put issues on the agenda and constantly monitored the situation on the ground. Such a solid network brought the UN human rights monitoring system onto the ground to collect first-hand information and to report back to the UN Human Rights Council. However, the government has taken very little action to follow up recommendations of their reports, particularly the harmonisation of domestic law in accordance with international human rights instruments and the establishment of an independent complaint mechanism (Nowak 2008, 2010: 77).

In a similar vein but in a more national setting, the Papua lobby was able to secure strong support from Eni Faleomavaega, the US Congressman from American Samoa. The congressman organised a congressional hearing in Washington DC in September 2010 to discuss the human rights situation in Papua, inviting Papuan representatives and experts to appear. While this was the first special hearing for Papua ever organised by Faleomavaega within the US Congress, the impact is already significant. This action symbolises Papuans' capability to cross the boundaries of the nation-state of Indonesia to express their *memoria passionis* in the world's most powerful nation to mobilise solidarity of outsiders. Papuans were not permanently confined as abjects at the margins of the nation-state. On the contrary, they were able to successfully secure some support within US politics and more importantly, assert their identity politics despite the denials of the Indonesian ambassador to the US, Dino Pati Djalal (Hernawan 2010).

A genealogy of torture 77

By the end of 2011, a convergence of all the contestation built enormous pressure on the SBY administration. Yudhoyono signalled a new approach towards Papua by responding to Papuans' appeal for dialogue. He installed a new government agency, *Unit Percepatan Pembangunan Papua dan Papua Barat* (UP4B), a unit that is mandated to accelerate development policy in Papua. An Indonesian observer[48] explains,

> He appointed Lieutenant General Bambang Darmono and Dr Farid Hussein, two figures who previously played a decisive role in ensuring necessary conditions for securing a peace agreement for Aceh, and the whole work is commissioned under the supervision of the Vice President Boediono.

Further, the President met with Papuan Church leaders twice since. However, until SBY finished his second term, his promise was never translated into action (Hernawan 2013).

The call for dialogue is not novel in the Papuan context. Since the meeting between President Habibie and the '100 team', the Papuans have continued to express their aspirations to follow up the initial 'dialogue' with the central government. However, these aspirations have met with little attention from Jakarta (Hernawan 2012).

Papuan Church leaders initiated the Papua Land of Peace framework as one possible line of communication with Jakarta. It is a model of conflict resolution which envisions Papua as a land free of all forms of violence. This movement managed to broaden its membership to include other faith leaders and thus became an inter-faith movement for peace. One of the key promoters explains that in recent years, this movement has declined mainly because of the lack of commitment among inter-faith leaders.[49] Another faith leader[50] argues that it is partly because of the failure of the inter-faith leaders themselves to come up with tangible proposals that grip the imagination of the public. The withering Papua Land of Peace campaign did not signal an end for peace movements in Papua. Instead, a new form arose under the name *Jaringan Damai Papua* (Papua Peace Network)[51] in 2010 under the leadership of Father Neles Tebay, a Papuan Catholic priest, and Muridan Widjojo, a researcher from LIPI. This network has been instrumental in clarifying the appeal for dialogue to the general public and has lobbied decision makers at the national level to be more receptive to peace dialogue, although consecutive governments have shown little interest in dialogue (Elisabeth *et al.* 2016).

Over the last two years, the current Joko Widodo (Jokowi)'s government has taken a number of important actions that illustrate the ways the Indonesian state revisits its relations with the abjected Papua. Among his various significant changes of policy towards Papua, one of the most important elements is the release of five Papuan political prisoners in May 2015[52] and the decision to open Papua for international observers, particularly journalists. The follow-up decision to release the rest of the political prisoners, however, met with strong resistance from the national parliament so that no further actions have been taken.

78 *A genealogy of torture*

Similarly, the decision to open Papua for international observers has been translated to escorted visits to Papua for international journalists by the Indonesian authorities.

Moreover, during 2016, we witnessed phenomenal incidents that confirmed the ongoing governance of torture of Papuans. The police arbitrarily arrested and detained more than 4,000 Papuans over six months in thirteen cities across Indonesia, not just inside Papua, including Dekai, Fak-fak, Jakarta, Jayapura, Kaimana, Makassar, Malang, Manado Manokwari, Merauke, Sentani, Wamena and Yogyakarta. Although most of the protesters were released within twenty-four hours, they were subjected to various forms of torture and inhumane treatment (The Coalition of Papua Itu Kita 2016). These patterns of police action never happened in the previous regime over the last four decades, suggesting the intensifying actions of the state authorities towards Papuans.

Despite the continuing Indonesian state's domination, in 2014 the abjected Papuans took a major step by consolidating all factions and formed new leadership under the name of the United Liberation Movement for West Papua (ULMWP) (2015). In only two years, this organisation has become a game changer. ULMWP has been effective in unifying Papuans inside and outside Papua. It has also been effective in mobilising support from Indonesian civil society and international actors that eventually draws strong reactions from the Indonesian state.

Papuans express their overwhelming supports to ULMWP as we can observe in various demonstrations led by Papuan youth such as AMP, KNPB or WPNA that resulted in arbitrary arrest by the police. The police arrest and detention, however, are capable enough to deter their determination because the young Papuan generation continues to raise their call for self-determination and even *merdeka*. This action has met with the rise of support from the Indonesian civil society. For the first time in Indonesian's civil society engagement with Papua, *Front Rakyat Indonesia* (FRI/the Indonesian People Front) for West Papua publicly supported the right to self-determination of Papuans and organised simultaneous rallies in major cities in Indonesia, including Jakarta, Yogyakarta, Makassar, Palu and Ternate, on 1 December 2016 to mark the Papuan historic day.[53] Without overstating this development, their actions signify a new turn within the civil society since the Front no longer uses the wordings of human rights in general but a specific but contentious term of 'self-determination'.

In a similar vein, at the international level, ULWP has gained international recognition from the sub-regional diplomatic forum in the South Pacific Melanesian Spearhead Group (MSG). During its 20th Summit in 2015, the MSG granted an observer status to the Papuan representatives under the United Liberation Movement for West Papua and thus officially recognised the existence of Papua as a nation (Hernawan 2015, 2016b). The international recognition went one step further when seven UN member-states, which might be considered politically and economically insignificant by international standards, raised the issue of Papua during the 71st Session of the UN General Assembly in 2016, illustrating the growing concerns of the Pacific neighbours of Papua (Hernawan 2016a).

The reactions from the Indonesian state were predictable. Domestically, it continues employing the mode of governance of torture to contain the Papuan public expression and their Indonesian solidarity movements, whereas in the international setting, it applies the diplomacy of denial while investing significant resources and personnel to delegitimise the credibility of ULMWP. The argument of interfering with Indonesia's sovereignty is the key message that Indonesian diplomats[54] argue through the MSG and the UN fora. These strategies have not shown effectiveness as the abjected Papuans have been able to penetrate the isolation of Indonesia. However, it might still be too early at this stage to draw a final conclusion regarding where these developments will lead. We still need to cautiously observe the developments.

Conclusions

This genealogical investigation has revealed that torture in Papua is not merely a technique to inflict excruciating pain on the body. Rather, it suggests a deeper meaning. It constructs the ways Papua has been governed by complex networks of domination that evolved since Papuans' first contacts with outsiders. Every node of domination, which includes kingdoms (Ternate and Tidore), nation-states (Dutch, Japanese, American, Indonesian), war, foreign investment and global markets (e.g. Freeport and BP enterprises), and security institutions that inscribe violence on bodies, has contributed not only to the production but also the maintenance and reproduction of the networks. Therefore, these networks of domination have become a mode of governance of domination. The governance of domination is interpreted as producing Papua as the abject. Abjected Papuans suggest an ambivalent and ambiguous mode of governance between claiming and denying Papuans and Papua. Although at the early stage, Papuans had managed to protect their boundaries, eventually they became the abject, dominated and constituted at the margins of the Netherlands and Indonesia.

Within a networked governance of domination, torture played a prominent role in shaping Indonesian military strategies of conquest, control and surveillance. The cornerstone of this governmentality is the 1969 Act of Free Choice. This UN-sponsored plebiscite laid foundations for more sophisticated and long-term networks of domination. In the last fifty years, these networks have grown into a massive and multilayered architecture of domination by colonising Papuan public space, incorporating technologies of war, installing hidden torture chambers, maximising the centrality of prison systems, displaying broken bodies in Papuan public space and waging divide-and-rule tactics through, for example, conflicting rules (e.g. *Otsus* and *pemekaran* laws) and recruiting proxies (e.g. militia). Therefore networks of domination have developed in adaptable ways, proving resilient and dynamic without compromising a core rationality: the territorial integrity of Indonesia.

However, this networked governance of domination is not absolute in nature, as Foucault suggests. Nor is the construction of the abject permanent, as Kristeva asserts. The Papuan experience has revealed persistent practices and ideologies

80   *A genealogy of torture*

of opposition to domination. Despite its limitations, the opposition deploys a wide range of strategies from armed (e.g. OPM) to non-violent resistance (e.g. refugees, NGOs and Churches); from political (e.g. Papuan Presidium Council) to cultural movements (e.g. the *Mambesak* music group); from domestic legal remedies (e.g. Komnas HAM) to international lobbying (e.g. international solidarity movements and Melanesian Spearhead Group); from secular narratives (e.g. human rights) to faith-based narratives (e.g. Papua Land of Peace framework) to reclaim the dominated Papuan space and to penetrate the boundaries of the Indonesian state. These nodes of opposition have merged into the game changer ULMWP, which has been effective in unifying and representing Papuans at international diplomatic fora.

In sum, this genealogical investigation suggests that torture in Papua constitutes a sophisticated architecture of domination, which is permanently in the making and persistently confronts burgeoning networks of opposition. These dynamics of two different modes of governance have shaped Papua and Papuans in the last half-century without any clear sign of resolution in the near future. The genealogical investigation has limits, however, since we have not analysed specificities in the characteristics of the long-term practice of brutality. This issue will be dealt with more fully in the following chapter, which will discuss the anatomy of torture.

Notes

1 For the full chronology see www.papuaweb.org/chrono/files/pre1945.html (accessed on 15 February 2017).
2 This stereotype has little changed as expressed by interviewees and helps shape the *habitus* of the Indonesian state apparatus towards Papuans (see Chapter 4).
3 Drawing on Feldman's (1991) study of violence in Northern Ireland, space is understood as a construct or product of power relations.
4 The first attack occurred between 21 July and 6 August 1947, about four months after the Linggajati Agreement was signed. This action caused the United Nations Security Council to intervene and both sides were invited to come to the negotiating table. This new round of negotiations resulted in the Renville Agreement of January 1948, which weakened the position of Indonesia and the principles of the Linggajati Agreement as the territory of the Republic was drastically reduced to Sumatra and Java under the so-called 'Van Mook line', the area under Dutch occupation. This agreement did not successfully stop the continuing fight between the Indonesian and Dutch militaries outside the negotiating table and led to the second military attack from 19 December to 5 January 1949.
5 The vast literature on Indonesian military history (Cholil 1971; Pusat Sejarah dan Tradisi ABRI 1995; Pusat Sejarah dan Tradisi TNI 2000a; Dinas Sejarah Militer Kodam XVII/Tjendrawasih 1971) portrayed the Dutch activities as an intervention into Indonesian sovereignty. Such action only galvanised the mobilisation of military and civilian power for launching a military attack to liberate Papua. This technique of power was carefully crafted by reviving the Defence Council, which drew the overall plan of military action. So it was not a coincidence at all that President Sukarno vehemently announced *Trikora*. Conversely, it was meticulously calculated including the date and place of the announcement to commemorate the Dutch military aggression towards Yogyakarta.

A genealogy of torture 81

6 The original version of Trikora is as follows: *[1] Gagalkan pembentukan negara Boneka Papua buatan Kolonial Belanda. [2] Kibarkan Sang Merah Putih di Irian Barat Tanah Air Indonesia. [3] Bersiaplah untuk mobilisasi umum mempertahankan kemerdekaan serta kesatuan Tanah Air dan Bangsa Indonesia.*

7 *Foreign Relations of the United States*, Vol. XXIII, Doc. 172, Conversation between President Kennedy and President Sukarno of Indonesia.

8 Interview with a retired Indonesian army officer III/E3 in Papua on 4 September 2010. This interview will be further analysed in Chapter 4 as the narrative of 'proceduralism', one of the four chief sub-narratives of domination.

9 Historians argue that the 1965–1966 massive massacre has become the darkest and bloodiest part of Indonesian history (Robinson 1995; Cribb 1990; Roosa 2008). Following the recovery of the bodies of the top army officers that were dumped in a dry well in Lubang Buaya, just outside Jakarta, Major General Suharto led the massive operation to eradicate Communism across the country. Some half a million people, mostly from Java and Bali (Cribb 2001; Roosa 2006; Robinson 1995), were massacred mostly because they were suspected of being members or associates of the Indonesian Communist Party (PKI). To date, no explanation of what happened is available to the public and any effort to reveal the history confronts enormous opposition. Some scholars argue that it was in fact Suharto's coup and the massacre was merely a pretext (Roosa 2006). One thing is clear: the spectre of Communism has been inscribed in the psyche of Indonesian society and the public display of broken bodies was introduced as a method of terror.

10 Suharto's New Order has constituted one of the main elements of the vast literature on Indonesian history. Scholars have analysed the genesis of Suharto's New Order, its relation to the East Timor occupation (Stanley 2008; Tanter *et al.* 2006; McDonald 2002), the dominant role of the Indonesian military in sustaining the regime (Jenkins 2010) and the collusion with Freeport McMoran (Leith 2003; Ballard 2001). However, there is limited analysis available that delves into the gravity of Suharto's machinery to institutionalise terror and surveillance across Papua.

11 The UN Administration compiled 156 complaints into six lists dated from 12 August 1968 until 30 April 1969. Fifty-three letters contained support for integration with Indonesia and rejected the plebiscite. These were mostly signed by civil servants, members of local councils or chiefs. One hundred and three letters expressed the opposite position. They were signed by university students, chiefs or Papuan political activists. Thirty-five of 103 letters explicitly reported political prisoners, disappearances, killing and repression of freedom of expression and association. Only one letter reportedly used the word 'torture' and few letters mentioned 'bombing'. While the data in the letters were not sufficient to count numbers of casualties, it was crystal clear that the Papuans were living under constant fear and that the UN presence was the only way out they could hope for.

12 Beside TPNG sources, a newspaper report, 'Unrest in West Irian', written by Peter Hastings for *The Australian*, 14 April 1967, confirms the level of fear as the result of tight control of Indonesia over the territory.

13 TPNG report 1969.

14 Interview with a Papuan refugee I/D7 in Port Moresby on 2 May 2010.

15 Interview with a victim in Merauke on 20 July 2010. Similar unpublished accounts have been collected by local NGOs in Manokwari following the 2nd Papuan Congress in 2000 entitled *'Benarkah Bangsa Papua Telah Diberi Kesempatan Untuk Menentukan Nasib Sendiri?: Penuturan tentang Kecurangan PEPERA di Manokwari'* [Is it true that the nation of Papua has been given a chance to exercise the right to self-determination? Narrative about the deception of the Act of Free Choice in Manokwari], confirming the coercive measures in conducting the Act of Free Choice.

16 The original version reads: *'Usaha-usaha yang ditempuh Kodam XVII/Cenderawasih dalam mensukseskan Pepera dapat dilaksanakan sesuai dengan persetujuan New*

82 *A genealogy of torture*

York. Hasilnya adalah rakyat Irian Barat tetap bersatu di dalam wilayah Republik Indonesia.'

17 Interview with victims III/A45 in Jayapura on 29 August 2010.

18 Interview with a chief III/D7 in Jayapura on 28 August 2010.

19 Interview with a chief III/D1 in Jayapura on 18 July 2010. The original lyric is 'Ifar Gunung is a detention centre. It is located at the edge of the mountain. When I was detained there. The Mount of Cyclops was high and the scenery was beautiful. I was sitting and musing' [*Ifar Gunung adalah tempat tahanan. Letaknya di pinggir gunung. Waktu aku dalam tahanan. Gunung Cyclops tinggi, indahnya pemandangan. Aku duduk dengan termenung*].

20 In this context the original word *pengaruh* (influence) is generally used by ordinary Papuans to describe the negative influence of an idea or ideology coming from outside that has serious impacts on the inside.

21 Interviews with two eyewitnesses III/B8 and III/B9 in Wamena on 4 August 2010. In separate interviews in Wamena on 31 July 2010, other eyewitnesses III/F2, III/F3 and III/A22, who lost members of their families because of the military operation in Wamena and its surroundings, confirmed this account.

22 During fieldwork in Biak, Sentani, Merauke and Papua New Guinea, many respondents shared similar stories as to what happened in Wamena.

23 Interview with a female survivor III/A23 in Wamena on 5 August 2010. During my interview, she confessed that she had mixed feelings towards the interview because she felt curious and suspicious, but also grateful that at last, an outsider had paid a visit to her and listened to her story.

24 Stuart Kirsch's analysis of the ethnographic representation of violence in Papua reveals the correlations between the stereotype of Papuan primitiveness and justification of militarisation in Papua. This theme will be further explored in Chapter 4.

25 *Kopassus* is the current name of the Special Armed Forces of the Indonesian army. During this period, however, its official name was *Kopassandha*.

26 Interview with an OPM combatant IV/D3 by phone on 8 September 2009.

27 Interview with a Papuan leader IV/D2 in Australia on 9 August 2009.

28 Elini Harris (2005) analyses the kidnapping tactic as a form of Papuan resistance and considers how it was represented in Australian media. She concludes that this tactic is ambiguous. Although this tactic managed to highlight the Papuan call for independence as the cause of Papuan resistance, it failed to significantly win support from the international community because the method was violent in nature. Ondawame (2010) acknowledges this ambiguity but asserts that this method is an OPM preference although it is 'inhumane' to many humanitarian organisations.

29 *Gerombolan Pengacau Keamanan* (GPK), a common term introduced during Suharto's New Order, means a movement that disrupts public order; in other words, criminals. This description deliberately aims to undermine the notion of the resistance and displace it into the sphere of criminality and thus renders the abject. That is, GPK was outcast and construed beyond the Indonesian state protection.

30 Representing the Catholic Church, I was personally present during the hearings between the Papuan delegation and the national authorities in Jakarta. I can recall that there was minimal attention and willingness from the authorities to follow up the report.

31 The Australian Broadcasting Commission television programme, *Four Corners*, investigated this intriguing incident in 1996 under the title 'Blood on the Cross' that revealed the use of the International Committee for the Red Cross in the Indonesian Military Operation that targeted the TPN-OPM. See www.abc.net.au/4corners/stories/s39706.htm (accessed on 15 February 2017).

32 For discussion of the hostage crisis and its impact on the mind of Papuans who construed this incident as the coming of 'the messiah', see Timmer (2000).

A genealogy of torture 83

33 Steven Suripatty was born and grew up in Fak-fak (South West Papua), actively involved in student activism at Cenderawasih University.

He had already been active during the student demonstration in 1996 following the killing of Dr Tom Wanggai [a lecturer at Cenderawasih University] by the Indonesian military. He was also active in our church choir and a great soccer player too. (Interview with Suripatty's fellow student IV/E5 in Australia on 27 May 2012)

34 Interview with a witness V/A2 in the United States in May 2011.

35 See Michael Cookson (2008: 45–54) for his analysis on the leaked top-secret document of the Indonesian Department of Home Affairs (the 2000 *Depdagri* document) which outlined a strategy to eradicate 'Papuan Conspiracy' since the 100 team met with President B.J. Habibie. One of Komnas HAM's findings of the 2000 Abepura case demonstrates that the *Depdagri* and other contemporary Indonesian government documents met the required criterion of being 'systematic' to constitute crimes against humanity (Komnas HAM 2001: 11).

36 The Papuan Task Force was voluntarily initiated by Papuans following the return of the '100 team' of Papuan leaders, who held the meeting with President B.J. Habibie on 26 February 1999. The original purpose was to provide protection to these representatives who received physical and psychological threats from the Indonesian security organisations (see van den Broek and Szalay 2001). Over time, this task force has evolved into a militia-like group equipped with a command structure, training, attributes and uniform. Although the task force is not armed, its appearance resembles a Brimob unit.

37 From my personal engagement with this process starting from the investigation stage as a member of the investigation team to the court hearings held in Makassar, South Sulawesi, it constituted major progress for civil society organisations in Papua and Jakarta to work together with the witnesses to provide testimony to the Indonesian human rights court. The 'Abepura' case was the first case ever brought to this court but failed to break the cycle of impunity within the Indonesian police force. However, some witnesses continue their work to help other victims and to raise awareness of unpunished human rights abuses. Later in 2008, they established *Bersatu Untuk Kebenaran* (United for Truth), a solidarity network among victims of human rights across Papua to unify their voices. Interviews with a victim III/A10 in Jayapura on 21 July 2010 and 13 July 2010; and a victim III/A30 in Biak on 10 August 2010.

38 Interview with a victim III/A36 in Wasior on 16 August 2010.

39 For a close analysis of the genesis of *Otsus*, see Agus Sumule (2003). He elucidates the role of a group of Papuan academics and intellectuals commissioned by the Governor of Papua, Jaap Solossa, to draft a Special Autonomy Bill for Papua under great time constraints and the political turmoil in Papua.

40 In *Kopassus untuk Indonesia*, Santosa and Natanegara (2010) do not mention this incident. However, this book explains how members of Kopassus were still posted at Indonesian foreign missions, such as the Indonesian embassy in The Hague between 2000 and 2003 'to monitor activities of RMS, OPM and G30 S/PKI fugitives'.

41 Interview with an observer II/C2 in Jakarta on 4 January 2011.

42 This footage appeared for the first time on YouTube on 17 October 2010 but then was removed the following day. On its press release dated 17 October 2010 (www.humanrights.asia/news/press-releases/AHRC-PRL-021-2010), the Asian Human Rights Commission acknowledged that it received the footage and then published it on its website at the same date. Similarly, the Fairfax News Media separately received the same footage and uploaded it on the same website (www.youtube.com/watch?v=uEis R8rFLOo&feature=related). By 11 July 2014, the viewers reached 146,756 hits.

43 See the first verdicts: Keputusan no. 186-K/PM.III-19/AD/XI/2010 for three soldiers reads 'guilty of acting together to disobey an order' [*bersalah telah melakukan tindak pidana militer secara bersama-sama tidak mentaati perintah atasan*] and Keputusan no. 187-K/PM.III-19/AD/XI/2010 for the platoon commander reads 'guilty of

84 *A genealogy of torture*

deliberately provides an opportunity to the military to disobey an order' [*bersalah melakukan tindak pidana dengan sengaja memberi kesempatan kepada militer untuk tidak mentaati suatu perintah dinas*] and the second verdicts: PUT/03-K/PM.III-19/AD/I/2011, PUT/04-K/PM.III-19/AD/I/2011, PUT/05-K/PM.III-19/AD/I/2011 read: 'guilty of committing a military crime of acting together to deliberately disobey an order' [*bersalah melakukan tindak pidana militer yang dengan sengaja tidak mentaati suatu perintah dinas yang dilakukan secara bersama-sama*].

44 Interviews with a middle-ranking police officer III/C16 in Papua on 18 August 2010 and a senior police officer III/C18 in Papua on 25 August 2010.

45 A retired senior Australian public servant explained that the decision to grant asylum was not uniquely made for Papuan asylum seekers. Several thousand people from a wide range of countries apply for refugee status within Australia every year. While approval rates vary, they can be as high as 80 per cent for nationals of some countries, depending on the circumstances in those countries. The controversy arose for two reasons: (1) they came on a boat without authorisation in the context of a pre-existing major domestic controversy about unauthorised boat arrivals bringing asylum seekers from Afghanistan, Iraq and Iran and (2) they intentionally made a very clear political statement on arrival at Cape York, which raised problems for Australia's relationship with Indonesia. As Australia is a signatory of the 1951 UN Refugee Convention, it has the core obligation not to return people who are found to be refugees to their country of origin (non-refoulement principle), which is also enshrined in Australia's domestic legislation. The Department of Immigration had to make a legal decision based on this international legal obligation and domestic legislation. These legal requirements were not well understood either within the Australian Government or by governments in the region. These factors, together with the very public difficulties that arose in the bilateral relationship with Indonesia, contributed to their cases being of an unusually high profile for an extended period. The decision-making process was conducted under intense public scrutiny and in a situation where the information available to assess the individual circumstances of the asylum seekers against conditions in Papua was very limited or outdated. (Interview with a retired senior Australian public servant IV/E6 in Canberra on 29 May 2012.)

46 The official title is 'Agreement Between Australia and The Republic of Indonesia on The Framework For Security Cooperation' (Australian Treaty Series 2008, ATS 3). In contrast to Indonesia, subsequently Australia had conducted a public inquiry under the 'Joint Standing Committee on Treaties' at the Australian Parliament that drew major attention across the country responding to the Lombok Treaty before it came into force on 7 February 2008.

47 From my personal and professional involvement in hosting these visits in conjunction with a coalition of Papuan NGOs, I found that the intelligence services made it very difficult for the Special Rapporteurs to talk with ordinary Papuans and NGOs. Intelligence agents made themselves visible in the hotel where the visitors stayed and tailed them wherever they went. Although we managed to have a meeting in a relatively free and secure environment, we had to take various measures to escape from the network of surveillance.

48 Interview with an Indonesian observer II/E2 in Jakarta on 6 January 2011.

49 Interview with a Papuan religious leader III/B19 in Jayapura on 1 September 2010.

50 Interview with a Papuan religious leader II/E14 in Jakarta on 3 January 2011.

51 See www.jdp-dialog.org.

52 See www.antaranews.com/en/news/99372/release-of-papua-political-prisoners-strategic-for-papua-development.

53 See www.cnnindonesia.com/nasional/20161129231806-20-176183/demo-dukungan-referendum-papua-digelar-1-desember (accessed on 15 February 2017).

54 www.abc.net.au/news/2016-09-26/indonesia-pacific-islands-spar-at-un-over-human-rights-autonomy/7878292.

References

ACFOA 1995, *Trouble at Freeport: Eyewitness Account of West Papuan Resistance to the Freeport McMoran Mine in Irian Jaya, Indonesia, and Indonesian Military Repression: January 1994–February 1995*, Australian Council For Overseas Aid (ACFOA), Canberra.

ALDP 2002, *Advokasi Rakyat untuk Wasior*, Aliansi Demokrasi untuk Papua, Jayapura.

Araf, A., Aliabbas, A., Manto, A., Reza, B.I., Satriya, C., Mahruri, G., Nurhasya, J., Simun, J., Safa'at, M.A. and Indarti, P. 2011, *Sekuritisasi Papua: Implikasi Pendekatan Keamanan terhadap Kondisi HAM di Papua*, Imparsial, Jakarta.

Aspinall, E. and Fealy, G. (eds) 2003, *Local Power and Politics in Indonesia: Decentralisation and Democratisation*, Institute of Southeast Asian Studies, Singapore.

Bahar, S., Sinaga, N.H. and Kusuma, A.B. (eds) 1992, *Risalah Sidang Badan Penyelidik Usaha-Usaha Persiapan Kemerdekaan Indonesia (BPUPKI), Panitia Persiapan Kemerdekaan Indonesia (PPKI) 29 Mei 1945–19 Agustus 1945*, Sekretariat Negara Republik Indonesia, Jakarta.

Ballard, C. 1995, 'Citizens and Landowners: The Contest over Land and Mineral Resources in Eastern Indonesia and Papua New Guinea', paper presented to Mining and Mineral Resource Policy Issues in Asia-Pacific Prospects for the 21st Century, The Australian National University.

Ballard, C. 2001, *Human Rights and the Mining Sector in Indonesia: A Baseline Study*, International Institute for Environmental Development, London.

Ballard, C. 2002a, 'The Denial of Traditional Land Rights in West Papua', *Cultural Survival Quarterly*, Fall, pp. 39–43.

Ballard, C. 2002b, 'The Signature of Terror: Violence, Memory and Landscape at Freeport', in B. David and M. Wilson (eds), *Inscribed Landscapes: Marking and Making Place*, University of Hawai'i Press, Hawai'i.

Ballard, C. 2013, '"Oceanic Negroes": British Anthropology of Papuans, 1820–1869', in B. Douglas and C. Ballard (eds), *Foreign Bodies: Oceania and the Science of Race 1750–1940*, ANU E-Press, Canberra.

Budiarjo, A. 1992, 'Linggarjati: Langkah Pertama Menuju Dekolonisasi Indonesia', in A.B. Lapian and P.J. Drooglever (eds), *Menelusuri Jalur Linggarjati: Diplomasi dalam Perspektif Sejarah*, Pustaka Utama Grafiti, Jakarta, pp. 9–20.

Chauvel, R. 2005, *Constructing Papuan Nationalism: History, Ethnicity, and Adaptation*, vol. 14, East-West Center Policy Studies East-West Center, Washington, DC.

Cholil, M. 1971, *Sedjarah Operasi: Pembebasan Irian Barat*, Pusat Sejarah ABRI, Jakarta.

Christianty, D.W., Kasim, I. and Dewi, T.N. 2007, *Pengadilan Pura-pura: Eksaminasi Publik atas Putusan Pengadilan HAM Kasus Abepura*, Lembaga Studi dan Advokasi Masyarakat, Jakarta.

Cookson, M.B. 2008, 'Batik Irian: Imprints of Indonesia Papua', PhD thesis, Australian National University.

Cribb, R.B. (ed.) 1990, *The Indonesian Killings of 1965–1966: Studies From Java and Bali*, Centre of Southeast Asian Studies Monash University, Clayton, Vic.

Cribb, R. 2001, 'Genocide in Indonesia, 1965–1966', *Journal of Genocide Research*, vol. 3, no. 2, pp. 219–39.

Djopari, J.R. 1993, *Pemberontakan Organisasi Papua Merdeka*, Grasindo, Jakarta.

Drooglever, P. 2009, *An Act of Free Choice, Decolonization and the Right to Self-Determination in West Papua*, One Word, Oxford.

86 *A genealogy of torture*

Elisabeth, A., Budiarti, A.P., Wiratri, A., Pamungkas, C. and Wilson, B. 2016, *Proses Perdamaian, Politik Kaum Muda, dan Diaspora Papua: Updating Papua Road Map*, Lembaga Ilmu Pengetahuan Indonesia, Jakarta.

Elsham Papua 2002, *Crime Against Humanity Under Act of Tracing and Annihilation in Wasior, Manokwari*, Elsham Papua, Jayapura.

Feldman, A. 1991, *Formation of Violence: The Narratives of the Body and Political Terror in Northern Ireland*, University of Chicago Press, Chicago, IL.

Foucault, M. 1980, *Power/Knowledge Selected Interviews and Other Writings 1972–1977*, The Harvester Press, Sussex.

Foucault, M. 1984, *Nietzsche, Genealogy, History*, Pantheon Books, New York.

Foucault, M. 2003, 'Governmentality', in P. Rabinow and N. Rose (eds), *The Essential Foucault: Selections from Essential Works of Foucault, 1954–1984*, The New Press, New York and London.

Gerrit, K. 2010, 'Robbers and Traders: Papuan Piracy in the Seventeenth Century', in J. Kleinen and M. Ossewiejer (eds), *Pirates, Ports, and Coasts in Asia: Historical and Contemporary Perspectives*, Institute of Southeast Asian Studies, Singapore.

Giay, L.J. 2011, 'Pemerintah Belanda, Orang Mee dan zending C&MA di Onderafdelling Wisselmeren 1938–1956', Bachelor thesis, Universitas Sanata Dharma.

Glazebrook, D. 2004, '"If I Stay Here There is Nothing Yet If I Return I Do Not Know Whether I Will be Safe": West Papuan Refugee Responses to Papua New Guinea Asylum Policy 1998–2003', *Journal of Refugee Studies*, vol. 17, no. 2, p. 205.

Glazebrook, D. 2008, *Permissive Residents: West Papuan Refugees Living in Papua New Guinea*, ANU E-Press, Canberra, A.C.T.

Graziano, F. 1992, *Divine Violence, Spectacle, Psychosexuality, and Radical Christianity in the Argentine 'Dirty War'*, Westview Press, Boulder, CO, San Francisco, CA, Oxford.

Harris, E. 2005, 'Kidnapping, West Papuan Resistance and the Australian Media', Honours thesis, University of Melbourne.

Hernawan, B. 2010, 'Why Papuan Leaders Went to the U.S. Congress?', *The Jakarta Post*, 7 October 2010, www.thejakartapost.com/news/2010/10/07/why-papuan-leaders-went-us-congress.html.

Hernawan, B. 2011, 'Managing Papuan Expectations After Handing Back Special Autonomy', *CIGJ Policy Paper*, vol. 16.

Hernawan, B. 2012, 'Jakarta-Papua Dialogue: Between a Rock and a Hard Place', *The Jakarta Post*, 11 June 2012, www.thejakartapost.com/news/2012/06/11/jakarta-papua-dialogue-between-a-rock-and-a-hard-place.html.

Hernawan, B. 2013, 'Quo Vadis the Peace Dialogue for Papua?', *The Jakarta Post*, 10 March 2013, www.thejakartapost.com/news/2013/03/10/quo-vadis-peace-dialogue-papua.html.

Hernawan, B. 2015, 'Contesting Melanesia: The Summit and Dialogue', *The Jakarta Post*, www.thejakartapost.com/news/2015/07/08/contesting-melanesia-the-summit-and-dialogue.html.

Hernawan, B. 2016a, 'Listening to the Pacific Beat on Papua', *The Jakarta Post*, www.thejakartapost.com/academia/2016/09/29/listening-to-the-pacific-beat-on-papua.html.

Hernawan, B. 2016b, 'ULMWP and the insurgent Papua', *Live Encounter*, 1 November 2016.

Hernawan, B. and van den Broek, T. 1999, 'Dialog Nasional Papua, Sebuah Kisah "Memoria Passionis" (Kisah Ingatan Penderitaan Sebangsa)', *TIFA Irian*, March, no. 12.

A genealogy of torture   87

Indonesian Evangelical Church, Catholic Church and Christian Evangelical Church 1999, *Human Rights Violations and Disaster in Bela, Alama, Jila and Mapnduma, Irian Jaya*, Timika.

Jenkins, D. 2010, *Soeharto dan Barisan Jenderal Orba, Rezim Militer Indonesia 1975–1983*, Komunitas Bambu, Depok.

Kirksey, S.E. 2012, *Freedom in Entangled Worlds: West Papua and the Architecture of Global Power*, Duke University Press, Durham, NC and London.

Kirksey, S.E. and Harsono, A. 2008, 'Criminal Collaboration? Antonius Wamang and the Indonesian Military in Timika', *South East Asia Research*, vol. 16, no. 2, pp. 165–97.

Kirsch, S. 2010, 'Ethnographic Representation and the Politics of Violence in West Papua', *Critique of Anthropology*, vol. 30, no. 1, pp. 3–22.

Koalisi LSM untuk Perlindungan dan Penegakan HAM di Papua 2003, *Laporan Awal Kasus Wamena 4 April 2003*, SKP Jayapura, ELSHAM Papua, Kontras Papua, ALDP, Koalisi Perempuan Papua, Elsam Jakarta, PBHI Jakarta, Jayapura.

Komnas HAM 2001, *Laporan Akhir KPP HAM Papua/Irian Jaya*, Komisi Nasional Hak Asasi Manusia, Jakarta.

Komnas HAM 2004, *Laporan Penyelidikan Tim* Ad hoc *Penyelidikan Pelanggaran HAM yang Berat di Papua*, Komisi Nasional Hak Asasi Manusia, Jakarta.

KOPKAMTIB 1977, *The Role and Function of KOPKAMTIB: The Operational Command for the Restoration of Security and Order*, by KOPKAMTIB.

Kristeva, J. 2002, *Revolt, She Said*, MIT Press, Cambridge, MA and London.

Lapian, A.B. 2009, *Orang Laut Bajak Laut Raja Laut: Sejarah Kawasan Laut Sulawesi Abad XIX*, Komunitas Bambu, Jakarta.

Lapian, A.B. and Drooglever, P.J. (eds) 1992, *Menelusuri Jalur Linggarjati: Diplomasi dalam Perspektif Sejarah*, Pustaka Utama Graffiti, Jakarta.

Leith, D. 2003, *The Politics of Power: Freeport in Suharto's Indonesia*, University of Hawai'i Press, Honolulu.

LP3BH 2001, *Laporan Pelanggaran Hak Asasi Manusia oleh Anggota Satuan Brimob di Kecamatan Wasior-Kabupaten Manokwari*.

Manuaron, K.A. 2001, *Laporan Seputar Wasior*, Gereja Kristen Injili di Tanah Papua, Wasior.

McDonald, H.E.A. 2002, *Masters of Terror, Indonesia's Military and Violence in East Timor in 1999*, Strategic and Defence Studies Centre, ANU, Canberra.

McWilliam, A. 2011, 'Marginal Governance in the Time of Pemekaran: Case Studies from Sulawesi and West Papua', *Asian Journal of Social Science*, vol. 39, no. 2011, pp. 150–70.

Münninghoff, H.F.M. 1995, *Laporan Pelanggaran Hak Asasi Terhadap Penduduk Lokal di Wilayah Sekitar Timika, Kabupaten Fak-fak, Irian Jaya, 1994/1995*, Keuskupan Jayapura, Jayapura.

Nowak, M. 2008, *Summary of Information, Including Individual Cases, Transmitted to Governments and Replies Received*, UN Human Rights Council, Geneva.

Nowak, M. 2010, *Report of the Special Rapporteur on Torture and Other Cruel, Inhuman or Degrading Treatment or Punishment, Manfred Nowak, Addendum: Follow-Up to the Recommendations Made by the Special Rapporteur Visits to Azerbaijan, Brazil, Cameroon, China (People's Republic of), Denmark, Georgia, Indonesia, Jordan, Kenya, Mongolia, Nepal, Nigeria, Paraguay, the Republic of Moldova, Romania, Spain, Sri Lanka, Uzbekistan and Togo*, United Nations Human Rights Council, Geneva.

Ondawame, O. 2010, *'One People, One Soul': West Papuan Nationalism and the Organisasi Papua Merdeka*, Crawford House Publishing, Adelaide.

88 A genealogy of torture

Osborne, R. 1985, *Indonesia's Secret War*, Allen & Unwin, Sydney, London, Boston, MA.

PGGP 2006, *Laporan Awal Kasus Bentrok Abepura, 16 Maret 2006: Luapan Konflik Masyarakat Papua terhadap PT Freeport Indonesia*, Persekutuan Gereja-Gereja di Papua, Jayapura.

Poulgrain, G. 2015, *The Incubus of Intervention*, Strategic Information and Research Development Centre, Petaling Jaya.

Pusat Sejarah dan Tradisi ABRI 1995, *Tri Komando Rakyat: Pembebasan Irian Barat (Trikora)*, Markas Besar Angkatan Bersenjata Republik Indonesia Pusat Sejarah dan Tradisi ABRI, Jakarta.

Pusat Sejarah dan Tradisi TNI 2000a, *Sejarah TNI Jilid III (1960–1965)*, Sejarah TNI Markas Besar Tentara Nasional Indonesia Pusat Sejarah dan Tradisi TNI, Jakarta.

Pusat Sejarah dan Tradisi TNI 2000b, *Sejarah TNI Jilid IV (1966–1983)*, Sejarah TNI Markas Besar Tentara Nasional Indonesia Pusat Sejarah dan Tradisi TNI, Jakarta.

Ramandey, F.B. and Keagop, P. (eds) 2007, *Menelusuri jejak kasus pemimpin bangsa Papua, Theys Hiyo Eluay* Cet. 1st edn, Lembaga Studi Pers dan Otsus Papua, Jayapura.

Ridhani, R. 2009, *Mayor Jenderal Soeharto Panglima Komando Mandala Pembebasan Irian Barat*, Sinar Harapan, Jakarta.

Robinson, G. 1995, *The Dark Side of Paradise: Political Violence in Bali*, Cornell University Press, Ithaca, NY.

Roosa, J. 2006, *Pretext for Mass Murder: The September 30th Movement and Suharto's Coup d'État in Indonesia*, University of Wisconsin Press, Wisconsin, MI.

Roosa, J. 2008, 'The Truths of Torture: Victims' Memories and State Histories in Indonesia', *Indonesia*, no. 85, p. 31.

Rutherford, D. 1999, 'Waiting for the End in Biak: Violence, Order, and a Flag Raising', *Indonesia*, vol. 67, April, pp. 35–59.

Saltford, J. 2003, *The United Nations and the Indonesian Takeover of West Papua, 1962–1969, The Anatomy of Betrayal*, 1st edn, RoutledgeCurzon, London and New York.

Samsudin 1995, *Pergolakan di Perbatasan: Operasi Pembebasan Sandera Tanpa Pertumpahan Darah*, Gramedia Pustaka Utama, Jakarta.

Santosa, I. and Natanegra, E.A. 2010, *Kopassus untuk Indonesia*, Red and White, Jakarta.

Saraswati, A. 1997, *Sandera, 130 Hari Terperangkap di Mapnduma*, Pustaka Sinar Harapan, Jakarta.

Schmitt, C. 1985, *Political Theology: Four Chapters on the Concept of Sovereignty*, MIT Press, Cambridge, MA.

Smith, A.E.D. 1991, 'Crossing the Border: West Papuan Refugees and the Self-Determination of Peoples', PhD thesis, Monash University.

Souter, G. 1963, *New Guinea: The Last Unknown*, Angus and Robertson, Sydney, London, Melbourne.

Stanley, E. 2008, *Torture, Truth and Justice: The Case of Timor-Leste*, Routledge, London and New York.

Start, D. 1997, *The Open Cage: The Ordeal of the Irian Jaya Hostages*, Harper Collins, London.

Sumule, A. 2003, 'Swimming Against the Current: The Drafting of the Special Autonomy Bill for the Province of Papua and Its Passage through the National Parliament of Indonesia', *The Journal of Pacific History*, vol. 38, no. 3, pp. 353–69.

Tanter, R. 1990, 'The Totalitarian Ambition: Intelligence and Security Agencies in Indonesia', in A. Budiman (ed.), *State and Civil Society in Indonesia*, Centre of Southeast Asian Studies Monash University, Clayton, Victoria.

A genealogy of torture 89

Tanter, R., van Klinken, G. and Ball, D. 2006, *Masters of Terror: Indonesia's Military and Violence in East Timor*, Rowman & Littlefield, Oxford.

The Coalition of Papua Itu Kita 2016, *Human Rights Situation in Indonesia Specific Focus on Human Rights in Papua*, Papua Itu Kita, Perkumpulan Belantara Papua, Jakarta Legal Aid Institute, Yayasan Pusaka, Yayasan Satu Keadilan, Jakarta.

Tim Kemanusiaan Wamena 2001, *Peristiwa Tragedi Kemanusiaan Wamena 6 Oktober 2000: Sebelum dan Sesudahnya, Sebuah Laporan Investigasi*, SKP Jayapura, Kontras Papua, Elsham Papua, LBH Jayapura, Jayapura.

Timmer, J. 2000, 'The Return of the Kingdom: Agama and the Millennium Among the Imyan of Irian Jaya, Indonesia', *Ethnohistory*, vol. 47, no. 1, pp. 29–65.

Timmer, J. 2008, 'Spectres of Indonesianisation and Secession in Papua', in P.J. Drooglever (ed.), *Papers Presented at the Seminar on the Act of Free Choice* Institute of Netherlands History, The Hague.

United Liberation Movement for West Papua 2015, *ULMWP Sebuah Profil: Persatuan dan Rekonsialiasi Bangsa Melanesia di Papua Barat*, Tim ULMWP, Jayapura.

van den Broek, T. and Szalay, A. 2001, 'Raising the Morning Star', *The Journal of Pacific History*, vol. 36, no. 1, p. 2001.

Visser, L. (ed.) 2012, *Governing New Guinea: An Oral History of Papuan Administrators, 1950–1990*, KITLV, Leiden.

Vlasblom, D. 2004, *Papoea: een Geschiedenis*, Mets & Schilt, Uitgevers.

Widjojo, M. 2009, *The Revolt of Prince Nuku, Cross-Cultural Alliance-making in Maluku, c. 1780–1810*, Brill, Leiden and Boston, MA.

Zocca, F. 1995, 'The West Papuan Refugees of Kiunga District', *Catalyst*, vol. 25, no. 1, pp. 60–104.

Zocca, F. 2008, 'Mobility and Changes in Cultural Identity Among the West Papuan Refugees in Papua New Guinea', *Catalyst*, vol. 38, no. 2, pp. 121–51.

4 The anatomy of torture

Introduction

In this chapter we will explore the specificities and characteristics of torture in Papua. The analysis so far suggests the Foucauldian notion of spectacularity. As a spectacle, visibility is central to torture in Papua. But visibility alone might not be sufficient to generate maximum terror. As Foucault illustrated by four stages of torture ritual, the ritual is usually performed in a controlled environment in which witnesses will be framed to interpret its symbolic meaning exactly as displayed by the torturer. In this sense, the context is inseparable from theatrical performance in that the context of the public display of torture determines the message conveyed to the audience.

Two recent instances of leaked footage of torture from Abu Ghraib and Papua exemplify the notion of visibility performed in a very different context and thus render different meanings. The first is the footage leaked from Abu Ghraib prison. This footage disturbed audiences worldwide. Images of the injured body were inadvertently leaked and then circulated widely through the media.[1] The public audience was not meant to see the actual event. Rather, this action was deliberately designed to be invisible and secretive. The original audience was very specific: interrogators, not the public. Therefore, once the footage was leaked to the public as a new audience, the effect and the meaning dramatically changed. If in the original design, the torture performance was construed as the display of the sovereign power of the US state to the detainees, in the new setting the meaning changed completely. The new audience perceived the performance as an act of illegality and immorality. Hence the display evokes public opposition and disgust rather than terror.

A contrary case comes from the Papuan context. It reveals a completely different experience with footage of torture distributed on YouTube.[2] Just as the US soldiers did not mean their brutality to be leaked to the public, Indonesian soldiers never intended the images to be circulated without limit. However, there is a clear distinction between the two crime scenes. The difference lies in the notion of audience. Abu Ghraib's torture was designed specifically for a very confined audience: the interrogators and inmates; whereas the Papuan torture was meant to be displayed to its immediate public audience: the family and the

The anatomy of torture 91

community of the tortured. So the notion of public display was deliberately generated even though it was limited. As the US soldiers lost control of the spectacularity of torture, so did the Indonesian soldiers once the video was leaked to YouTube (see Hernawan 2015, 2016).

This chapter, however, will deal with a different type of a public display of torture. It will analyse an unmediated daily phenomenon for Papuans. In this setting, the public can literally touch the sliced bleeding wounds, hear the agonised screams of survivors, feel fear and witness the theatrical brutality performed by torturers. This examination will focus on each element of the triangle of survivors-torturers-spectators to determine the specificities and characteristics of torture in Papua. To begin with, let us start with a brief clarification of key concepts.

Clarifying concepts of survivors-torturers-spectators

The notions of 'survivor, torturer and spectator' play a pivotal role in examining the torture files collected from my fieldwork. Therefore, it is necessary to define these three concepts used in this book.

Survivors

In the vast human rights literature, scholars identify the classical problem of the binary opposition of survivors *versus* victims. The literature centres on the notion of agency (Dunn 2005; Meyers 2011). The term 'victim' is seen by some commentators to denote powerlessness, passivity, innocence,[3] helplessness, even being 'pathetic' and thus lacking agency; whereas the term 'survivor' can be seen as entailing the opposite. The latter suggests capacity, being pro-active, self-reliance, being 'heroic' and thus enjoying agency to endorse change. Survivors are perceived as 'fully agentic, responsible individuals who are bearers of recognized rights' (Meyers 2011: 267). However, scholars agree that both notions overlap in the sense that there is a degree to which an individual is being subjected to domination and forced to become a 'survivor' although s/he has the capacity to recover and regain her or his agency (Dunn 2005: 23–4).

Informed by this complexity, in this book I will use the term 'survivor' to highlight the capacity of the abject to regain agency. Drawing on Metz's analysis of the power of *memoria passionis* for generating change for those who survived Auschwitz, the notion of 'survivor' helps capture the politics of hope embedded in the notion of the abject which Kristeva herself failed to advocate for. In the case of torture in Papua, survivors denote those who have been treated as the abject by the torturers and constituted at the margins of the Indonesian nation-state as 'foreigner'. The Indonesian state has exercised a technology of domination to exclude and claim Papua at the same time. This ambiguous and ambivalent relationship has characterised 'the art of governing' Papua in the last fifty years.

92 *The anatomy of torture*

Torturers

In a similar fashion, conceptualising the 'torturers' in this book derives from the whole debate of defining perpetrators or offenders as those who commit crimes. However, torture is not an ordinary crime. Rather, it is an extraordinary crime and falls under crimes against humanity under international human rights law. For instance, Article 7 of the Rome Statue explicitly lists torture as one of ten major crimes that fall under the jurisdiction of the International Criminal Court. Consequently, torturers are not ordinary offenders. They are conceived not only as a threat to a particular community in a particular location but more importantly, they constitute a threat to humankind, the whole community of human beings. Hence torturers should be subject to the universal jurisdiction of the International Criminal Court (ICC).

In relation to crimes against humanity, another element of torture which features prominently in international human rights law is the involvement of a 'public official' or 'policy' element. Steven Dewulf problematises this element by referring not only to major UN documents but also international court decisions such as the International Criminal Tribunal for the Former Yugoslavia (ICTY) and the International Criminal Tribunal for Rwanda (ICTR). Referring to Article 1 CAT, Dewulf argues that 'public official' is a very broad concept. It covers 'all officials, agents, private contractors and others acting in an official capacity of on behalf of the State, in conjunction with the State, under its direction or control, or otherwise under color of law' (Dewulf 2011: para 236). Further, he asserts, 'It is not necessary that the perpetrator himself is such an official or acted in an official capacity. It suffices that a (distant) link exists between the perpetrator and the authorities' (Dewulf 2011: para 237).

In relation to the question of public official, Hannah Arendt's (1963) compelling account on the trial of the Nazi commander Adolf Eichmann is relevant here. It illustrates the complexity of comprehending crimes against humanity and those who commit these crimes. Her argument of banality of evil illustrates that 'public officials' as perpetrators, such as Eichmann, are just ordinary people. They are not born as monsters. Just as in the Holocaust Nazism turned Eichmann into an instrument of killing, so too in the context of torture, the state institutions turn ordinary people into torture operators. Penny Green and Tony Ward's study on state crime summarised key elements in the literature of torture that explain why ordinary people become torturers: authoritarian institution, ideology, strong obedience to authority and being 'either fiercely anti-communist or attracted to fascist ideology' (Green and Ward 2004: 140–1). The study, however, found that the element of technical training in the conduct of torture is not a necessary condition to produce torturers. Rather, the whole nature of brutalising and humiliating during training for torturers plays a decisive role in creating 'systemic desensitisation' of torturers to acts of violence (Green and Ward 2004: 141). In other words, a formation period of members of the state security services is very instrumental to the creation of torturers (Kelman 2005; Kelman and Hamilton 1989; Peters 1985: 184).

The anatomy of torture 93

Taken together, torturers denote ordinary people who are turned into torturers through systemic desensitisation while they go through professional training when they join state security institutions. This training not only enables them to commit crimes against humanity but also establishes a link to the state authorities and ideology.[4]

Spectators

Spectators denote those who look upon or witness torture. Drawing on Graziano's study of an abstract audience of torture in Argentina's Dirty War, the notion of witnessing ranges from gazing in a literal sense to a symbolic sense and to an abstract sense. In a literal sense, witnessing means seeing and even engaging with an actual event. In a symbolic sense, witnessing is watching a representation of a torture event mediated and filtered by the media. In an abstract sense, however, witnessing can only draw on an idea of torture based on knowledge of sites and events of torture, although this knowledge is suppressed or surrounded by denials (Graziano 1992: 78).

However, Diana Taylor (1997) posits that witnessing is not necessarily a one-way act of watching. In the concluding remarks of her study on witnessing disappearances in Argentina's Dirty War, Taylor underlines the fluidity and reciprocity of witnessing in the sense that the onlooker and the looked do not hold permanent positions. The looking subject can simultaneously become an object, the looked, by other onlookers and these onlookers become objects of others etc.

> There is no stable footing here: the viewing subject is also the object of the gaze; the outsider is incorporated into the play of looks. We were all looking, looking at each other looking. The same scopic structure that situates the object to be looked at puts 'us' in the picture. We are all caught off balance in the spectorial gaze, suddenly aware that the object of our gaze is also a subject who looks back, who challenges and objectifies us.
>
> (Taylor 1997: 261)

While Taylor suggests the notion of intervention embedded in witnessing, Cohen's analysis of the bystander[5] contradicts her. Based on his study of mechanisms of denials of those who commit atrocities, he proposes the notion of bystanders as 'the descriptive name given to a person who does not become actively involved in a situation where someone else requires help' (Cohen 2001: 69). Therefore, Cohen reveals an element of 'non-intervention' in witnessing. Nonetheless, the notions of intervention, non-intervention and reciprocity will all be used in this book to identify patterns of spectators in the case of Papuan torture. This multifaceted ambiguity in the conception of spectatorship will come to be seen as a fertile resource in the analysis of this book (see Levine 1985).

94 *The anatomy of torture*

Torture survivors: constructing the abject[6]

This section explores whether the intersection between class, ethnicity and gender plays an instrumental role in engendering the abjection in the Papuan torture. Ethnicity is understood as 'a concept which signifies and symbolizes social conflicts and interests by referring to different types of human bodies' (Omi and Winant 2002: 123). Class refers to models of social stratification in which people are grouped into a hierarchical structure. Gender denotes cultural constructs of feminine and masculine characteristics which represent power relations within a society (Peterson 1992; Scott 1986; Skjelbæk 2012). Among the three categories, ethnicity is broadly discussed by Foucault, Kristeva and Metz in relation to Fascism whereas class and gender are less discussed.

Class

The Torture Dataset reveals the top five occupations of survivors: 146 cases (35 per cent) farmers, fifty-nine cases (14.5 per cent) students, eighteen cases (4.4 per cent) company employees, seventeen cases (4.1 per cent) civil servants at village level and twelve cases (2.9 per cent) fishermen (see Figure 4.1).

They work as subsistence farmers or fishermen, low-level public servants or company employees. Farmers in a context like Papua, which is already ranked the poorest province in Indonesia,[7] refer to the lowest class not only in political but also in economic terms. Farmers suggest the notion of powerlessness, poverty and vulnerability vis-à-vis the power of the state and global capital. These characteristics illustrate that the survivors of torture in Papua rarely come

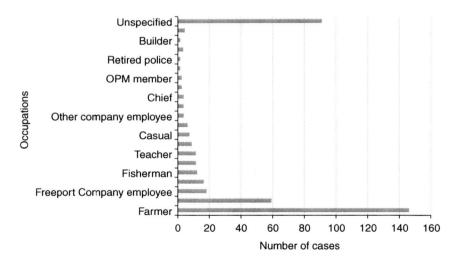

Figure 4.1 Survivors based on occupation.
Source: $n=431$, Hernawan database.

from higher classes. They are mostly from the lower class who have very limited access to public services and justice systems.

Further, even though only 14.5 per cent (students) represents the middle class, it is important to highlight this fact because high school and university students largely shape the future generation of Papuan intellectuals. Targeting this particular group of the population will have a strategic impact on social control over the Papuan future. Torturing this class may cause traumatic consequences in the psyche of future Papuans which may undermine their identity formation.

It is important to highlight the fact that in a very small number of cases survivors also include nurses, chiefs, church workers, OPM members etc. However, it is instructive to highlight the fact that OPM members are not a high percentage of torture survivors (0.05 per cent). Given the guerrilla character of the Papuan resistance historically, as well as the technology of war, this figure is not surprising. OPM members are highly mobile, hide in difficult geographical terrains for their safety or are based outside Indonesian territory (e.g. PNG), and are thus less likely to be captured and subjected to torture. In other words, torture in Papua targets civilians. This element is very important to constituting crimes against humanity as the ICTY Appeal Chamber declared.[8] William Schabas's analysis on the ICTY judgements concludes that the category 'civilian' does not mean that victims have to be civilians but it includes combatants who are not in a combat situation when the attack occurs (Schabas 2006: 190–1).

The issues of powerlessness, poverty and vulnerability are even greater when it comes to the geographical location where the survivors reside, as demonstrated in Figure 4.2.

Thirty per cent of the survivors live in urban centres compared to 68 per cent in rural areas. These figures mirror the latest Indonesian government census of 2010, which records that 23.5 per cent of the Papuan population live in urban areas, and 76.5 per cent in rural areas. Under the ongoing '*pemekaran*' policy, which has created new local governments, urban–rural boundaries have become

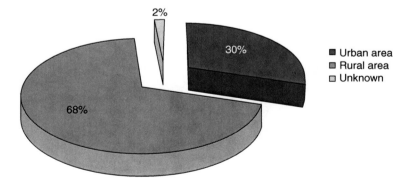

Figure 4.2 Survivors based on residence.
Source: $n=431$, Hernawan database.

96 *The anatomy of torture*

blurred. However, this reality does not mean that the poverty gap between urban and rural inhabitants has become less obvious.

In the Papuan context, the intersection between class, welfare and indigeneity is crucial. Its importance has been reflected around the discussion of Special Autonomy. On the one hand, the Indonesian government persistently argues that development policy is the right way to improve the welfare of Papuans who mostly live in poverty; but on the other hand, many Papuans and observers argue that this package has failed to meet its objectives.

A study of Papua's development under Special Autonomy by economists Budi Resosudarmo and Frank Jotzo (2009) reveals that the economic benefits of this package largely go to the migrants who constitute 38.2 per cent of urban population. In contrast, in rural areas of Papua, where the migrants only constitute 10.4 per cent of the population, the majority-indigenous Papuans (89.6 per cent) live in poor conditions (Resosudarmo, Napitupulu and Manning 2009: 47). Based on this figure and the figure that shows the majority of the survivors live in rural areas, it is reasonable to argue that most of the survivors also live in poverty even during the Special Autonomy regime.

The data in Figures 4.1 and 4.2 have led to a conclusion that the majority of survivors are the powerless, vulnerable, poor and isolated. Therefore, survivors do not have the capacity to defend themselves through legal, economic and political means. This reality is also evident in Figure 4.3, which shows the types of prosecution for survivors.[9] Most survivors (58 per cent) have never been prosecuted. This fact may suggest that torture mostly functions as a form of punishment and terror because the torturers had little intention of prosecuting their victims in court. This analysis is further supported by the fact that only 10 per cent of the survivors were sentenced and 1 per cent had the chance to appeal. This evidence is important for us as it demonstrates that torture is not primarily used to gain confession or collect strategic information as the utilitarian mode of torture functions. On the contrary, torture has mostly been used to exhibit the domineering power of the Indonesian state over Papuan bodies. As Foucault suggests, this kind of power shows little interests in the judicial mechanisms because

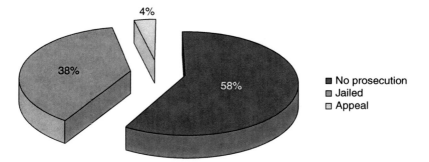

Figure 4.3 Prosecution of torture survivors.
Source: *n*=431, Hernawan database.

The anatomy of torture 97

its major concern is to reactivate power, not to re-establish justice (see Chapter 2).

Whereas these characteristics are very common among torture survivors, they show patterns of state terror targeting the lowest classes of the Papuan population. This finding is different from a survey jointly undertaken by Jakarta-based NGOs, Kemitraan and LBH Jakarta, which argues that torture survivors come from educated and well-off classes of Papuans (Kemitraan and LBH Jakarta 2012: 28–30). While this survey has usefully addressed the question of public intolerance to torture, it suffers from a number of methodological problems. Based on fifty-nine respondents, the data collection was limited to those who were serving jail terms in three prisons in Papua. It was also confined to a one-year period of 2011 and thus leaves out the broader pattern of imprisonment as part of the Indonesian national prison system (see Chapter 3). Moreover, the survey has not dealt with torture outside prisons, such as those committed in police stations, military detentions, other government facilities and public space. Only in the last few years, torture has been expanded to target Papuan activists and university students on a large scale while the existing pattern of torturing villagers remains.

Geography and ethnicity

Geographically, and based on their traditional land rights, survivors can be divided into highlanders (Table 4.1) and coastal people (Table 4.2) as shown in Figure 4.4. The highlanders are Papuan inhabitants who live in the central highlands from the District of Nabire in the west to the District of Pegunungan Bintang in the east (see Map of Papua). Papuan highlanders constitute 71 per

Table 4.1 List of Papuan highlander survivors

No.	Tribes	Province	Number of cases
1	Amungme	Papua	88
2	Mee	Papua	71
3	Western Dani	Papua	55
4	Dani	Papua	39
5	Moni	Papua	26
6	Nduga	Papua	15
7	Muyu	Papua	4
8	Lani	Papua	3
9	Ayamaru	West Papua	2
10	Arfak	West Papua	2
11	Yali	Papua	2
12	Ketemban	Papua	1
13	Damal	Papua	1
14	Mandobo	Papua	1
	Sub-total		313

Source: n=431, Hernawan database.

98 *The anatomy of torture*

Table 4.2 List of Papuan coastal survivors

No.	Tribes	Province	Number of cases
1	Wondama	West Papua	43
2	Biak	Papua	41
3	Serui	Papua	12
4	Yapen-Waropen	Papua	4
5	Doreri	West Papua	3
6	Fak-Fak	West Papua	2
7	Sorong	West Papua	1
8	Bintuni	West Papua	1
9	Sentani	Papua	1
	Sub-total		109
	Sub-total highlanders		313
	Unidentified		21
	Total		431

Source: $n=431$, Hernawan database.

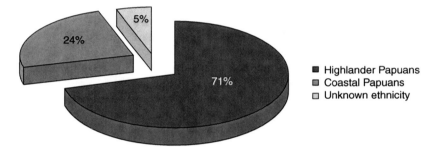

Figure 4.4 Survivors based on ethnicity.
Source: $n=431$, Hernawan database.

cent of the survivors in comparison to 24 per cent living in coastal areas (5 per cent not known). Papuan highlanders are one of the key elements that will make up the patterns of survivors as will be further explored below.

Ethnicity

Figure 4.4 also demonstrates that a very high percentage of the torture survivors are Papuans (both highlanders and coastal people). Their combined figures are 95 per cent Papuan with ethnic identity remaining unclear for 5 per cent. This smaller percentage likely includes non-Papuans. The question of non-Papuan survivors emerged when one ex-Indonesian army soldier[10] shared his story during my fieldwork. Recalling his working experience near the Papuan border around Jayapura, he explained that the practice of torture applied to anyone who passed an army checkpoint at the Indonesian border with PNG regardless of ethnic

The anatomy of torture 99

background.[11] This testimony contradicts the statistical figures. So we must be open to the possibility of a pro-Papuan bias in the way these databases are constructed. On the other hand, if we look back at our genealogical investigation (see Chapter 3), this phenomenon might make sense for two reasons. First, abjection is not limited to Papuans but also includes those who engage with the abjected Papuans and the abjected zones. The Indonesian border with PNG is considered an abjected zone. So anyone, including non-Papuans, will be subjected to torture regardless of their ethnic background whenever they cross the border into the abjected zone. Moreover, we have found no evidence that a non-Papuan experienced torture without having any engagement with Papuans. Second, in this context torture becomes routine, procedural and not very spectacular. So it makes little sense to keep records on who has been tortured in the army checkpoints because this was not the main purpose of torturing the bus drivers and their passengers. Nonetheless, this gap highlights another limitation of my Torture Dataset. That is, it is biased towards filtering out non-Papuan cases of torture.

The high rate of the Papuan highlanders experiencing torture suggests different treatment by the Indonesian security services. Although the central highlands is not the only area in Papua where the Indonesian security forces apply the technology of war, it has experienced a longer period of war-like circumstances and more intensive militarisation in recent years compared to other parts of Papua (see Chapter 3). For instance, two additional army battalions have been stationed permanently in the highlands since 2004.[12] Although the role of the military in Indonesian politics has declined dramatically across Indonesia, this action suggests that the colonisation of the Papuan space has not diminished. On the contrary, it is still on the rise (see Markas Besar TNI 2006). The contemporary records show that clashes between TNI and/or the police and the OPM mostly occur in the highlands (from Jayawijaya to Puncak Jaya regions) which is home to a dense Papuan population.

Another important question that one can pose is whether ethnicity has become a basis for torturing Papuans. While the question will be dealt with fully under the section 'The torturers' below, it can be said at this stage that ethnicity does not feature very much. However, this does not mean that racial stereotyping has no role in the mindset of the Indonesian state apparatus. On the contrary, Papuans have historically been constructed as 'black' and associated with animality, notably labels of 'monkey' or 'pig'.[13] These labels signify the notions of disgust and impurity embedded in the concept of abjection.

Kirsch's analysis of the correlation between ethnographic representation of Papuan primitiveness and state-sponsored violence is instructive here. His analysis unveils that the stereotype of stone-age Papuans labelled as 'inherently violent' was already constructed by the Dutch colonial regime, then adopted and reproduced by Indonesia as a post-colonial state through media representation and tourism.[14] However, the impact is much more detrimental than just a construct. The image has been 'used to justify militarisation of the province and the violence of the Indonesian regime' (Kirsch 2010: 16). This analysis finds parallels in the following passages.

100 *The anatomy of torture*

A non-Papuan informant, who worked as a state prosecutor, expressed his racial stereotyping by juxtaposing the Dayaks in Kalimantan and Papuans as follows:

> The people here are too demanding, don't follow the rule, come to work but don't work, don't want to be developed, and are jealous with the migrants ... we [migrants] feel sad here of being treated as a second-class citizen by the local government. The government's priority is on the locals whereas the migrants are only in the second ... the Dayaks have the same things. They want independence. The difference is they are committed to work, to learn from the migrants so they are developed; whereas here, if you give them a book to read, they don't want to read it. This is a clear indication that they don't want to learn because books are the source of knowledge.[15]

Although this passage has nothing to do with torture, it illustrates the general attitude and the *habitus* of the Indonesian state apparatus towards Papuans. The informant clearly emphasises laziness, underdevelopment and backwardness not only in comparison with migrants in Papua but also with Dayaks in West Kalimantan. It suggests that Papuans are even more inferior than the Dayaks who are considered inferior in relation to 'migrants'. Hence, while the informant appreciates the Dayaks, he actually reinforces his superiority over both Papuans and the Dayaks.

In a different way, a Papuan informant, who works as a senior state prosecutor, illustrates internalisation of racial stereotyping into his worldview:

> I came to Java, got educated in Java until became smart. I got a job as a public servant in Java, lived in Java, understand Javanese culture and speak Javanese, to 'kill' the Javanese. ... In a negotiation, you need an argument. If you deal with Javanese using the Papuan ways, definitely you'll lose because it doesn't match to each other ... I often hear people call me 'black, monkey, kill him'. This has made us hate each other. This has prompted us to fight to death.[16]

Implicitly he accepts the reality that the Javanese culture is superior to Papuans so that he forced himself to master the Javanese culture to resist its dominance. These two expressions (black and monkey) are typical racial stereotypes that have shaped relationships between Papuans and non-Papuans and between the Indonesian state apparatus and Papuans. When it comes to torture, this element plays a role in constructing survivors as less human, perceived as deserving death ('kill him').

Gender

Figure 4.5 shows that male survivors (87 per cent) constitute the majority of survivors as opposed to only 13 per cent females. If we combine the elements of

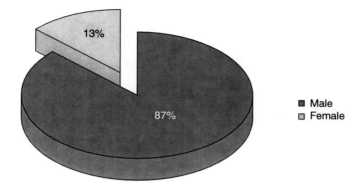

Figure 4.5 Survivors based on gender.
Source: $n=431$, Hernawan database.

geography, ethnicity and class, we come up with the patterns of Papuan torture survivors which are mostly ethnically Papuan, highlanders, farmers, civilians and males.

Further, when it comes to female survivors, the nature and impacts of torture are different. Figure 4.6 demonstrates that rape is the dominant method of sexual torture committed against women. Twenty-eight per cent of female survivors have been raped as opposed to only 5 per cent who experienced other forms of sexual torture without rape. The combined figure of rape and other forms of sexual torture (33 per cent) is slightly higher than non-sexual torture (30 per cent). For males, these figures are 9 per cent for stripping and genital torture with no cases of rape, and 91 per cent for non-sexual torture (see Figure 4.7). This fact may suggest that in reality, these two different forms of torture overlap. A relatively high percentage of unknown data suggests that the primary sources of my Dataset lack detailed description of the methods of torture as already discussed in Chapter 1.

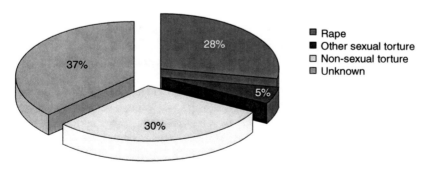

Figure 4.6 Torture against women.
Source: $n=54$, Hernawan database.

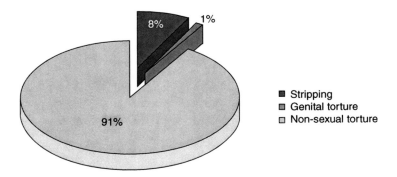

Figure 4.7 Torture against male survivors.
Source: *n*=377, Hernawan database.

The fact that rape features dominantly as a method to sexually torture Papuan women is striking. This constitutes the second pattern of torture. The phenomenon might be related to the strategy of conquest introduced by the Indonesian state when it gained control over Papua in 1962. This correlation between rape and war resonates with a broader pattern of the use of rape as a weapon of war in combat zones such as Bosnia Hersegovina,[17] Sierra Leone, Rwanda,[18] Democratic Republic of Congo and Timor-Leste (CAVR 2005: Chapter 7.7). In all these contexts, rape has been declared as a crime against humanity and violations of the laws of war. Drawing on an empirical study of female survivors of torture referred to the Medical Foundation for the Care of Victims of Torture, a London-based NGO, Michael Peel analyses the purpose and motive of rape as a method of torture:

> The *purpose* of the rape is to humiliate the victim, and to intimidate others. It may be to obtain information from a third party. It is the reason the authorities have to condone or encourage the rapes, which are never purposeless. Rape is committed for a combination of *motives* including exercise of power, the infliction of humiliation, and lust, and even the perpetrator is not likely to know which is predominant.
>
> (Peel 2004: 12, my emphasis)

Peel's analysis illuminates the experience of the Papuan abject in the sense that the exercise of the Indonesian sovereign power over Papuan female bodies has resulted in production of the abject, the most extreme form of disgust and humiliation. Rape is never purposeless. In the Papuan context where women who are culturally understood as a symbol of Papuan life, torturing and raping women can also have a strategic purpose. That is to reinforce the notion of impurity which has been embedded in the perception of abjected Papuans. Kirsch's analysis on the correlation between stone-age representation and violence against

The anatomy of torture   103

Papuan women discloses misogyny. 'By representing West Papuan women as cannibals whose unrestrained sexuality poses a threat to men and modernity, the state claims legitimacy for its violence against women while attempting to conceal the violence of development' (Kirsch 2002: 67).

Although many archives have recorded experiences of sexual torture of female survivors, an analysis of the phenomenon remains limited. To fill this knowledge gap, a recent joint study of Komnas Perempuan, ICTJ Indonesia and the MRP (Komnas Perempuan 2010) sheds new light on this issue. The study covers the period of 1963–2009 and examines 261 files of violence against Papuan women, broader than just sexual torture. This study found two types of violence, state violence in 138 files and domestic violence in ninety-eight files. Fourteen women suffered both. The study not only confirms the pattern of the Papuan torture, but more importantly, shows the ways in which Papuan women are vulnerable to multiple abuses even in their own families, with family domination compounding state violence.

These findings resonate with the testimony of a female torture survivor collected during the fieldwork. She shared her suffering from experiencing multiple forms of torture including sexual torture and witnessing other survivors who were being raped or executed.

> On 13 August 1968, my husband was just released from detention but then he fled to the bush to hide because the army came to our village and raped our women. The men had gone. I was arrested and was forced to show where my husband was hiding. I said I didn't know. Then I was electrocuted, tied up with barbed wire and was forced to join the patrol with three other women. Every time I fell down on my walk they hit me like a pig. During the patrol, I was forced to drink muddy water mixed with fagot and chili. For two days, I had to leave my baby unattended at home. Actually I knew the cave where they were hiding but if I had told the soldiers, all of them would have been killed. If such a thing had happened, I would have been responsible to God. Then I thought I'd be better if I died. God would have received me. I witnessed Mr Petrus' arrest. He was then tied up onto a tree and was shot. But they missed him so the soldiers stabbed him and dumped him into a ditch.
>
> Back to the village, Anton, an Ambonese soldier, raped me under the gunpoint. Other women were ashamed [to tell the story] because it was taboo. But I acknowledged it. It was not my fault! So why I should be ashamed! I also told my husband when I visited him in his hiding place. He burst into tears because he was so sorry with me.[19]

This example is not an unusual kind of female survivor's story. It seems an unusually powerful one rather than typical. Only 28 per cent of females were raped. In contrast to male survivors, this survivor had to suffer from pre-existing gender imbalances encapsulated in the word 'taboo' on top of the physical and psychological pain she suffered from the torturers. She clearly indicates that she is not

104 *The anatomy of torture*

the only survivor but her fellow survivors chose to keep silent[20] because of cultural constraints. These survivors do not want to expose themselves as persons who breached a sexual taboo that results in suffering of social sanctions. The taboo contains the notions of impurity, defilement and disgust which resonate with the notion of abjection. Therefore, when the female informant broke the taboo by confessing her story to her husband, she took a great risk. She exposed herself to a risk that the husband might have despised her because of the sexual abuse she suffered. Fortunately, her husband did not blame her whatsoever and even accepted her unconditionally. This support provided safety and protection which helped her rebuild her shattered life (see Herman 1992).

In their study of rape during the war in Bosnia,[21] Bülent Diken and Carsten Lausten (2005) explored the ways in which rape has transformed survivors into an abject. Drawing on Kristeva's theory of abjection, Diken and Lausten illustrate the gravity of rape which is not found in other forms of sexual torture. In a pessimistic and speculative way, they argue that rape is so traumatic because it invades the innermost intimacy of survivors and transforms their innermost being into an abject. 'One of the most horrible things one can do is to invade the interior, to fill it. In the interior everything becomes abject, because nothing properly belongs there' (Diken and Lausten 2005: 121). These scholars believe that the act of penetrating survivors has not only transformed the survivors into an abject but more importantly, into an agent of their 'own desubjectivication', a process of dehumanisation, as the survivors have no way to escape from their own interiority and privacy once the filth has forcefully intruded inside the survivor's intimacy. The survivor has been forced to become an agent that produces their own shame and humiliation permanently. In the case of female survivors, Diken and Lausten conclude that 'the rape survivor is forced into total passivity, reduced into an abject of penetration and, in the case of successful impregnation, to an incubator for enemy seed' (Diken and Lausten 2005: 122).

This analysis is useful for two different reasons. First, it helps us understand why rape survivors, particularly women, have suffered from multiple forms of torture. Rape destroys both the public and private lives of female survivors and transforms survivors into an abject. When this brutality is deliberately displayed by the enemy soldier to the relatives and families of the survivor, such an act can achieve the most destructive impacts on the survivors' subjectivity because many survivors suffer from isolation and rejection from their communities long afterwards. These survivors have been seen as filth, impurity and taboo. They undermine 'our well-established distinctions, our culture and our identity' (Kristeva 1982: 69).

Second, the data highlight the stark contrast between the Papuan experience of rape and Diken and Lausten's analysis of abjection in the Bosnian context. The Papuan experience unveils that while many women survivors succumb to torture and have been silenced, many others manage to reclaim their agency (see Chapter 5). This evidence suggests that these women are not converted into a permanent abject or 'total passivity' as Diken and Lausten describe. Rather, while they have become abject, they proactively rebuild their shattered lives and

The anatomy of torture   105

eventually regain agency. Further, even in the Bosnian post-conflict situation, an empirical study of rape conducted by Inger Skjelbæk reveals the power of the victims to 'redefine their social identities in the post-conflict sociopolitical space' (Skjelbæk 2012: 142). This finding reveals agency, the essential element to craft a new and better future, and thus contradicts Diken and Lausten's speculative argument. Skjelbæk also acknowledges the important role of communal support in rebuilding victim identities, which resonates with Metz's solidarity.

Among cases of male survivors, however, rape is not found. Moreover, sexual violence (stripping and genital torture) only occurs in a very small percentage (9 per cent) as opposed to 91 per cent of survivors who experienced non-sexual torture (see Figure 4.7). The method of 'stripping' as a form of sexual torture is not limited to politically motivated torture. Rather, it is a common practice among the Indonesian police whenever they arrest and detain criminals suggesting the notion of *habitus*. Again this suggests the recording bias discussed earlier. If this form of torture is routine, it may not be oriented to shock and awe and may be used routinely with non-Papuan common criminals.

The data in Figures 4.6 and 4.7 are only partially consistent with two caveats on an analysis of sexual violence summarised by Elizabeth Stanley's study of torture in Timor-Leste (2008). First, she argues rape is often portrayed merely as a private act by officers and thus confined to individual crime, as opposed to interpreted as a systematic and institutionalised crime. Second, female survivors are frequently only associated with sexual violence. This understanding, Stanley argues, overlooks the facts of multiple forms of violence experienced by female survivors of torture. Moreover, sexual violence not only targets women but also male survivors since violence is all about domination and thus does not discriminate between victims (Stanley 2008: 30–1). On the second caveat, while the Dataset certainly shows multiple forms of violence against female survivors, the ratio of these other forms of violence to sexual abuse is dramatically lower for women compared to men.

Drawing on the Papuan historical background in which the strategy of conquest constitutes a key element of the governmentality of torture, the ways in which rape has been used as a predominant method of sexual torture against women (Figure 4.6) suggest non-coincidence. On the contrary, the significant prevalence of rape, minimal prosecution of survivors (Figure 4.3) and the very high percentage of involvement of members of the Indonesian security services (discussed further below) demonstrate the element of institutionalisation, as Stanley argues. The element of 'systematic' use is harder to assess as the Torture Dataset lacks details of the element of 'planning' in using rape to torture women as we have seen in other contexts such as Argentina or Chile. No evidence is presented either of a formal state policy[22] to use rape. The sheer high incidence of rape of female torture survivors is, however, suggestive of a systematic phenomenon.

In relation to Stanley's second caveat, Figure 4.7 shows that sexual torture is rare for men but not exclusively used against women. As in Stanley's Timor data, techniques of sexual torture against men in a hidden setting were found in

106 *The anatomy of torture*

Papua, particularly prior to *reformasi*. During my fieldwork, a former OPM member shared his story of being tortured in military detention in Papua in the 1970s.

> We were forced to eat shit, drink pee. I was electrocuted in my testicles, bum and legs because they thought I was a [OPM] commandant. Around 2 a.m. in the morning, they then started the interrogation and again I was forced to hold the wire. The torture we experienced was unbelievable but thank God, we survived because of God. I was detained from May 1973 until 17 August 1977 and then was released and returned to Governor Pattipi. They told me, 'You were the perpetrator'. So they grilled me because they didn't want to hear who I actually was. My seniors, who were with me in the detention, have already gone to God now.
>
> Then in *Kodim* ... oh, my God! ... for 6 months I didn't see the sunlight. I could not understand this atrocity and my tears flowed. After 6 months, I was transferred to the Military Police detention. Three other fellow detainees are still alive now. We were detained during the war. God protected me. I'm still alive. I put cotton on my ears as a memorabilia of what I inherited from my detention.[23]

This story exemplifies multiple forms of torture, particularly electrocuting genitals, as a form of sexual torture on male survivors, to force him to confess that he was an OPM commander. While it illustrates the heinous treatment of the Indonesian military towards a Papuan combatant, this story also suggests the existence of the human will to resist and even to transcend an extreme condition. The belief system of the informant became a vehicle to transform his traumatic experience into resilience to survive.

In sum, Papuan torture survivors are constructed as the abject from five main characteristics: farmers, Papuans, highlanders, civilians and males. While there may be some biases in the Torture Dataset, all these trends are extremely strong. In other words, the governmentality of torture has reinforced the notions of 'stone-age living in a state of nature, of perpetual warfare, and of uncontacted populations that resist their incorporation to the state' (Kirsch 2010: 16). It also reinforces notions of abject women as discarded, defiled sexual objects. These characteristics provide a fertile ground for the Indonesian state apparatus to commit torture, as will be further discussed below.

The torturers: representing the sovereign

Informed by the notion of the ordinariness of torturers, the influential role of their professional formation and their links with the state authorities, this section will identify persons who commit torture, their institutional affiliations, technologies of torture, reasons of torture, political regimes in relation to torture and finally locations of torture.

Who are the torturers?

Figure 4.8 gives empirical evidence that torturers are mostly members of the Indonesian state security apparatus: TNI and the police. This is the third pattern. They comprise 65 per cent military personnel, 34 per cent police officers and only 1 per cent militia. Drawing on the historical analysis of the colonisation of Papua (see Chapter 3), these figures are not surprising. The Indonesian state security services have played a central and direct role in governing Papua in the last half-century. In such a controlled environment, it can be expected that members of TNI, the police or Indonesian intelligence commit torture to assert their power and/or to infuse terror.

The disturbing element of the results in Figure 4.8 lies in the fact that the Indonesian state has become an agent of terror and brutality. Instead of delivering services and protection, the Indonesian state apparatus is willing to resort to terror and brutality as a mode of governance rather than to legal and democratic procedures. As we will see in the following section, this reality is even more disturbing as the practice has been basically unchallenged in the last fifty years. Moreover, we will conclude that the brutality and terror have been institutionalised and normalised.

What did the torturers do?

In deploying torture, the torturers use physical and psychological methods that include stealth and scarring torture, somatic, psychological and pharmacological torture as well as deprivation of basic needs torture and different types of beatings.[24] Although these methods are distinguishable in theory, they are inseparable in practice since most frequently the torturers have used them simultaneously or consecutively against survivors. Sexual torture, for instance, targets both the body and the psyche of survivors.

Tables 4.3, 4.4 and 4.5 depict various methods of torture based on the three different categories developed by psychiatrists.

It is evident from Table 4.3 that the most frequently used physical torture is 'beating', followed by 'kicking'. These techniques are far more frequent than

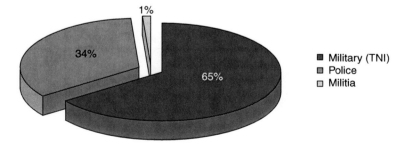

Figure 4.8 Description of the torturers.
Source: $n=431$, Hernawan database.

108 *The anatomy of torture*

Table 4.3 Physical methods of torture

No.	Methods	Frequency
1	Beating	246
2	Kicking	103
3	Burning part of the body	28
4	Rape and gang rape	15
5	Push-up exercises	15
6	Stabbing	14
7	Shooting	10
8	Dragging	7
9	Forced labour	6
10	Electric shock	5
11	Mutilation	4
12	Stomping	4
13	Sexual slavery	3
14	Pulling out fingernails	2
15	Other sexual assault	1

Source: $n=431$, Hernawan database.

Table 4.4 Psychological methods of torture

No.	Methods	Frequency
1	Pouring water	20
2	Stripping	34
3	Drowning	18
4	Public humiliation*	15
5	Mock execution	7
6	Pouring fuel	4
7	Detention in toilet full of faeces	2

Source: $n=431$, Hernawan database.

Note
* Public humiliation includes being paraded on city streets and forced to do unpaid maintenance work on public facilities and unpaid work in military or police compounds.

Table 4.5 Deprivation of basic needs

No.	Methods	Frequency
1	Starvation	17
2	Standing in the sunlight	8
3	Sleeping on wet floor	5
4	Property destroyed	4
5	Restriction of medical treatment while in detention	4
6	Solitary confinement	3

Source: $n=431$, Hernawan database.

The anatomy of torture 109

any other forms of torture. These methods may not require specific training and funding. As the vast majority of torturers are members of state organisations that are authorised and trained to use force, any application of force could derive from their social upbringing, professional training, *habitus*, the environment and the customs of the security services.[25] Therefore, it is not a surprise that members of TNI and the police turn their bodies into weapons.

In terms of psychological torture (Table 4.4), the techniques of using water (both pouring and drowning) and humiliation (stripping and public humiliation) constitute four major methods frequently used to torture Papuans. Despite its low frequency, parading as part of public humiliation is important to highlight here. This method exhibits the notion of spectacularity of torture as Foucault illustrates with the public execution of Robert Damiens (see Chapter 2). So does mutilation, especially of forms that leave a long-term trace, like the very long common practice of burning part of the body, but also with some of the less common practices, like pulling out fingernails. The Torture Dataset reports that parading is commonly mixed with physical torture and in some cases, this method involves severe physical torture that has led to the death of the tortured. However, Papua is not unique. Timor-Leste's experience under Indonesia revealed the same pattern (CAVR 2005: Chapter 7.4). Therefore, it can be concluded that parading and other forms of public humiliation have been institutionalised within the Indonesian state security services and play a role of communicating the sovereign power of the Indonesian state.

The Torture Dataset does not record any indications that the water techniques constitute 'waterboarding', a method designed not to leave physical marks on the body.[26] The US experience of torture reveals that any application of waterboarding requires specific training to be able to perform and reach the desired goals. Such requirements do not fit into the reality of the limited funding and skills of the Indonesian state security services. Moreover, if low cost and simple techniques of torture are already effective to generate terror, there is no reason to use costly techniques such as waterboarding.

In line with the principles of low cost and simple techniques of torture, exposing human nakedness through stripping seems effective. As previously indicated, this humiliation technique is commonly practised by the Indonesian state security apparatus to break down survivors' mental condition. It was experienced as especially humiliating by female survivors in the Torture Dataset. Survivors were forced to breach Papua's taboo, which regards public display of sexuality as forbidden and thus such exposure will cause them public humiliation. Since most cases of torture were committed in the public arena, this humiliation technique can reach maximum effect.

In a similar vein, unpaid work in a military or police post under constant surveillance might cause public humiliation. Although, this technique does not necessarily constitute torture per se, in light of Article 1 and 16 of UNCAT, the former UN Special Rapporteur on Torture Manfred Nowak and Elizabeth McArthur (2006) argue that this treatment can constitute 'cruel, inhuman, and degrading treatment' (CIDT) which is also absolutely prohibited. The authors

110   *The anatomy of torture*

interpret torture and CIDT as two distinct but inseparable acts. As opposed to other scholars and the European Court of Human Rights, the authors argue that 'the decisive criteria for distinguishing torture from CIDT is not the intensity of the pain or suffering inflicted, but the purpose of the conduct and the powerlessness of the victim' (Nowak and McArthur 2006: 150). Therefore, the authors conclude, 'any infliction of severe pain or suffering for a specific purpose as expressed in Art. 1 CAT amounts to torture' (Nowak and McArthur 2006: 151). Hence, any survivors exposed to this technique are likely to suffer CIDT as they are not in any position to resist members of TNI or police who humiliate them. Just as parading, so too these forms of public humiliation amount to torture (and are so counted in the Torture Dataset) if the infliction of pain or suffering meets the criteria outlined in Article 1 CAT.[27]

Under the category of deprivation of basic needs (Table 4.5), starvation is the most common method. However, the statistics do not show high frequency in comparison to physical methods. This figure is understandable as most torture in Papua has been committed in the public arena. Therefore, it would not require much space to detain them and requires low costs in providing meals for detainees. Nevertheless, in light of Nowak's argument, this treatment can amount to torture if intentional severe pain or suffering, the public official element and a specific purpose are involved.

Another element of deprivation of basic needs that requires analysis is solitary confinement. While this is a normal practice in all prisons for the purpose of protecting particular prisoners from others, the Papuan experience reveals that this function is harnessed into another method of torture. Despite the low percentage, this method has been deployed against Papuan political leaders who were captured and punished by Indonesian authorities as we have seen in the ways in which the Indonesian national prison system has been used as part of the governmentality of torture (see Chapter 3). The latest legal interpretation of this phenomenon by the UN Special Rapporteur on Torture Juan Méndez confirms the Papuan experience of solitary confinement constitutes torture since it was designed as punishment for a prolonged period, reduced social contact to a minimum and caused unhealthy physical and psychological conditions (Méndez 2011: para. 81).

In reflecting on the overall methods of torture, Rejali's compelling empirical study *Torture and Democracy* (2007) is relevant. This research has specifically examined the methods of torture from its invention, and the ways it has been used by different kinds of political regimes. He argues that generally torturers use methods that are easily accessible to them such as their own bodies, their equipment, particularly weaponry, and anything available and moveable in their immediate surroundings, such as furniture, wooden instruments, stones etc. These instruments are low cost and the use of them does not require any specific training. 'The availability, habit and memory shape how torturers choose' (Rejali 2007: 19). Philosopher Elaine Scarry (1985) argues that essentially in a torture situation, everything assimilated into the process of torture can be converted into a weapon. In particular, she identifies three main forms of human civilisation, including technology, cultural events and civilised nature. Instead of using the term 'torture', Scarry argues torturers in Brazil, for instance, use the term 'the telephone' to suggest that they were not torturing a human being because it was just a telephone or 'the plane ride' in Vietnam. Similarly, torturers in Argentina[28] use the term 'the dance' for torture or 'the birthday party' in the Philippines to resemble a cultural event (Scarry 1985: 44). In a similar vein, legal philosopher David Luban (2007) critically reveals the involvement of professions in US torture, particularly lawyers, psychologists, psychiatrists and anthropologists. These professions help explore conditions and methods that in a certain context would constitute degrading treatment, such as the role of anthropologists in suggesting the use of dogs, women and nakedness in Abu Ghraib prison or the role of psychologists and psychiatrists in designing, training and applying 'waterboarding techniques'. This revelation underscores the vulnerability of professions vis-à-vis the sovereign power of the world's most powerful state which has led to compromising the ethical rules of those professions. Sovereign power is more than capable of turning professions into weapons of torture.

Rejali's analysis is consistent with the low standard of equipment, training and funding of the Indonesian state security apparatus, except at senior levels. It is publicly known and officially acknowledged that both the Indonesian military and the police force have long suffered from very low funding from the national budget (Reiffel and Pramodhawardhani 2007: 95–100). These circumstances do not allow them to employ high-tech methods, pharmacological methods or any methods that require specific training and significant financial support. Hence, the fourth pattern of torture in Papua is that it is constituted by techniques that only require low cost and low skills.

Why did the torturers commit torture?

Figure 4.9 shows us that four major reasons are recorded in the Torture Dataset as justifications of torture. It is obvious that accusation has been considered sufficient for torturers to commit torture in Papua in the last half-century. These include accusation of killing members of security services or company employees, demonstration, accusation of being a member of OPM and accusation of attacking government installations.

Furthermore, we can also identify that four types of accusation or labelling involve political dimension as they relate to state authorities or corporations that contribute to maintaining state interests in Papua. These reasons suggest that torture in Papua is mostly politically motivated and has been committed to justify any acts of the Indonesian security apparatus against anyone who is perceived as an enemy of the Indonesian state. Therefore, it is predictable that any acts or individuals associated with TPN-OPM are likely to be subjected to torture when they confront TNI or the police. If torture relies on low-skilled, low-cost methods, why is the impact overwhelming? The answer to this question can be referred back to the colonisation of Papuan space in the previous chapter. Torture as a technique is simple and cheap but when the technique is weaved together with a sophisticated architecture of domination, the impact can be devastating.

112 *The anatomy of torture*

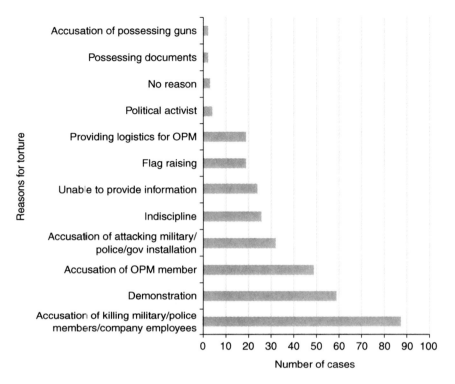

Figure 4.9 Reasons for torture.
Source: $n=431$, Hernawan database.

On the other hand, accusation as the basis for torturing Papuans reveals the lack of professionalism of the Indonesian security apparatus, who rely on the use of coercion with complete impunity[29] to handle allegations of crimes instead of forensic investigation as part of the rule of law and international human rights law. The widespread use of torture not only strengthens the perception of the implementation of the state of abjection in Papua but also undermines the ability of the Indonesian judiciary to uphold the rule of law as part of Indonesia's democratisation.

In the context of Indonesia's democratisation,[30] it is instructive to underline another major reason for torture: involvement of individuals in public demonstrations. This reason is an important indicator of how torturers have acted above the law as demonstrations are part of freedom of expression enshrined by the Second Amendment of the 1945 Indonesian Constitution, domestic laws, and international human rights instruments ratified by Indonesia. For instance, thirteen civilians were arrested, detained and tortured by the police of Papua when they participated in a rally to demand the closure of Freeport mine on 16 March 2006 (see Figures 4.10 and 4.11) (PGGP 2006).

Figure 4.10 Bruised Papuan students.
Source: courtesy of Septer Manufandu.

Figure 4.11 The suspects were being held in a parade.
Source: courtesy of Septer Manufandu.

114 *The anatomy of torture*

Another example of torturing demonstrators occurred in Jayapura in October 2011. Following the Third Papuan Congress, TNI and the police raided, arrested, detained and tortured some 380 people before they were released overnight. It is important to note that beatings and other forms of torture delivered on the spot in public are usually not recorded (including in the Torture Dataset). This underreporting serves to understate the proportion of torture occurs in public space. Only five leaders were detained, prosecuted, convicted and jailed (PGGP and Elsham Papua 2011). This is a public attack and public humiliation whereby Papuans were rounded up, tortured and detained by the Indonesian state security services (see Figure 4.12). These state institutions have no hesitancy to publicly humiliate and torture Papuans who already surrender to their authority. In comparison to the general pattern of targeting the low class of farmers and highlanders as above identified, torturing of participants of the Third Papuan Congress has revealed a new element that previously we had never discovered, namely criminalisation of the peaceful pro-independence activity.

In sum, the fifth pattern of torture in Papua is that it is regularly based on unproven and one-sided accusations by the Indonesian security services.

Another crucial element that needs to be highlighted is the fact that Figure 4.9 does not code any reasons for torture related to ethnicity. While racial stereotyping is pervasive in Papuan polity and society, this figure suggests that ethnicity

Figure 4.12 Participants of the Third Papuan Congress rounded up by the Indonesian State Security Services.

Source: ELSHAM Papua.

is not a basis for targeting torture but as a colouring element. Papuans have been tortured not primarily because they are labelled 'black, monkey or pig' but because they have been perceived as an enemy, which threatens the Indonesian sovereign power. However, the fact of a very high percentage of Papuans being tortured as opposed to non-Papuans, which likely makes up some of the 5 per cent unknown ethnicity (Figure 4.4), suggests a correlation between ethnicity and torture. More specifically, the racial stereotyping informs the ways in which Indonesian security services treat Papuans. Hence, it can be argued that ethnicity plays a significant role in the mindset of the torturers which help them desensitise and neutralise their ethical identities (Kelman 2005).

Further, it is important to highlight the ways in which private sectors (e.g. Freeport mine) have enjoyed equal protection from the security apparatus to that enjoyed by state organisations. Any attempt to disrupt their operations has met exactly the same brutal reaction from TNI and/or the police as if such an act occurred in state installations. The torture files not only recorded the Indonesian security apparatus committing torture within the Freeport area in 1995 (Münninghoff 1995) and 2009 but also some timber companies operating in Papua (Elsham Papua 2002; Komnas HAM 2004; LP3BH 2001).

When did torture occur?

Figure 4.13 shows torture has been committed against Papuans across all political regimes. Out of 431 codified cases of torture, 42 per cent occurred during *reformasi*, which is the period between the fall of Suharto's New Order in May 1998 and the enactment of the Special Autonomy Law for Papua in November 2001. This transition period records the highest frequency of torture. It is followed by the second highest (37 per cent) during the New Order period during 1967 to 1998. The third highest is the *Otsus* era which constitutes 19 per cent of the total figure and finally, the lowest is the Sukarno period (1963–1967) which only constitutes 2 per cent of the total number.

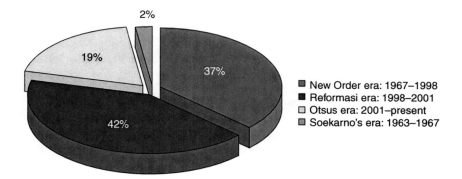

Figure 4.13 Regimes and torture.
Source: $n=431$, Hernawan database.

116   *The anatomy of torture*

This description might not follow the common maxim that an authoritarian regime causes the highest number of torture survivors (e.g. Argentina, Chile or South Africa). There are two possible explanations for this phenomenon. First, the three-year transitional period of 1998–2001 witnessed ongoing instability and lawlessness across Indonesia that marked a short period of *reformasi* following the fall of the dictator Suharto (Braithwaite *et al.* 2010). In the case of Papua, these conditions might have become a justification for the security apparatus to act on their own policies to defend the state because the central government was in a crisis of legitimacy and unable to control its own apparatus. Rooted in the authoritarian legacy of the New Order, the Indonesian security forces, both TNI and the police, deployed harsh measures, notably killing and torture, to deal with Papuan political aspirations. These were expressed through raising the Morning Star flag in a number of places and occasions and through Papuan gatherings.[31] In other words, the persistence of torture by security forces from Sukarno to the present day suggests that the use of force, including torture against Papuans, has become institutionalised in the culture of the security forces and as such has persisted since 1999 when the national governments were democratically elected.

The second possible explanation is that during this particular period, civil society organisations had gained momentum to operate with far greater freedom to monitor and document ongoing violence. This might contribute to the highest rate of cases of torture reported during the *reformasi* era and subsequently reduced cases during the *Otsus* era. In other words, monitoring and public scrutiny might have largely contributed to this phenomenon. Nonetheless, the magnitude of the pattern of highest recorded cases of torture during *reformasi* still makes it reasonable to define the sixth pattern of torture in Papua in that under conditions of lawlessness and political transition, the Indonesian state apparatus has heavily relied on torture as a technique to handle secession movements.

During the *Otsus* era, however, cases of torture remain significantly high. The genealogical investigation has revealed the ambiguity of *reformasi* towards change and the continuity of the authoritarian legacy from the previous regimes that maintain the sovereign power of Indonesia. The video of torture on YouTube exemplifies this pattern. Therefore, torture in its ten patterns is unlikely to disappear in the near future unless a structural shift in the governance of Papua occurs. It is relevant to highlight Rejali's thesis which argues that torture is unlikely to disappear even in liberal democracy because torture will take form in clean and hidden techniques.

Nonetheless, overall the fifty years of state-sponsored torture evoke the key element of crimes against humanity, namely policy. Machteld Boot (2002) outlines the logic of policy. First, he outlines the 'systematic or widespread' requirements drawing on the ICTR and the ICTY judgements. In the ICTR's view systematic means 'thoroughly organized and following a regular pattern on the basis of a common policy involving substantial public or private resources' (Boot 2002: 479). The *Blaskić* judgement[32] of the ICTY further specifies the systematic element by outlining four criteria:

The anatomy of torture 117

1 the existence of *a political objective*, a plan pursuant to which the attack is perpetrated or an ideology, in the broad sense of the word, to destroy, persecute, or weaken the community;

2 the perpetration of a criminal act on *a very large scale against a group of civilians* or the *repeated and continuous* commission of inhumane acts linked to one another;

3 the preparation and *use of significant public or private resources*, whether military or other; and

4 the *implication* of high-level political and/or military authorities in the definition and establishment of the methodical plan (para 203, my emphasis).

I have argued that these elements are essentially applicable to Papua. The term 'widespread' refers to the scale of the acts perpetrated or to the number of victims (Boot 2002: 479; Schabas 2006: 192). In the words of the ICTY, it is the 'cumulative effect of a series of inhumane acts or the singular effect of an inhumane act of extraordinary magnitude' (para 206). It suggests large scale and high frequency of practice, something that has been demonstrated for Papua.

Finally, deduced from the two criteria, both tribunals interpret that the policy for crimes against humanity need not be formalized. In *Tadić* Judgment,[33] the ICTY stated that 'if the acts occur on a widespread or systematic basis that demonstrates a policy to commit such acts'. Similarly, the ICTR asserts that 'the requirement that the attack must be committed against "civilian population" inevitably demands some kind of plan, the discriminatory element of the attack is, by its very nature, considered only possible as a consequence of a policy' (Boot 2002: 482). Therefore, in Boot's view, policy is a synonym of 'plan' or 'systematic'.

Furthermore, Schabas (2006: 195) identifies another fundamental element of the ICTY judgement of the *Blaskić* case which will be important to further analysis of this book: there is no need for perpetrators to have detailed knowledge of the crimes. Rather, a general knowledge would suffice.[34] This element will be useful to assess the degree of innocence or guilt as will be represented by the multilayered narrative of domination (see Chapter 5).

Taken together, the history of Papuan torture outlines the political strategy of conquest, domination and terror against Papuan civilians (Chapter 3). Papuan torture practice has repeatedly targeted Papuan farmers, highlanders, civilians and males and females for sexual violence. The practice has only involved members of the Indonesian state security services as perpetrators (Figure 4.8) and their facilities (Figure 4.14) which implies the involvement of high-level political and/or military authorities. The Torture Dataset also records 431 cases of torture suggesting a large scale of unpunished acts (Figure 4.15) of torture. Therefore, drawing on the ICTY and the ICTR judgements, such a long-term and unpunished practice of state-sponsored torture can only be possible if there is a plan or policy (see Chapter 3). This is the seventh pattern.

118 *The anatomy of torture*

Where did they torture?

Location of torture plays a central role in shaping the practice as a spectacle. Figure 4.14 shows that only 4 per cent of torture cases occurred in private areas in contrast to 27 per cent in public space. The latter includes marketplaces, community centres, Churches' backyards and any other open space around the survivors' residence. Further, 3 per cent and 4 per cent of torture cases occurred outside the military and police installations, respectively, but still within their compound. In this case, the public can still witness torture events as the Indonesian state security apparatus shows little effort to hide them and thus these events fall under the category of public.

Twenty-four per cent and 12 per cent of cases occurred inside police and military installations, respectively. This phenomenon requires analysis here. Drawing on Graziano's study of invisible torture in Argentina as a form of spectacular torture, torture committed inside the TNI and police installation is not entirely hidden. Rather, it only constitutes an open secret. We have seen how total disappearances combined with releases coming out with burnt or scarred bodies to display to friends and/or families contribute to this. While the actual events of torture were hidden from the public, the Papuan public already have specific knowledge of torture practices in these locations from the history of the domination of the Indonesian state. Therefore, the partial invisibility and inaudibility of torture do not minimise the message of terror to the public. On the contrary, they maximise the effect of terror by maximising the level of secrecy to generate the abstract notion of spectacularity. Taken together, cases of torture as spectacle (both secret and public) constitute 82 per cent of the total number of cases or 46 per cent excluding all the cases inside military bases and police stations. This shows the central element of a spectacle: public display of the injured body. This phenomenon constitutes the eighth pattern of Papuan torture.

Drawing on this evidence, it can be argued that the power of spectacle does not lie in the act of inflicting actual pain and suffering but more in the act of communicating such an experience through the display of mutilated bodies

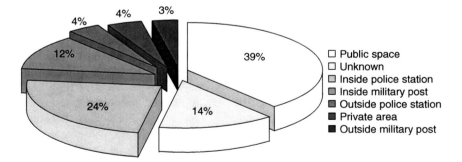

Figure 4.14 Locations of torture.
Source: $n=431$, Hernawan database.

The anatomy of torture 119

(Rothenberg 2003). Monstrous atrocity inscribed on the body is only a means to transmit a social policy, as Foucault suggests. Such power explains the reality of the unrestrained power of the Indonesian state apparatus which is more than capable of penetrating the judiciary and turning the rule of law into the rule of abjection and the rule of spectacle. The element of spectacularity is not unique to Papua. Aceh and the former Indonesian province of East Timor have experienced a similar degree of public brutality. CAVR (2005: Chapter 7.2) documentation clearly identifies the public display of the body to generate terror to the whole community of East Timor under Indonesian rule. However, in these two contexts, the notion of spectacularity gained less attention. In her study of torture in Timor-Leste, Stanley (2008: 82), for example, acknowledges this pattern but does not go any further to analyse the performative element of torture.

Figure 4.15 confirms that the sovereign enjoys almost complete impunity since in 71 per cent of cases, none of the torturers were ever brought to justice, in 5 per cent those who were brought to the court were eventually acquitted and 24 per cent of cases have pending torture charges. From the archives, there is very minimal information available regarding the final status of the pending cases. The current pending cases are cases of extrajudicial killings, torture, rape and destruction of property committed by TNI in Wamena in 2003 and by the police in Wasior in 2001. Hence, they have been pending for many years and it is reasonable to surmise that they were instituted at the time to give the appearance of an operating rule of law. A decade on, we can report no substance to the rule of law in relation to them.

Furthermore, Figure 4.15 suggests that the Indonesian judicial system is not capable of holding torturers accountable. The establishment and the increase of military infrastructure across Papua and close surveillance of civilians have left limited free space for an impartial and free judiciary because Papua has been constructed an abjected zone. Under this status not only law but, borrowing Kristeva's words, meaning has collapsed. Hence, the visibility of torture in such a context makes sense because the public display of torture is not performed in a context where the rule of law applies. On the contrary, the performance of

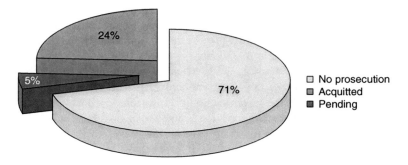

Figure 4.15 Prosecution for the torturers.
Source: $n=431$, Hernawan database.

120 *The anatomy of torture*

torture is being staged in an abjected zone in which Papuan public space has been militarised and thus dominated by the technologies of war, strategies of conquest and procedures of control and surveillance of TNI underpinned by the ideology of the territorial integrity of Indonesia. In this context, the Indonesian security services have full confidence to do anything, including committing torture in public, because law can only have limited impacts on their conduct.[35] In other words, TNI and the police manage to reach their targets in communicating the message of the sovereign power of the Indonesian state.

In ensuring the effectiveness of the torture ritual, Papuan public space is extremely strategic for the Indonesian state. Controlling and dominating public space is a *conditio sine qua non* for TNI and, to some extent, the police to convey the message of the awe of the Indonesian state, particularly after the separation of East Timor and the resolution of Aceh which left Papua as the only area where the culture of violence persists despite domestic and international scrutiny. The following testimony from a middle-ranking military officer confirms this analysis. Opposing an argument of dismantling the territorial commands of the army as part of TNI reform,[36] even as he advocates reform he implicitly suggests that such a proposal will simply uproot the existence of the Indonesian army and is thus implausible:

> The territorial command of the army is the display of the power of the army. So there is no way it can be or should be dismantled. *Kodim*, for example. It needs reform in terms organisation and functions so as to not use intimidation [against Papuans]. Today soldiers have become teachers, farmers, dealing with natural disaster.[37]

While he implicitly acknowledged that territorial commands such as *Kodim* did commit 'intimidation' in the past and thus need reform, he maintains the unconditionality of this territorial command. This argument is crucial to illustrate the internal dynamics of Indonesian military reform. Despite the TNI reform agenda sanctioned by law, the territorial command remains unchallenged. A number of key senior army generals who advocated have been sidelined. In the Papuan context, this fact suggests that the strategy of militarising the Papuan space will only continue in the near future (Araf *et al.* 2011; Markas Besar TNI 2006). The element of colonisation of public space which has led to almost complete impunity[38] constitutes the ninth pattern of the Papuan torture.

In sum, the torturers are members of the Indonesian security apparatus. They have instituted torture as the way to govern Papua over half a century. Regime change has limited impact on the governmentality of torture since the practice remains common. This evidence supports the argument of governmentality of torture as torture is not limited to inflicting pain on the bodies of the tortured. Rather, it is about communicating the message of terror.

The spectators: gazing at the spectacle

Although Papuans have been treated as an abject and Papuan space has been militarised for half a century, this does not necessarily make Papua completely dominated. Some key elements of Papuan society intervene, as illustrated in Figure 4.16. Forty-nine per cent of cases involve local NGOs in exposing torture (Papuan and Indonesian national NGOs combined), 31 per cent of cases involve the churches of Papua and 20 per cent involve international NGOs. These organisations not only investigate, document and submit cases of torture to relevant authorities but also provide humanitarian assistance to torture survivors. Drawing on human rights narratives introduced in Papua in the mid-1980s, these organisations adopt a clear stance to expose the immorality and illegality of the spectacle of torture to seek redress (Humphrey 2002: 33).

Figure 4.16 also shows how local actors,[39] particularly Papuan churches and human rights NGOs, have been instrumental in exposing the immorality and illegality of torture. The combined figures of churches and local NGOs constitute 80 per cent as opposed to the role of international NGOs which only uncovered 20 per cent of torture cases. This statistic indicates the capability of local actors at confronting torture in Papua. Further this evidence provides empirical grounds for the Kristevan notion of 'revolt' in that turning back to local capacity to generate energy for change is a reality. Drawing on their *memoria passionis*, abjected Papuans are able to organise for themselves a network that enables them to speak for themselves using human rights and social justice narratives. Human rights discourse became a vehicle to mobilise international solidarity movements that put pressure on international political bodies, like the United Nations. The churches of Papua, in particular, have played an effective role not only in amplifying the voices of abjected Papuans but more importantly, in formulating Papua Land of Peace as a framework that connects Papuans' suffering to international church networks. This framework has been a vehicle to transform the energy of *memoria passionis* into social movements which recently sought dialogue with the central government (see Chapter 3). In sum, Figure 4.16 suggests the tenth pattern of the Papuan torture: local actors play a more instrumental role in exposing torture than international actors. This finding challenges both Kristeva, who believes that the abject remains marginalised

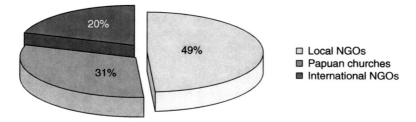

Figure 4.16 Who exposed torture in Papua?
Source: Hernawan database.

122 *The anatomy of torture*

permanently, and Foucault, who suggests that domination only leaves limited space for agents to manoeuvre. It confirms Metz's analysis of *memoria passionis*.

International NGOs, such as Amnesty International, Human Rights Watch, Franciscans International and International Church network, have played a different role in exposing the immorality of the spectacle of torture. As they are not allowed to work inside Papua, their role is bridging the initiatives of the local NGOs and churches with the international community of conscience. Their contribution in international lobbying and advocacy has been strategic in turning the logic of the spectacle of torture upside down. Whereas in the Papuan context, the spectacle of torture has been generated by TNI and the police to convey the message of the sovereign power of the Indonesian state, these NGOs turned this logic on its head. They use exactly the same spectacle to expose the illegality and immorality of the Indonesian state. Spectacularity has been the tipping point to convert the notion of the sovereign power into a message of immorality and illegality of acts of torture committed by the Indonesian state. An international church-based NGO worker illustrates the power of this international advocacy as follows:

2001–2003 was the height of our work. Indonesia was nervous of what we were doing because we were able to put things on the agenda in The Hague, New York, Geneva, Berlin, not so much in Brussels. We had an international lobby, worked in a coordinated way, could push same things at the same time. This network not only focused on Papua but also military budget. BIA [the Indonesian Military Intelligence Agency][40] was not much interested in this [the military budget] but when it came to Papua, they were very interested. But we were churches so they can't say we're communists.[41]

This assertion reveals the effectiveness of the international network of lobby and advocacy for Papua at the time. The key success lay in the effectiveness of simultaneous mobilisation of supports in the centres of decision-making in Europe and the US to put pressure on Indonesia. Moreover, this network consisted of church-based organisations which minimised any possibility of being discredited as Communists by Indonesian military intelligence. While Papua was not the only issue on their lobbying agenda, it was a sensitive issue for the Indonesian military. In a similar vein, during the 2012 Universal Period Review (UPR) of Indonesia by the UN Human Rights Council, twelve of twenty-five countries highlighted specific human rights conditions of Papua, including political prisoners, ongoing impunity, restrictions of freedom of expression and restricted access for journalists to visit Papua.[42]

In the context of lobbying and advocacy, one might pose a question of the role of Komnas HAM. Komnas HAM is not recorded in the torture archives as an organisation which took the first initiative to expose torture. Under Indonesian law, Komnas HAM has the role and obligation to receive and verify any complaints of human rights allegations submitted by Indonesian civil society. If Komnas HAM is provided with sufficient preliminary evidence by a complainer, it may conduct a subpoena investigation that can lead to prosecution by the Attorney General's Office. One of the rare examples of how Komnas HAM and the Attorney General filed a case to the Indonesian human rights court occurred in 2002. This is called the 2000 Abepura case of extrajudicial killing and torture alleged against the police of Papua. While Komnas HAM had recommended twenty-five police officers to stand trial, only two senior police officers were brought to court by the Attorney General office and both were acquitted (see Figure 4.15).

This case is important not only because it is the only[43] human rights case that has ever been heard by the Indonesian permanent human rights court to date, but more importantly, it has become a precedent for holding TNI and the police accountable for human rights abuses across Indonesia. Even though the result was a big disappointment for victims and human rights groups, the court hearings of the Abepura case sent a message to the Indonesian security services that their misconduct could no longer go unnoticed. Once again NGOs had taken over the logic of spectacularity for the benefit of survivors by exposing alleged human rights abuses. The court hearings also indicated some progress with domestic remedies for victims of human rights abuses although it had done little to change the cycle of impunity.

The flip side is that the court hearings also exemplify further abjection processes for the witnesses. Coming to the court for the first time in the foreign soil of Makassar far removed from their homeland, many witnesses felt alienated. They immediately confronted the gaze and gesture of the panel of judges who looked down on and even made fools of them whenever they were not able to speak in formal-standard Indonesian. Instead of being restored, their dignity was even further undermined by the Indonesian human rights court (ELSAM 2007).

Another important element of exposing torture is the role of the churches in Papua. Figure 4.16 records an influential role of the churches in exposing torture (31 per cent of cases). This significant figure is consistent with the historical background in which the churches have been the driving force of resistance to Indonesian state domination through non-violent means prior to the establishment of secular Papuan NGOs in the 1980s.

In conclusion, the spectators here are those who engage with the survivors. Some chose to intervene to bring Indonesian state brutality to light but some may just be silent. Further, the Dataset does not record the element of bystander such as the ways the broader Indonesian public responds to Papuan torture. This problem of ambiguity of witnessing, however, will be dealt with more fully in the following chapter when we discuss the internal dynamics of actors and their relationships with one another.

Conclusion

The examination of the anatomy of torture has unveiled ten patterns that constitute and exhibit asymmetric power relations of the three main actors: survivors, torturers and spectators in the abjected space of Papua in the last half-century.

124 *The anatomy of torture*

First, most of the victims are Papuans, farmers, males, civilians and highlanders that live in the rural areas, which now include Papuan activists and their supporters. Only a few cases involve victims that were OPM members or OPM leaders. Second, rape features as a predominant method to sexually torture Papuan women. Third, almost all torturers are members of the Indonesian state security apparatus: TNI and the police. Fourth, techniques of torture only require low cost and low skills. Fifth, torture in Papua is regularly based on unproven and one-sided accusations by the Indonesian security services. Sixth, under conditions of lawlessness and political transition, the Indonesian state apparatus has heavily relied on torture as a technique to handle secession movements. Seventh, drawing on the ICTY and the ICTR judgements, fifty-year and unpunished practices of state-sponsored torture constitute a crime against humanity. Eighth, most cases constitute both public and secret spectacle of the sovereign power of the Indonesian state. Ninth, the colonisation of public space has led to virtually complete impunity and perpetuated torture practice in Papua. The tenth pattern of the Papuan torture: local actors play a more dominant role in exposing torture than international actors.

The kind of spectacularity of torture marks a stark contrast with the leaked Abu Ghraib and Papua videos. The Papuan experience has revealed that survivors constitute the most marginalised people in terms of class, ethnicity and gender. Situated in Papua, whose people are among the most marginalised group of the Indonesian population on Human Development indicators, survivors experience additional multiple levels of marginalisation, including frequent experience of imprisonment, that have placed them in the most vulnerable sector of the Papuan population. Survivors were not suppressed entirely but remained visible precisely because they are used as a means to convey a message of terror from the torturers to a broader audience.

The torturers, who are mostly found in the Indonesian security services, communicate a message of the sovereign power of the Indonesian state through the survivors of torture. In contrast to the Argentinian experience of the Dirty War where the bodies disappeared, Papuan bodies mostly remain visible, rendering a spectacle for a broader audience, the spectators. The spectators witness the asymmetric power relations between the torturers and the survivors inscribed on the bodies of the survivors. The acts of the torturers in denying but at the same time retaining the survivors have reinforced the notion of the abject and generated public knowledge of torture as an open secret. Through these ambivalent actions, Papuans have been constructed as the abject through torture.

However, in contrast to Kristeva's notion of the powerless abject, Papuan experience has provided us with evidence that the abject is not powerless. On the contrary, the survivors have revealed their human qualities that are capable of resisting, transforming and even transcending their suffering into energy for change. Further, with the support of spectators, the survivors are even able to take over or harness the technology of the spectacle. Instead of conveying the message of the sovereign power of the Indonesian state, the survivors have used the spectacle to expose the illegality and immorality of torture to seek redress.

The anatomy of torture 125

In this context, the role of spectators, particularly NGOs and churches, becomes crucial. The collaboration of the survivors with engaged spectators on occasions has effectively turned the logic of spectacularity of the sovereign state of Indonesia upside down. It must be said, however, that this has happened in only a tiny fraction of the cases in the Torture Dataset. This collaboration then infuses a new notion into the logic of spectacularity, namely illegality and immorality. With the new message, the survivors and spectators mobilise support to engage other non-engaging spectators to build solidarity with the Papuan torture survivors and work towards change. This movement resists Foucault's awesomeness of the sovereign power. Instead of being paralysed and dominated by the sovereign power of Indonesia, the joint project of the Papuan survivors and their spectators has crafted a new beginning of 'revolt' in a Kristevan sense, which means a social process to renew the life of the mind and society. The Papua Land of Peace framework has become a manifestation of this project to create a better and just future for Papuans.

While this chapter has examined the structure of torture in Papua, it has not discussed in detail the internal dynamics of the three actors and how these actors interact with one another. Chapter 5 will further explore internal dynamics of survivors, torturers and spectators and mechanisms that structure their interactions. Once the context of torture, the structure of torture, the logic of torture and the internal dynamics and mechanisms of actors are identified, the whole networked governance of torture in Papua can be more fully understood.

Notes

1 It was not until 28 April 2004 that the US Media became interested in hidden torture practised in Abu Ghraib prison by US soldiers when the TV programme *60 Minutes II* for the first time broadcasted this atrocity which had begun in early 2004.
2 See Figure 3.6 in Chapter 3.
3 See Bumiler (1988: 72–5) on the discussion of three models of survivor ideology critiquing the notion of 'innocent victims' as ideological 'masks' in legal reasoning. The three models are: 'sacrifice' to highlight the noble connotation of victimhood as martyrdom; 'exclusion' which denotes that victims are a source of evil that is perceived to pose a threat to dominant culture (e.g. witches) and 'distortion' to underscore the notion of irrationality which underpins victims' behaviour.
4 Chapter 5 will further explore the complexity of the dynamics of the state authorities and perpetrators.
5 American social psychologists John M. Darley and Bibb Latané examined the failure of thirty-eight people who watched the killing of Kitty Genovese in the middle of a street in a residential section in New York City without any action. They laid the foundation of this study by concluding that 'the more bystanders to an emergency, the less likely, or the more slowly, any one bystander will intervene to provide aid' (Darley and Latané 1968: 378). They identify three possible reasons for this: (1) if only one bystander is present in an emergency, he may intervene because the help must come from him. If there are, however, more people present, responsibility to act would be shared so that the pressure to intervene will be weakened and finally, no one helps; (2) potential blame may be diffused because the more people present, 'the punishment or blame accrues to any individual is often light or nonexistent'; and (3) if others are present but their behaviour is not closely observed, any one bystander will

126 *The anatomy of torture*

assume that one of those other bystanders has taken any action to help. Therefore, he will think that his own action will be redundant because he assumes 'somebody else must be doing something'.

6 An earlier version of some parts of this section has been published in my previous work including 'Torture as a Mode of Governance: Reflections on the Phenomenon of Torture in Papua, Indonesia', in M. Slama and J. Munro (eds), *From 'Stone-Age' to 'Real-Time': Exploring Papuan Temporalities, Mobilities, and Religiosities*, ANU Press, Canberra and 'Torture as Theatre in Papua', *International Journal of Conflict and Violence*, vol. 10, no. 1, pp. 77–92.

7 The 2013–2016 data of the Indonesian Statistical Bureau recorded that by September 2016, 37.33 per cent and 37.07 per cent of the rural population of Papua Barat and Papua provinces, respectively, are poor as opposed to some 5.69 per cent and 4.21 per cent of the population in urban areas of Papua Barat and Papua provinces, respectively (www.bps.go.id/linktabledinamis/view/id/1219, accessed on 15 February 2017). Overall, during the period of 1996–2010, two provinces of Papua are ranked among the lowest in terms of the Human Development Index (www.bps.go.id/linktable dinamis/view/id/909, accessed on 15 February 2017).

8   [T]he expression "directed against" is an expression which "specifies that in the context of crime against humanity the civilian population is the primary object of the attack." In order to determine whether the attack may be said to have been so directed, the Trial Chamber will consider ... the means and method used in the course of the attack, the status of the victims, their number, the discriminatory nature of the attack, the nature of the crimes committed in its course, the resistance to the assailants at the time and the extent to which the attacking force may be said to have complied or attempted to comply with the precautionary requirements of the laws of war.

(See Kunarac *et al.* IT-96–23/1-A para. 91)

9 It should be noted here that the Torture Dataset only recorded imprisonment as the only form of punishment. Other forms of punishment such as civil monetary penalties are not recorded. This might illustrate a limit of the Dataset.

10 Interview with an ex-Indonesian army soldier I/A6 on 17 May 2010 in Papua New Guinea. Further analysis on this testimony will be discussed in Chapter 5.

11 My twelve-year professional experience concurs this practice of indiscriminate excessive use of force to anyone associated with the abjected Papuans.

12 Army battalion 756 is stationed in Wamena and battalion 755 is in Timika.

13 Racist stereotyping has been common for Papuans in various aspects of their daily encounters with the mainstream culture. In sports, for instance, when Persipura, the popular Papuan soccer team, played Jepara on 19 December 2007 the spectators called Jack Komboy, Persipura goal keeper, 'monkey' (*Bintang Papua Online*, 21 December 2007). A stronger comment posted by Dzulfikry Imadul Bilad, an ITB university student, on his Facebook page following the soccer match between Persib and Persipura on 2 May 2010 triggered a strong backlash from the Papuan community in Bandung. There were some 500 reactions on Facebook and it was widely covered by the media (metrotvnews.com, 19 May 2010). He wrote: 'Damned you Papuans, you can only play soccer with your muscle not your brain. Uneducated, idiot, black, but still alive ... damned Papua...!!!' [*Dasar Orang Papua, Bisanya Tarkam Pake Otot Bukan Pake Otak Maen Bolanya, Ga Sekolah, Bodo2, Udah Itam Hidup Lagi. ... Sialan Lu Papua.!!!*]. Bandung Institute of Technology banned him from attending lectures as a sanction even though the Papuan community demanded his expulsion from the university.

14 Rupert Stasch's (2011a) research on the Korowai has revealed the role of international media and tourism in reinforcing the stereotypes of 'primitive' and 'stone-age' Papuans within a global setting. Stasch's other work (2011b), however, further

disclytes that tourists and the Korowai are symmetrically positioned in their perceptions of each other. While tourists perceive the Korowai's nudity as the state of origin,
fulfilling their desire for reenactment of the first state of humanity, the Korowai perceive tourists as the source of funds that bring them material benefits. In other words,
both benefit from their encounters with one another. This provides a stark contrast
with the circumstances of torture in which the elements of aesthetic enjoyment and/or
symmetric relations rarely exist. In a similar vein, some international solidarity groups
for Papua tend to use 'primitive images' to represent Papuans.

15 Interview with a state prosecutor II/C11 on 2 August 2010 in Papua. Similar remarks
feature also in interviews with Indonesian postgraduate students in Australia IV/E7
and IV/E8 in October 2012 in Australia.

16 Interview with a senior state prosecutor II/C20 on 26 August 2010 in Papua.

17 See Case (IT-96–23 and 23/1 para. 150) regarding Foca's case involving three
Bosnian Serbian army (VRS) commanders: Kunarac, Kovac and Vukovic. ICTY convicted and punished them for committing crimes against humanity and rape: '[S]ome
acts establish per se the suffering of those upon whom they were inflicted. Rape is ...
such an act ... Sexual violence necessarily gives rise to severe pain or suffering,
whether physical or mental, and in this way justifies its characterisation as an act of
torture. Severe pain or suffering, as required by the definition of the crime of torture,
can thus be said to be established once rape has been proved, since the act of rape
necessarily implies such pain or suffering.' Geoffrey Robertson highlights the importance of this decision, stating, 'One of the most notable achievements of the ICTY has
been to identify and to stigmatize rape as a war crime rather than a spoil of war'
(2006: 392). This recognition did not happen to similar crimes committed by the
Nazis, the Russian army under Stalin in Eastern Europe or Pakistani soldiers against
some 200,000 Bengali women.

18 See Case no. ICTR-96–4-T regarding Jean-Paul Akayesu, a mayor of Taba commune,
who was found guilty of genocide. Akayesu not only refrained from stopping the killings, but personally supervised the murder of various Tutsis. This case is important to
highlight since ICTR states that rape could be a genocidal act.

19 Interview with a female survivor IIA/33 on 11 August 2010 in Papua.

20 Silence features prominently in torture setting both at individual and societal levels.
Scholars have critically examined this common phenomenon and the difficulty to
represent it (Améry 1980; Dawes 2007; LaCapra 2001; Scarry 1985).

21 Among the variety of techniques of sexual torture in conflict and war situations, rape
is one of the most researched. The study of rape as a weapon of war demonstrates that
it has been deployed by enemy soldiers as an effective strategy of subjugation not
only over individuals but also communities (Diken and Lausten 2005; Rothenberg
2003; Semelin 2007). Diken and Lausten (2005), who explore the use of rape as a
weapon of war in Bosnia (1992–1994) and in civil wars in Rwanda, Liberia and
Uganda, argue that

> the prime aim of war rape is to inflict trauma and thus to destroy family ties and
> group solidarity within the enemy camp. Apart from demoralization of the enemy,
> war rape can also become an integral aspect of ethnic cleansing.
>
> (Rothenberg 2003)

> The study of 100 women from twenty-four countries seeking asylum in the UK
> reveals that rape is the most common form of sexual torture. Many of them were
> raped and sexually assaulted numerous times, frequently by multiple perpetrators
> (Smith and Boyne 2009). For a different view see Human Security Research
> Group (2012).

22 For a critical discussion on various views of policy requirement in crimes against
humanity see Thomas O. Hansen (2011).

128 *The anatomy of torture*

23 Interview with a male survivor IIA/15 on 20 August 2010 in Papua.

24 There is no consensus among scholars on how to categorise torture. Rejali (2007), for instance, divides it into two areas based on any marks left on the body: stealth and scarring torture. However, this categorisation fails to grasp the differences between physical and psychological torture. Peters applies three categorisations: somatic, psychological and pharmacological torture (1985: 169–71). Psychologists and psychiatrists from the International Rehabilitation Centre for Torture (Punamäki *et al.* 2010), in particular, deploy four different categories to emphasise differences between physical, psychological, deprivation of basic needs torture and different types of beatings. While confirming these differences, Reyes (2007), a physician and psychologist from the International Committee of the Red Cross who played an instrumental role in formulating the Istanbul Protocol, emphasises the equal impacts of all types of torture.

25 See Chapter 5, which will further explore motives of the torturers.

26 Waterboarding is an interrogation technique in which the survivor is made to feel as if he or she is drowning and thus is expected to give required confession or information to interrogators. The sensation of drowning is achieved by placing the survivor on an inclined board with feet elevated above the head. The suspect's face is then covered with a piece of cloth or cellophane and water is poured onto the face. The cloth limits or completely halts the flow of air into the survivor's lungs, causing them to collapse and the survivor to gag. While water does not actually enter the lungs, due to the position of the body, it does enter all other cavities of the head, thereby causing the sensation of drowning. Apart from the sensation of drowning, waterboarding has other serious effects such as asphyxiation and hyponatremia. Asphyxiation or lack of oxygen can cause the survivor to lose consciousness and can ultimately lead to brain damage. Death can occur due to hyponatremia, an imbalance of salts in the blood caused by swallowing too much water. Other immediate effects include extreme stress reactions that manifest through elevated heart rate and gasping for breath, while long-term effects include depression, panic attacks and post-traumatic stress disorder. Although waterboarding leaves no physical marks on its survivor, the possible side effects require that the technique is carried out by experts following specific instructions. Often these proceedings are supervised by a doctor to prevent accidental death. (Atlas of Torture Online: www.univie.ac.at/bimtor/glossary/129, accessed on 15 February 2017). The UN Committee Against Torture declared 'waterboarding' as torture (CAT/C/USA/CO/2 para. 24).

27 The latest interpretation of this article by the UN Special Rapporteur on Torture Juan Méndez (2012) further expands the definition of torture and CIDT by including death penalty and solitary confinement. He argues that while death penalty per se is not violation of the right to life, the death row phenomenon or methods of execution is because this method 'involves unnecessary suffering and indignity' (para. 29). 'The death row phenomenon is a violation of article 7 of the International Covenant on Civil and Political Rights, and of article 1 or article 16 of the Convention against Torture and Other Cruel, Inhuman or Degrading Treatment or Punishment, depending on the length of isolation and severity of conditions. The anxiety created by the threat of death and the other circumstances surrounding an execution, inflicts great psychological pressure and trauma on persons sentenced to death. A prolonged stay on death row along with the accompanying conditions constitutes a violation of the prohibition of torture itself' (para. 78). Nowak also concurs with this interpretation (2012).

28 For a critical and comprehensive analysis on the ways the Argentinian junta of the Dirty War generated a constructed reality through introducing and imposing a new language to its state security apparatus, see Feitlowitz (1998).

29 For instance, the then-Indonesian Chief of Army General Ryamizard Ryacudu (now the Indonesian Minister of Defence) publicly praised the soldiers who killed Theys Elluay as heroes (see Chapter 3). See www.radioaustralia.net.au/international/2003-04-24/murderers-praised-by-indonesias-top-soldier/705416, accessed on 15 February 2017.

30 Freedom House lists torture as one of the main criteria to assess the level of rule of law in a country concerned; see Puddington (2012).

31 For a critical reflection on this period see van den Broek and Szalay (2001).

32 Tihomir Blaškić was a former army general and commander at the Croatian Defence Council (HVO) who was sentenced to nine years' imprisonment by ICTY for the biggest massacre committed by the Croatian army under his command in Ahmići, as a non-legitimate military target, in April 1993 (see case no. IT-95–14).

33 Duško Tadić was a Serbian Democratic Party leader and a former member of the paramilitary forces supporting the attack on the district of Prijedor, including the Omarska, Trnopoje and Keraterm concentration camps in the beginning of 1992. He was sentenced to twenty-five years' imprisonment by ICTY for crimes against humanity, breaches of Geneva Conventions and violations of the customs of war (see case IT-94-1-T).

34   It follows that the *mens rea* specific to a crime against humanity does not require that the agent be identified with the ideology, policy or plan in whose name mass crimes were perpetrated nor even that he supported it. *It suffices that he knowingly took the risk of participating* in the implementation of the ideology, policy or plan. This specifically means that it must, for example, be proved that: [a] the accused willingly agreed to carry out the function he was performing; [b] that these functions resulted in his collaboration with the political, military or civilian authorities defining the ideology, policy or plan at the root of the crimes; [c] that he received orders relating to ideology, policy or plan; and lastly [d] that he contributed to its commission through intentional acts or by simply refusing of his own accord to take the measures necessary to prevent their perpetration.

       (See the Blaškić case IT-95–14-T, para. 257, my emphasis)

35 In his recent doctoral thesis on professionalism of the Indonesian military, Robertus Purwoko Putro (2012), an Indonesian airforce middle-ranking officer, concludes that the problem of impunity is deeply entrenched not only in the structure of the Indonesian army but more importantly, in its psyche. In combination with the historical legacy of the military domination in Indonesian politics particularly during the New Order, the culture of impunity within the Indonesian military has seriously undermined their professionalism. This conclusion supports the notion of *habitus*, as will be elaborated further in Chapter 5.

36 Interviews with a middle-ranking Indonesian officer, IV/C2 on 10 June 2010 in Australia and with a retired Indonesian army general, II/E4 on 24 June 2010 in Jakarta support reform.

37 Interview with a middle-ranking Indonesian army officer, IV/C1 on 15 June 2010 in Australia.

38 In the torture literature, the problem of impunity for systematic torture is not novel. Pervasiveness and massive scale of atrocity often pose serious obstacles to address the crime. In many contexts, truth commissions that were established following the collapse of an authoritarian regime to collect evidence necessary for prosecutions were not necessarily able to penetrate long-established power relations emanating from state power. From Indonesia's history of atrocity in Timor-Leste, CAVR (2005) and Commission for Truth and Friendship (CTF) (2008) resulted in a similar conclusion. Both found that the Indonesian state apparatus was guilty of orchestrating and committing crimes against humanity. However, when it comes to the question of accountability, only a handful of perpetrators were tried and only a few of them were convicted and sentenced. Similarly, in the US context, the policy-makers that authorised the use of torture against terrorist suspects have never been prosecuted despite the vibrant public debates and campaign condemning the use of torture against these suspects.

130 *The anatomy of torture*

39 It is interesting to note that the Torture Dataset has no record of individuals exposing torture cases. If it is an individual like the Catholic Bishop of Jayapura, he acts as a representative of an organisation, not as an individual.
40 BIA is different from BIN (*Badan Intelijen Negara*/the Indonesian State Intelligence Body). The former operates specifically under the army whereas the later answers to the President of Indonesia.
41 Interview with a Dutch NGO worker V/B6 on 2 May 2011 in the Netherlands.
42 An unpublished note by Franciscans International, 'Universal Periodic Review of Indonesia Statement Related to West Papua and Papua, United Nations, 23 May 2012'.
43 Despite the continuous pressure of the Indonesian human rights groups, the Indonesian parliament only approved two ad hoc tribunals to hear cases of the Tanjung Priok massacre of 1984 and the Timor-Leste case of 1999. In both court hearings, all of the senior perpetrators ultimately enjoyed impunity.

References

Améry, J. 1980, *At the Mind's Limits: Contemplations by a Survivor on Auschwitz and its Realities*, Indiana University Press, Bloomington and Indianapolis, IN.

Anderson, B. 2006, *Imagined Communities: Reflections on the Origin and Spread of Nationalism*, Verso, London and New York.

Araf, A., Aliabbas, A., Manto, A., Reza, B.I., Satriya, C., Mahruri, G., Nurhasya, J., Simun, J., Safa'at, M.A. and Indarti, P. 2011, *Sekuritisasi Papua: Implikasi Pendekatan Keamanan terhadap Kondisi HAM di Papua*, Imparsial, Jakarta.

Arendt, H. 1963, *Eichmann in Jerusalem: A Report of the Banality of Evil*, Faber and Faber, London.

Boot, M. 2002, *Genocide, Crimes Against Humanity, War Crimes: Nullum Crimen Sine Lege and the Subject Matter Jurisdiction of the International Criminal Court*, Intersentia, Antwerp, Oxford, New York.

Braithwaite, J., Braithwaite, V., Cookson, M. and Dunn, L. 2010, *Anomie and Violence: Non-Truth and Reconciliation in Indonesian Peacebuilding*, ANU Press, Canberra.

Bumiler, K. 1988, *The Civil Rights Society: The Social Construction of Victims*, The Johns Hopkins University Press, Baltimore, MD and London.

CAVR 2005, *Chega! The Report of the Commission for Reception, Truth, and Reconciliation Timor-Leste*, The Commission for Reception, Truth, and Reconciliation Timor-Leste (CAVR), Dili.

Cohen, S. 2001, *States of Denial: Knowing about Atrocities and Suffering*, Polity Press, Cambridge.

Commission for Truth and Friendship 2008, *Per Memoriam ad Spem: Final Report of the Commission for Truth and Friendship (CTF) Indonesia – Timor-Leste*, Commission for Truth and Friendship Indonesia and Timor-Leste, Denpasar.

Darley, J.M. and Latané, B. 1968, 'Bystander Intervention in Emergencies: Diffusion of Responsibility', *Journal of Personality and Social Psychology*, vol. 8, no. 4, pp. 377–83.

Dawes, J. 2007, *That the World May Know: Bearing Witness to Atrocity*, Harvard University Press, Cambridge, MA and London.

Dewulf, S. 2011, *The Signature of Evil: (Re)Defining Torture in International Law*, Intersentia, Cambridge-Antwerp-Portland.

Diken, B. and Lausten, C.B. 2005, *Becoming Abject: Rape as a Weapon of War*, vol. 11, Body & Society.

The anatomy of torture 131

Dunn, J.L. 2005, '"Victims" and "Survivors": Emerging Vocabularies of Motive for "Battered Women Who Stay"', *Sociological Inquiry*, vol. 75, no. 1, pp. 1–30.

ELSAM 2007, *Ekspose Hasil Eksaminasi Putusan Pengadilan Abepura dan Timor Timur*, Lembaga Studi dan Advokasi Masyarakat (ELSAM), Jakarta.

Elsham Papua 2002, *Crime Against Humanity Under Act of Tracing and Annihilation in Wasior, Manokwari*, Elsham Papua, Jayapura.

Feitlowitz, M. 1998, *A Lexicon of Terror, Argentina and the Legacies of Torture*, Oxford University Press, Oxford, New York.

Graziano, F. 1992, *Divine Violence, Spectacle, Psychosexuality, and Radical Christianity in the Argentine 'Dirty War'*, Westview Press, Boulder, CO, San Francisco, CA, Oxford.

Green, P. and Ward, T. 2004, *State Crime: Governments, Violence and Corruption*, Pluto Press, London and Sterling, VA.

Hansen, T.O. 2011, 'The Policy Requirement in Crimes Against Humanity: Lessons from and for the Case of Kenya', *The George Washington International Law Review*, vol. 43, no. 1, pp. 1–41.

Herman, J.L. 1992, *Trauma and Recovery*, Basic Books, New York.

Hernawan, B. 2015, 'Torture as a Mode of Governance: Reflections on the Phenomenon of Torture in Papua, Indonesia', in M. Slama and J. Munro (eds), *From 'Stone-Age' to 'Real-Time': Exploring Papuan Temporalities, Mobilities, and Religiosities*, ANU Press, Canberra, http://press.anu.edu.au/wp-content/uploads/2015/04/8.-Torture-as-a-Mode-of-Governance-Reflections-on-the-Phenomenon-of-Torture-in-Papua-Indonesia.pdf.

Hernawan, B. 2016, 'Torture as Theatre in Papua', *International Journal of Conflict and Violence*, vol. 10, no. 1, pp. 77–92.

Human Security Research Group 2012, *Human Security Report 2012: Sexual Violence, Education, and War Beyond the Mainstream Narrative*, Simon Fraser University, Vancouver.

Humphrey, M. 2002, *The Politics of Atrocity and Reconciliation, From Terror to Trauma*, Routledge, London and New York.

Kelman, H.C. 2005, 'The Policy Context of Torture: A Social-Psychological Analysis', *International Review of the Red Cross*, vol. 87, no. 587, pp. 123–34.

Kelman, H.C. and Hamilton, V.L. 1989, *Crimes of Obedience Toward A Social Psychology of Authority and Responsibility*, Yale University Press, New Haven, CT and London.

Kemitraan and LBH Jakarta 2012, *Penyiksaan di Bumi Cenderawasih*, Kemitraan and LBH Jakarta, Jakarta.

Kirsch, S. 2002, 'Rumour and Other Narratives of Political Violence in West Papua', *Critique of Anthropology*, vol. 22, no. 1, pp. 53–79.

Kirsch, S. 2010, 'Ethnographic Representation and the Politics of Violence in West Papua', *Critique of Anthropology*, vol. 30, no. 1, pp. 3–22.

Komisi Kebenaran dan Persahabatan 2008, *Per Memoriam Ad Spem*, Komisi Kebenaran dan Persahabatan Indonesia – Timor-Leste, Denpasar.

Komnas HAM 2004, *Laporan Penyelidikan Tim* Ad hoc *Penyelidikan Pelanggaran HAM yang Berat di Papua*, Komisi Nasional Hak Asasi Manusia, Jakarta.

Komnas Perempuan 2010, *Stop Sudah! Kesaksian Perempuan Papua Korban Kekerasan dan Pelanggaran HAM 1963–2009*, Komisi Nasional Anti Kekerasan terhadap Perempuan, Majelis Rakyat Papua, ICTJ, Jakarta.

Kristeva, J. 1982, *Powers of Horror: An Essay on Abjection*, Columbia University Press, New York.

LaCapra, D. 2001, *Writing History, Writing Trauma*, The Johns Hopkins University Press, Baltimore, MD and London.

132 *The anatomy of torture*

Levine, D.N. 1985, *The Flight from Ambiguity: Essays in Social and Cultural Theory*, University of Chicago Press, Chicago, IL and London.

LP3BH 2001, *Laporan Pelanggaran Hak Asasi Manusia oleh Anggota Satuan Brimob di Kecamatan Wasior-Kabupaten Manokwari*.

Luban, D. 2007, 'Torture and Professions', *Criminal Justice Ethics*, vol. 26, no. 2, p. 2.

Markas Besar TNI 2006, *Rencana Strategis Pembangunan TNI Tahun 2005–2009*, Markas Besar Tentara Nasional Indonesia, Jakarta.

Méndez, J.E. 2011, *Interim Report of the Special Rapporteur of the Human Rights Council on Torture and Other Cruel, Inhuman or Degrading Treatment or Punishment*, United Nations, New York.

Méndez, J.E. 2012, *Interim Report of the Special Rapporteur on Torture and Other Cruel, Inhuman or Degrading Treatment or Punishment*, United Nations, New York.

Meyers, D.T. 2011, 'Two Victim Paradigms of the Problem of "Impure" Victims', *Humanity*, Fall, pp. 255–75.

Münninghoff, H.F.M. 1995, *Laporan Pelanggaran Hak Asasi Terhadap Penduduk Lokal di Wilayah Sekitar Timika, Kabupaten Fak-fak, Irian Jaya, 1994/1995*, Keuskupan Jayapura, Jayapura.

Nowak, M. 2012, 'What's in a Name? The Prohibitions on Torture and Ill Treatment Today', in C. Gearty and C. Douzinas (eds), *The Cambridge Companion to Human Rights Law*, Cambridge University Press, Cambridge, pp. 307–28.

Nowak, M. and McArthur, E. 2006, 'The Distinction between Torture and Cruel, Inhuman or Degrading Treatment ', *Torture*, vol. 16, no. 3, pp. 147–51.

Omi, M. and Winant, H. 2002, 'Racial Formation', in P. Essed and D.T. Goldberg (eds), *Race Critical Theories: Text and Context*, Blackwell Publishing, Malden, MA.

Peel, M. 2004, *Rape as a Method of Torture*, Medical Foundation for the Care of Victims of Torture, London.

Peters, E. 1985, *Torture*, Blackwell, New York.

Peterson, V.S. 1992, 'Introduction', in V.S. Peterson (ed.), *Gendered States: Feminist (Re)Visions of International Relations Theory*, Lynne Rienner Publishers, Boulder, CO and London.

PGGP 2006, *Laporan Awal Kasus Bentrok Abepura, 16 Maret 2006: Luapan Konflik Masyarakat Papua terhadap PT Freeport Indonesia*, Persekutuan Gereja-Gereja di Papua, Jayapura.

PGGP and Elsham Papua 2011, *Tragedi Lapangan Zakheus*, Persekutuan Gereja-gereja di Papua (PGGP) and Elsham Papua, Jayapura.

Puddington, A. 2012, *Freedom in the World 2012: The Arab Uprisings and Their Global Repercussions*, Freedom House, Washington, DC.

Punamäki, R.-L., Samir R. Qouta and Eyad El Sarraj 2010, 'Nature of Torture, PTSD, and Somatic Symptoms Among Political Ex-Prisoners', *Journal of Traumatic Stress*, vol. 23, no. 4, pp. 532–6.

Putro, R.A.P. 2012, 'The Professionalism of the Indonesian Military', PhD thesis, University of New South Wales.

Reiffel, L. and Pramodhawardhani, J. 2007, *Out of Business and On Budget: The Challenge of Military Financing in Indonesia*, The Brookings Institution, Washington, DC.

Rejali, D. 2007, *Torture and Democracy*, Princeton University Press, Princeton, NJ and Oxford.

Resosudarmo, B.P., Napitupulu, L. and Manning, C. 2009, 'Papua II: Challenges for Public Administration and Economic Policy Under Special Autonomy', in B.P.

The anatomy of torture 133

Resosudarmo and F. Jotzo (eds), *Working with Nature against Poverty*, Institute of Southeast Asian Studies, Singapore, pp. 59–73.

Reyes, H. 2007, 'The Worst Scars are in the Mind: Psychological Torture', *International Review of the Red Cross*, vol. 89, no. 867, pp. 591–617.

Robertson, G. 2006, *Crimes Against Humanity: the Struggle for Global Justice*, Penguin Books, Camberwell.

Rothenberg, D. 2003, '"What We have Seen has been Terrible": Public Presentational Torture and the Communicative Logic of State Terror', *Albany Law Review*, vol. 67, no. 2, pp. 465–99.

Scarry, E. 1985, *The Body in Pain: The Making and Unmaking the World*, Oxford University Press, New York, Oxford.

Schabas, W. 2006, *The UN International Criminal Tribunals: The Former Yugoslavia, Rwanda and Sierra Leone*, Cambridge University Press, Cambridge.

Scott, J.W. 1986, 'Gender: A Useful Category of Historical Analysis', *The American Historical Review*, vol. 91, no. 5, pp. 1053–75.

Semelin, J. 2007, *Purify and Destroy*, C. Hurst & Co, London.

Skjelbæk, I. 2012, *The Political Psychology of War Rape: Studies from Bosnia and Herzegovina*, Routledge, London and New York.

Smith, E. and Boyne, J. 2009, *Justice Denied: The Experiences of 100 Torture Surviving Women of Seeking Justice and Rehabilitation*, Medical Foundation for the Care of Victims of Torture, London.

Stanley, E. 2008, *Torture, Truth and Justice: The Case of Timor-Leste*, Routledge, London and New York.

Stasch, R. 2011a, *Toward Symmetry in Study of Tourists' and Visited People's Experiences: Nudity and Payment in a New Guinea 'Cannibal Tours' Setting*, University of California Press, Berkeley, CA.

Stasch, R. 2011b, 'The Camera and the House: The Semiotics of New Guinea "Treehouses" in Global Visual Culture', *Comparative Studies in Society and History*, vol. 53, no. 1, pp. 75–112.

Taylor, D. 1997, *Disappearing Acts: Spectacles of Gender and Nationalism in Argentina's 'Dirty War'*, Duke University Press, Durham, NC and London.

van den Broek, T. and Szalay, A. 2001, 'Raising the Morning Star', *The Journal of Pacific History*, vol. 36, no. 1, p. 2001.

5   Theatre of torture

Introduction

So far this book has dealt with the macro-structural analysis of the politics of torture in Papua. It examines torture as a mode of governance: the interplay between the *rationalities* of constructing the post-colonial state of Indonesia and maintaining its territorial integrity and *techniques* of domination consisting of strategies of conquest, war, torture, surveillance, divide-and-rule tactics etc. However, as Foucault argues, governance also involves multiple types of agency with actors representing their heterogeneous narratives. Hence it is time for us to analyse other layers that constitute the governance of torture: the individual and the social.

Informed by Kristeva's analysis of the abject and Metz's theory of *memoria passionis*, we will delve into two essential layers of the governance of torture in Papua. First, we will explore the dynamics of individual actors to identify the impacts of torture on individuals as recorded in their narratives. There are three categories of actors (survivor, perpetrator and spectator) which the interviews suggest can be represented by three different narratives (suffering, domination and witnessing), respectively. Each narrative is found not to be a single entity. Rather, it consists of layers of sub-narrative. First we will analyse each layer of each sub-narrative to illustrate the ways in which different rationalities of the practice of torture in Papua have different impacts on individuals involved in the practice. Second, we will elaborate the interactions among the three actor types involved in the torture setting to further clarify the logic of spectacularity which features prominently in the governance of torture in Papua. In exploring these interactions, the theory of motivational postures as developed by Valerie Braithwaite (2014) will be deployed.

In examining the dynamics of individual actors and interactions among actors, the metaphor of theatre[1] will be used to illustrate their complex relationships as a form of theatricality. In an overview of the concept of theatricality, Tracy Davis and Thomas Postlewait (2003) summarise its development, usage and claim to validity. They define theatricality as

> a mode of representation or a style of behavior characterized by histrionic actions, manners, and devices, and hence a practice; yet it is also an

interpretative model for describing psychological identity, social ceremonies, communal festivities, and public spectacles, and hence a theoretical concept.

(Davis and Postlewait 2003: 1)

The benefit of the metaphor of theatre is its effectiveness for conceptualising the dynamics of individuals and the social as performance by exploring their psychological identities, social behaviour, rationalities that underpin the interactions and power relations that frame their relationships (see Goffmann 1956). Moreover, as the Torture Dataset already suggests, the framework of performance will be beneficial to explore the notion of spectacularity that underpins the practice of torture in Papua. The metaphor of theatre will help us analyse actors, roles, script and stage as distinct but interrelated and inseparable units of analysis. The metaphor of theatre will illustrate the dynamics of multiple agencies as 'actors', their multilayered narratives as 'scripts', their fluid interactions with one another as 'roles' as well as their interactions with the structural power as 'stage' in the torture practice in Papua. This metaphor is also effective to demonstrate that theoretically there is only a little space available to evade the theatre of torture as represented by 'exceptions' (see Figure 5.1). On the contrary, every individual plays a role in the torture setting directly or indirectly although this role may change over time depending on different scripts that an individual plays.

Theatre of torture as an ideal type

As the method of triangulation has been discussed in Chapter 1, this section will only highlight the implementation of triangulation of data in this chapter. Triangulation has been deployed as a means to critically engage with complex and competing scripts as represented by the three main actors of the torture model: survivors, perpetrators and spectators. Drawing on 214 individual and seven group interviews, the analysis aims at identifying a model that illustrates the ways in which each actor represents herself, interacts with other actors and exercises power relations among them. In other words, triangulation of data helps disclose the theatre of torture below (Figure 5.1).

In identifying the theatre of torture, I have worked inductively by comparing, identifying, selecting and summarising common features of various scripts until I reached a level where no new fundamental elements can be added into the theatre of torture. Drawing on CDA which explores power relations and inequality in language, the theatre of torture encapsulates common patterns of worldviews and systems of meaning elicited by interviewees. However, instead of carefully analysing transcripts and visual recordings to identify four elements (vocabulary, grammar, cohesion and text structure) of a text, the approach adopted here is different. The approach only analyses vocabulary and cohesion to capture the patterns of worldview and systems of meaning. Moreover, this takes into account frequencies of the ways in which the three chief narratives (suffering, domination and witnessing) and their sub-narratives have been

136 *Theatre of torture*

narrated by interviewees. Overall, there are sixteen distinct narratives identified based on the main themes elicited by interviewees. Each sub-narrative represents a particular script in most cases embraced by a number of interviews indicated by a numeric indicator in each circle in Figure 5.1.

The next section of the chapter uses an interview with just one individual to illustrate each of the sixteen types of narratives. Figure 5.1 shows that for some types of scripts, many other interviews could have been used to illustrate its relevance to understanding torture, while for others only a couple could have been used. For one script, the perpetrator script of pleasure, the case presented is actually the only one in the data. While this means we certainly must be careful not to sensationalise this script based on an n of 1, there is still significance in the fact that it at least exists. Moreover, we must not read too much into the quantitative frequency of different types of scripts beyond noting that certain among them are unusually widespread. Social desirability biases are likely to drive these frequencies in important ways. One reason we think the perpetrator script of pleasure is noteworthy even with an n of 1 is that reporting that one takes pleasure in the suffering of a torture victim is hardly as noble a way of thinking about one's actions as the alternatives.

The narrative of suffering is represented by thirty-four interviews which illustrate the script of victim, twenty-seven interviews for the script of warrior, twenty-two interviews for the script of agent and four interviews for the script of secondary victim. The narrative of domination is represented by eighteen interviews which encapsulate the script of proceduralism, three interviews for the script of *habitus*, two interviews for the script of denial and one interview for the script of pleasure. The narrative of witnessing is represented by forty-three interviews of the script of caregiver, twenty-two interviews of the script of observer, three interviews of the script of bystander and two interviews of the script of beneficiary. Given their complexity and nuances, thirty-one narratives not only fit into one of the ideal types of script below but into two or more sub-narratives. For example, a narrative of a state actor represents a mixture between a script of proceduralism and denial at the same time. Another example is a script of beneficiary which represents converged scripts of victim and agent because the identity of a beneficiary generally stems from a warrior and then becomes an agent before it ends with a beneficiary. But it does not stop there. A beneficiary identity oscillates between victim, agent and beneficiary as we will see in the discussion below. Moreover, there are two interviews that signify two types of narratives from survivors that do not fit into any of sixteen narratives. These exceptions are the narratives of forgetting and wandering which will also be discussed further below.

While the theatre of torture model in Figure 5.1 has been generated inductively from my reflection upon empirical experience on the ground in Papua, as a metaphor, the theatre of torture could be seen as an ideal type[2] in a Weberian sense. In Weber's view, 'ideal types are not normatively exemplary but they are pure constructs of relationships that we conceive as "sufficiently motivated," "objectively probable" and thus causally "adequate" in the light of our nomological

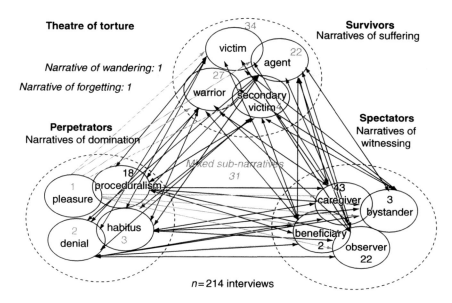

Figure 5.1 Theatre of torture model.

knowledge'. The sixteen types in Figure 5.1 are abstractions that fail to capture all of the complexity in the data on torture in Papua, and in particular the utter uniqueness of each individual's story and their (and others') experience and interpretation of the phenomenon of torture. Ideal types are valuable as cognitive means, to the extent that they lead to knowledge of 'concrete cultural phenomena in their interconnections, their causes, and their significance' (Ringer 1997: 111–12).

As an ideal type, we will see that the model in Figure 5.1, for example, forces us to consider the logic of the possibility of the existence of forty-eight different channels of influence in the model. This excludes the dense interconnections that we have already begun to describe between different survivor narratives (e.g. between victim, agent and warrior scripts), different types of spectators and different types of perpetrator narratives. Surprisingly, interrogation of the 214 interviews then leads to the discovery of thirty-one mixed sub-narratives of the forty-eight possibilities as actually existing in the data. Two narratives of exception (wandering and forgetting), however, do not fit into any of the forty-eight possibilities but they still belong to the theatre model. So actually what we are engaging with here is not pure ideal typical Weberian sociology, but what Thomas Scheff (1990) calls 'abduction', seeing what we can learn by shuttling back and forwards between induction and deduction. As an ideal type, the theatre of torture aims to illustrate multiple interactions and mutual influence among different actors and their scripts.

There are two types of relationships here: (1) dynamics among the four sub-narratives internal to one narrative and (2) external dynamics of sub-narratives

138 *Theatre of torture*

to other narratives. We already described the first type interaction among the four sub-narratives or scripts within one major narrative (e.g. survivor, agent, warrior and secondary victim under the narrative of suffering). The external dynamics are much more complex. Each arrow represents a two-way relationship between one sub-narrative of one narrative and another sub-narrative of another narrative. Each narrative develops eight possible relationships with eight other sub-narratives of two other narratives. For example, the sub-narrative of agent can have four relationships with the four sub-narratives of the narrative of witnessing and the four sub-narratives of the narrative of domination, simultaneously. Similarly, the sub-narrative of *habitus* builds relationships with the four sub-narratives of the narrative of suffering and the four sub-narratives of the narrative of witnessing. This pattern of relationship possibilities applies to every sub-narrative in the theatre model. The script of pleasure, however, only has a one-way relationship with the four survivor sub-narratives. There are no cases in the data where victims or caregivers enjoy pleasure from torture. If each of twelve sub-narratives has eight external relationships, in total we can have ninety-six possible relationships. But this is a double counting because in reality a two-way relationship constitutes only one relationship, not two (e.g. the relationship between agent and bystander is exactly the same as bystander and agent). Therefore, ninety-six must be divided by two, which means forty-eight relationships. Taken together, all relationships constitute a theatre of torture which exerts mutual influence among actors.

Empirically, however, some narratives are more influential than others. For example, the scripts of victim, warrior and agent are much more widespread in the data than the script of secondary victim. Therefore, these scripts have more power to influence the narrative of domination or the narrative of witnessing. Similarly, the scripts of caregiver and observer are more common than the scripts of beneficiary and bystander. As a result they also have a lot of influence over narratives of domination and suffering in ways we will illustrate below. Finally, the script of proceduralism is far more dominant than other scripts of domination and thus more commonly shapes and is shaped by both narratives of suffering and witnessing. Let us now put some flesh on the bones of this model by exploring a single case of each narrative to explore the meaning of the dynamics of actors.

Dynamics of actors: survivors, perpetrators, spectators

This section will delve into the narratives of suffering, domination and witnessing that are produced and reproduced by the three actors involved in the governance of torture in Papua: survivor, perpetrator and spectator. In the theatre of torture these three actors are equally important, interdependent and mutually influential. However, among the three actors, it is only perpetrators that represent and manifest the power of the state.

A theatre can only perform properly if all actors can perform their various roles according to their scripts. As already analysed in Chapter 4, the survivors are all ethnically Papuans. They are constructed as abjects by members of the Indonesian security apparatus as the perpetrators. However, the previous analysis has also demonstrated that survivors and perpetrators are not in an equal position. On the contrary, they are situated in a context like Papua where the policy of domination and the colonisation of public space have applied for the last half-century. In this context, the perpetrators are more than capable to influence and even turn survivors into abject rendering the notion of a spectacle of power rather than the other way around, the survivors towards the perpetrators. However, if only two actors perform their 'scripts' without any presence of spectators, it would not be a spectacle. Both of them need spectators who play an instrumental role to fulfil the logic of theatricality by exposing and resisting torture as identified in Chapter 4. Let us analyse each narrative of torture below.

Narrative of suffering

For the Papuan torture survivors, we will see that suffering is the central theme of their narratives. Suffering has been produced through pain inflicted upon their bodies and minds by the Indonesian security apparatus (see Chapter 4). During my fieldwork, respondents have used storytelling to elicit their stories of suffering from their memories since most of their stories have not been written. This act of remembrance is not a linear process. Rather, it constitutes spiral trajectories that incorporate different meanings produced by the survivors and their interactions with two other actors.

This section will categorise stories from survivors according to themes that are recurrently narrated, particularly innocence, humiliation, anger, fear and anxiety but also hope for justice, freedom and, broadly defined, 'a better future'. The interviews show four different layers of sub-narratives representing four different interpretations and rationalities of suffering: victim, agent, warrior and indirect victim.

The first and predominant notion of suffering is 'victim'[3] represented by the story of Benny, an Amungme elder who does not speak Indonesian.

> I knew nothing but all of a sudden, they came and arrested me. I am an elder, a chief. I signed [the contract with Freeport] so the whole world can eat. I got arrested. Thank God I'm still alive. The Amungme people feed them from all over the world. The whole world! But why was I arrested. I signed the agreement but received nothing from Freeport.
>
> In 2009 I was having lunch and discussing dowry with my family. All of a sudden the police raided and six of us got arrested. They [the police] punched me, kicked me on my chest so I resisted because I knew nothing. I cried to God 'My Lord, the Indonesian police are going to shoot me.' I saw my daughters terrified and crying and so I told them, 'Pray all of you.' All of them were scared because of so many shootings and then we were brought to the police station.

140 *Theatre of torture*

I was wondering why I got arrested not somebody else who is fighting for Papuan independence. I didn't work for it. It's not me. They had to arrest those big people. I am just <u>an ordinary man,</u> <u>did not know anything.</u> I'm a <u>chief</u> who signed the agreement [with Freeport company]. <u>No respect.</u> See we were arrested like <u>animals,</u> like <u>pigs.</u> Got arrested and thrown into the detention. This is a <u>gift</u> from <u>Freeport?!</u>

I keep wondering <u>why I got arrested?!</u> My family thinks the same. I won't forget this forever. I am hurt with this thought. I'm <u>innocent</u> but why was I arrested and also my children. The one who can see <u>things</u> through is only the Father in heaven.

During the detention period, no food, no water, no sleep for two days. No poo because we couldn't get out, locked up. So we pee in a bottle. For twenty days, we were locked up before we were allowed to get out to go the toilet and do some laundry. We <u>knew nothing</u> but we were punished like <u>animals</u> for four months.[4]

In this story Benny repeatedly claims his innocence by stressing the phrases 'not knowing', 'wondering', 'knew nothing', 'why was I arrested', although he only once uses the word 'innocent'. Benny structures his stories based on the priorities of values and norms he embraces. He starts by asserting his role as 'a chief' or an 'elder', who not only has the highest social status in his worldview but more importantly, has entered an agreement with Freeport McMoran to allow this company to extract the wealth in his land. This worldview constitutes his script. It determines the ways he interprets the world. As a chief, he knows exactly that he has the authority, responsibility but also the willingness to 'feed the whole world'. This phrase signifies his responsibility as a chief to look after his community and the world.

Therefore, when the Indonesian police raided his house and brutally and illegally[5] arrested him and his family who were neither armed nor showed resistance to the arrest, his worldview was turned upside down. His script records his experience as excessive humiliation because he was treated like an animal in front of his family and community. For Benny the act of dehumanisation is considered much worse than the violent act itself. Such a thing is totally unacceptable to his worldview as it is simply an act of dehumanisation of an Amungme chief and not upholding the law.

In his excerpts, Benny only mentioned very briefly his situation in Timika police custody. Perhaps he was not so concerned with what happened to his body because his major attention was on defending his dignity. This humiliating experience sticks to his mind as he said that he would 'never forget'. He cynically summarises his experience as 'a gift from Freeport', which can be interpreted to mean that his counterpart in the agreement did nothing when he was subjected to a brutal reality. Based on his Melanesian worldview of signing an agreement between two parties, he assumes that both he and Freeport are bound by the agreement to protect each other's lives against a common enemy. Hence, in Benny's view, Freeport passivity not only signalled complicity to torture but even betrayal of the agreement.

Theatre of torture 141

I call this narrative a script of victim as this resonates with the notion of 'pathetic victim'. Benny's story of victimhood resonates with the typology of victim as previously discussed in Chapter 4. It illustrates qualities of victims such as 'innocence, passivity, vulnerability, individuality, integrity and articulacy' (Doak 2008). This type of victimhood invokes compassion from its audience. However, being passive, 'pathetic' victims rarely represent themselves in any public appearance to demand justice from the Indonesian state or to campaign for *merdeka*.

The second notion of suffering is the 'warrior' based on excerpts from Frans, a member of the OPM who resides in exile in Papua New Guinea.

> I'm one of the founders of the [OPM] movement together with Papuan members of the Indonesia army and police.
>
> 11 February 1984: we originally planned to move for a national rebellion but there was an argument among ourselves because the members of the police had not received salary so they could not move their families. But those who were in the army had done that. The plan was 5 February but many opposed this because it was the gospel day.[6] So we changed to the 11th.
>
> But there was a leak because some army soldiers married non-Papuans and their wives asked them why they had to go for picnic on their own while the men did not come along. We ran out of time and so they told their wives.
>
> 12 February 1984: the Indonesian army came and arrested me and took me to Aryoko [army command in Jayapura]. I was really worried because at the time Aryoko meant death. I was interviewed from 7 o'clock in the morning until 5 in the afternoon. But I asked for a break so I could come to my office at JDF and it was permitted. In Aryoko I was beaten up with a military belt until my teeth were crushed and kicked on my shin and my back. They hit my car too until it was badly damaged.
>
> My uncle, Yohanes – not sure whether he managed to go back to his home village safely now – had been arrested earlier and he had confessed to them what I had done. They used this confession against me. He had been already beaten badly so he confessed. Then I made my confession too.
>
> Admiral Siregar called me to KODAM and he asked me about my support to 'the people in the jungle.' I explained that I provided support for both groups to keep them in a balanced position. While we were talking, suddenly a radio call came in. 'OPM is going to make a coup' so the commander issued an order of the status of highest alert. I was allowed to go home but before leaving, I asked him a letter of guarantee to protect me from any further arrest. But he only told me, 'If you come back, just tell the guards that you have seen me.'
>
> During my time in the camp in East Awin, I had been offered an opportunity to get a citizenship from the PNG government. But I rejected it. I belong to Papua and I can only accept citizenship from Papua.[7]

142 *Theatre of torture*

Just like Benny's story, so too does Frans's narrative start with an explanation of his worldview as a leader and his plot to organise what he calls 'a national rebellion' against Indonesian authority in the late 1960s and end with his story in the refugee camp. He use the words 'plan', 'move', 'movement', 'a leak', 'a national rebellion' to describe his context in which he played a role as a leader. Although he had been tortured, obviously he could ask for a break from his torturers and it was granted and also he met the admiral in an amicable conversation. These facts might indicate that his role was significantly influential to guarantee his torturers that he would not escape their brutal measures. He also knew places around Jayapura in the 1960s that were designated for torture and even to kill those who were categorised as OPM hardliners. So when he was arrested, he had known that torture and death were inevitable consequences for his cause.

During my interview, his pitch remained stable throughout our conversation. This might be interpreted as meaning that the whole story was something he had thought through. He did not explain the torture part in great detail. Rather, he moved to his conversation with the admiral. At the end, he underlined his identity of belonging ('I belong to Papua') that has led him and his family to live in a stateless situation to date ('I can only accept citizenship from Papua').

In sum this is a typical script of a warrior who believes that torture is only a sacrifice for his or her cause. These social and political conditions constitute Frans's worldview that influences the ways he interprets his experience of torture. So when he presents himself to an audience like me, he orders his stories according to his priorities of norms and values to support his role as a warrior. That is why the most important aspect of his utterance is his leadership, his plot, his struggle for *merdeka*, not the details of his experience of being tortured. His suffering both from torture and being a refugee is located at the bottom of his stratification of values because it is simply an expected sacrifice for his role. However, later we will learn from Michael's narrative that even a warrior can switch his narrative to that of a beneficiary.

The third notion of suffering is the script of 'agent' represented by Anna,[8] a woman who has experienced multiple traumatic experiences and managed to come to terms with these experiences. She is now working as a local coordinator of a local NGO X. This group has the mission to organise survivors of human rights abuses across Papua to speak for themselves and to fight for justice.

> In 1998,[9] I was arrested on the street and was thrown into a truck and then was brought to KODIM. I was interrogated by a group of army soldiers with a painted face. They lit a candle and burnt my hands. They sliced my arms with their bayonets and hit my back and the back of my neck with a rifle butt because I fed the boys who raised the flag. I was released and then arrested again by the police. They took my statement and I was charged with treason but never brought to court.
>
> My father was shot dead in Dok II Jayapura by the Indonesian military during the martial law when I was still a kid. Subsequently, my mother was arrested and electrocuted until she was paralysed when she was released

Theatre of torture 143

from the military detention. Later on she was completely crippled before dying a while ago.

A friend called me an 'extraordinary woman' because I survive multiple violence. My parent was shot dead, I was tortured, and now my husband is having affairs with another woman in East Java.

During conducting our research on the situation under martial law July–August 1999, I collapsed. I fell over and fainted because I could not stand the overwhelming stories. The boys who were accompanying me were panicked and gave me massage with oil and said '*mama*, be strong.' Following this research in Northern Biak, I had a feeling of hatred and anger whenever I saw army soldiers. I had great difficulty to speak after the 1998 incident.

Fortunately Father Bob kept inviting me for dinner in his place and we had nice conversations until I overcame this problem. However, hatred is still inside me and I am easily triggered.

About my case? No follow-up after people [NGOs and researchers] came and collected information. They didn't give the victims any update. Eventually we joined a local NGO. It's a slow process, as we don't have enough money and skills.

I always start with a prayer with victims to make me strong before we share our stories. I also make jokes to bear the stories.

In her excerpts, Anna summarises her personal transformation experience from being voiceless to become an agent. She underlines key words that explain her experiences of torture such as 'arrested', 'torture', 'sliced', 'hit', 'burnt' and also 'charged without trial', More importantly, she presents her family background that suffered similar brutality of torture – her mother 'electrocuted' until permanently paralysed after her father had been shot dead by the Indonesian security forces. This traumatic experience was still in her mind on the day I interviewed her. Even now she continues to suffer from domestic violence.[10]

However, she did not give up or join the voiceless. Instead she joined a local NGO. Her journey was far from easy. She still has to manage 'anger' and 'hatred'. For quite some time, she lost her ability to speak. Only because of the help of a Catholic priest who invited her for dinner and facilitated conversations did she regain her speaking ability. She experienced what she calls 'collapse' when she was confronted with 'overwhelming stories' of suffering collected from her fellow survivors. This story suggests a common symptom of post-traumatic stress disorder (PTSD) as Anna's body and consciousness become numb (Allodi and Randall 1985; Herman 1992).

Regaining her capacity to speak marked her transformation process. Anna emerged from the level of a defeated survivor and became an agent. Anna passionately dealt with her fellow survivors to collect their narratives of suffering. At the same time, she managed to keep a critical distance by presenting these stories in a way that the outside world would comprehend. This meant that she had to meet criteria of truth that the world would accept. However, she emphasised that she did not hear any feedback from those who came to her and

144   *Theatre of torture*

collected her stories. Eventually, this fact led her to join a local NGO to speak up for herself and her fellow survivors. The whole process of transformation illustrates the ways in which her memory of suffering generated energy for change. Anna's script of mobilising the collective memory of fellow survivors suggests a role of an agent who cares for her fellow survivors as well as formal justice processes. That is why she also underlines feedback from NGOs or individuals who collect their stories.

The key elements of her transformation are the role of faith,[11] jokes and the role of the priest who invited her for dinner. In every encounter with other survivors, she explained that she starts with 'a prayer to make me strong' and 'makes jokes' to help bear the stories. These two coping mechanisms function at different levels. Prayers help her craft a mental space that enables her personality to confront her own and other survivors' suffering. She uses jokes to technically go through the stories of brutality: she could only make jokes in front of other survivors. This engagement with fellow survivors has exposed Anna to the *memoria passionis* which she shares with them. This has become the transforming and tipping point for Anna. It has driven Anna's sense of solidarity to mobilise other people's solidarity with the torture survivors. Anna's experience, however, is not unique or instantly crafted. Rather, it is situated and rooted in a broader religious experience of a Christian prayer group 'Deborah and Barak'. This group was established on 13 March 1998 in Biak by families of the survivors of the martial law era in Papua[12] to support each other and to draw inspiration from the Bible.[13] In the book of Judges Chapter 4 and 5, Deborah and Barak are two biblical figures who led the Israelites to successfully counter attack the Canaanites prior to the formation of the kingdom of Israel. During this era, Israel was ruled by judges and Deborah was the only female judge. Barak was the commander under her leadership. The way in which the Biak prayer group associates itself with these biblical figures clearly illustrates its vision of resistance, not of surrender as commonly expressed by defeated survivors of torture. Hence, Anna's transformation experience has been part of the larger communal process of survivors who draw on their *memoria passionis* to aim for liberation.

Anna's experience and her religious community are inseparable from the role of the Catholic priest who invited Anna for dinner and conversations. His act exemplifies the act of creating a safe environment as Judith Herman (1992) argues. This environment not only enables Anna to regain her confidence and to make sense of her personal history but more importantly, to reconnect her shattered world with the world of meanings. The role of the priest confirms the element of the influential role of the churches in Papua in exposing torture as already identified in Chapter 4. Its healing[14] and advocacy roles[15] are crucial both at individual and communal levels to create a safe environment necessary for building shattered lives of torture survivors as well as to expose state-sanctioned brutality.

Anna's narrative represents an ideal type of a survivor who has gone through traumatic experiences of torture and has found ways to overcome her memories with storytelling, sharing her experiences with other survivors, engaging in

Theatre of torture   145

voluntary work to organise survivors and using a spiritual framework to guide her until she regained the status of the subject or an agent (Herman 1992: 213). The trauma is not totally eradicated because she truthfully acknowledges that anger and hatred are still inside her but she has moved beyond traumatic memory. She lives with *memoria passionis* which gives her a source of energy to rebuild her past, not as a haunting history but as a foundation to craft a better future.

The fourth script of suffering is 'indirect victim' represented by a younger generation of Papuans who only inherit scripts of torture and other forms of brutality as legacies from their parents. Most of them did not experience any torture or other brutal attack from the Indonesian security services but they inherit stories of suffering from their parents who fled Papua because of persecution. They live quiet lives after experiencing torture or engage in resistance movements to raise the issues of the brutality committed by the Indonesian security forces. Markus is a young man who was born, grew up and lives in PNG as a Papuan refugee:

> I found it very difficult to organise young Papuans here. I think many of them just didn't want to get involved because they were ignorant with the struggle of our parents. They had struggled until today so where the youth would go [to learn the history of the Papuan struggle]. How can we respond if someone raises a question what the contribution of the second generation of the Papuan refugees? I believe we need to continue the struggle of our parents. I tried to talk to them about this but they didn't listen to me.
>
> Similarly, I found difficulties talking with our parents. It is very rare that they share their stories with us so that the second generation would understand and get involved. But the young Papuans are divided into groups according to ideologies. This makes us difficult to be united. As a younger generation, we should be neutral, nurturing the good side and leaving behind the bad side.
>
> My observation found three major obstacles to our development: leadership, management and funds. We don't have leadership. Everybody walks on his or her own. There is no management or financial backup that supports our initiatives.[16]

Markus's story also starts with his role as a leader of the Papuan students living in PNG who experiences difficulties in organising his fellow young Papuans. In describing his stories, he uses the words 'difficult', 'organise', 'involve', 'young Papuans', 'struggle' that indicate his vision as a young leader to take responsibility in promoting the cause of Papua in his context. His difficulties are not limited to youth but also to parents who do not 'share' their stories with the younger generation. So Markus argues that this fact has contributed to the lack of interest among young Papuans in promoting stories about the Papuan struggle for independence.

In the whole story, Markus did not mention a word about the past because obviously he did not possess it. His memory is confined to his family's living

146   *Theatre of torture*

experience on foreign soil, PNG. Therefore, his orientation is towards the future, not the past. This becomes his stratification of norms and values which he uses to assess his dire situation. He clearly expresses his concerns over three issues that have become the stumbling blocks ('divide, ideologies, obstacles') to the development of young Papuans, including leadership, management and funds. He has the ability to reflect on the 'struggle' that the Papuan older generation has fought for. His former role as a student leader has guided him to present himself as one who looks to the future and offers a vision for his 'second generation'. Like Frans, he does not mention the dire conditions of the daily reality that the Papuan refugees have to confront in PNG. This sub-narrative may also suggest that Markus interprets his living conditions as a price for his cause.

All four types of scripts reveal different perceptions and interpretations of torture based on different worldviews that influence and even determine the ways the actors express and perform themselves in the theatre of torture. For the survivors, torture is a traumatic event. It leaves a scar on their bodies and their minds. However, for the agent, torture has been transformed into *memoria passionis* and the capacity to empower others who live with a traumatic memory to create a better future. In the case of the warrior, torture is a matter of sacrifice necessary to achieve victory such as 'freedom', 'international attention to the cause of Papua', 'Papuan political struggle'. Similarly, for the indirect victims, despite the absence of personal experience of torture, the story they inherit from their parents has become the memory of suffering. This collective memory has inspired and empowered these actors to create a better future for Papuans living as refugees with a liminal identity.

Benny's story of anger and remembrance demonstrates what psychoanalyst Judith Herman calls 'hyperarousal' and 'intrusion'. 'Hyperarousal' means a PTSD symptom by which a torture survivor suffers from the state of permanent alert as if the danger might return at any time. Therefore, his or her body develops physiological reactions such as 'startles easily, reacts irritably to small provocations, and sleeps poorly' (Herman 1992: 35). 'Intrusion', on the other hand, is one of the three major PTSD categories that explain a situation where a traumatised person confronts a persistent pattern of reliving the event as if the event is recurring in the present (Herman 1992: 37). Benny could not resume his normal life as the event sticks in his mind. Although he was released and has never been charged, no redress is available to him to restore his worldview that has been severely damaged. The state did not take any responsibility for rehabilitation of his reputation as a chief or make an apology to him. Therefore, he has to travel a long way to recovery.

Anna's symptoms of numbness and anxiety are common among torture survivors not only in Papua or other parts of Indonesia (Larson-Stoa 2010), but also around the world (Herman 1992; Stover and Nightingale 1985).[17] In her compelling analysis of the phenomenon of numbness caused by torture, Elaine Scarry illustrates the effectiveness of torture in destroying the connection between a torture survivor and the world of meaning. Torture not only severely damages the body of torture survivors through pain but also destroys the capacity of individuals to make sense of their world because achievements of human civilisation (such as medicine and trials) have been converted into torture devices (Scarry 1985). As a result, torture survivors are silenced (Améry 1980). Herman calls this symptom 'contrition', another PTSD category where 'the system of self-defense shuts down entirely. This helpless person escapes from her situation not by action in the real world but rather by altering her state of consciousness' (1992: 42). Anna's physiological reaction suggests that her bodily function being utterly shut down temporarily helps her to cope with her traumatic experience.

However, at the later stage of her recovery, Anna's story illustrates the power of *memoria passionis* at work. Anna's remembrance of her brutal experience does not end in preserving the architecture of memory of her past. Rather, she explored and treated the past as a source of transcendental transformation. This process paved the way for change and liberation. Her memory became a memory of suffering, a subversive energy which aims to turn the status quo upside down. Therefore, the memory of suffering is dynamic and has become her driving force to rebuild her shattered life. Drawing on the energy of *memoria passionis*, she rewrites her script as an agent who regained control of herself.

This transformative experience did not occur to Benny, Frans or Markus. All of them still suffer from PTSD in different stages. Benny continues to suffer from 'hyperarousal' and 'intrusion' whereas Frans and Markus remain at the stage of disconnection. 'Disconnection' suggests a different element of traumatic memory. It means complete disengagement from the world as the basic assumption of safety and trust with a relational life has been destroyed. Herman asserts, 'Traumatic events have primary effects not only on the psychological structures of the self but also on the systems of attachment of meaning that link individual and community' (Herman 1992: 51). In the case of Frans, he decided to physically disconnect with his past by fleeing the country, seeking refuge in PNG. He crafted a new liminal identity as a new script, on a foreign soil to give meaning to his past according to his new belonging (Glazebrook 2008; Kirsch 1997; Malkki 1995). Having inherited the legacies of torture from his parents, in contrast to Frans, Markus wants to reconnect with the past by bridging his new identity and his parents' history. However, he develops his liminal identity by disconnecting himself from his daily reality in PNG in which Papuan refugees have been treated as stateless people and thus are granted few rights. These three types of scripts (survivor, warrior, secondary victim) represent the ways in which survivors of torture rebuild their lives based on selectivity of truth and memories.

Overall, the four types of scripts not only refer to ideal types that represent the wide variety of perceptions of torture among survivors but also illustrate different impacts of torture on individuals. Diagnosis of the four scripts reveals that not every torture event necessarily generates abjection. It is only the script of survivors which largely produces the notion of abjection whereas the three other scripts (agent, warrior and secondary victim) suggest the notion of agency to different degrees.

Not every survivor's narrative is adequately represented by the four scripts (victim, agent, warrior and secondary victim). My findings reveal two types of

148 *Theatre of torture*

scripts that do not fit any of the narratives in Figure 5.1. One has been named a script of 'wanderer', the other a script of 'forgetting'. Each of them derives only from one single interview. This fact illustrates the limits of my data. However, without dramatising their significance, both scripts indicate the extent one can potentially escape from the governmentality of torture, loosening Foucauldian chains.

A script representing the wanderer derives from a narrative of Ester,[18] a Papuan woman who resides in the border camps located at the Indonesian border with PNG. Her script does not fit into Figure 5.1.

> I have an Indonesian ID card. My husband works as an Indonesian public servant but my parents and siblings live here as refugees in PNG. So we decided to have a place at the border because it's easier for me to cross the border to see my parents and to go back to Papua to see her children and husband.

Knowing that non-citizens in PNG, like Papuan refugees, are not entitled to public education services, she sent her son to a university and other children to school in Jayapura. Although Ester never experienced any mistreatment from the Indonesian security services, she experiences dire living conditions in her parents' place as refugees. Moreover, unlike Anna or Frans, Ester never gets involved in any activism. She is mother and wife for her family who diligently looks after her family on both sides of the political border.

This script seems ordinary. However, a caregiver[19] who looks after Papuan refugees in the border area of Indonesia-PNG reveals that there are a large number of 'wanderers'. He explains, 'Officially the refugees are settled in Iowara camp [under UNCHR]. [There are] about 2,500 of them and not much change in terms of their number. But some 5,000–6,000 live in the border camps'. Further, this caregiver explains the ways the Catholic Church in this area got involved in taking care of Papuan refugees in the first place, 'No choice for the Church. They came, dying and sick along the border. Also most of them are Catholic, about 85%'. Despite my inability to assess the conditions in the camps, overall, the script of wanderer indicates an important variable to test the validity claims of Figure 5.1 in that not every story can fit the model. More importantly, this script may indicate the existence of a space free of domination which both Foucault and Kristeva fail to see.

The significance of the narrative of wanderer is not confined to a geographical notion but more importantly addresses power relations. Ester's narrative suggests a stronger level of agency in that she manages to both physically move between two distinct political spaces (Indonesia and PNG) and to manoeuvre between the domineering power of the Indonesian state and a state of freedom. To a degree, other scripts allow limited space to evade the domineering power of the Indonesian state.

The second exception is the script of 'forgetting' elicited by Willy,[20] a young man who was stabbed with a bayonet on his left arm by a member of Brimob during a police raid in 1999. The scar remains visible. During my interview, Willy narrated his story with low and stable pitch, suggesting that he was not under much pressure to tell his candid view on the incident that happened to him. He summarises his experience:

> I have forgotten the past because it happened long time ago and I am young so I don't have any mental pressure. I just enjoy my life. But if I see Brimob, I am still afraid of them and can't go nearby any police officers. Perhaps my friends can do it but I just can't.

It is important to highlight Willy's competing interpretations to understand the dynamics of forgetting. On the one hand, he claims that he has 'forgotten' his past and 'enjoys his life' but on the other hand, fear remains inside him whenever he comes across Brimob or any police officers. Following Herman's analysis, this phenomenon is common among torture survivors, and not an extraordinary case. Trauma remains but it is a matter of managing its impact to get on with survivors' lives (Herman 1992). Willy's experience may illustrate the ways he manages his trauma. His script, however, does not fit into any of the twelve scripts in Figure 5.1. He explains that he enjoys his life but unlike Anna, he is not involved in any activism of organising other survivors. Unlike Frans, he did not join in any armed resistance movements as a *warrior* to militarily retaliate against Brimob. He does not embrace the script of the secondary victim either. The puzzle of the dynamics of *forgetting* may derive from the dynamics of managing trauma in that Willy experienced a transition from 'disconnection' to agency, similar to the process that Anna went through. Willy admitted that a sense of 'fear' remains with him but unlike Benny, he has reconnected his systems of meaning with the reality around him and thus he gets on with his life. In this sense, Willy's script of *forgetting* may resonate with the script of *agent* although it may be limited to a sense that Willy regained his agency without necessarily extending it to empower other survivors. Willy's script suggests that he retains the meta-narrative of the 1999 event. What he forgot is his perception and interpretation about the event, not the event itself. Even though his script exemplifies the most identifiable element of forgetting, this element is not entirely absent from all other sub-narratives. Other narratives have been reconstructed from the memory of the interviewees who experience and/or perceive torture, not during the actual event. Therefore, it is natural that some elements of their stories have been forgotten or even suppressed as a result of the sensory-psychological mechanisms of trauma. This phenomenon may put limits on Metz's theory of *memoria passionis* in a sense that this memory does not necessarily lead to emancipation unless it is mobilised as a collective force.

Narratives of domination

Drawing on testimonies from members of TNI and police officers who served in Papua in the era of the 1960s, and the 1980s to the present era, the narratives of

150 *Theatre of torture*

domination illustrate their experiences, perceptions and rationalities in relation to the practice of torture in Papua. Based on the degree of the responsibility of perpetrators, four different scripts[21] were identified: proceduralism, *habitus*, denial and pleasure. These ideal types will further clarify identities of perpetrators from the Torture Dataset.

The first and predominant script of domination is 'proceduralism'.[22] This type derives from a story narrated by Jono, a retired Army Special Unit officer who served in Papua before the Act of Free Choice in 1969. Although his recollection of his past remained very clear when he told his story, he did not share many details:

> At the time I was in charge of a combat intelligence unit and had to be in disguise. The training I had to take was really really heavy: trained to steal documents like a pick pocket without being spotted and other sorts of training. In Papua, my job was to arrest members of the OPM and to take them to KODAM. So I invited him to take a walk with me around here [village] and then disappeared. Another unit took him somewhere else. This applied to the hardliners. But for those who were more approachable, we provided vocational training on agriculture.[23]

This short excerpt encapsulates the important elements of his script. He describes his role by using the words 'job', 'combat intelligence', 'training', 'arrest', 'take'. He precisely portrays his narrative as fulfilling his job. It was just a procedure. Nothing was taken personally. His highly demanding training, divisions of labour among different units within the Indonesian army, the differentiation of targets between the OPM 'hardliner' and the sympathisers – all feed official procedures. Therefore, it is understandable that during my interview, Jono's pitch and body language remained calm and relatively stable because he could simply reproduce an official script that he had embraced.

Jono's worldview is a lot harder to assess. What can be identified is that his disconnectedness is his personal baggage. It shows the ways he separates any personal engagement from his professional life. Jono simply carried out what was necessary as it was prescribed. He knew that once he targeted the hardliners, they would disappear. He implicitly suggests that he knew all the procedures by describing the ways to eliminate targets, the agents who were involved and the locations that were used. These elements were not randomly ordered but on the contrary, followed a standard procedure. It is he who played a decisive role in identifying targets and not the other unit because he had to determine whether a suspect deserved life or death. Therefore, it is not surprising that he did not mention any moral judgement in the centrality of his role to determine life and death of those who were considered the enemies of the Indonesian state, even though these events occurred almost fifty years ago. He remains firm that his responsibility was simply to follow orders.[24]

Hence, Jono's brief script is revealing. It confirms the element of 'systematic' or 'policy' as we already identified in Chapter 4 as the seventh characteristic of

Theatre of torture 151

torture in Papua. The script disclosed that the Indonesian state deliberately introduced torture as a mode of governing Papua since the beginning of its administration in the 1960s.

The second script of domination is *habitus*. It comes from Lubis, a police officer who served in Papua during my fieldwork. He testified that torture remains prevalent, unpunished and deeply rooted in the culture and training of the police force. This perpetuates crimes of obedience (Kelman and Hamilton 1989). However, Lubis reveals that scarring methods have changed into more stealth and untraceable techniques (see Rejali 2007) and there has been little reform to eradicate this institutionalised violence.

> Torture is still everywhere but notably in Papua because of the low level of education [of the people]. Hit [a suspect] first, then interview [him/her]. Such a thing still exists in Java too. When I was in the police academy, I saw our senior put a table foot on a suspect's toe. The table was made of steel. Of course, the foot was punctured; or pulling fingernails. But it changed now. It leaves no marks. Slapping or punching doesn't leave any mark. You wash your face and it's gone. So the practice is still there but using *'pola manis'* [soft approach].
>
> The police academy contaminated my attitude. I used to be a bad boy with violent behaviour but had stopped before joining the police force. When I did my training at the police academy my past behaviour came back because of the atmosphere. I did shoot a criminal until he had to have amputation but that's it. I stopped. I have not hit anybody including my boys since then because if an officer hits somebody, soldiers will follow this example.[25]

Lubis puts the pervasiveness of torture practice very bluntly not only in Papua but across Indonesia, even though he refers to the utilitarian mode of torture. He describes the techniques of coercive interrogation by 'pulling fingernails' or 'put a table foot on a suspect's toe' as common. More importantly he blames his 'seniors' and 'the police academy', which led to rampant torture across Indonesia because exemplary torture practices have developed a kind of habit and culture. However, Lubis sets the boundaries between his personal moral standard and the practice within the police academy. He describes his formation in the police academy as 'contaminating', suggesting that his 'purity' has been spoiled during his introduction into the world of the Indonesian police force. He believes that before and after his socialisation time in the police academy, his purity is better maintained.

Lubis demonstrates his ambiguous standards of morality. On the one hand, he claimed that his standards of morality do not tolerate any form of coercion or violent behaviour. On the other, he has done nothing to intervene in any torture committed in front of him by his senior. Lubis simply blamed his *habitus* as responsible for undermining his standards of morality.[26] In other words, Lubis is not prepared to take any personal responsibility for his ambiguous moral standards and pretends to maintain his innocence by differentiating his claimed

152 *Theatre of torture*

high personal moral standard from the low institutional moral standard of the Indonesian police. He illustrates this situation with the word 'contaminated'. Moreover, Lubis's ambiguity also illustrates the script of interpretive denial at play. He denies the reality of his complicity in the practice of torture.

In sum, Lubis's story exemplifies the ways in which *habitus* can deeply affect individuals. They lose control over their ethical identity once they are positioned as a subordinate of a powerful institution,[27] like the Indonesian police force. This institution is more than capable of imposing a different standard of morality so that individuals simply neutralise and normalise their exposure to torture and other forms of violent behaviour. Torture is no longer considered brutal and primitive but something normal, state-sanctioned and thus institutionalised.

The third type of script of domination is denial. Ahmad, an army general who recently served in Papua, exemplifies this. To understand Ahmad's script, Stanley Cohen's theory on three levels of denial (2001: 7–8) is relevant. Cohen distinguishes three types: 'literal denial, interpretive and implicatory denial'. *Literal denial* means assertion that something never happened or is not true. The emphasis of denial is on the fact or the knowledge of the fact. *Interpretive denial* means providing an alternative interpretation or meaning of a fact or knowledge of a fact. So, the raw facts are not totally rejected but simply construed in a different way of understanding. *Implicatory denial* does not deny the facts or their interpretations. Rather, it simply emphasises the disconnection between the facts or their interpretations from the subject. Ahmad states:

> Human rights violations happened in the past. But was it true that the troops shot at the people? If the military were attacked, they would have fought back. Is it a violation of human rights? It is a violation if they [the military] do act arrogantly over those who are not in power.[28]

Ahmad started his script by drawing a temporal boundary between the present and the past. Although he did not specifically respond to the question of torture, he asserts that human rights abuses 'happened in the past' but even then, he questions the truth ('was it true?') of any shooting by the 'troops'. In his view, if such a thing had occurred, it would have been merely a matter of self-defence because the troops only responded to an attack. He indicates some degree of knowledge on human rights principles when he argues that a violation of human rights occurs when the army 'do act arrogantly' and thus abuse their power against 'those who are not in power'.

For Ahmad, human rights violations did not really happen. He denied twice. First, he categorically denied that human rights violations continue to occur today by saying they 'happened in the past' (literal denial). Second, he denied by saying it was a form of self-defence by referring to 'were attacked' and 'fought back' (interpretive denial). The double layers of denial indicate a level of sophistication as he did not say that human rights violations did not happen. He knew from the public discourse that the Indonesian army has been subjected to fierce public criticisms of their history of abuses in Papua and other parts of Indonesia.

Theatre of torture 153

As a senior army officer, he would know that the time when the army could dictate the public discourse was over and he has to employ different strategies to counter public criticisms to TNI. His script as denial is clear here in that Ahmad claims minimal responsibility.

The fourth script is 'pleasure' stemming from a story of Karel, a former member of the Indonesian army, who now resides in PNG. He shared his story of his former duty in early 1980s around the Jayapura area. The script of pleasure illustrates the highest degree of responsibility of a torturer even though it is represented by only one interview in Figure 5.1.

> It was a common practice that everybody had to have a travel pass to go anywhere: visiting their families in another village or even for going to their gardens etc. From Borowai to Genyem, there were a number of checkpoints and every single vehicle must report: national ID and travel pass. It was a must! If not, we would do whatever we like. When Papuans came in, then the non-Papuans personnel would treat them. They kicked them. Force them to crawl, to run, do push-ups. We were watching. On the other time, when transmigrants came in and didn't bring proper documents … ehm … that's our cup of tea. We made them really, really bad. We didn't shoot anybody but we did whatever we like. It's just a game for us, just for fun. Nothing else because we didn't have anything to do and our commander couldn't do much. He let us go. Yes, for the first time, there was an order but then it had become a common practice as if it was the main duty; but [actually it was not]. The bus drivers kept their heads down as low as possible. It didn't matter whether he was from Flores, Makasar, Java, Papua … we treated them all the same: badly. The same thing with us. It didn't matter where we were from, Makassar, Ambon, Java, Papua – all were army personnel and we acted as an army regardless of our ethnic background. We were under the one Indonesian army corp. That's all.[29]

Karel started his story using the term 'common practice' to indicate his *habitus*. He uses the phrase 'whatever we like' and the words 'treat', 'army', 'watching', 'game', 'fun', asserting his domineering position. Such a position presumes that coercion is normalised and even 'fun' like 'watching a game'. His testimony demonstrates that inflicting pain on the bus drivers and commuters who were not able to present proper travel documents was acceptable to his superior and fellow army soldiers. He uses the word 'treat' to describe coercive acts of forcing the victims to crawl, to run or to undergo corporal punishment. Karel makes it clear that he and his group did not want to kill them but 'just to make them suffer'. Death was not the ultimate goal. Rather, the pleasure of theatrically exhibiting power was the ultimate goal.

By depicting the act of torture as a common practice and an enjoyable game, Karel reveals his script of *habitus* and pleasure that shapes the meaning of his narratives. In contrast to Jono, who sharply divided his personal and public life, Karel reveals no differentiation between personal and public life. Pleasure and

154 *Theatre of torture*

conformity with his group constituted his personal baggage that determined how he carried out torture. Although Jono and Karel show a similar pattern in which they did not mention any moral judgements in their stories, Karel showed a strong sense of remorse when I interviewed him almost twenty years after the actual event.

Two other important elements need to be highlighted here: the type of survivors and the notion of spectacularity in torture. Karel mentioned that the survivors were not only indigenous Papuans. Some of them were non-Papuans who happened to be in the wrong place at the wrong time. This fact is consistent with the previous analysis of the identities of survivors (see Chapter 4) which suggests that some of the survivors were not indigenous Papuans. However, the abjection framework helps explain the reason why torture has also been committed against non-Papuans. The non-Papuans experienced torture not because of their identities as non-Papuans but because of their act of crossing the abjected zones: the Indonesian borders with Papua New Guinea. So once non-Papuans are associated with or become part of the abject, they are treated as abject and thus at risk of torture. In this sense, it can be argued that torture against non-Papuans also constitutes the symbolic mode of torture in that it does not seek information or confession as the utilitarian mode aims for. Rather, it aims to exact the domineering power of the Indonesian state over the body of the non-Papuans to tame them.

If we put all four scripts (denial, proceduralism, *habitus*, pleasure) under the lens of the crimes of obedience theory, we will unveil a deeper relationship between individuals and institutions in a torture setting. One should not forget that individuals who committed torture are members of state-sanctioned institutions such as TNI or the Indonesian police. The theory of crimes of obedience will help explain the linkage between individuals, institutions and institutionalisation of torture in the Indonesian security services in the last half-century.

Herbert C. Kelman and Lee Hamilton (1989) developed the social-psychological theory of crimes of obedience to explain how soldiers can commit genocide. They explore the relationships between individuals and institutions in which the latter play a strong role in influencing and even reshaping the ethical identity of individuals who belong to an institution. Then in a later work, Kelman (2005) applies the framework to torture. He defines

> a crime of obedience: a crime that takes place, not in opposition to the authorities, but under explicit instructions from the authorities to engage in acts of torture, or in an environment in which such acts are implicitly sponsored, expected or at least tolerated by the authorities.

This framework is a useful tool to explain the process by which individuals such as Ahmad, Jono, Lubis and Karel embrace different scripts of the narrative of domination.

In the torture context, Kelman elucidates two different levels of social processes facilitating torture: policy formation and policy implementation (Kelman

Theatre of torture 155

2005: 128). Each part has three successive stages which show different degrees of influence. At the level of policy formation, the first step is the development of three justifications or rationalities that are used by perpetrators to justify their actions. The arguments include 'combating OPM' (Jono), 'searching for travel documents' (Karel) and 'combating crimes' (Lubis). Second is professional development[30] in which the agents of torture had to undergo intensive training to develop their capacity. The Lubis case provides the clearest example of the development of specific skills of torture within the Indonesian police academy. His case demonstrates that torture is deeply institutionalised not by written guidelines but by habituated practice. Finally, the policy formation leads to targeting those who are considered 'enemies of the State'. This formulation is fundamental to shape the mindset of the torturers so that torture becomes normalised. However, the development of mindset and capacity to commit torture will not necessarily lead to the actual practice of torture unless the implementation level is fulfilled.

At the level of implementation, the first phase is *authorisation*. It began when Jono was sent to Papua with a mission to eradicate the OPM or when Karel's commander gave him an order or Lubis's senior showed him an example of interrogation techniques. Then *routinisation*[31] as the second phase follows. For Jono the script of 'proceduralism' helps routinise torture whereas for Karel, the script is a 'common practice' and for Lubis the script is 'the atmosphere'. Routinisation helps neutralise the ethical identity of torturers such as members of TNI and the Indonesian police. Eventually, the level of implementation comes to the *dehumanisation* phase where Jono believes what he did was part of a chain of command to fulfil his mission in eradicating the OPM hardliners. There was no personal consideration or judgement involved. In a more explicitly verbal expression, Karel describes his act of torture as 'just for fun' and part of 'the game'. Similarly, Lubis believes that torture is simply everywhere and nothing has changed except that the Indonesian police force use the 'soft ways'. The element of *dehumanisation*, the ultimate stage of the implementation of crimes of obedience, constitutes the rationale of constructing the notion of enemy. Dehumanisation converts the subject into the abject and thus deprived the victim of his or her subjectivity and human dignity. In the last half-century history of the militarisation of Papua, there is no question that the OPM is defined as an enemy of the Indonesian state. This official position of the Indonesian government condones mistreatment and torture against OPM members if they are captured (see Chapter 3).

Moreover, the crimes of obedience framework helps illuminate the processes in which the element of 'systematic', as identified in Chapter 4, has been developed, maintained and eventually institutionalised within the Indonesian security services in the last half-century. The framework is useful not only as a complement to the archival materials but more importantly as a fuller explanation of the interaction between individuals and institutions in a torture context. The framework also helps identify thirty-one mixed scripts that the perpetrators embrace not as separate and unrelated sub-narratives. Rather, they are closely

156 *Theatre of torture*

intertwined and interdependent. The policy formation and policy implementation are legal concepts that help reveal the ways in which mixed scripts of denial, proceduralism, *habitus* and pleasure have merged into layers of motivation to commit torture.

Narratives of witnessing

The last actor type involved in the torture theatre is spectators, who hold the script of witnessing. This sub-section will analyse four types of spectators based on their roles and arguments: caregiver, observer, beneficiary and bystander.

The first and predominant script of witnessing is 'caregiver', represented by Siti. The caregiver represents those who directly and willingly engage with survivors as they share *memoria passionis*. Siti worked for a Jakarta-based NGO and is involved in advocating for the rights of Papuan victims at the national and international levels.

> All [previous engagement with victims] have made a very deep impression in my life, notably trust building. To build trust with victims is not an easy job. They have long experiences with previous projects from various NGOs and other organisations.
>
> Does it fail or succeed? From the legal point of view, the legislation provides us with a very limited space. Finding new evidence to re-open a case such as the Abepura case of 2000 is extremely difficult. The document produced by the ad hoc investigation team for Abepura is much better that the one produced by the ad hoc team for Wasior and Wamena because the team for Wasior and Wamena did not go to the crime scene, did not visit the victims, and eventually the dossier got stuck in the Attorney General's office. There was no follow-up from Komnas HAM after I quit my job. This resulted from the lack of capacity and commitment of my former organisation. I'm quite pessimistic.
>
> A success story is the establishment of a solidarity group X. In this organisation, the victims themselves helped each other to learn how to build a solidarity organisation, to learn human rights, to be sensitive to human rights issues. X organises events to commemorate tragedies in Papua, cooperates with the regional office of the Ministry for Justice and Human Rights, looks after political prisoners, and talk to university students to educate them. They are able to raise the meanings and values of human rights to the public attention.[32]

Siti starts her story with a description of her long journey to build trust with Papuan victims. She uses the words 'deep impression', 'trust', 'build', 'long experience', 'not easy' to describe her passion to build trust with victims before she could establish respectful relationships with them. Once it was established, she felt humbled because she was accepted into the community of victims. Then she moved on to reflect on her engagement with the Indonesian legal system, which she describes with the words 'limited', 'difficult', 'got stuck', 'no follow up', 'pessimistic'. She summarises her experience with the word 'pessimistic' to capture the inadequacy of law to deliver justice for the victims of human rights abuses. Finally, Siti identifies a success story, the establishment of the organisation X, which Anna also mentioned earlier. Siti highlights important elements that show the organisation X has played an effective role: taking care of its fellow victims and political prisoners and organising activities of remembrance.

Siti's script shows the strong influence of survivors. Her work focused on building trust with the victims, working through the justice system, helping them organise the organisation X and supporting their initiatives. Siti exemplifies Metz's category of solidarity at play which puts an emphasis on grassroots work rather than engaging political and judicial systems. The network of solidarity lays the ground for a politics of hope (Ashley 1998: 163). Therefore Siti's priority is clear: the injured body, not an anonymous and formal system such as the judiciary.[33] Therefore, for Siti, the establishment of organisation X constitutes a milestone for the victims to regain their positions as the subject. For her, this achievement is considered much more important than legal issues such as long delays in prosecution by the Attorney General. Based on her 'personal baggage', she produces and reproduces a script of caregiver which consists of solidarity, compassion and empathy towards survivors. This script resonates with the tenth characteristic of Papuan torture in which local actors play a more direct and dominant role in dealing with torture.[34]

The second and highly significant script of witnessing is the 'observer', represented by Dewa, who has done extensive research on Papua:

I imagine 'torture' as an expression that has been used to label any parties who were labelled as the enemy of the State, the traitor. In Papua, there are only two categories: separatist and non-separatist. Those who hold the power to make a definition, include the Ministry for Foreign Affairs, BIN [the intelligence body] and *Polhukam* [the ministry for political and social affairs]. All of these are military dominated institutions.

'Separatism' for me is a domain of meaning of Papua that includes the notion of untrustworthy, easily bought, opportunistic, drunkard, aggressive. This labelling has formed a cycle of meaning. But dialogue can break the cycle. So in Papua, if somebody is considered 99% NKRI but an incident happens, then all good reputation will be wiped out. The categorisation of 'ours and not ours' is the main and the only criterion to select Papuan leadership. This is *the* criterion, nothing about capacity of leadership. This has generated a paradigm of separatists and the Papuans mimic this pattern by meticulously defining 'who belongs to *merdeka* and who does not'.

This has become a cycle of violence. It also occurs among OPM activists in regards to TNI. This type of violence occurs under the reading of state-sponsored violence. Various conflicts occur in Java and other parts but these cannot be included in state-sponsored violence.[35]

158 *Theatre of torture*

Dewa expresses his worldview by using the words 'torture', 'expression', 'label', 'separatist', 'criterion', 'definition', 'cycle', 'violence'. These vocabularies summarise his argument on the relationships between torture and the state control mechanisms. Dewa defines torture as an 'expression' or a 'label', which has been used by the Indonesian state apparatus to define the enemy of the State. This category plays a decisive role in screening candidates for the Papuan leadership and in determining whether an incumbent leader can stay in a government office. Dewa frequently uses the word 'cycle' to illustrate the ongoing dynamics of constructing the image of the enemy who deserves severe punishment from the state. It is not a single event. Rather, it is a self-recreating process and maintained by three major Indonesian state agencies, the Ministry for Home Affairs, the Indonesian Intelligence Body and the Ministry for Politics and Security Affairs. This analysis is important because it illustrates that TNI and the Indonesian police are not the only institutions responsible for labelling Papuans as separatists. Other Indonesian government institutions are not immune from such stereotyping (see Chapter 3).

Furthermore, Dewa argues that the state control mechanisms have been able to permeate the psyche of Papuans who then adopt the way in which the Indonesian state constructs its enemy.[36] In Dewa's analysis, the binary opposition of 'us and them' is no longer the monopoly of Indonesian authority. Papuans have adopted the same polarised mindset of defining 'friends and foes'. Those who support their cause for *merdeka* are considered friends but those who do not are foes, as if there is no grey area.

Dewa reveals his script of witnessing as an observer who focuses on understanding and explaining a complex structure of social and political reality of torture in Papua. Therefore, he presents his observation to an audience without necessarily involving his personal judgement. He is well aware that his 'observer' script has to demonstrate the principles of objectivity and comprehensiveness.

The third script of witnessing is the 'beneficiary' represented by Michael, a returnee from Papua New Guinea. This category draws on the concept of beneficiary developed by Robert Meister (2002) to explain a group of people who benefit from a regime change because they manage to secure their position to always be part of the ruling class, regardless of ideology or political affiliations. They 'received material and social advantage from the perpetuation of the old regime and continuing well being in the new order' (Meister 2002: 96–7). Michael summarises his view:

> The integration [of Papua with Indonesia] caused people to leave their homes. Many killings happened. My people remain traumatised. After *reformasi*, the situation calmed down. Everybody made mistakes, including the Dutch. It all happened after the war so it was the era of liberation.
>
> If I were looking for a good life, I might have been still there [in PNG]. But change has to be made from within. That's why I came back because Indonesia has changed. Let us be part of it. Politics is all about compromise. Democracy is the best way to compromise. The Papuan struggle needs to compromise. This must be part of the struggle.

Theatre of torture 159

Klemens [a prominent Papuan leader] takes the path that our elders took it before. I appreciate that but it is <u>nothing new</u>. We had called for *merdeka* until we had *mubes* [the Papuan deliberation] and the [Papuan] Congress even we went to the [State] palace [in Jakarta]. We have delivered resolutions after resolutions. All were answered with <u>the Special Autonomy Law</u>. For me, this is the answer although it is not 100% implemented. But politics is just like that. It is all about implementation now. The Papuan leaders are *'setengah hati'* [half-hearted] particularly those who have never been part of the struggle.

<u>Referendum [for Papua]</u>? Is there any way to get there? We don't need to follow Timor-Leste. No need to lie to each other! Is it [referendum] possible? I told the Papuan activists about this. What Vanuatu has been doing is <u>not new</u>. The UN mechanisms are not like the Sentani market.[37] Everybody knows that. But I respect this aspiration out of my sympathy.[38]

Michael depicts his worldview by referring to a historical event: the integration of Papua into Indonesia. However, he did not use the technical term 'the Act of Free Choice' but simply 'integration'. Despite the major Indonesian military operation leading to the integration (see Chapter 3), Michael only briefly mentioned 'killings' and 'traumatised people' without further elaboration. He quickly moved his theme into his justification of his return to Papua. He believes that the world has changed for the better as he frequently uses the word 'change'. He illustrates change with reference to *'reformasi* and the Special Autonomy', two important events which have reshaped the relationship between Papua and Jakarta. However, as already discussed in Chapter 3, Special Autonomy remains problematic and Michael recognised this.

Explicitly Michael wants to be 'part of it [the change]'. This reference suggests his role as beneficiary because he wants to be part of the new regime. That is why he puts emphasis on 'compromise' because there is 'nothing new'. Further, he downplays the idea of 'referendum' or *'merdeka'* by using phrases like 'no way to get there', 'no need to follow Timor-Leste' and 'not like the Sentani market'.

Michael's story illustrates the ways in which a beneficiary manages to secure its position to be on the side of the new regime regardless of its political or ideological differences. For a beneficiary, the main point is to secure his or her material and social advantage, not the survivors. Even though Michael shares the struggle for Papuan independence, he decided to compromise his ideology of *merdeka* and complied with Indonesian authority. He believes that independence ideology belongs to the past. This reference resonates with memory of transfiguration, a type of memory that Metz criticises because it disconnects the past with the present and the future. This type of memory is only paralysing because it does not generate energy for liberation. Furthermore, Michael's narrative exemplifies the transformation of the script of warrior to the script of a victim to the script of beneficiary. However, this narrative is unstable. Rather, it continues to oscillate between the three scripts as it justifies and legitimises the existence of the script of beneficiary.

160 *Theatre of torture*

In Meister's critiques of human rights discourse during a regime change the 'beneficiary' script falls under a grey area because this group of people is less identifiable in comparison to perpetrators or actors for two reasons: (1) human rights discourse puts a heavy emphasis on endorsing 'passive supporters of the old regime to become active opponents – a category in which some beneficiaries may fall'. The discourse assumes that beneficiaries can cleanse themselves through this process to support national healing. So the focus is to incorporate all elements that support a transition from the old regime to a new regime; and (2) the reality is that a new democracy does not start with new citizens. This means the new regime has no alternative but to include those who served the old regime, including beneficiaries (Meister 2002: 97). Drawing on his own personal experience as a Holocaust survivor, Primo Levi (1986) shares Meister's critique. He disclosed the complexity and delicacy of the beneficiary phenomenon by highlighting the fact that in extremely asymmetric power relations, such as in a Nazi concentration camp, a detainee was in a very vulnerable position. In such a circumstance, collaboration is an inevitable strategy to survive. Further, Levi describes an argument that believes the more oppression there is, the more resistance is 'hagiographic and rhetoric' (Levi 1986: 43). In other words, such an argument is just an illusion. He illustrates the ways in which many detainees collaborated with the guards of the Nazi camps simply to secure their food supply for several months in advance. Similarly, many agreed to work as camp guards to protect their lives and the lives of their families.

The fourth script of witnessing is the 'bystander'. The bystander effect is a social-psychological phenomenon in which individuals do not take action to help those who are in an emergency situation where other people are present (Darley and Latané 1968). Under this circumstance, responsibility among onlookers is shared, diffused and eventually, leads to no action. The bystander model of witnessing demonstrates a neuro-psychological phenomenon which Freud calls 'blindsight'. This is a phenomenon of knowing and not knowing a thing or knowing a thing to avoid knowing it. This phenomenon plays an instrumental role in denial (Thomas 2011: 8–9).

Bahar, an Indonesian journalist, depicts his observation of the nature of bystanders in regards to torture videos broadcast on the online media.

> When global online media, the Australian media, and the CNN published the torture videos from Papua, the Indonesian TV [channels] were silent. None of them covered the incident. They only started covering this brutality when the court-martial hearings began.[39]

Bahar's vocabulary of 'silent', 'coverage', 'media' and 'hearings' focuses on and values exposing truths. He also refers to the torture videos with the word 'brutality'. For him, such footage may only confirm his assumption of violent behaviours of the army, which turned out to be beyond imagination. He illustrates the passivity of the Indonesian media as a form of bystander. Further, he demonstrates that this media only started their coverage once the military had conducted court hearings.

Theatre of torture   161

In Bahar's script, the silence[40] of the Indonesian media represents the passivity of larger segments within Indonesian society towards a serious problem in Papua, which he wants to break up. Implicitly he argues that the domestic media should have been the one who exposed the graphic footage and should not have waited until the authorities intervened. In other words, Bahar's view on investigative journalism is at odds with the bystander script, which colluded with the state narrative.

As the media represents the attitude of their audience, Indonesian TV channels, in Bahar's view, represent literal denial by their audience. This audience denied the existence of torture in Papua until Indonesian authority acknowledged the reality. The implication of this analysis might be that a large proportion of Indonesian society might believe that atrocity in Papua never happened unless state authority tells them to believe this.[41] However, this suggestion needs specific research to carefully measure the bystander phenomenon, which goes beyond the scope of this book.

Similar to the survivors and the perpetrators, the spectators contain layers of sub-narratives and contradictions in producing truths of witnessing. The act of witnessing torture does not produce one single meaning. Rather, it contains layers of meanings that often compete with one another and even the thirty-one scripts in Figure 5.1 are mixed between caregiver, observer, bystander and/or beneficiary. The following section will further explore the complexity of the dynamics of these multiple layers when they interact in the theatre of torture.

Interactions of survivor-perpetrator-spectator

This section will further elaborate interactions between the three actors – survivor, perpetrator and spectator – to illustrate asymmetric relations that construct and govern their relations. These interactions will further disclose the ways in which torture plays a role as a mode of governance as shown in Figure 5.1.

Interactions between survivor and perpetrator

As discussed in Chapter 3, the context in which survivors interact with perpetrators is the militarisation of Papua with almost complete impunity. The intensity of interactions between each layer of the two narratives of suffering and domination is not the same. Among the four scripts of the narrative of suffering, *agent* and *warrior* are more engaged with other actors whereas *survivor* and *secondary victim* are less. Anna and Frans are examples that confirm this. For Anna and Frans, torture is unable to stop them advocating their causes for human rights and aspirations for *merdeka*, respectively, because they believe that these are the most important values for them. Similarly, for Markus, the dire conditions of refugee life only strengthen his commitment to educate the young Papuans to speak for the Papuan cause. On the contrary, for Benny, human rights agendas or aspirations for *merdeka* are not his ultimate values. So when the Indonesian police tortured him, his reaction indicated some degree of compliance to

162   *Theatre of torture*

authority before he eventually isolated and removed himself from the public. However, these scripts do not necessarily explain how torture governs the interactions between survivors and perpetrators.

The interaction between individuals and an authority can be explained by the motivational postures theory developed by Valerie Braithwaite (2014; Braithwaite, Murphy and Reinhart 2007). This theory reveals the types of compliance and resistance of individuals in relation to authority, which helps to explain the interactions between survivors and perpetrators in the torture context. Braithwaite defines motivational postures as 'socially shared thoughts and feelings that become organized into well-crafted signals to authority about different kinds of approval of and deference to authority'.[42] The theory is also applied to negotiate 'new relationships with authority' (Braithwaite 2014).

Grounded in empirical evidence from the area of tax compliance and aged care regulation under a democratic regime, Braithwaite discovered five dimensions of motivational postures:[43] commitment, capitulation, resistance, disengagement and game playing. *Commitment* means a posture of embracing authority because of the belief that authority does good for individuals. *Capitulation* conveys a message of surrendering to authority in letter but not in spirit. Despite different degrees of compliance to authority, *commitment* and *capitulation* demonstrate openness for collaboration with authority. *Resistance* is a motivational posture that opposes authority. It explicitly shows hostility towards authority by taking actions against authority. *Disengagement* is a motivational posture that resists authority by avoiding any relationship with authority. Finally, *game playing* is a motivational posture that shows disagreement with authority by trying to change and manipulate the rules of the game any time an actor wishes to do so. This actor simply aims to show its capability to force authority to follow its agenda rather than the other way around.

Anna and Frans's responses to torture and Markus's attitude to the dire conditions of refugee life in PNG show the motivational posture of *resistance*. They express an opposition to Indonesian authorities who tortured them or to the impoverished conditions in refugee life in PNG. In contrast, Benny's response indicates *disengagement*. He withdrew from any engagement with the Indonesian authorities and preferred to go back to his quiet life, although he may continue living with traumatic memory. From the Torture Dataset (see Chapter 4) there is little evidence that any survivor demonstrates *commitment* to Indonesian authority. On the contrary, as John Braithwaite *et al.* (2010) argue, many Papuans show the motivational posture of *capitulation* to Indonesian authority. This element has contributed to the stalemate of conflict resolution in Papua in that many combatants simply *capitulated* to Indonesian authorities rather than *committed* to peace given that a peace agreement or institutions of peace are non-existent in Papua (Braithwaite *et al.* 2010: 141).

However, as already examined, the narrative of domination that the Indonesian authority conveys to Papuans is not a monolithic story. Rather, it consists of four different layers of script: denial, proceduralism, *habitus* and pleasure. Among them, Karel's *pleasure* is a script that suggests a pro-active approach to

Theatre of torture 163

torture, although this is not the most common script. Torturers take personal responsibility when they justify their acts of torture for pleasure. From the motivational postures perspective, pleasure resonates with *commitment* in that perpetrators commit torture because they believe it necessary. They enjoy it. On the other hand, the three other scripts illustrate more of a capitulation approach in that perpetrators commit torture because of their sense of obedience to authorities. As above described, members of TNI or the Indonesian police may not necessarily embrace the attitude that torture is justified. Hence, the scripts of Ahmad's *denial*, Jono's *proceduralism* and Lubis's *habitus* find parallels in the motivational posture of *capitulation*. Members of TNI or the Indonesian police commit torture because they cannot resist their superiors and their structural commands and doctrines. They comply with the letter of the doctrines although they may not necessarily embrace the spirit of the doctrine.

Interactions between survivors and spectators

As a response to the long-term practice of torture, Papua has also experienced long-term resistance. The resistance is not limited to armed struggle represented by OPM but spreads more broadly. It covers Papuan political and social movements, including international solidarity groups, as elaborated in Chapter 3. Those who have witnessed the Papuan experience of torture share the narrative of witnessing. However, just as the narrative of suffering constitutes different scripts or sub-narratives, so too does the narrative of witnessing contain different layers of script. These layers require analysis to determine their relationships with the narrative of survivors in order to understand the correlation between witnessing and visibility.

Michael Humphrey (2002) argues that visibility of atrocity is a paradox. On the one hand, the visibility communicates and transmits the message of terror from the abuser to the broader audience but on the other hand, this act can result in the 'recognition of suffering victims, for compassion and care' (2002: 91). This recognition will evoke empathy and moral responsibility to care. This argument speaks to the first model of witnessing: that of the *caregiver*. Siti's *caregiver* exemplifies the moral values of recognition, compassion and care for the Papuan victims of torture. Siti immersed herself in *memoria passionis* to experience its emancipatory energy. The script of caregiver also engages in broadening solidarity networks to expose the illegality and immorality of torture to end torture in Papua. Caregivers deliver humanitarian assistance and engage the Indonesian justice systems as well as international human rights mechanisms accessible to them.

The genealogical analysis in Chapter 3 already reveals fundamental contributions of the *caregiver* to the Papuan resistance movement. One of the important examples that Siti specifically refers to is the establishment of a solidarity group X. This action illustrates the degree of *commitment* of caregiver to *agents* not only at the practical but also at the strategic level. The organisation X constitutes a new form of social resistance in that the Papuan survivors themselves are fully

164 Theatre of torture

in charge of their narratives. By endorsing the organisation X, the caregiver empowers *agents* to be equal partners in their social resistance. This approach is completely different from the common approach of a caregiver who tends to represent agents, warriors, survivors or secondary victims. This approach puts agents in a more powerful position than when they are represented by caregivers by rehabilitating the ability of agents to reconnect with the world of meaning.

In a less engaged fashion, Dewa's *observer* suggests a significant degree of recognition, compassion and care for the Papuan victims of torture. His analysis of the cycle of violence in Papua contributes to the exposure of the illegality and immorality of torture in Papua. Just as Siti's script, so too Dewa's suggests the motivational posture of *commitment*. However, in the Papuan context the relationships between *observer* and *survivors* vary. While *agents* can easily cooperate with *observer*, it may not always be the case for a *warrior, victim* or *secondary victim*. My own experience of being expelled from East Awin refugee camp in PNG by some of the Papuan refugees (see Chapter 1) suggests the motivational posture of *resistance* towards the observer. Similarly, the saga of a team of scientists who were taken hostage by OPM in 1996 in the central highlands of Mapnduma, Papua illustrates the degree of hostility towards *observers* (see Chapter 3).

The interactions between *survivors* and *secondary victims* with an observer are more cooperative and frequently mediated by *agents*. One of the criticisms that an agent such as Anna mentioned is the lack of information that both *caregiver* and *observer* give back to survivors. However, Benny's script of victim suggests the motivational posture of *disengagement* not only from authority but from the public, including *observers*. My interview would have been impossible without the mediation of agents because Benny had deliberately withdrawn from the public once his worldview was turned upside down by the Indonesian police.

The patterns of interactions between bystander and beneficiary with survivors tend to show the motivational postures of *disengagement* and *game playing*, respectively. Bahar's observation of the phenomenon of the bystander towards the narrative of suffering is consistent with the lack of awareness and understanding of the general public about Papua (see Chapter 3). Similarly, Michael's script as beneficiary illustrates the ways he downplays the narrative of suffering of his own people. He engages with the suffering Papuans simply for his own material and social benefits, not for the benefits of Papuans. Michael's argument that Indonesia has changed towards democracy and his reference to Special Autonomy only justify his *game playing*. He is capable of manipulating the narrative of suffering, which he was personally part of as a returnee, and to articulate his script to convince Indonesian authority.

This analysis reveals a fundamental element of building an agenda for emancipation. The analysis suggests that only caregivers and observers can cooperate with agents to build a strategic alliance for emancipation. These three types of scripts show *commitment* to each other necessary to build a network of solidarity. They reveal three chief potentials for emancipation. First, they share common goals of exploring *memoria passionis* to craft a better future for Papua.

Second, they endorse participation of survivors to be in charge of their own emancipation (e.g. organisation X). Finally, they also explore available legal and political mechanisms for better recognition and protection for survivors. These three elements break the ground for crafting institutions of hope[44] fundamental for peacebuilding.

On the other hand, there is little evidence that *bystanders* and *beneficiaries* will bring about emancipation. On the contrary, either script *disengages* with, manipulates or *plays the game* with the Papuan memory of suffering. As Metz already identifies, the beneficiaries believe that their memories of transfiguration belong to the past. These memories are only histories now. They do not have connections with the present, let alone influence over the future. The *bystanders* show little interest in sharing the Papuan memory of suffering. The media representation of the narrative of suffering seems unable to bridge the gap between the Papuan survivors and the broader audience both nationally and internationally. This phenomenon confirms scholars' analyses that witnessing torture is ambiguous and does not necessarily lead to compassion, recognition and care for torture survivors (Cohen 2001; Humphrey 2002; Linfield 2010; Sontag 2003).

Interactions between perpetrators and spectators

The narrative of domination is predominant in Papua and has little changed in the last fifty years. However, there is room for the Papuan resistance to man-oeuvre. This has developed significantly *post reformasi*. The interactions between perpetrators and spectators are situated in the dynamics of domination and resistance which characterise the mode of governance of torture in Papua. In a similar fashion to the interactions between perpetrators and survivors, the rela-tionship between perpetrators and spectators is asymmetric. The narrative of domination is not equal to the narrative of witnessing in that the latter has less power to influence the former.

As already analysed, among the four scripts of domination, the script of *pleasure* is the most pro-active motivation to commit torture. This script also exemplifies the clearest way of presenting torture as performance to a broader audience. The element of theatricality features prominently in a setting where Karel committed torture at the Indonesian border with PNG rather than the *habitus* of the Indonesian police academy where Lubis developed his profes-sional capacity. The performative element of torture is made visible to witnesses who embrace different scripts (caregiver, observer, beneficiary and bystander) to interpret the message of terror delivered through the practice of torture in Papua. This notion of spectacularity evokes the symbolic mode of torture as the common pattern in Papua.

In contrast, the scripts of *denial* and *proceduralism* illustrate the degree of *disengagement* of the perpetrators with the broader audience. Both Ahmad's *denial* and Jono's *proceduralism* avoid any suggestion that they have any con-nection with the practice of torture. In referring to the practice of torture, Ahmad

166 *Theatre of torture*

uses a more generic term, 'human rights abuses', rather than 'torture', whereas Jono draws the line between his intelligence team and the execution team. By doing so, Ahmad and Jono aim to erect an impenetrable barrier between the witnesses and the secretive world of the Indonesian security services. Therefore, these two scripts suggest the ability of the narrative of domination to hide torture, which is more consistent with the utilitarian mode of torture.

This illustration confirms the genealogical analysis in Chapter 3 that both utilitarian and symbolic modes of torture coexist and overlap. However, the symbolic mode has been adopted by the Indonesian security services as the basis to develop the mode of governance which includes various technologies of domination including conquest, war, utilitarian techniques of torture, divide-and-rule tactics etc. This governance of torture results in the creation and maintenance of the atmosphere of terror which is deeply entrenched not only in the political structures but also at the individual psyche and societal level.

From the perspective of the narrative of witnessing, both *caregiver* and *observer* resist the practice of torture. In conjunction with *agents*, they have developed an alliance of solidarity networks inside and outside Papua to confront the spectacular performance of torture presented by the script of pleasure. The specific role of this alliance is monitoring and networking. Monitoring focuses on measuring the conditions of Papua against national and international legal standards using human rights narratives. On the other hand, networking leads to organising nodes of alliances for change inside and outside Papua. The network mobilises and consolidates support among caregivers, observers and bystanders who are willing to join caregivers and observers. The genealogical analysis suggests that monitoring roles have more success than networking. Proselytising bystanders remains a big challenge. The challenge lies in the fact that the bystander *disengages* with the scripts of pleasure and other scripts (denial, proceduralism, *habitus*) of the narrative of domination. Bahar's observation of the slow and minimal response of the Indonesian national media to the video of torture suggests the posture of *disengagement* of the general public towards state-sanctioned brutality.

This observation finds a parallel in Susan Sontag's study (2003) of the response of the general public to the representation of war through photography and in Humphrey's analysis (2002) of the reasons why witnessing atrocity does not necessarily evoke empathy. Sontag examines the phenomenon of the bystander of war in the context of mediated interaction through photography. She argues that spectators only capture the glimpse of an event and it immediately fades away. So an event of atrocity like war or torture is less likely to enter the awareness of spectators (Sontag 2003: 20). Humphrey interprets this issue from a different perspective. He argues that in contrast to the victims of natural disasters who are considered innocent, the survivors of state violence are construed as having a lesser degree of innocence and even seen with scepticism (Humphrey 2002: 93). The survivors are tainted by the notion of guilt infused by the narrative of domination. Therefore, these survivors gain less attention from the general public.

Theatre of torture 167

Michael's script of *beneficiary* suggests that he capitulates to Indonesian authority. While Michael underlines the traumatic experience of his people and his own experience as a returnee, he perceived that Indonesia has changed from an authoritarian to a democratic regime. Hence, he decided to maximise the opportunity of Special Autonomy for Papua provided he is able to access material and social benefits from Special Autonomy. While Michael's argument is not entirely invalid, he downplays the reality of the failure of the Special Autonomy. Michael is identifiable and visible but many beneficiaries remain quiet and stay in the background, as Meister argues.

However, the lesson learnt from the conflict in Timor-Leste during Indonesia's annexation contradict Meister's argument. The script of *beneficiary* in the Timor-Leste context was far from elusive. Rather, it was made highly visible through the formation and operation of proxies or militias who committed 25.6 per cent of the total amount of violent cases (CAVR 2005: Chapter 6, para 111). East Timor militias capitulated to the Indonesian dominating power and were willing to partake in committing atrocities against their own people. CAVR makes it clear that this was a deliberate strategy of TNI as an unsuccessful tactic to maintain the territory following the referendum in 1999. It is not unlikely that a similar strategy has been deployed by the Indonesian security services to respond to the Papuan aspirations for *merdeka*. The genealogical analysis already unveils the formation and operation of militias as a proxy of TNI and/or the intelligence services. Despite their insignificant role in committing actual torture, TNI proxies such as *Barisan Merah Putih* [Red and White Group] have actively engaged in Papuan politics. If the low-level conflict in Papua continues, it is not implausible that East Timor's pattern of violence will be replicated in Papua.

In sum, the interactions between perpetrators and spectators reveal two major potentials for liberation and violence simultaneously. An alliance of *agents*, *caregivers* and *observers* is the most likely to play a monitoring role to resist the pervasiveness of the narrative of domination of the Indonesian state. Similarly, this alliance has been effective in exposing the immorality of torture to the broader audience to mobilise solidarity. Moreover, this alliance has been instrumental to lay the ground of hope despite the gap of Papuan leadership, which remains unresolved.

On the other hand, the interaction between perpetrators and spectators can build an alliance between the rationality of *pleasure* and the argument of the *beneficiary*, which has generated and maintained a cycle of violence. The empirical evidence both from Timor-Leste and Papua illustrates the ways the domineering power of the Indonesian military deployed a deliberate strategy to recruit civilians as their proxies. This historical context poses a serious challenge for crafting a peacebuilding strategy, which will be further explored in the next chapter.

168 *Theatre of torture*

Conclusions

Our examination of the theatre of torture has unveiled three main elements that have constructed, underpinned and nurtured torture as a mode of governance in Papua. First, the examination has revealed the work of *memoria passionis* of the survivors illustrated in four types of impacts of torture on individuals who have been subjected to it. The scripts of *survivor, agent, warrior, secondary victim, wandering* and *forgetting* suggest different degrees and intensity of the work of *memoria passionis* and thus agency. Second, the analysis has also identified the ways in which perpetrators justify their state-sanctioned brutality against Papuans. The scripts of *proceduralism, habitus, denial* and *pleasure* have become rationalities of torture represented at the individual level. However, these rationalities constitute integral elements of the broader narrative of domination conveyed by the macro-structural power of the Indonesian state. The dynamics of the narratives of suffering and domination render asymmetric power relations between the Indonesian state and Papuans. The multilayered dynamics are not framed in a vacuum. On the contrary, as the metaphor of theatre suggests, these constitute the performance of power relations and have been witnessed by multilayered audiences as the third element of the theatre of torture. Witnessing torture in Papua has rendered four different interpretations, comprising *caregiver, observer, beneficiary* and *bystander* interpretations. These four scripts shape the ways spectators respond to torture in Papua. Figure 5.1 reveals that the most common narratives represented in the Torture Dataset are caregiver (forty-three), victim (thirty-four), warrior (twenty-seven), agent (twenty-two) and observer (twenty-two). The dominant narrative among perpetrators was proceduralism (eighteen).

The alliance of caregiver, observer and agent has manifested the consolidation of the energy of *memoria passionis* to resist the domineering narrative of the Indonesian state as represented by the logic of spectacularity of torture. Despite the gap in the Papuan central leadership, the alliance has also identified three elements necessary for institutionalising hope for Papua's emancipation: shared goals for emancipation, survivors' participation in their own emancipation and engagement with available legal and political mechanisms.

The genealogical investigation uncovers a confrontation between the alliance of emancipation and an alliance of domination. The latter consists of the rationality of pleasure and the beneficiary phenomenon. Drawing on the logic of the spectacularity of torture, this alliance of domination continues to implement a policy of terror by exploiting Papuan bodies in pain, leaving a little space of freedom as an exception.

The Torture Dataset reveals multilayered elements of torture that constitute a mode of governance. Chapters 3 and 4 have delved into the macro-structural layer of power relations at the state level in which the dominating power of Indonesia has constructed Papua as an abject. Drawing on the metaphor of theatre, the analysis of this chapter has pondered the multiple impacts of the governance of torture at the level of the individual psyche to understand the dynamics of

Theatre of torture 169

different narratives, rationalities and interpretations of torture in Papua. The analysis has also disclosed the impacts of the governance of torture on the Papuan society. The interactions of the narratives of suffering, domination and witnessing have not only shaped but sometimes even determined the interactions between survivors, perpetrators and spectators who represent different narratives. The final part of the book will reimagine possibilities for building a peace framework, drawing on the existing Papua Land of Peace framework. By strengthening the Papua Land of Peace framework, the book will conclude with a theatre of peace as a strategy to address the theatre of torture in Papua.

Notes

1 The metaphor of theatre is the basis for generating the concept of theatricality. This concept is commonly used in the social sciences to explain 'all aspects of human life' coded as a system of meanings (Davis and Postlewait 2003: 1). All three theorists used in this book – Foucault, Kristeva, Metz – use the metaphor of theatre in their work to analyse interactions between individuals, society and polity. Both Foucault and Metz use the Latin term *theatrum philosophicum* (Foucault 1997: 216) and *theatrum mundi* (Metz 1980: 105), respectively; whereas Kristeva simply uses the term 'theatre' (Kristeva 1997).

2 Ideal type is closely associated with Max Weber. An ideal type is formed from characteristics and elements of the given phenomena, but it is not meant to correspond to all of the characteristics of any one particular case. It is not meant to refer to perfect things, moral ideals or statistical averages but rather to stress certain elements common to most cases of the given phenomenon. Weber himself wrote

> An ideal type is formed by the one-sided *accentuation* of one or more points of view and by the synthesis of a great many diffuse, discrete, more or less present and occasionally absent concrete *individual phenomena*, which are arranged according to those onesidedly emphasized viewpoints into a unified *analytical* construct.
>
> (Shils and Finch 1949: 90, original emphasis)

3 There is only one equivalent Indonesian word for 'victim', 'survivor' and 'sacrifice', namely '*korban*'. Therefore, the differentiation of meaning depends on the context to which a speaker refers.

4 Interview II/A4 in Papua on 3 July 2010. The themes of bitterness, self-isolation and self-removal are not exclusive for survivors living inside Papua. The themes are also common among some Papuan refugees I/D6 (interview on 2 May 2010) who had already fled Papua into PNG or the Netherlands (V/E7 on 12 May 2011). The themes suggest that geographical boundaries and distance may not necessarily generate a sense of personal safety. A variation was found in an interview with a male survivor III/A16 in Papua who eloquently narrated his experience of torture but explicitly resisted specifying the details of how he was tortured. This phenomenon resonates with Elaine Scarry's frame of 'resisting representation' (1994) as a direct impact of torture on survivors' ability to talk.

5 SKP Timika, a local Catholic Church-based organisation, reported that the police used force illegally to raid, arrest and detain Benny and his relatives (2009).

6 On 5 February 1885 German Christian missionaries Carl Ottow and Johan Geissler arrived in the island of Mansinam, offshore from Manokwari, the provincial capital of West Papua province. The Evangelical Christian Church of Papua (*GKI Tanah Papua*) mark this as the date when Papua was baptised a Christian land.

170 *Theatre of torture*

7 Interview I/D10 with a Papuan refugee in PNG on 15 May 2010. A similar experience was elicited from interview V/A1 on 23 April 2011 in the US. Although this warrior is physically and legally safe under the protection of the US legal system, his new US citizenship has also become a barrier to the extent he has limited access to visit his extended family in Papua. A similar script of warrior is also found among women refugees in PNG elicited from interviews I/A14, I/A15, I/A16, I/A17 and I/A18 on 29 May 2010.

8 Interview with a survivor II/A20 in Papua on 11 August 2010. A similar theme of agency is also found in separate interviews III/A9 on 12 July 2010 and III/10 on 21 June 2010 in Papua.

9 See Chapter 1.

10 Interview with a caregiver III/B11 in Papua on 12 August 2010 confirms the continuous domestic violence that Anna has to suffer.

11 As psychologists discovered, it is common that belief systems play an important role in coping with traumatic experience (Orosa *et al.* 2011).

12 Interview with survivors II/A28 in Papua on 11 August 2010.

13 Interview with a survivor II/A20 in Papua on 11 August 2010.

14 Interviews with caregivers I/B3 on 30 April 2010, I/B4 on 5 and 6 May 2010 and I/B7 on 17 May 2010 in PNG illustrate how the role of the Catholic Church in PNG is crucial in providing humanitarian, health, education and legal aid for Papuan refugees since they only constitute 'permissive residents', not 'citizens', with few rights granted by PNG government. The role of UNHCR is limited not only in terms of targeted refugees but also its continuation. UNHCR only provides humanitarian aid to those who live inside the Iowara refugee camp in the Western Province of PNG whereas most Papuan refugees live outside this camp and spread out across PNG.

15 Interview with Christian pastors II/B15 and II/B16 on 18 August 2010 in Papua who share their regular programme of remembrance to commemorate violent incidents in their parish to create a collective memory of the incidents as part of rebuilding the social cohesion of their parish.

16 Interview I/A8 with a Papuan refugee in PNG on 17 May 2010. An interesting variation is elicited from interview V/A3 on 29 April 2011 in the Netherlands in which the interviewee expressed her mixed scripts. She states, 'I'm from West Papua but now I'm Dutch. My home is Holland. When I arrived in Papua, everybody was crying but then soon I realized no McDonald, no buses. It was not comfortable. I was expected to kiss the ground but I didn't do it immediately. Only after a while, I then kiss the ground in the beach. I have to concentrate here in Holland. Make myself strong and help others. This is a Melanesian principle. We need to be strong to be able to help others.'

17 Autobiographical accounts of torture survivors have been widely published. A famous account of Henri Alleg (1958), a French journalist during the French war in Algeria, was banned in France and had to be published outside the country. It reveals the systemic use of torture by the French government to eradicate the Algerian resistance movement, although it was proven ineffective. In a similar fashion, but less known, accounts of female torture survivors, such as a Catholic nun who survived torture in Guatemala (Ortiz 2007) and an Iranian woman journalist who was forced to marry her torturer to survive (Nemat 2007), illustrate the complexity of traumatic experiences of torture at the personal and individual level. Being a woman, the torture experience of rape marks female survivors with the notion of disgust and impurity, among other torture effects, which resonates with the notion of Kristeva's abjection (see Chapter 3). A more recent account of torture survivors was written by David Hicks (2010), an Australian man who was arrested by the US army in Afghanistan and then detained in Guantanamo Bay before being released without trial. On 17 October 2012, the US Federal Court ruled that the detention in Guantanamo Bay for providing material support to terrorism was invalid because it was applied retroactively. His account also illustrates the power of memory to reclaim agency and craft a better future.

Theatre of torture 171

18 Interview with a woman wanderer I/A11 in PNG on 5 May 2010.
19 Interview with a caregiver I/B4 in PNG on 5 and 6 May 2010.
20 Interview with a male survivor III/A41 in Papua on 19 August 2010.
21 For a critical discussion solely on the dynamics of perpetrator narratives, see Leigh Payne (2008).
22 The proceduralism argument finds parallel in Hannah Arendt's analysis of the famous trials of Adolf Eichmann, a Nazi leader who was convicted of crimes against the Jewish people with intent to destroy them (1963: 244). Eichmann argues that he did not do anything wrong because he just fulfilled his *duty* to follow orders to transport Jews to the concentration camps. He claimed he had no knowledge of what would have happened with the Jews.
23 Interview II/E3 with a retired Indonesian army officer in Papua on 4 September 2010. Although he admitted that he was eighty-six years of age during my interview, he remained very much aware of selecting which part of his stories he could share with me. He did not want to go into any details about the ways he was trained as an intelligence agent, the procedures to deploy him or the methods for eliminating the OPM hardliners.
24 In July 1961, three months after Adolf Eichmann's trial began, Stanley Milgram, a social psychologist from Yale University, conducted an experiment that measured obedience to authority. While his methods were controversial, the result is authoritative. He concludes

> Ordinary people, simply doing their jobs, and without any particular hostility on their part, can become agents in a terrible destructive process. Moreover, even when the destructive effects of their work become patently clear, and they are asked to carry out actions incompatible with fundamental standards of morality, relatively few people have the resources needed to resist authority.
> (Milgram 1974: 6)

25 Interview III/C16 with a middle-ranked police officer in Papua on 18 August 2010.
26 A separate interview with a senior police officer III/C18 conducted in Papua on 25 August 2010 independently confirmed Lubis's *habitus* but drew a different conclusion that resonates more with the script of denial. He states, 'the environment is influential. So there is no such thing as systematic'.
27 See a recently published testimony of Glenn Carle, an ex-CIA interrogator and torturer, who illustrates the entanglement of *habitus*, ethical identity and personal decisions. Instead of succumbing to the state ideology, Carle decided to maintain his ethical identity and made a decision not only to leave the CIA but also to publish his testimony despite heavy censorship from the CIA (2011: 290).
28 Interview with an Indonesian army general, II/C24, in Papua on 2 September 2010. Variations of the denial argument include 'there is no complaint so far' (interview with a middle-ranking police officer III/16 in Papua on 21 July 2010); 'there is no torture, for sure, because there is no complaint' (interview with a middle-ranking police officer III/C2 in Papua on 6 July 2010); 'there is no omission! Such a thing might have happened in the past but certainly not today' (interview with a middle-ranking police officer II/C1 in Papua on 8 September 2010); 'it is just exaggeration' (interview with a middle-ranking army officer III/C13 in Papua on 3 August 2010).
29 Interview I/A6 with a former army soldier in PNG on 17 May 2010.
30 The element of 'professional development' resonates with groupthink theory, a previous study by Irving L. Janis. Janis unveiled this psychological phenomenon in which a member of a group of people tends to conform to the collective desire of the group. By minimising conflict and differences with the collective interests of the group, a member aims to secure his or her belonging to the group. Janis defines this symptom as 'a mode of thinking that people engage in when they are deeply involved in a cohesive in-group, when the members' strivings for unanimity override their motivation to realistically appraise alternative courses of action' (1982: 9).

172 *Theatre of torture*

31 The element of 'routinisation' constitutes the main object of the theory of techniques of neutralisation developed by Gresham M. Sykes and David Matza (1957). They identified five types of justifications for committing crimes: *the denial of responsibility* in which offenders blame their circumstances that force them to commit crime; *the denial of injury* in which offenders insist that their action do not cause any harm; *the denial of victim* in which offenders believe that victims deserve any action against them; *the condemnation of the condemners* in which offenders blame those who criticise them and describe these criticisms as unfair; and *the appeal to higher loyalties* in which offenders argue that their actions are beneficial if they are put in perspective.

32 Interview II/B1 with a caregiver in Java on 16 September 2010. There are some variations of engaging with survivors. An interview with a caregiver V/A4 on 11 May 2011 in the Netherlands illustrates the difficulty of juggling Papuan political factionalism and building Papuan solidarity in an international public. Sometime factionalism caused significant damage to the effort of building Papuan solidarity. Another interview with an international caregiver V/B3 on 29 April 2011 in the Netherlands reveals the preference to engage with Papuans living inside Papua rather than those in exile.

33 Interviews with caregivers who are lawyers (II/B3 on 9 July 2010 in Papua; II/B7 on 28 July 2010 in Papua) suggest that while they realise the limits of the corrupt Indonesian justice system, they maximise the available legal window of opportunity to defend their clients.

34 Interviews II/B4 on 10 July 2010 and B/5 on 12 July 2010 in Papua with other caregivers reveal their limited resources (funding, management, networking, English language skills) which put serious constraints on their capacity to provide legal assistance and to work with survivors.

35 Interview with an academic II/E2 in Jakarta on 21 June 2010. A similar sympathetic observer can be identified from separate interviews with other academics V/E1 and V/E2 on 9 May 2011 in the Netherlands. Another type of observer is more detached rather than engaging with survivors. These observers deal with the issue of Papua simply because it is her or his job as an analyst and a foreign diplomat. Interview II/E15 on 17 January 2012 and II/E16 on 19 January 2012 in Jakarta, III/E4 on 11 January 2012 in Papua, V/E4 (on 3 May 2011), V/E5 (on 5 May 2011) and VE9 (16 May 2011) in the Netherlands illustrate the script of proceduralism weaved with the script of 'observer'. In these interwoven scripts observers just follow orders or procedures to monitor Papua issues and thus personal engagement is considered irrelevant and might even jeopardise their professional standard. Therefore, for an observer, witnessing can be much more ambiguous than what Dewa represents.

36 The genocide literature identifies defining and dehumanising the enemy as one of the most important strategies of those who are in the position of formulating policies or delivering orders. This strategy is deliberately designed to neutralise personal and moral judgement among the operatives. So when an actual order to kill is delivered, the operatives have embraced the belief that they are not only doing the right thing and a noble mission but more importantly they eliminate non-human enemies (Semelin 2007).

37 The Sentani market is a local market 40 km outside Jayapura, the provincial capital of Papua. Being a local market, it is modest in size; a variety of actors are involved and a variety of commodities. By referring to this illustration, Michael simply emphasises the stark contrast between the modest Sentani market and UN mechanisms, which are considered enormously complex machinery.

38 Interview III/F5 in Papua on 4 September 2010. Interview III/D6 in Papua on 21 August 2010 independently confirms this pattern although this interviewee does not necessarily agree with Michael's stance. See Santosa and Rizal (2010) for a recent example of an edited volume containing various personal testimonies of Papuan figures who advocate for the Indonesian state narrative.

Theatre of torture 173

39 Interview II/E3 with an Indonesian journalist on 24 February 2011 in Australia.

40 Drawing on Stuart Kirsch's anthropological study, the correlation between bystander and silence is not limited to the media. Rather, it goes deeper into the production of knowledge of Papua. Kirsch argues that there is a divide between Southeast Asian and Pacific studies which covers Papua. While the former tend to be drawn to courtly tradition which to some extent has been appropriated by the state, the latter largely ignore the state. The divide has led to the marginalisation of political violence in the anthropological research on Indonesia, particularly in outer islands (2002: 54). Similarly, in the recent study of peacebuilding in Timor-Leste, John Braithwaite *et al.* (2012) have critically disclosed that 'misplaced realism' embraced by neighbouring countries of Indonesia, like Australia, not only had failed to appreciate the power of the weak but, more importantly, had condoned the deliberate colonial strategy of the Indonesian state which caused the loss of hundreds of thousands of lives of East Timorese.

41 In the Indonesian political context, during the fortieth anniversary of the 1965 massacre, which killed more than 500,000 people labelled 'Communist' (Cribb 2001), both state and non-state actors (e.g. Nahdhatul Ulama, one of the largest Muslim organisations in Indonesia) refused to offer an apology to the victims (*Kompas*, 15 August 2012, http://nasional.kompas.com/read/2012/08/15/20243252/PBNU.Tolak. Permintaan.Maaf.kepada.Korban.Tragedi.65, accessed on 15 February 2017). In 2016 vigilante groups such as Front Pembela Islam (the Defender Front of Islam) held a large demonstration in Jakarta to put pressure on the government to refuse to apologise to the victims (www.thejakartapost.com/news/2016/06/03/thousands-rally-in-protest-of-alleged-revival-of-pki.html, accessed on 15 February 2017). President Joko Widodo affirmed the government refusal to offer an apology (www.thejakartapost. com/news/2016/06/28/i-wont-apologize-to-pki-jokowi-dismisses-rumors.html, accessed on 15 February 2017). This attitude illustrates not only the degree of collusion between state and non-state actors to destroy those who are labelled as the enemy of the state but, more importantly, the deliberate intention of the state to kill its own citizens without any legal justification. This state-sanctioned brutality and its surrounding denial suggest that it is all about reactivating power, not seeking justice, as Foucault analyses.

42 This theory derives from social identity theory, a major strand of a social psychology, which deals with the dynamics of social groups developed by John Turner (1987) and Henri Tajfel. The maxim of this theory is that the behaviour of individuals and social groups is influenced by their social identities. Therefore, it is natural that an individual has multiple and fluid identities depending on different social groups to which s/he belongs.

43 These motivational posture models draw on an empirical study in a context of democracy. For our analysis here, these models have their limits, particularly in explaining the 'grey area' of beneficiary. Although most characteristics of the beneficiary refer to the posture of capitulation, this posture is limited to explaining the element of 'no choice' to escape the network of domination as in Primo Levi's illustration with the Nazi concentration camp (1986). Similarly, the posture of disengagement is useful to explain some elements of the script of bystander. However, it does not explain the whole nature of ambiguity of bystanders who tend to know but at the same time do not know a thing.

44 These elements of building institutions of hope resonate with Valerie Braithwaite's analysis of institutions of hope (2004) which outlines three distinct but inseparable elements to institutionalise hope: shared goals, collective efficacy and democratic institutions.

174 *Theatre of torture*

References

Alleg, H. 1958, *The Question*, J. Calder, London.

Allodi, F. and Randall, G.R. 1985, 'Physical and Psychiatric Effects of Torture: Two Medical Studies', in E. Stover and E.O. Nightingale (eds), *The Breaking of Bodies and Minds: Torture, Psychiatric Abuse, and the Health Professions*, W.H. Freeman and Company, New York, pp. 58–78.

Améry, J. 1980, *At the Mind's Limits: Contemplations by a Survivor on Auschwitz and its Realities*, Indiana University Press, Bloomington and Indianapolis, IN.

Arendt, H. 1963, *Eichmann in Jerusalem: A Report of the Banality of Evil*, Faber and Faber, London.

Ashley, J.M. 1998, *Interruptions: Mysticism, Politics, and Theology in the Work of Johann Baptist Metz*, University of Notre Dame Press, Notre Dame, IN.

Braithwaite, J., Braithwaite, V., Cookson, M. and Dunn, L. 2010, *Anomie and Violence: Non-Truth and Reconciliation in Indonesian Peacebuilding*, ANU Press, Canberra.

Braithwaite, J., Charlesworth, H. and Soares, A. 2012, *Networked Governance of Freedom and Tyranny: Peace in Timor-Leste*, ANU E-Press, Canberra.

Braithwaite, V. 2004, 'The Hope Process and Social Inclusion', *The Annals of The American Academy of Political and Social Science*, vol. 592, pp. 128–51.

Braithwaite, V. 2014, 'Defiance and Motivational Postures', in G. Bruinsma and D. Weisburd (eds), *Encyclopedia of Criminology and Criminal Justice*, Springer, New York.

Braithwaite, V., Murphy, K. and Reinhart, M. 2007, 'Threat, Motivational Postures and Responsive Regulation', *Law and Policy*, vol. 29, no. 1, pp. 137–58.

Carle, G. 2011, *The Interrogator: A CIA Agent's True Story*, Scribe, Melbourne.

CAVR 2005, *Chega! The Report of the Commission for Reception, Truth, and Reconciliation Timor-Leste*, The Commission for Reception, Truth, and Reconciliation Timor-Leste (CAVR), Dili.

Cohen, S. 2001, *States of Denial: Knowing about Atrocities and Suffering*, Polity Press, Cambridge.

Cribb, R. 2001, 'Genocide in Indonesia, 1965–1966', *Journal of Genocide Research*, vol. 3, no. 2, pp. 219–39.

Darley, J.M. and Latané, B. 1968, 'Bystander Intervention in Emergencies: Diffusion of Responsibility', *Journal of Personality and Social Psychology*, vol. 8, no. 4, pp. 377–83.

Davis, T.C. and Postlewait, T. (eds) 2003, *Theatricality*, Cambridge University Press, Cambridge.

Doak, J. 2008, *Victims' Rights, Human Rights and Criminal Justice, Reconceiving the Role of Third Parties*, Hart Publishing, Oxford and Portland, OR.

Foucault, M. 1997, 'Theatrum Philosophicum', in T. Murray (ed.), *Mimesis, Masochism, and Mime: The Politics of Theatricality in Contemporary French Thought*, University of Michigan Press, MI, pp. 216–38.

Glazebrook, D. 2008, *Permissive Residents: West Papuan Refugees Living in Papua New Guinea*, ANU E-Press, Canberra, A.C.T.

Goffmann, E. 1956, *The Presentation of Self in Everyday Life*, University of Edinburgh, Edinburgh.

Herman, J.L. 1992, *Trauma and Recovery*, Basic Books, New York.

Hicks, D. 2010, *Guantanamo: My Journey*, William Heinemann, Sydney.

Humphrey, M. 2002, *The Politics of Atrocity and Reconciliation, From Terror to Trauma*, Routledge, London and New York.

Janis, I.L. 1982, *Groupthink: Psychological Studies of Policy Decisions and Fiascoes*, 2nd edn, Houghton Mifflin, Boston, MA.

Kelman, H.C. 2005, 'The Policy Context of Torture: A Social-Psychological Analysis', *International Review of the Red Cross*, vol. 87, no. 857, pp. 123–34.

Kelman, H.C. and Hamilton, V.L. 1989, *Crimes of Obedience Toward A Social Psychology of Authority and Responsibility*, Yale University Press, New Haven, CT and London.

Kirsch, S. 1997, 'Refugees and Representation: Politics, Critical Discourse, and Ethnography along the New Guinea Border', in M. Morgan and S. Leggett (eds), *Mainstream(s) and Margins: Cultural Politics in the 90s*, Greenwood Press, London.

Kirsch, S. 2002, 'Rumour and Other Narratives of Political Violence in West Papua', *Critique of Anthropology*, vol. 22, no. 1, pp. 53–79.

Kristeva, J. 1997, 'Modern Theatre Does Not Take (a) Place', in T. Murray (ed.), *Mimesis, Masochism, and Mime: the Politics of Theatricality in Contemporary French Thought*, University of Michigan Press, MI, pp. 277–81.

Larson-Stoa, D. 2010, 'Effect of Therapy on Depression, Anxiety, Somatization, and Functioning in Indonesian Torture Survivors', Master of Arts thesis, University of South Dakota.

Levi, P. 1986, *The Drowned and Saved*, Sphere Books Ltd, London and New York.

Linfield, S. 2010, *The Cruel Radiance: Photography and Political Violence*, University of Chicago Press, Chicago, IL and London.

Malkki, L.H. 1995, *Purity and Exile: Violence, Memory, and National Cosmology Among Hutu Refugees in Tanzania*, University of Chicago Press, Chicago, IL and London.

Meister, R. 2002, 'Human Rights and the Politics of Victimhood', *Ethics and International Affairs*, vol. 16, no. 2, pp. 91–108.

Metz, J.B. 1980, *Faith in History and Society Toward a Practical Fundamental Theology*, Burns & Oates, London.

Milgram, S. 1974, *Obedience to Authority: An Experimental View*, Tavistock Publications, London.

Nemat, M. 2007, *Prisoner of Tehran, One Woman's Story of Survival Inside a Torture Jail*, John Murray, London.

Orosa, F.J.E., Brune, M., Huter, K., Fischer-Ortman, J. and Haasen, C. 2011, 'Belief Systems as Coping Factors in Traumatized Refugees: A Prospective Study', *Traumatology*, vol. 17, no. 1, pp. 1–17.

Ortiz, D. 2007, *The Blindfold's Eyes: My Journey from Torture to Truth*, Orbis Books, New York.

Payne, L.A. 2008, *Unsettling Account: Neither Truth Nor Reconciliation in Confessions of State Violence*, Duke University Press, Durham, NC and London.

Rejali, D. 2007, *Torture and Democracy*, Princeton University Press, Princeton, NJ and Oxford.

Ringer, F. 1997, *Max Weber's Methodology: The Unification of the Cultural and Social Sciences*, Harvard University Press, Cambridge, MA and London.

Santosa, A.E. and Rizal, Y. (eds) 2010, *Integration: A Done Deal, Critical Comments on Papua Road Map*, Pusat Studi Nusantara, Jakarta.

Scarry, E. 1985, *The Body in Pain: The Making and Unmaking of the World*, Oxford University Press, New York, Oxford.

Scarry, E. 1994, *Resisting Representation*, Oxford University Press, New York and Oxford.

Scheff, T.J. 1990, *Microsociology: Discourse, Emotion and Social Structure*, University of Chicago Press, Chicago, IL and London.

176 *Theatre of torture*

Semelin, J. 2007, *Purify and Destroy*, C. Hurst & Co, London.

Shils, E.A. and Finch, H.A. (eds) 1949, *Max Weber on the Methodology of the Social Sciences*, The Free Press of Glencoe, New York.

SKP Timika 2009, *Laporan Awal Kasus Penembakan di PT Freeport Indonesia Tanggal 8–31 Juli 1999*, Sekretariat Keadilan dan Perdamaian Keuskupan Timika, Timika.

Sontag, S. 2003, *Regarding the Pain of Others*, Farrar, Straus and Giroux, New York.

Stover, E. and Nightingale, E.O. (eds) 1985, *The Breaking of Bodies and Minds: Torture, Psychiatric Abuse, and the Health Professions*, W.H. Freeman and Company, New York.

Sykes, G.M. and Matza, D. 1957, 'Techniques of Neutralization: A Theory of Delinquency', *American Sociological Review*, vol. 22, no. 6, pp. 664–70.

Thomas, N. 2011, 'On Turning a Blind Eye and a Deaf Ear: Society's Response to the Use of Torture', *International Journal of Group Psychotherapy*, vol. 61, no. 1, pp. 7–25.

Turner, J. 1987, *Rediscovering the Social Group: A Self-Categorization Theory*, Basil Blackwell, Oxford.

6 Theatre of peace

Reimagining 'Papua Land of Peace'

Introduction

Our examination of torture has revealed that torture constitutes a mode of governance. The governance of torture contains not only one single monolithic power relation but three different interrelated layers of asymmetric power relations: macro-structural, micro psychic-individual and mezzo-communal levels. Therefore, the framework of the theatre of torture is a useful tool for us to analyse the three different areas of power relations as represented by the complex interactions of the narratives of survivors-perpetrators-spectators. However, the foregoing discussion has not dealt with the question of *how* we can address and possibly dismantle the governmentality of torture to create a theatre of peacebuilding as a means to craft a 'better future' for Papua.

This is a very challenging question as the history of Papuan peacebuilding is still in the making. Therefore, this chapter will not pretend to provide a definite answer. Rather, it will explore possibilities of strengthening and maximising the existing theatre of peacebuilding in Papua. As opposed to the theatre of torture which is heavily influenced and to a large extent governed by the domineering power of the Indonesian state, the theatre of peacebuilding will build on Metz's theory of *memoria passionis* and theology of revolt as a politics of hope. We will start by reviewing the Papua Land of Peace framework to assess its strengths and limitations before exploring the challenges of building peace in a prolonged conflict situation like Papua informed by three different empirical studies: Susanne Karstedt's Violent Society Index, John Braithwaite's *Peacebuilding Compared*, and Erica Chenoweth and Maria Stephan's study on non-violent resistance. Drawing on the narratives of *warrior, agent, caregiver* and *observer* (see Chapter 5), we will then analyse three alternative narratives (solidarity, healing, and revolt). This lays foundations for the architecture of the theatre of peacebuilding as a long-term and holistic strategy to dismantle the theatre of torture facilitated by a permanent national truth and reconciliation commission for Papua (TRCP).

Why Papua Land of Peace?

As the historical context of Papua Land of Peace has already been discussed in Chapter 3, this section will only highlight the philosophy and architecture of Papua Land of Peace as a movement. The emphasis on 'movement' is important to highlight to capture the dynamics and open-ended nature of Papua Land of Peace while simultaneously underscoring its notions of fragility, interruption and limitations.

Van den Broek and colleagues (2005) encapsulated the reflections of Papuan representatives on the concept of Papua Land of Peace during their deliberations in Jayapura in 2001. Forty organisations representing almost all sectors of Papuan civil society, government and the private sector explored the philosophy of Papua Land of Peace before formulating a broad concept of freedom which is defined as 'the desire to liberate themselves from all forms of oppression' (2005: 7). This philosophy derives from a deep understanding of the complex social, cultural, economic and political situation of Papua. These conditions became the basis to define Papua Land of Peace as 'a social condition, not just a geographical area which is free from violence within a war zone' (2005: 7). In other words, freedom has become the basis upon which Papuans want to build and establish 'a land of peace', a social construction of reality of Papua. This conceptualisation is fundamental as it provides an alternative to the governmentality of torture which has been embedded in the ways Papua has been governed in the last half-century. There are nine elements[1] summarised here that constitute the pillars of the architecture of Papua Land of Peace (2005: 9–21) (see Figure 6.1):

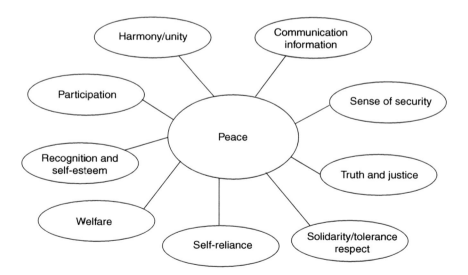

Figure 6.1 The architecture of Papua Land of Peace.
Source: van den Broek *et al.* (2005: 8).

1   Participation is described as taking an active role in the public sphere 'to build the world around us'. The emphasis of being an agent for one's own history resonates with the narrative of agent under the theatre of torture.

2   Harmony/unity is an element that highlights the importance of protecting the environment for the future sustainability of human life. This concern derives from long-term experience with extractive industries in Papua, such as Freeport Indonesia, which have caused enormous environmental and social damage.

3   Communication and information are interrelated elements concerning access to reliable sources of information and the freedom to communicate given that the Papuan social and political landscape is often coloured by misleading information which often leads to over-expectation.[2]

4   Sense of security refers to living peacefully and enjoying safety as a basic right for Papuans. Given that Papua has been heavily militarised, this element aims at drawing the distinction between human security and state security affairs.[3]

5   Truth and justice refers to an element of clarifying Papuan political history to establish the historical truth of the territory. This element constitutes a major unresolved dispute between the Indonesian state and Papuans in that Papuans demand a review of the history of its integration into Indonesia whereas the Indonesian state claims that there is no need to conduct such a thing because the history is final.[4] 'There must be dialogue in regard to Papuan history by all involved parties to rediscover the historical truth of the territory. At the very least, dialogue will create an opportunity to clarify truths and untruths, therefore, open a way for the truth to be understood and accepted' (van den Broek, Korain and Kambayong 2005: 17).

6   Solidarity/tolerance/respect refers to an embrace of togetherness and differences that mark the nature of the Papuan community. 'Solidarity is also determined by a sense of equality and shared commitment to those values respected by all human communities, such as truth, peace, justice etc.' Solidarity becomes the basis for tolerance and respect in that these attitudes provide 'a basic tool for reconciliation and permanent mutual acceptance in the community' (van den Broek, Korain and Kambayong 2005: 11).

7   Self-reliance is a quality of being in charge of one's own life. This element stems from the phenomenon of Papuan dependence on Indonesian government aid and projects which has greatly undermined the capacity of Papuans to craft their own future.

8   Welfare refers to 'material and spiritual satisfaction where no one needs to suffer from hunger, poverty or disease' (van den Broek, Korain and Kambayong 2005: 13). This is a universal basic need which directly relates to state policies. One of the criticisms of Special Autonomy for Papua is the failure of this package to significantly improve the living standards of Papuans. This criticism is echoed in various analyses including Benny Giay's and Neles Tebay's work discussed below as well as in various public demonstrations.

180 *Theatre of peace*

9   Recognition and self-esteem: restoring Papuan dignity which has been suppressed for half a century. 'It is clear that self-esteem of the Papuan people
has been suppressed to the point that it has almost ceased to exist. Many
Papuans have begun to feel inferior because they are regarded as ignorant
and primitive' (van den Broek, Korain and Kambayong 2005: 18).

Inspired by this broad framework, Giay further developed the Papua Land of
Peace framework with his vision of *Menuju Papua Baru: Beberapa Pokok
Pikiran Sekitar Emansipasi Orang Papua* (Towards a New Papua: Thoughts on
Papua Emancipation) (2000)[5] which encapsulates his vision of emancipation,
freedom and liberation; the essential elements of the philosophy of Papua Land
of Peace. He traced back the ways Papuans perceive liberation and emancipation
by identifying two main elements: structure and substance of emancipation.
Under 'structure', he identifies four different perceptions of liberation ranging
from 'ordinary people', Papuans of the 1960s and Papuan NGOs, to contemporary Papuan nationalists. Giay argues that ordinary Papuans simply conceive liberation as 'Indonesia, go home!' (Giay 2000: 17, my translation). This
phrase encapsulates the sense of reclaiming the agency of abjected Papuans, as
Kristeva suggests. Being marginalised and dominated by the Indonesian state, in
Giay's view, ordinary Papuans envision the new Papua as a geographical space
that is free from outsiders, particularly Indonesians. However, Giay does not
provide a critical analysis of whether this approach is viable in the current geo-
politics or in what ways Papuans can reclaim their identity simply by expelling
Indonesians. Similarly, he does not provide justification when he describes
Special Autonomy as a concept of a power structure to govern Papua proposed
by Papuan NGOs (Giay 2000: 19). In fact, despite the Papuan NGOs' feedback
to the legal drafting of the Special Autonomy Law as required by the Indonesian
legal system, this law is an Indonesian law formulated by the Indonesian parliament as a representative of the state power. In other words, it is the state which
formulates the law, not an NGO.

The third concept derives from the 1960 political context which envisioned
an independent state of Papua as part of the Kingdom of the Netherlands. Giay
notes that this concept had been 'destroyed' by the Indonesian state (Giay 2000:
17). This concept is interesting in the ways that it resonates with a post-colonial
state that is not able to sever ties with its former coloniser. Finally, Giay outlines
the last concept which he calls 'an independent state of West Papua' (*Negara
Papua Barat Merdeka*). This concept derives from the formulation of the nation-
alist Papuans who lost their faith in the nation and government of Indonesia
because they believe that 'The nation of Indonesia is a real coloniser' (Giay
2000: 20, my translation). Giay continues to identify key state institutions
including Papua territory as the replacement of the former Netherlands New
Guinea and the structures of executive and legislative powers which assume
authority and responsibility to govern the territory. Giay, however, does not
elaborate this concept any further in a way that we can sense the degree of feas-
ibility of this political structure for Papua given it is a province of Indonesia, not

Theatre of peace 181

an independent state. Nevertheless, these four political alternatives represent a variety of political views of Papuans towards a political framework of their future.

The second element that Giay discusses is the substance of the New Papua. Drawing on a number of analyses, Giay lists ten elements that constitute the New Papua (Giay 2000: 21–7, my translation):

- Recognition-access-demilitarisation
- Freedom to take initiatives
- Protection of the land and the nation of Papua
- Priority given to Papuans to rehabilitate their identity
- Back to Papuan history and celebrating Papuan identity symbols[6]
- Reconciliation and collective trauma healing
- *Papuanisasi*:[7] reclaiming agency and self-reliance
- Demilitarisation of Papua
- Multiculturalism
- Development based on ethical and human rights standards.

I found interesting parallels between Giay's and Foucault's analysis on the link between tertiary education in Papua and the production of knowledge that produces, reproduces and underpins asymmetric power relations between Indonesia and Papua. Giay situates his analysis in the context of what he calls 'colonialised Papua' in which Papuans are in the stage of 'transition' and have been forced to change almost instantly from a traditional and fragmented tribal society to a society governed by the power of the state, the rationality of economic development and the global market. 'In the West, this process happened naturally for more than a millennium, whereas in Papua, the people were forced to rush and if necessary, just in a few years' (Giay 2000: 94, my translation). As a result, transition has become a form of domination in which outside influence and actors intervene in the traditional structures of Papuans in the form of violence and colonialisation to enforce change. Giay refers to the Indonesian government policy of development as an example of this domination project: 'It is not surprising that in Papuans' view *development*[8] has become an instrument of justification of all extortion, expropriation and killing' (Giay 2000: 95, my translation and emphasis). As a counterbalance to domination, *development* gave birth to the ideology of *Papua Merdeka* (independent Papua) stemming from the interrelations with the Indonesian state security services who force Papuans to adopt development. In turn, this ideology has even caused a new problem when the Indonesian state perceived it as a threat and used it as '*a "licence"* to arrest, jail, and kill any Papuans with an excuse of treason, rebels and disintegration' (Giay 2000: 96, my emphasis).

In this context, Giay argues that the role of the tertiary education in Papua is ambiguous and ambivalent. On the one hand, tertiary education has the capacity to empower and transform Papuans as a collective to be able to confront change and interruption caused by development. Furthermore, tertiary education can

182 *Theatre of peace*

play a role in a critique of domination in that it can unveil the structure of domination controlling Papua; universities can make Papuans aware of their own situation as colonised people and make them aware that they have to work together to reclaim their position as subjects.

On the other hand, the same education institutions can reproduce state narratives and maintain the status quo. Giay refers to an example of the erection of the State University of Cenderawasih in Papua in 1963 which he describes as 'implementation of an agenda to *indonesianise*[9] Papua'. In a similar vein, the institution maintains the status quo by 'not accommodating change and the social dynamics of the Papuan society. It confines itself from the society because it fixed on the past and social values of the past' (Giay 2000: 96, my translation). While Giay's analysis resonates with Foucauldian notions of governmentality in which knowledge and power are inseparable and interrelated, this analysis independently accords with the historical analysis of the genealogy of torture in this book (Chapter 3).

The latest development of the Papua Land of Peace framework has been by Neles Tebay in his *Dialog Jakarta-Papua, Sebuah Perspektif Papua* (Jakarta-Papua Dialogue, A Papuan Perspective) (2009). He specifically elaborates the element of 'truth and justice' under the architecture of Papua Land of Peace by promoting the idea of *dialogue* as a means 'to create Papua Land of Peace' (Tebay 2009: 26–7). His proposal is based on his analysis of five major elements that have largely contributed to Papua conflicts: (1) state violence, (2) the failure of Special Autonomy to uplift the welfare standard of Papuans, (3) Indonesian government inconsistency in implementing Special Autonomy, (4) distrust of Papuans towards the Indonesian government and (5) the decline of international support for the Indonesian government.

Just as Giay's analysis has identified militarisation and state violence as a major problem, so with Tebay's. However, Tebay further argues that the long-term militarisation of Papua has only caused more and more conflicts, not a solution. 'Violence has only increased the number of victims and problems. Therefore the conflict resolution in Papua through peaceful means, namely dialogue, is an urgent need to prevent further bloodshed in the future' (Tebay 2009: 2, my translation). This argument reflects Tebay's deep conviction of the value of dialogue as the only means to break the culture of violence. However, the following section, which discusses challenges of Papua Land of Peace, will provide empirical evidence that dialogue in itself will not entirely and immediately end violence and domination in the long term.

Tebay posits that dialogue is a means to bridge the unbridgeable positions between the Indonesian state, which firmly holds the position of '*NKRI* is a nonnegotiable price', and the OPM, which equally firmly holds the position of '*Merdeka*, a nonnegotiable price'. If both sides retain these positions, Tebay suggests, even until

> the end of the world, the Papuan conflicts will not be solved peacefully. Jakarta-Papua dialogue will not happen. The nonnegotiable attitude will

Theatre of peace 183

only cause death for both sides whereas we want to hold dialogue because we respect the value of life.

(Tebay 2009: 26, my translation)

Tebay's analysis identifies the fundamental ideological differences between the narrative of the Indonesian state and the narrative of Papuans. He proposes that both sides need to step out from their own boxes to be able to engage with each other. He even becomes very explicit to the Papuan audience by emphasising the need to exclude the call for *merdeka* from the agenda of dialogue (see Chapter 3) which met with strong criticisms from some Papuan leaders.[10] If we look back to the history, this statement is strategic in that Tebay might want to avoid any repetition of the failure of the 1999 'national dialogue' between the 100 team of Papuan representatives and the President of Indonesia. During this meeting, the delegation called for *merdeka* and immediately terminated the meeting because President Habibie asked them to return home and rethink their request. As a result, the window of opportunity was closed, leaving Papua without any conflict resolution (see Chapter 3).

Further, Tebay sets out the goals and the ways he measures dialogue as conflict resolution. First, he outlines four elements that set the boundaries of conflict resolution for Papua:

- 'Papua conflicts have to be solved peacefully and not with any violent means;
- Papua conflicts have to be solved comprehensively and not partially;
- Papua conflicts have to be solved in a dignified manner and with mutual respect, so that no one can lose face;
- It has to include follow-up and concrete actions of the agreement'

(Tebay 2009: 24, my translation)

Tebay highlights four chief conditions of dialogue, namely *peacefulness, comprehensiveness, respect* and *concreteness*. In his view, these four elements are deemed crucial to rehabilitate relationships between the Indonesian state and Papuans which have been characterised by asymmetric power relations, domination and abjection. However, the emphasis on comprehensiveness and the holistic nature of conflict resolution will have to face the complex reality of multi-polar violence, multilayered challenges of peacebuilding and non-violent resistance presented by Karstedt, Braithwaite and Chenoweth and Stephan, respectively, in the following section.

Second, he sets out seven criteria to measure the successes and failures of Jakarta-Papua dialogue, emphasising the centrality of a peace 'agreement' between Jakarta and Papua:

- the government and Papuans reach agreement on the criteria of Papua Land of Peace which both sides will commit to fulfil together with all elements of Papuan civil society;

184   *Theatre of peace*

- the government and Papuans reach agreement on fundamental issues which have to be solved to create Papua Land of Peace;
- the government and Papuans reach agreement in regard to root causes of the fundamental issues identified by both sides;
- the government and Papuans reach agreement in regard to solutions to address the fundamental problems and their root causes and facilitate the creation of Papua Land of Peace;
- the government and Papuans reach agreement in regard to prevention of the recurrence of fundamental problems;
- the government and Papuans reach agreement in defining roles of all stakeholders involved in creating Papua Land of Peace;
- the government and Papuans reach agreement in follow-up and concrete actions to further implement their agreement

(Tebay 2009: 31–2, my translation)

The emphasis on peace agreements is not unique for Papua. Rather, it resonates with recent empirical studies at a global level (Human Security Research Group 2012; Karstedt 2012) which show the effectiveness of peace accords in reducing violence, as will be further discussed in the following section.

As part of his effort to elaborate the Papua Land of Peace framework, Tebay not only put his ideas into writing. He has also translated his thoughts into practice by establishing *Jaringan Damai Papua* (Papua Peace Network) in 2010 in conjunction with LIPI (the Indonesian Institute of Science).[11] The Papua Peace Network has actively organised dialogues among Papuans, Papuans with non-Papuans living in Papua, and Papuans and the Indonesian government (see Elisabeth *et al.* 2016).

Taken together, Papua Land of Peace and its evolution offer an alternative system to the governmentality of torture. Just as governmentality involves an interplay between rationalities, technologies of power and actors, so too does Papua Land of Peace. As its rationality, the framework envisions a New Papua of emancipation and freedom from all forms of oppression. Rooted in the Papuan *memoria passionis*, the framework has become the theatre of peacebuilding for Papua which is underpinned by nine pillars or principles of peace as opposed to technologies of domination. The framework also involves actors who tirelessly promote peace, including Papuan Church leaders, LIPI, JDP and the broader civil society organisations as opposed to the Indonesian state security services who enforce domination. Furthermore, JDP has been instrumental and committed to promote dialogue as the means to pave the way to develop positive peace.

While Papua Land of Peace outlines a new Papua based on emancipation and freedom, this framework confronts political challenges and theoretical limits. Despite overwhelming support from the Papuan community, politically the framework has been seen as unconvincing by some Papuan activists and leaders in accommodating *merdeka* aspirations. They narrowly misunderstand peace as passivity and non-resistance. Some of them even believe that the terminology has been corrupted by the Indonesian security apparatus to silence Papuans

Theatre of peace 185

whenever they call for justice and now dialogue (see Chapter 3). This suspicion is not without justification. A proponent for the idea of dialogue shares his experience: 'Before the idea of dialogue was accepted by SBY [early 2012], I was under constant surveillance and intimidation from *intel*. Now, even *Kopassus* invite me for their public fora discussing the issue of dialogue'.[12] While this experience illustrates some degree of openness of the Indonesian security apparatus towards the issue of dialogue, it also suggests that the security apparatus carefully confines the public discourse of dialogue. Other sources independently confirmed this: 'The government has put pressure on LIPI to not talk about dialogue anymore', whereas another source at the Indonesian National Parliament revealed, 'SBY is only good at public image. But behind closed doors, he remains against dialogue. We tried to convince him but it just hit a stone wall'.[13]

When the regime changed, many would expect more progress on the government side. Another dialogue proponent, however, reveals the opposite:

> UP4B did not support dialogue ... In comparison to SBY, though, Jokowi has a better sense [on Papua]. He picked two of 11 LIPI recommendations on Papua without consulting his cabinet. Unfortunately he is not able to control his [cabinet] ministers.[14]

This observation is crucial as it summarises the ebbs and flows of dialogue in the last two political regimes that do not make very much progress.

Theoretically Papua Land of Peace suffers from three major limitations: (1) its utopian vision of the New Papua, (2) its teleological belief in emancipation and (3) its understanding of peace as a monolithic and static social construct. The utopian nature of Papua Land of Peace lies in the fact that the framework aims at reconstructing the current social and political configuration of Papua into an idealised and possibly romanticised Papua governed by freedom. The notion of 'free from all forms of oppression' suffers from absolutism and romanticism in that freedom is perceived as an absolute, static and pure condition. In reality, however, such a condition rarely exists. Perhaps reconfiguring power relations to ensure greater agency and equitable power relations and maximise realisation of the nine elements of the architecture of Papua Land of Peace may forge freedom in a more dynamic, relational and progressive sense.

Jason McLeod's assertion on the centrality of 'a grand strategy for change' in Papua is relevant here. He elaborates the ways of generating change through six elements, namely 'increased movement participation, enhanced strategic skilfulness, greater unity, the ability to attract greater support within Indonesia, internationalisation of the struggle and taking advantage of political opportunities' (2015: 194). McLeod investigates recent developments of Papua that reflect significant change inside and outside Papua that meet the six criteria above.

The framework also assumes that emancipation is a teleological process which can be achieved through dialogue. This process assumes that once dialogue occurs and reaches agreement on a new deal of power sharing, domination and violence will eventually disappear. This assumption overlooks the nature of

186 *Theatre of peace*

domination and violence which never escapes both conflict and post-conflict society, as will be discussed in the following section. The vast literature on truth commissions and the following empirical studies illustrate that domination and violence only change their forms and appearance from state-sponsored to domestic violence or from state crimes to communal violence after a society has gone through a transition period.

Similarly, peace should not be understood as a static and monolithic condition of a society. Rather, it is a multilayered and dynamic process which is character-ised by fragility and discontinuity (see Lederach 1997). As I will explore further in the following sections, peace as a process contains three layers of narratives which address different levels of power relations of the theatre of torture. At the macro-structural level, a peacebuilding narrative will provide the narrative of 'revolt' to counter the narrative of domination. Revolt in this context should not be restricted to a merely political status such as revolution or *merdeka*, but more broadly. It conceives Kristevan notions of revolt in which it restores asymmetric power relations into fair and equitable relations. At the individual-psychic level, a peacebuilding narrative should offer the narrative of healing to challenge the process of abjection. At the community level, Metz suggests peacebuilding should promote and forge the narrative of solidarity. This element aims to rehabilitate relationships among members of the Papuan community marked by violence and to transform relationships into bonds based on respect and hope.

Reimagining Papua Land of Peace

Building on the previous criticism of Papua Land of Peace, this section and the following will reimagine Papua Land of Peace in two parts: the nine pillars and the core tenet (see Figure 6.2). In essence, reimagination aims to dismantle the culture of domination and at the same time build a new culture of peace. Informed by the vast literature of organisational culture, this ambition essentially deals with 'culture change'. Hence, it needs to carefully take into account key assumptions of culture change as ambiguous, complex and paradoxical (Morgan 1986), fluid and multilayered processes (Deal and Kennedy 1988; Schein 1985), and threatening an established culture (Deal and Kennedy 1988: 157). Despite their disagreement[15] of defining stages of culture change, these scholars agree that a clear vision is fundamental, the role of leadership is critical and story-telling is influential (Shearing and Ericson 1991). This body of literature not only helps us understand complexity in culture change but, more importantly, helps strengthen Papua Land of Peace by incorporating the most relevant ele-ments of these literatures.

Informed by the culture change literature, the following discussion will analyse three recent empirical studies which have explored complex challenges to change cultures of domination towards cultures of peace. First is Susanne Karstedt's 'Violent Society Index' (VSI) (2012) that measures the continuing violence by combining three different variables together: multiple forms of viol-ence, multiple actors in and of violence and the relation to mass atrocities and

Theatre of peace 187

mass violence. Second is John Braithwaite's *Peacebuilding Compared* which demonstrates various trajectories of peacebuilding as 'partial and *longue durée*' (Braithwaite 2011). In twelve case studies of peacebuilding in Asia and the Pacific so far, Braithwaite found that the trajectory for peacebuilding takes a different path in a different context. This study is beneficial to assess and strengthen the pathway of Papuan dialogue in that it provides a horizon of a fragile path to peace. Finally, Erica Chenoweth and Maria Stephan's (2011) study of non-violent resistance concludes that relying on non-violent struggle is empirically more successful than waging violent resistance. This study will strengthen the Papua Land of Peace framework by providing a broader empirical ground for the effectiveness of the politics of hope based on non-violent struggle.

Karstedt's VSI addresses the changing nature of mass violence and mass atrocity by offering 'a new approach to the multifaceted nature of contemporary mass violence that ultimately aims at providing contextualized instruments of early warning and risk assessment' (Karstedt 2012: 501). Karstedt has established two types of indices: VSI(40) and VSI(30), respectively. The VSI(30), which is based on a sample of seventy-three countries, includes homicide data, and the VSI(40), which is based on a sample of 103 countries, does not include homicide over the period of three decades (1976–2010). Building on the concept of multi-polar violence (see Gerlach 2010), she further identifies four different but strongly and positively intercorrelated types of violence: *interpersonal violence* which covers lethal violence in personal conflicts, *state violence* which focuses on state-sponsored violence such as torture, killings, disappearances and political imprisonment, *terrorist attacks* which comprise attacks that target unarmed victims, and *battle deaths in state-based internal armed conflicts* which covers state actors and paramilitary groups and guerrillas (Karstedt 2012: 503). Karstedt also underscores a discrepancy between proliferation of violence and peacebuilding which further disclosed the complexity of peacebuilding in the long run based on four major identified patterns: (1) 'the rapid motion of mass violence versus the slow motion of peacebuilding, (2) the dynamics of violence versus long-term causal factors, (3) micro-dynamics versus macro-level, (4) shifting involvements and boundaries between violent actors and victims' (Karstedt 2011).

What is the relevance of this study to our discussion here? Although Karstedt's study does not directly address violence in the Papuan or Indonesia context, the longitude and latitude nature of her study is instructive to the case of Papua peacebuilding in two ways. First, one empirical finding is that peace accords[16] and power sharing significantly contribute to the reduction of at least three types of violence: state violence, terrorist attacks and battle deaths. The implication of this finding provides an empirical ground for Papuans' call for peace dialogue in that dialogue is most likely to contribute to significant reduction of violence in Papua. However, the second element of this study simultaneously shows that peace accords and power sharing do not necessarily stop violence in the longer term. These two mechanisms seem insufficient to institutionalise peace in the long run. A decrease of state violence can be easily

188 *Theatre of peace*

replaced by a surge of homicide, as in Colombia in recent years. Similarly, the 2002 peace accord in Sri Lanka only reduced state violence for a short period before the highest level of violence in the country's history. The implication of Karstedt's comparative study poses a serious question to the pathway of dialogue currently advocated by many Papuans who believe that dialogue will end all forms of oppression. This objective may be overly ambitious and less feasible. Similarly, the Papua Land of Peace framework as a whole may suffer from the lack of any careful calculation if it does not take into account the fact of continuing violence in any given situation.

By learning from Karstedt's study, the Papua Land of Peace framework can be strengthened by appreciating the fluid and changing nature of violence regardless of the social and political change, particularly the fact that in many conflict situations, state violence becomes the most resilient form of violence to eradicate (Karstedt 2012: 509). If Papua Land of Peace incorporates Karstedt's analysis, the next question is *how* this revised framework can be developed to prevent recurrence of violence and build peace in the *longue durée*. To fill this gap, we need another lens that can offer a pathway to craft a more long-term peace. This is where Braithwaite's study comes into play.

Braithwaite's *Peacebuilding Compared*[17] aims at deciphering sixty armed conflicts around the world to understand successes and failures of peacebuilding. So far the project has completed twenty-six cases of armed conflicts based on a model of sequencing truth, justice and reconciliation. Braithwaite built a model of high-integrity truth-seeking and reconciliation which begins with the stage of establishing the truth of armed conflict before moving into reconciliation and ending with justice (Braithwaite 2011). These three stages of what he calls 'a theory of truth and prevention' are based on three different stages of politics. It starts with 'politics of trust' followed by 'politics of hope' and ends with 'politics of accountability'. However, he acknowledged that none of his case studies fits the model (Braithwaite 2011: 136; Braithwaite and Nickson 2012: 445). Therefore, he revised his argument, stating that 'truth, justice, and reconciliation can come in all possible sequences' (Braithwaite and Nickson 2012: 447).

Drawing on the case studies of Bougainville (Papua New Guinea), Indonesia, Timor-Leste and Solomon Islands, Braithwaite and Nickson (2012) identify four different ways of sequencing truth-justice-reconciliation. In the case of Bougainville (see Braithwaite *et al.* 2010) the authors found that the sequence is reconciliation first followed by local truth and restorative justice. Indonesian peacebuilding (see Braithwaite *et al.* 2010) is framed as mostly non-truth and reconciliation, without justice. With the exception of Papua, all major conflicts in Indonesia following the fall of President Soeharto in 1998 have been settled but truth and justice remain elusive. In the case of Timor-Leste (see Braithwaite, Charlesworth and Soares 2012) the sequence is mostly truth and reconciliation followed by little justice despite the establishment of the Commission of Reception, Truth and Reconciliation (CAVR). The last case study is Solomon Islands (see Braithwaite *et al.* 2010) which is framed as justice followed by truth and reconciliation. The authors considered the Solomon Islands 'exceptional' in that a prosecutorial approach was largely employed to establish punitive justice as a response to violence in the period 1998–2003.

Based on these empirical findings, Braithwaite and Nickson propose a thought-provoking idea in the context of transitional justice literature,[18] namely a permanent Truth and Reconciliation Commission (TRC), although they do not specify whether this is national or international,[19] equivalent to the International Criminal Court. A permanent TRC 'that keeps its doors open for a century has the option of educating survivors that truth, justice and reconciliation are partial accomplishment of the *longue durée*' (Braithwaite and Nickson 2012: 475). By establishing a permanent TRC, reconciliation processes are not limited to the period of a TRC which lasts only for a short period of time. The permanent presence of a TRC may help institutionalise peace in a more sustainable way by providing unlimited space and time for survivors to come and share their stories whenever they feel ready. Furthermore, the authors also argue that a permanent TRC can become a focus for educating future generations about the *memoria passionis* of their forebears (Braithwaite and Nickson 2012: 475). Similarly, for perpetrators, a permanent TRC might assist those who seek immediate forgiveness from survivors to close their own histories and memories and to realise that there is no need to hurry, as space remains open as long as the TRC operates. Moreover, it is up to survivors to decide whether they are ready to reconcile with perpetrators, if ever.

Within the Papuan legal context, the idea of a permanent TRC resonates with the existing legal requirement of Article 46 of the Special Autonomy Law of 2001 which stipulates establishment of TRC for Papua:

> In order to strengthen the national unity and integrity it shall be established a Commission of Truth and Reconciliation in the Province of Papua.[20]

Although this article suggests a statist orientation ('national unity and integrity') for a Papuan TRC, legally and politically it provides a window of opportunity to look into silenced Papuan history. Moreover, under Article 45[21] para 2, the TRC is seen to be established in conjunction with two other legal mechanisms: a commission on human rights and a human rights court.[22] Combined together, all these mechanisms will proffer a promising opportunity for Papua. After over a decade of the Otsus enactment, none of these requirements have come into existence. Therefore, legally and politically the Papua Land of Peace framework still has to confront the non-existent political will of the government to implement laws it has passed.

At the analytical level, the idea of a permanent TRCP might fill the gap of *how* a reimagined Papua Land of Peace framework can be translated into practice as a remedy to the governance of torture. By taking into account multi-polar violence and a permanent TRCP combined, the Papua Land of Peace framework can be empowered in two ways. First, the framework will not take for granted that violence will vanish once a peace accord or dialogue or power sharing is achieved. Instead, Papua Land of Peace will be able to provide a strategy to

190 *Theatre of peace*

broaden the network of peacebuilding by empowering the local peacemaking initiatives as we learnt from Braithwaite's *Peacebuilding Compared*. Second, by adopting a permanent TRCP, Papua Land of Peace might not only address individual and communal levels of peacebuilding but also macro-structural levels of peacemaking. This TRCP might contribute to what Papuans have called 'rectifying history of Papua' (*pelurusan sejarah Papua*). This might be an opportunity to establish truths of *memoria passionis* of Papuans not only for Papuans but also for Indonesia as a nation. As Braithwaite's project on Indonesian peacebuilding suggests, Indonesian reconciliation has greatly suffered from non-truth and injustice. In this case, a permanent presence of TRCP might be able to contribute to establishing truth in the long run. Furthermore, at the individual and community level, a permanent TRCP might provide unlimited space and time for both survivors and perpetrators to be educated in the reality of partial truth and the long-term and complex processes for reconciliation.

However, the political situation in Indonesia and Papua shows that a peace negotiation seems to be a distant prospect despite continuous calls from inside and outside actors (Hernawan 2012). In this context, a proposal of establishing a permanent TRCP may not be the highest priority of the present Indonesian government. Therefore, the social and political situation of Papua remains fragile and the increasing level of violence may not be easily contained (see International Crisis Group 2012). In this situation, the third empirical study by Chenoweth and Stephan is pertinent to envisage a new ground.

As Chenoweth and Stephan's main argument has been summarised in Chapter 1, in this section I will underscore the key findings of four key studies that the authors use to structure their arguments: the 1979 Iran revolution and the Philippines as two successes, Palestinian Territories as one partial success and Burma as one failure of civilian resistance (at the time). In these four case studies all armed resistance failed.

The four case studies presented by Chenoweth and Stephan illuminate the Papua Land of Peace framework. That is, paths for peace for Papua can be much strengthened by following the patterns of successful non-violent resistance. First, non-violent resistance would be able to establish a wide range of participants with a shared vision of post-conflict governance to secure its path to democratic transition as an end-game as we learn from the experiences of Iran, the Philippines, Palestine and Burma. Initiated and promoted by Papuan Church leaders, the Papua Land of Peace campaign has embraced a broad range of participants from different religious, ethnic and professional backgrounds to share *memoria passionis*. However, this initiative has withered away and has been taken over by the Papua youth and students movements, particularly AMP and KNPB.

Second, during the transition period as experienced by the Iranian revolution and Philippines people's power, the resistance needs to maintain strict discipline of only embracing non-violent means to press their demands to maintain their reputation to a broader audience. This discipline will also be an effective means to convince security forces to shift their loyalty and become an ally for the resistance. Moreover, this strategy requires state accountability through non-violent

Theatre of peace 191

means rather than the other way around. The late Dutch Papuan leader Viktor Kaisiepo's critical comments encapsulate the high risk of the use of armed resistance in the Papuan struggle.

> My objection to armed struggle is principle and practical. Principally, I believe that armed struggle has to be controlled by politics. If not, it will have no chance to win … In a practical sense, a military group without any discipline will have no result for Papuans. Armed struggle costs food or women, but aren't they aware that villages where the rebels rely on are very vulnerable to the revenge of the Indonesian military because of the support they give?[23]
>
> (Kaisiepo 2012: 266–7)

Third, unity of leadership and diversity of strategies and tactics play a key role in forging change. Given the long history of Papuan factionalism, the Papuan leaders decisively made a historic step by establishing ULMWP on 6 December 2014 that consolidates Papuan national movements both inside and outside Papua (Hernawan 2016). ULMWP has been effective in promoting the cause of Papua at the international level since it obtained observer status from the Melanesian Spearhead Group. The status reflects international recognition of the abjected Papuans who have been neglected since the UN closed the chapter of Papua in the 1960s (see Chapter 3).

Fourth, the element of international sanction plays a decisive role in the case of the successful Philippines change just as its absence is critical to failures in peace processes, such as with Israel-Palestine. Since 2014, the leaders of the MSG and the PIF have shown their commitment to contribute to finding a peaceful solution for Papua's conflicts by extending their offers to Jakarta to facilitate dialogue between Papua and Jakarta (Hernawan 2015). They have also raised the urgency to address the human rights problems of Papua to the UN General Assembly in 2016, suggesting that Papua is gaining traction both at regional and international diplomatic fora (Hernawan 2016).

Papuan experience suggests that these four lessons from non-violent resistance around the world pose serious implications for Papuan movements. If they want to fulfil their dream, they need to answer these four chief challenges adequately.

Despite these limitations, McLeod's investigation has revealed encouraging findings. In line with Chenoweth's and Stephan's findings, McLeod provides us with five recent case studies from Papua in which non-violent resistance worked well: the Papua Land of Peace campaign, the long strike of Papuan Freeport union in Timika and the campaign to 'hand back' Otsus in Jayapura, public declaration of independence in October 2011, and the campaign for the Melanesian Spearhead Group membership[24] (McLeod 2015: 193). In all of these examples, a non-violent campaign was proven effective to push the agenda for change. He concludes that 'the movement has secured a number of important gains and been hampered by strategic deficiencies and the movement's marginal international

192 *Theatre of peace*

position. However, this only emphasizes the point that civil resistance is a promising framework for securing further advances' (McLeod 2015: 233).

Informed by the insights of the three empirical studies, Papua Land of Peace can be further strengthened as visualised in Figure 6.2. Multi-polar violence and domination needs to be taken into account as a continuous challenge for peace in any given situation.

Inspired by the three abovementioned empirical studies, the four pillars of the Papua Land of Peace framework have been revised and strengthened in this model: (1) participation should involve broader constituencies than just indigenous Papuans, (2) truth and justice would envision the establishment of TRCP, (3) solidarity should mobilise support from both the international community and world leaders to support the peace process in Papua and (4) self-reliance and leadership is critically needed to discipline and guide a Papuan non-violent movement. Apart from these pillars, we can see, at the centre of the model, peace is no longer perceived as one monolithic process. Rather, it constitutes cascades of peace which will be discussed below. The cascades of peace will be translated into TRCP as a model of the theatre of peacebuilding.

Cascades of peace

Let us now move to the core tenet of the theatre of peacebuilding represented by the circles of 'peace' at the centre of Figure 6.2. As outlined in Chapter 2, the Kristevan notion of revolt encapsulates a broader sense than 'opposition' or

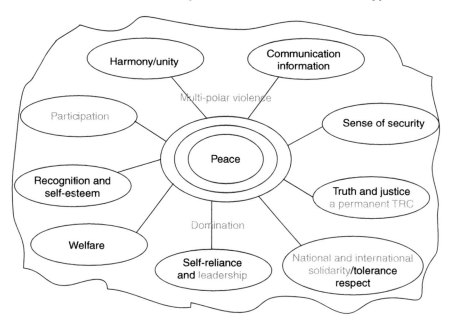

Figure 6.2 Theatre of peacebuilding.

Theatre of peace 193

'resistance'. It contends the notion of renewal of all dimensions of a society. Revolt contains a highly dynamic process of change to reclaim agency. The element of 'process' resonates with the core idea of peace used in our examination here which is inspired by Lederach's concept of peacebuilding (see Chapter 1). Grounded in *memoria passionis*, which can be institutionalised into a permanent TRCP, peace has become cascades of peace processes. These consist of three distinct but inseparable peacebuilding processes: the macro-structural (narrative of *revolt*), individual level (narrative of healing) and communal level (narrative of solidarity) which constantly evolve and interact with one another. Building on the foregoing discussion, Figure 6.3 illustrates one way of reimagining societal and political transformation of Papua from the theatre of torture to the theatre of peacebuilding. The foundation, inspiration and guidance of this transformation is *memoria passionis* which is translated and instituted into TRCP. The following analysis will explain the key elements of this transformation.

Figure 6.3 centres on *memoria passionis* as the basis of transformation from the theatre of torture to the theatre of peacebuilding. At the top, TRCP is founded to incorporate and manifest the history of Papuan suffering. The red arrows coming out from *memoria passionis* illustrate the influence, intrusion and interruption of the memory to all layers of transformation: macro-structural, micro-individual and mezzo-communal in both the theatre of torture and the theatre of

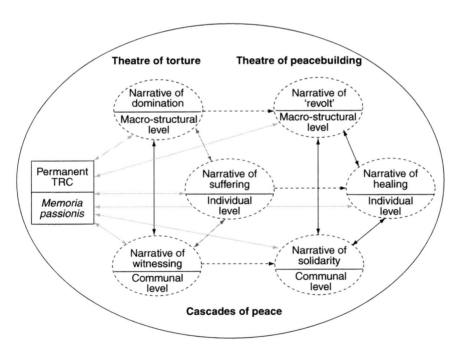

Figure 6.3 A model of transformation from the theatre of torture to the theatre of peacebuilding.

194   *Theatre of peace*

peacebuilding. Therefore, *memoria passionis* has become the root and the guidance of the transformation. It can enable change from the narrative of domination to the narrative of revolt, from the narrative of suffering to the narrative of healing, and from the narrative of witnessing to the narrative of solidarity. The whole process of transformation is governed by the motivational posture of commitment to peace[25] as the only way to guarantee the process of dismantling the governance of torture to the governance of peace. The following sections will elucidate four key elements of Figure 6.3, namely the TRCP and the three key peace narratives (revolt-healing-solidarity).

A permanent TRC for Papua?

Transitional justice scholars (Bisset 2012; Freeman 2006; Hayner 2011; Smyth 2007) identify four chief objectives of transitional justice: reconstruction of truths of the past; delivery of justice; the rule of law and democratic reform; and the establishment of durable peace. Within this framework, however, scholars and activists are divided between those who advocate for prosecutorial and punitive justice (e.g. ad hoc tribunals, hybrid tribunals, the International Criminal Court) (Akhavan 2009; Cassese 1998) and those who give more priority to restorative justice (truth and reconciliation commission) for equally complex reasons. There is not any fixed recipe for this as the recipe should be context specific.

Nonetheless, both sides agree that both forms of justice can be complementary. More importantly, transitional justice is a framework that requires multiple justice mechanisms to adequately address atrocities. In practice, however, restorative justice[26] in the form of TRC has become a preferable vehicle to implement the four chief objectives in a post-conflict situation. In the context of political transition, criminal prosecution commonly suffers from the limits of authority imposed by a former authoritarian regime which tries to maintain its impunity as a trade-off for reform. For instance, the case of Cambodia illustrates a prolonged thirty-year negotiation before the hybrid court came into existence. Even then, this court can only try a few of the former Khmer Rouge regime (Hayner 2011: 204–6). Technically, criminal prosecution centres on perpetrators, not victims. As a result, victim stories will be treated as secondary as long as they support evidence admissible to the court. Moreover, the court can only focus on specific cases of a number of individuals who held ultimate responsibility for atrocities (Akhavan 2009: 631), not on a broader historical pattern of abuses. Financially, the prosecution also confronts its limits to try as many perpetrators as possible. As a result, this process can only select the most responsible perpetrators, leaving the others to be dealt with by the TRC.

TRCs, on the other hand, have more capabilities to address multiple past human rights abuses. Politically, this framework seems to be more acceptable for former authoritarian regimes as it focuses on documenting stories from victims, not punishing perpetrators. The case of South Africa TRC illustrates how the adoption of amnesty provision became the best feasible deal between the ANC and the former apartheid regime before the South African TRC could commence (Boraine 2000: Chapter 8; Hayner 2011: 27; Kiss 2000: 68). Technically, TRCs are more interested in identifying a broader historical pattern of human rights abuses and focus on victim stories. Furthermore, at the end of a TRC's term, they have to provide recommendations and conclusions for the transition period to democracy. Financially, TRCs share similar constraints as criminal prosecution. That is why the terms of TRC are temporary, up to three years.

If TRCs and courts proffer two different ways of dealing with the past, are they compatible or complementary? In contrast with some writers who argue that TRCs and courts are complementary, Alison Bisset argues, '[T]ruth commissions and trials are neither truly complementary nor entirely incompatible' (Bisset 2012: 188). To manage the discrepancies between the two, she suggests coordination of the two approaches as equal partners at the operational level to promote effective coexistence of them with the following principles: 'as distinct institutions; without obligations that link their procedures; on the basis of equality; under an agreement that regulates their operations; with the possibility of recourse to an independent resolution mechanism in the event of dispute' (Bisset 2012: 189–90).

In her analysis of framing transitional justice as a response to 'extraordinary evil', Miriam Aukerman elaborates this discussion further. She argues that a response to mass atrocities cannot be established a priori. Rather, it should be formulated a posteriori depending on the objective conditions that require a particular mechanism to respond. If the objective is to target individuals, retributive justice might be the most appropriate mechanism to fulfil the objective. However, if the objective is to rebuild and transform society, she suggests that other mechanisms, such as deterrence, rehabilitation, restorative justice and social solidarity, might be more adequate (Aukerman 2002: 95).

This analysis responds to the intention of our analysis here. It deals with the question of transforming and rebuilding Papuan society for positive peace. This metamorphosis platform is inspired by the Papua Land of Peace framework. While this framework would certainly deal with torturers as individuals, they are not the only priority of the theatre of peacebuilding. Rather, whole layers of the Papuan society must be reformed. Therefore, since Papuan society is targeted, our discussion here adopts a TRC as a way to initiate peace processes in Papua in the long term. It goes even further by exploring Braithwaite's proposal to establish a permanent TRC since it has to confront multi-polar violence as an ongoing challenge (Karstedt 2012). This proposal is relevant not only to Papua but may also be applicable to the whole Indonesian context. However, in the burgeoning literature of transitional justice, we can only find temporary TRCs (Freeman 2006; Hayner 2011). So this proposal and the following contextualisation in the Papuan setting will require an empirical ground to test the effectiveness of TRCP.

The literature of transitional justice (TJ) centres on three fundamental issues of TRC as reflected in the name: truth, justice and reconciliation. In regard to the question of truth, TJ scholars (Freeman 2006; Hayner 2011; Humphrey 2002;

196 *Theatre of peace*

Smyth 2007; Wilson 2001) agree that truth is constructed, partial, selective, biased and fragmented. In addressing this complex problem, the South Africa TRC, for instance, not only identified one type but instead four types of truth: forensic truth which refers to legal evidence; narrative truth which refers to oral histories or storytelling; dialogical truth which is produced through a social process of interaction; and restorative truth which repairs the damage of the past and prevents recurrence in the future (Smyth 2007: 25–8). This comprehensive effort was meant to capture the whole picture and anatomy of the apartheid regime to dismantle its architecture and craft a new democratic South African society. Despite these sophisticated efforts, Richard Wilson's analysis on the legal framework of the South African Commission reveals two unresolved problems that greatly influenced the production of truth: the limited mandate of the commission and the nature of the commission itself (Wilson 2001: 34–41). Although the South African TRC had the widest mandate of any truth commission, the mandate was limited to 'the extreme events and not upon the everyday, mundane bureaucratic enforcement of apartheid'.

In a broader perspective, Priscilla Hayner's study (2011) on twenty-one truth commissions shed more light on the selectivity of truth. First, she argues that the selectivity is not only a matter of the types of past abuse but also the gap of analysis on the role of international actors in domestic violence (Hayner 2011: 78). Second, she points out the limits of the commissions to address the root causes of the past abuses because they were preoccupied with descriptions of acts (Hayner 2011: 80). Third, she identifies that violence against women is generally underreported because of cultural reasons or the lack of understanding of the commissioners (Hayner 2011: 86). Based on this analysis, Hayner reached a conclusion on truth production via the commissions that:

> Truth commissions are virtually never smooth, pleasant, well-managed, well-funded, politically uncomplicated bodies. On the contrary, most struggle daily with a barrage of methodological, operational, and political problems, and operate under extreme pressures of time, under the heavy moral and emotional weight of their task and the risk of damaging error in their conclusions.
>
> (Hayner 2011: 210)

To make it more complicated, Braithwaite's *Peacebuilding Compared* has already revealed an empirical finding for the question of truth-seeking. Although establishing truth plays an instrumental role in delivering justice or in largely contributing to peace, it does not necessarily lead to justice. The case studies of Timor-Leste and other contexts illustrate this. If truth and justice are problematic, does reconciliation face a similar problem?

Michael Ignatieff's (1996) pessimistic comments problematise the capacity of TRC to come to terms with the past. He believes, 'A truth commission cannot overcome a society's division' (Ignatieff 1996: 113). The truth-seeking is not a process of rediscovering

Theatre of peace 197

a sacred text which has been stolen and vandalised by evil men and which can be recovered ... The past is an argument and the function of truth commissions is ... simply to purify the argument, to narrow the range of permissible lies.

(Ignatieff 1996: 113)

Just as in Benny's story who experienced 'intrusion' and 'hyperarousal' (see Chapter 5), a nation experiences a similar phenomenon. Ignatieff contends,

The past continues to torment because it is *not* past. These places are not living in a serial order of time, but in a simultaneous one, in which the past and the present are a continuous, agglutinated mass of fantasies, distortions, myths and lies.

(Ignatieff 1996: 119–20)

In Ignatieff's view, all of these psychological dynamics occur at the individual level, not at the national level. Therefore, '[n]ations, properly speaking, cannot be reconciled to other nations, only individuals to individuals. Nonetheless, individuals can be helped to heal and to reconcile by public rituals of atonement' (Ignatieff 1996: 121). In other words, reconciliation, according to Ignatieff, can only occur at the individual level as he believes that a nation does not have a psyche. These comments may point to a hopeful direction to start TRCP as 'public rituals of atonement'.

Aukerman (2002), Freeman (2006), Hayner (2011) and Minow (1998, 2000) all identified the question of reconciliation as complex, just as are the two other questions of truth and justice. Historically, not every truth commission adopts the element of reconciliation, but those who adopted this mandate (e.g. Chile, Morocco, Peru, Sierra Leone, South Africa and Timor-Leste) have found it a difficult mission (Hayner 2011: 182). In a broad sense, the concept of reconciliation derives from religion (Lederach 2001; Minow 1998)[27] but in the context of TRC, Hayner describes it as 'developing a mutual conciliatory accommodation between antagonistic or formerly antagonistic persons or groups' (Hayner 2011: 182). This description suggests the notion of dynamics between two conflicting parties but some TJ scholars emphasise that this dynamic is not an event. Rather, reconciliation is a process (Aukerman 2002; Hayner 2011) in the *longue durée* (Braithwaite 2011).

Having discussed the complexity of establishing truth, delivering justice and promoting reconciliation, we might ask *how* this discussion may contribute to imagining a permanent TRC for Papua. There are two major approaches to answer this question: legal-political and theoretical.

First is the legal-political approach. As already suggested, under the 2001 Special Autonomy Law Papua was granted a provision that stipulates the establishment of TRC in conjunction with a commission on human rights and human rights court. None of them, however, came into existence. Similarly, in the province of Aceh, a comparable provision has never been translated into practice

198   *Theatre of peace*

except the Truth and Reconciliation Commission despite trust of the victims towards the capability of the TRC.[28] At the national level the law of TRC was annulled by the Constitutional Court following the judicial review on the provision of unfair amnesty submitted by a group of NGOs (Hayner 2011: 235). This legal-political context suggests that a TRC remains a distant reality not only for Papua but also for Indonesia as a whole. Despite de facto reconciliation which occurred at individual and communal levels in most conflicts after the 1998 *reformasi* except Papua (Braithwaite *et al.* 2010), the pattern of impunity and denial to bring the history of past injustice into the public consciousness has little changed. For example, despite sufficient evidence presented to the court, the ad hoc tribunal for Timor-Leste failed to establish justice and so did the Indonesian human rights court for the 2000 Abepura case. In both cases all (TNI and police officer) indictees were acquitted and some on appeal (ELSAM 2007). A recent test of embedded impunity was a strong statement from the Widodo government rejecting a proposal to offer an apology for the 1965 massacre. This suggests that the Indonesian state is not yet prepared to review its meta-narrative to incorporate people's narratives, which are fragmented, hidden and localised.

On the other hand, a permanent state body to deal with serious issues in Indonesia is not novel. Komnas HAM, for instance, encapsulates the way in which the Indonesian state deals with human rights abuses in the past, the present and the future. Law 39/1999 on Human Rights has empowered Komnas HAM to operate as a state-sanctioned body to undertake subpoena investigation and prosecute human rights allegations. The law also guarantees the authority of Komnas HAM even though its recent corruption allegation[29] has seriously undermined its credibility. As a state body, Komnas HAM has been logistically equipped with sufficient resources by the state. Similarly, the Indonesian Anti-Corruption Commission (KPK) has become an effective mechanism to combat endemic corruption with the Indonesian state institutions under Law no. 30/2002. In other words, establishing the TRCP in the Indonesian legal-political context is not impossible. In fact, the provision of the TRCP combined with a commission on human rights and a human rights court is important to highlight. It suggests a vision of developing comprehensive transitional justice mechanisms which can potentially address the four main objectives of transitional justice as abovementioned.

Drawing on lessons of effective peacemaking at the community level in Bougainville, Timor-Leste, Aceh, Poso and Maluku to reconcile survivors and perpetrators, it can be argued that a multilayered and bottom-up TRCP could be a promising option for Papua. This local TRCP might be able to accommodate local wisdom and the role of traditional elders and religious leaders as mediators as well as sanctions. Hence, it will encourage local ownership and participation. This grassroots level of TRCP, however, needs to be linked up with a more authoritative and state-sanctioned and preferably internationally sanctioned TRC in accordance with Indonesian government administrative structures: sub-district, district, provincial and national levels. This strategy can be used to address different levels of power relations that may require different degrees of

Theatre of peace 199

power to intervene. Furthermore, an element of international monitoring[30] can be incorporated into this model of TRC to ensure its impartiality and reception by Papuans whose trust in the Indonesian government has significantly declined.

If a permanent TRC is established, one should also be aware of the risk of institutionalisation which we already learnt from both Komnas HAM and KPK. Under Law 39/1999, selection processes for Komnas HAM commissioners are the subject of national parliament's approval. Therefore, any political parties that have interests in Komnas HAM will make sure that their interests are represented within Komnas HAM. If this happens, Komnas HAM can suffer from the lack of integrity to represent survivors of human rights abuses. In the short term, while this TRCP will have the potential to create and foster a fertile ground for dialogue between Jakarta and Papua, it has to confront another risk: multilayered distrust from Papuans towards any formal-institutional initiative from the Indonesian state. To address this risk, the TRC needs to demonstrate its independence of the policy of the state institutions, particularly the Indonesian military, police and government.

Michael Humphrey's (2002: 108–9) observation on this bias is relevant here. Apart from logistical issues and public attention, he argues that a truth commission is a state project and thus it is the state that 'determines who will be acknowledged as a victim'. The state also selects what can be heard, what can be said and what can be remembered. He compares the Argentine and the South African truth commissions. The Argentine Commission was designed to provide a legal basis to prosecute the leaders of the Argentinian junta. As a result, the whole procedure was very legalistic and the report only focused on three types of abuses: kidnapping, disappearance and torture. Other types of abuses were dismissed (Freeman 2006).

Second, at the theoretical level, TRCP can be seen as a logical consequence of peacebuilding which has been understood as a process rather than an event. It embodies a concrete and tangible proposal to address multi-polar violence which continues in any given situation (Karstedt 2012). In conjunction with a commission on human rights and human rights court (criminal justice), TRCP would provide comprehensive justice mechanisms which allow survivors, perpetrators and observers to come to terms with each other and collaboratively transform the narratives of domination-suffering-witnessing into the narratives of revolt-healing-solidarity.

TRCP would have to allow a long-term inductive process in which the Papuan context will determine an appropriate order of truth-justice-reconciliation. Survivors should be given an ample chance to have high-integrity conversations to discuss and determine this matter. Similarly, perpetrators and spectators should be given equal access to testify to the commission. TRCP should also consolidate non-violent responses to extreme and ongoing violence in transitional societies, like Papua, into a state-sanctioned body which guarantees the process of change.

Furthermore, a permanent TRCP would be able to respond to Hayner's major concerns of future development of TRCs that (1) TRCs might risk being badly

200 Theatre of peace

established with a weak mandate and personnel and (2) TRCPs may be ineffective at influencing policy (Hayner 2011: 236). As a response to the first concern, the fact that the TRCP provision under the Special Autonomy Law has never been realised suggests that there is no hurry to establish a TRCP. This context would allow mature deliberation and public debate within the Papuan community to formulate the most feasible format for a TRCP. As a response to the second concern, like Komnas HAM and KPK, a permanent TRCP should allow more space and opportunity to engage in effective dialogue with policy-makers to ensure the implementation of its recommendations in the long run.

The following sections will not outline any practicalities of a permanent TRCP. Rather, they will explore fundamental processes which must happen to transform the theatre of torture into the theatre of peacebuilding. Facilitated by a permanent TRCP, this transformation can be conceptualised in the shift from narratives of suffering-domination-witnessing to the narratives of healing-solidarity-revolt. Now that a possible vehicle for the realisation of this shift in the TRCP has been identified, we can return to fleshing out the theoretical ambitions of this shift.

Narrative of healing

The first element of the theatre of peacebuilding is the narrative of healing.[31] This narrative derives from the narratives of *agent* and *caregiver* in that they proactively engage with survivors to empower them to reclaim their agency. The narrative helps to reassemble the shattered world of meaning of survivors so they can make sense of their traumatic experience of torture and move on. The narrative of healing works against the process of abjection in that it aims to embrace survivors and to reintegrate them into their community. While the abjection process has caused exclusion and colonisation, the narrative of healing transforms suffering into energy for change which can be used to break the boundaries between the abject and the subject. In other words, the narrative of healing means incorporation of the abject into the subject, or social inclusion. This is Anna's story (see Chapter 5).

The incorporation of the abject goes beyond the level of recognition of the suffering of abjected Papuans. While the latter has become part of TRCP objectives, the former suggests a radical demand: to reconstruct the whole society to be able to accommodate the abject as a new integral element of the imagined subject of Indonesia. The TRCP can facilitate this demand since the TRCP would operate under state-sanction and be equipped with resources and networks to embody the narrative of healing in two levels. At the societal level, the TRCP would be able to break the silence of Papua. The TRCP should be able to translate and amplify the Papuan *memoria passionis* into a language that can be understood by a broader audience (national and international). Sanctioned by state authority, TRCP would be able to influence decision-making processes at the various levels of the government. TRCP should even be able to sanction state institutions to incorporate the Papuan *memoria passionis* into the meta-narrative

Theatre of peace 201

of the state. For instance, TRCP can facilitate the process of rewriting the history of Indonesia by incorporating the narratives of Papuan torture survivors. The Truth and Friendship Commission with Timor-Leste (2008) has set a precedent for this. One of its findings is that the Indonesian state is found guilty and responsible for the violence in Timor-Leste following the referendum. It also developed the ideas of institutional accountability of the military and intelligence services.

At the individual level, the incorporation of the abject stories will create a safe environment that will enable torture survivors to reconnect with the outside world as a safe, meaningful and respectful world for them. Anna's story exemplifies this. By sharing *memoria passionis* and recognition of the stories by a broader audience, individuals might be assisted by the permanent TRCP to regain their capacity to make sense of the outside world (Staub 1998: 234). This is the meaning of the healing narrative at the individual level. Furthermore, the same process not only affects survivors but also perpetrators. The TRCP should provide an ample space for perpetrators to also share their stories and to listen to the stories of the survivors and vice versa. This encounter might lead to meaningful dialogue between survivors and perpetrators. If this happens, the narrative of healing can be a 'precondition for reconciliation' (Staub 1998: 235). This process also illustrates an important role of an attentive and sympathetic community in eliciting the narrative of healing at both individual and communal levels.

This process, however, requires trust between Papuans and the TRCP. This is a great challenge. The Papuans' long experience of being ruled under the governmentality of torture has led them to distrust any formal state institution. Therefore, while a permanent TRCP can be a useful means to re-craft trust, this project may first require a concerted effort to secure trust[32] with Papuans before it can operate in a meaningful way to embody the narrative of healing.

One way to build trust at the societal level through TRCP is to institutionalise reparation as outlined by various UN documents[33] (Echeverria 2012; van Boven 2012). In international law and practice, van Boven argues that reparation means 'a requirement of justice to restore harm and damage caused by a wrongful act' (van Boven 2012: 694). It consists of three elements: *the right to know* which guarantees survivors to know what happened; *the right to justice* which requires the state to carry out impartial trials; and *the right to reparation* which outlines the state obligation to provide restitution, compensation, rehabilitation, satisfaction and guarantees of non-repetition and prevention. In conjunction with a human rights commission and a human rights court, TRCP will have a chance to address these three elements of reparation. By facilitating reparation the TRCP will have a concrete and tangible means to measure its work in developing trust between Papuans and the Indonesian state; Papuans and the TRCP; and the TRCP and the Indonesian state.

202 *Theatre of peace*

Narrative of solidarity

This second element of the theatre of peacebuilding is the narrative of solidarity. Drawing on the narratives of *caregivers* and *observers*, the narrative of solidarity addresses the community level of the cascades of peace. Informed by Metz's concept of solidarity, this narrative aims to create a safe environment for the abject to reconnect with the world of meaning and thus gradually regain their subjectivity. Being subjected to the process of abjection, Papuans not only have been treated as non-persons and lost their dignity but also many of them believed they are indeed non-persons. Drawing on Chenoweth and Stephan's study, which highlights the ways in which international solidarity plays a significant role in (not) pushing for change, the narrative of 'solidarity' can be broadened to mobilise international solidarity movements.[34] In the case of Timor-Leste, for instance, the international solidarity movements played an instrumental role in amplifying and maximising the networked governance of resistance which ended violence and built peace (Braithwaite, Charlesworth and Soares 2012).

Papuan experience suggests something different. So far the international solidarity movements for Papua have not been as effective in mounting pressure on the global policy-makers to pay attention to Papua. On the contrary, it is Papuan local initiatives that play a key role in peacebuilding. For instance, we have learnt that local organisations, particularly the Papuan Churches and Papuan NGOs, have been instrumental in disclosing the governmentality of torture and advocating for the interests of the survivors both at the national and the international levels (see Chapter 5). In a similar vein, the ULMWP would not have been effective if the Papuan grassroots had not strongly supported their leaders in representing them in the MSG. These empirical findings suggest that the international solidarity movements are not a game changer but a catalyst for change as long as local actors take the lead. This remains an integral struggle within the Papuan community.

In the context of TRCP, this mechanism will have the capacity to broaden the narrative of solidarity by breaking the silence of Papua. TRCP will have the obligation to communicate and amplify the stories narrated by survivors, perpetrators and spectators to a broader audience. Despite all the challenges in reconstructing truth through a TRC, TRCP will have a state authority to document the history of Papua which minimises lies and denial and thus penetrates the cycle of impunity. This process will educate not only perpetrators but also bystanders, beneficiaries and observers alike. They will be exposed to the *memoria passionis* of Papuans which has been established as an official and state-sanctioned document. This opportunity may pave the way to restore fractured relationships between survivors, perpetrators and spectators.

Fostered by the work of TRCP, the narrative of solidarity can promote a number of core values of Papua Land of Peace, particularly 'self-reliance', 'recognition and self-esteem' and 'sense of security'. The narrative of solidarity provides a fertile ground for abjected Papuans to rehabilitate the element of self-reliance and leadership which has been seriously undermined by the governmentality of torture. By crafting and gradually expanding an 'island of civility' (Kaldor 2006), the narrative of solidarity could empower Papuan combatants to reintegrate into their communities and, vice versa, their communities will be empowered to accept and reintegrate them. Hence, the sense of security and self-esteem might be restored for both sides.

In parallel, the narrative of solidarity at the local level forges a broader engagement of international solidarity. This network has been helpful in facilitating the local initiatives in exposing the hidden story of Papuans to the attention of the international audience. This process will reinforce the pillar of 'recognition' of the architecture of Papua Land of Peace, which might help rehabilitate and then develop and foster Papuan self-esteem. Finally, the narrative of solidarity might help improve the sense of security among survivors since they can maximise the existing local support network as well as embrace a global support system.

In other words, the narrative of solidarity can have a broader impact on the individual and community levels. The engagement of caregivers and agents with survivors in everyday life shows positive impacts on incorporating the abject into the subject (see Chapter 5). This engagement breaks the boundaries set by the subject who prevents the abject from transgressing. At the communal level, the narrative of solidarity helps mobilise bystanders and beneficiaries as they are encouraged by genuine engagement with survivors. In other words, the narrative of solidarity endorses the motivational posture of commitment to work with survivors to reclaim their agency. However, the current politics may not work for the survivors, agents, caregivers and observers. The increase of militarisation and isolation of Papua suggests a surge of the narrative of domination. In this context, the following narrative may offer one alternative.

Narrative of revolt

The last element of the Papuan peacebuilding model is the narrative of revolt. It aims to dismantle the governmentality of torture in Papua and revive the rule of law and democracy. This task is enormously complex since it has to interrupt the institutionalised domination surrounded with almost complete impunity consisting of a strategy of conquest, war, torture, *divide et impera* tactics etc. (see Chapter 4). As both organisational culture and TJ literatures suggest, structural transformation will confront formidable challenges from interested parties, particularly the Indonesian security services. Hence, as Hayner already highlights, TRCP will definitely confront enormous challenges to penetrate the governmentality of torture. However, if we put this daunting task as the long-run aim and combine it with various TJ mechanisms, the struggle might craft a chance for TRCP to penetrate the governance of torture in Papua in an incremental way. Given its permanent status, TRCP will not have to rush to complete its daunting tasks in two or three years as TRCs normally do. Instead, TRCP will be privileged to fulfil its obligations to install a new regime of accountability step by step. There are at least two major areas that can be identified: storytelling and accountability enforcement.

204 *Theatre of peace*

First, storytelling is crucial to create a liberating space for all involved in the theatre of torture (survivors, perpetrators and spectators). This space lays the ground for reconfiguring power relations that will allow greater agency and equitable relations among all actors. TRCP would have the authority to create this space where perpetrators (and two other types of actors) should be treated respectfully so they would be confident to publicly (or privately) testify their truth of their past misconduct to TRC. This public testimony is crucial to join together pieces of truth collected by a TRC from different sources, particularly survivors and spectators. As the timeframe of a permanent TRC is limitless, perpetrators would be assured that it would not be necessary to seek immediate reconciliation with survivors. They need to learn the *memoria passionis* of survivors to situate their confessions into survivors' expectations. Survivors then will be given a chance to assess whether they accept the perpetrators' testimony. As perpetrators of abuses in the Papuan context are mostly state actors, their testimony would be crucial to draw a new policy that prevents any recurrence of those state-sponsored abuses.

This process can craft a liberating space for both perpetrators and survivors. Testifying to the TRCP can be a way of healing trauma for perpetrators who genuinely confess their misconduct and a way to rebuild their lives for those who have been subjected to the domination of the state. In this sense, transformation can occur and start with the individual level and may permeate a broader level: community and political structure. The transformation can also be liberating for the Papuan community because they can witness the public testimony of perpetrators who gradually generate a spectacle of liberation as a counter to the spectacle of the sovereign power of the state. If these two levels (individual and community) of liberation proceed thanks to the work of a permanent TRC, perpetrators may become agents of change in their own institutions and community. In the long run, this permanent TRC might incrementally endorse change at the macro-structural level and be the guardian of this transformative process to reach a holistic approach of revolt even though it may not entirely escape the multi-polar violence and domination.

Liberating space resonates with Giay's discussion on the broader meaning of *merdeka* as discussed in the previous section. This is the governing principle of the new Papua that he envisions. In more concrete terms, Giay has elucidated ten elements of the New Papua. One critical element to this discussion is demilitarisation of Papua. This remains the hardest element to dismantle even under the Indonesian *reformasi*. Militarisation is entrenched into a broader culture of the Papuan society which goes beyond the military organisation itself.

In this context, Shearing and Ericson's analysis is relevant. These scholars have examined the importance of storytelling to generate culture change in the context of police culture. The authors found that we can see police culture as 'not a book of rules, albeit informal cookbook rules, but as a story book' (Shearing and Ericson 1991: 489). Generating change in this context would be more effective by providing empirical examples through stories for three reasons. First, police stories function as analogous reasoning to respond and to act.

Second, police stories create a vocabulary of precedents that guide police to act. Finally, police stories 'use silences to establish a worldview that provides a way of seeing and experiencing a world' (Shearing and Ericson 1991: 492). This analysis illustrates the centrality of storytelling in penetrating a self-centred world of domination, as we found within the Indonesian security apparatus (see Chapter 5).

Second, at the level of accountability enforcement, TRCP would need to develop a more robust mechanism of accountability than one that simply relies on the existing Indonesian legal framework.[35] Fisse and Braithwaite's (1993: 140–54) analysis on pyramidal enforcement can inspire TRCP's formulation in progressively ensuring compliance for perpetrators and their institutions. These scholars outline six levels of pyramidal enforcement gradually moving from persuasion to punishment: (1) persuasion, advice, warning, (2) civil monetary penalties, (3) voluntary disciplinary or remedial investigation, (4) court-ordered disciplinary or remedial investigation, (5) corporate criminal sanctions and (6) corporate capital punishment.

This book will not discuss the details of any proposed model of accountability for TRCP. Such an exercise would need separate and careful elucidation which goes beyond the scope of this thesis. Figure 6.4 simply visualises the basic ideas of a pyramid of accountability. If TRCP is established in Papua, it can further explore applicability within the Papuan peacebuilding context which is still in the making. Inspired by the regulatory pyramid developed by Braithwaite (2002: 30–1), the following model will operate from the base of the pyramid (Level 1) as a form of persuasion and move to an upper level (Level 2) which tends to be

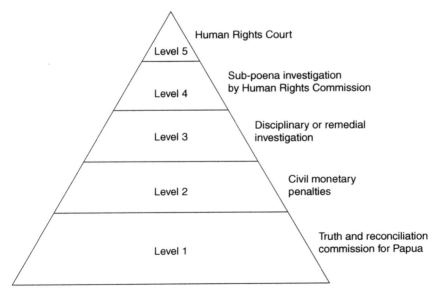

Figure 6.4 Pyramid of accountability.

206 *Theatre of peace*

more punitive only when the former fails to assert compliance from perpetrators and their institutions. The higher the enforcement goes, the more rigid form of punishment applies. In this respect, this model aims to integrate three separate elements – restorative justice, deterrence and incapacitation – into a single model to compensate for the weaknesses of one theory with the strengths of other theories (Braithwaite 2002: 32). In this context, the weaknesses of storytelling to persuade perpetrators and their institution to testify before TRCP will be covered by the pyramid of enforcement which involves strengths from deterrence and incapacitation of criminal enforcement (human rights commission and human rights court). This integration would hopefully ensure accountability of individuals and institutions for their involvement in the governmentality of torture in Papua.

Level 1

TRCP may convene public hearings for perpetrators to persuade them to confess their misconduct. If they voluntarily tell TRCP their stories which meet the standard criteria of the truth-seeking, TRCP will allow reconciliatory processes with relevant survivors and their families.

Level 2

TRCP will impose civil monetary penalties for institutions and individuals who do not provide comprehensive and honest testimonies to TRCP.

Level 3

Disciplinary or remedial investigation undertaken upon agreement with TRCP (accountability agreement), coupled with an accountability report.

Level 4

Subpoena investigation conducted by a human rights commission, coupled with an accountability report.

Level 5

Prosecution of perpetrators and institutions undertaken by a human rights court, with imprisonment for individual perpetrators and liquidation for institutional punishment. This might mean complete abolition of Brimob and Kopassus as units of the Indonesian security state.

This model might be a useful way to explore a possible integration of various transitional justice mechanisms, particularly a human rights commission and a human rights court to dismantle the governmentality of torture in Papua.

Theatre of peace 207

Concluding remarks

Reimagining Papua Land of Peace needs to take into account two conflicting realities as two sides of the same coin: the reality of domination and multi-polar violence as well as the reality of peacemaking. Violence and domination rarely escape our everyday life, but at the same time peacemaking also finds its way to work against violence. Both elements seem to constitute inseparable but antagonistic human conditions in any given situation.

It is not the ambition of Papua Land of Peace to capitulate to the reality of multi-polar violence which exists in Papua across time. Rather, the framework deliberately aims to dismantle structures of oppression by broadening spaces of peace characterised by the nine pillars of Papua Land of Peace. This vision can be achieved by institutionalising _memoria passionis_ of Papuans into TRCP. The purpose is to dismantle the theatre of torture to build the theatre of peacebuilding. Through TRCP, _memoria passionis_ might have a permanent delivery vehicle to transform narratives of domination-suffering-witnessing into the narratives of revolt-healing-solidarity.

The transformation, however, is not perceived as a teleological process or TRCP alone. Rather, it follows the logic of _memoria passionis_: interruption and revolt; and should be dealt with through interconnected TJ mechanisms, particularly a human rights commission and a human rights court. These processes constitute cascades of peace: layers of peacebuilding processes that constantly influence asymmetric power relations to generate equitable power relations. As a result, the peacebuilding processes aim at renewing every element of the society and polity which have been subjected to domination and abjection. This process suggests a dynamic and perhaps circular process in that a process of dismantling the governmentality of torture can be repeated or moved backward first before moving forward.

Nonetheless, one should realise that this is just the beginning of reimagining the Papua Land of Peace framework. The framework should be further informed with and tested by the ongoing efforts of Papuan civil society in building a political space for Jakarta-Papua dialogue and its prerequisites, such as openness to demilitarisation and _Papuanisation_.

Notes

1 In his doctoral thesis published in the Journal _Point_ as a single edition, Neles Tebay names the elements slightly differently. He only identifies eight elements, including awareness and respect for plurality, justice, unity, harmony, solidarity, togetherness, sincere fraternity and welfare (Tebay 2012).
2 Rumour is a common phenomenon in Papua. Given the lack of clear information mixed with over-expectation, many Papuans often believe that rumours are reality. For example, around 2000 there were rumours that the then-UN Secretary-General Kofi Annan would visit Papua and deliver independence for Papua. See van den Broek _et al._ (2005: 12).
3 In Giay's analysis, he specifically calls for demilitarisation. Although this call is not unique, it echoes and renews Papuans' call for demilitarisation.

208 *Theatre of peace*

4 One of the clearest formulations of the position of the Indonesian government on this issue can be seen in a document titled 'Questioning the Unquestionable: An Overview of the Restoration of Papua into the Republic of Indonesia' published by Permanent Mission of the Republic of Indonesia to the United Nations (Morgan 2003). This document specifically addresses the question that Papua is finished and a non-issue at the UN level.

5 For the background and a critical reflection on the influence of Giay's book on Papuan politics in 2000, see Cookson (2008).

6 Giay elaborates further this element in his booklet '*Mari Mengambil Alih Kendali Kehidupan, Memperjuangkan Pemulihan Negeri Ini*' (Let's Take Over the Control of Life, Struggling for Restoring The Country) (2008).

7 '*Papuanisasi*' is a term originally introduced into Papua post *reformasi* by the Indonesian government to explain its programme of filling government positions in Papua with more indigenous Papuan civil servants, not migrants. When Papuans held their 2nd Congress in Jayapura in 2000, the Congress infused and broadened the notion into a deeper meaning: reclaiming agency and be a master of their own land. Being involved in the whole process of Papuan emancipation, Giay's contribution to this development has been critical.

8 The English word 'development' has a broader notion than the Indonesian equivalent '*pembangunan*' which Giay refers to. The latter has a closer connotation with an ideology of economic development which narrowly puts strong emphasis on growth and physical indicators of success.

9 The Indonesian verb is '*Indonesianisasi*' which conceives the notion of infusing identity change into Papua and Papuans. This verb becomes an antonym of '*Papuanisasi*'.

10 Interview I/D2 in Port Moresby on 29 April 2010.

11 In parallel with Papua Land Peace movement, LIPI conducted research to explain the root causes of conflicts in Papua and propose a solution for them that resulted in a model of analysis called 'Papua Road Map'. It identifies four key problems: (1) marginalisation and discrimination, (2) failure of government development, (3) state violence and human rights violence and (4) history and political status of Papua. Based on this understanding, LIPI proposes four different solutions for each issue: (1) recognition by affirmative policy, (2) a new paradigm of development policy aiming at improving the welfare standards of Papuans, (3) reconciliation and human rights court to improve political relations between Jakarta and Papua and (4) dialogue to provide a space for negotiations between Jakarta and Papua (Widjojo 2010).

12 Interview III/D3 in Papua on 3 January 2012.

13 Interview II/C4 phase 2 in Papua on 30 January 2012.

14 Interview II/E18 in Jakarta on 13 October 2015.

15 The classical work of Terrence Deal and Allen Kennedy (1988) divides organisational culture into four types based on behaviour: work-hard, play-hard culture; tough-guy macho culture; process culture; and bet-the-company culture. Edgar Schein (1985: Chapter 12) uses three levels of culture. The deepest is the set of 'basic assumptions' of the nature of reality, human nature, human activity and human relations. The second and middle level is 'values' which are defined as 'what ought to be'. The top level is the 'artefacts and creation' which consist of technology, arts, and visible and audible behaviour patterns. From this framework, Schein outlines a very detailed mechanism of culture change that involves eleven stages. Hence, Schein's framework is considered the most comprehensive taxonomy of culture change.

16 The 2012 Human Security Report concludes that even a failed peace negotiation contributed to reducing violence (Human Security Research Group 2012: 178–9).

17 See http://regnet.anu.edu.au/research/research-projects/details/534/peacebuilding-compared-project and http://johnbraithwaite.com.

18 Hayner (2011: 216) examines various practices of TRCs which have existed. One of the common practices is that they were all temporary and lasted between two and three years. The reason is to keep momentum, focus and political and public attention.

Theatre of peace 209

19 Michael Scharf (1997: 380) is among the few who advocates for a permanent international TRC equivalent connected to the International Criminal Court based on a treaty. He puts forward four reasons to justify his proposal: '1) superior sufficiency of funding; (2) a greater perception of neutrality; (3) less susceptibility to domestic influences; and (4) greater speed in launching investigations'. This proposal is vulnerable for a number of reasons. First, since it is based on a treaty, it will be subject to prolonged negotiations among the UN member-states to agree on another international jurisdiction. Second, the financial superiority might be questionable. In contrast to ICC which prosecutes a limited number of individuals, a TRC is designed to collect and document testimonies from as many victims as possible. Therefore, it will require many more resources to support such a large operation. Third, neutrality of TRC is important. However, the reconciliation process occurs in a local context. This requires as much a sense of ownership as possible which is crucial to enable storytelling. Being located outside this context, a TRC may not be so effective to build a sense of ownership among local actors. Fourth, as it is based on a treaty, its jurisdiction may entirely rely on the ratification of the UN member-states. If this is the case, victims of a country which does not ratify this treaty may not be able to access this mechanism. Likewise, this TRC will not be able to launch any investigations.

20 The original text reads, '*Dalam rangka pemantapan persatuan dan kesatuan bangsa di Provinsi Papua dibentuk Komisi Kebenaran dan Rekonsiliasi*'.

21 The text reads, 'In order to fulfil the obligation as required by para 1, the government shall establish a national commission on human rights, human rights court and truth and reconciliation commission according to the laws' (*Untuk melaksanakan hal sebagaimana dimaksud pada ayat (1), Pemerintah membentuk perwakilan Komisi Nasional Hak Asasi Manusia, Pengadilan Hak Asasi Manusia, dan Komisi Kebenaran dan Rekonsiliasi di Provinsi Papua sesuai dengan peraturan perundang-undangan*).

22 It should be noted here that both a human rights commission and human rights court for Papua stipulated by Special Autonomy Law are different from the existing Komnas HAM and the Indonesian human rights court.

23 The Indonesian version reads: *Keberatan saya terhadap perjuangan bersenjata bersifat prinsipiil dan praktis. Secara prinsipiil saya merasa, bahwa satu perjuangan bersenjata harus dikendalikan secara politis, karena kalau tidak, ia tidak memiliki peluang untuk menang. ... Dilihat secara praktis, satu gerakan militer yang tidak berdisiplin tidak akan menghasilkan apapun bagi orang-orang Papua. Perlawanan bersenjata menuntut makanan atau wanita, akan tetapi sadarkan dia, bahwa kampong-kampung tempat bergantung para pemberontak sangat rentan terhadap balas dendam tentara Indonesia, karena 'bantuan yang sudah diberikan'?*

24 The rally coincided with my fieldwork in Papua in 2010. From my direct observation of the rally, it was highly organised by the Papuan leaders so it went peacefully without any violent incidents. It was tense at one stage when the Chief of Police of Jayapura Municipality deployed a Brimob unit to disperse the crowd. However, the Papuan leaders managed to maintain strict discipline of their crowd to stick to non-violent means. Furthermore, they were also able to convince the Chief of Police that they had only delivered their statement to the provincial parliament and would take responsibility for any damage that might have occurred. Moreover, some members of the Parliament also took a clear position that they took responsibility on the matter. After the rally finished, the police even provided the demonstrators with transport to take them to their homes around Jayapura.

25 It also means eschewing the motivational posture of capitulation in favour of revolt and moving from the motivational postures of gaming the Indonesian state corruptly for personal advantage and disengagement to solidarity and healing.

26 For a comprehensive theoretical analysis of the effectiveness of restorative justice see Braithwaite (2002: Chapter 3).

210 Theatre of peace

27 Lederach (2001) outlines five aspects of reconciliation: (1) centrality of trust building, (2) accompaniment which emphasises presence and sharing of common humanity, (3) humility which means understanding of one's place and one's humanity, (4) restoring the fabric of community and (5) wandering in a desert which means rethinking our timeframes seriously in relation to healing processes.

28 See www.modusaceh.co/news/tingkat-kepercayaan-korban-jadi-tantangan-kkr-aceh/index.html, accessed 15 February 2017.

29 See www.thejakartapost.com/news/2016/10/29/graft-allegations-hit-komnas-ham.html, accessed 15 February 2017.

30 An international and national mixture of administering TRCs is not uncommon. Although most TRCs are staffed by national staff, El Salvador and Guatemala TRCs, for example, were established by UN decisions and staffed by the UN personnel although they worked independently from the UN (Hayner 2011: 211–15).

31 In the literature of torture, healing relates to the issue of trauma, which constitutes one major preoccupation of the study of torture both in a theoretical and practical sense (see Chapter 5).

32 Valerie Braithwaite (1998: 51–7) outlines the complex process of developing trust between individuals and institutions. She identifies two inseparable types of trust: harmony and security trust, which are both institutionalised in our society. Harmony trust refers to communal norms in which community and relationships between individuals, and between individuals and their communities, are central. This type of trust emphasises sharing of values rather than the functions of organisations. Conversely, security trust centres on institutions or performance. In this case, exchange norms are crucial. Therefore consistency, competence and reliability are all central. In the case of Papua, security trust has been seriously undermined by the governance of torture. The security trust requires careful work to rebuild its performance.

33 UN GA resolution 60/2005: the Basic Principles and Guidelines on the Right to a Remedy and Reparation for Victims of Gross Violations of International Human Rights Law and Serious Violations of International Humanitarian Law (Reparation Principles); Article 14 Convention Against Torture; an Updated Set of Principles for the Protection and Promotion of Human Rights through Action to Combat Impunity (Impunity Principles).

34 For a critical discussion on reconceptualising civil society and its critical role in peacebuilding at the global political context after 9/11, see Kaldor (2003).

35 In strengthening the Indonesian legal system, it is crucial to consider Anna Kurniasari's doctoral thesis which analyses the weaknesses of the existing Indonesian legal framework to combat torture. She argues that the gap in the legal framework can be strengthened by criminalising torture through adopting a new law on combating torture in Indonesia. Her analysis identifies critical issues that have contributed to the reality that torture is not punished. These include: delayed introduction of the new Indonesian Criminal Law; no harmonisation of laws that can accommodate Indonesian ratification of the UN Convention Against Torture; problems of impunity; public misunderstanding of the nature of torture; and public ignorance (Kurniasari 2012: 438).

References

Akhavan, P. 2009, 'Are International Criminal Tribunals a Disincentive to Peace?: Reconciling Judicial Romanticism with Political Realism', *Human Rights Quarterly*, vol. 31, no. 2009, pp. 624–54.

Aukerman, M.J. 2002, 'Extraordinary Evil, Ordinary Crime: A Framework for Understanding Transitional Justice', *Harvard Human Rights Journal*, vol. 15, pp. 39–97.

Bisset, A. 2012, *Truth Commissions and Criminal Courts*, Cambridge University Press, Cambridge.

Theatre of peace 211

Boraine, A. 2000, *A Country Unmasked*, Oxford University Press, Oxford.

Braithwaite, J. 2002, *Restorative Justice and Responsive Regulation*, Oxford University Press, Oxford and New York.

Braithwaite, J. 2011, 'Partial Truth and Reconciliation in the *Long Durée*', *Contemporary Social Science*, vol. 6, no. 1, pp. 129–46.

Braithwaite, J., Braithwaite, V., Cookson, M. and Dunn, L. 2010, *Anomie and Violence: Non-Truth and Reconciliation in Indonesian Peacebuilding*, ANU Press, Canberra.

Braithwaite, J., Charlesworth, H., Reddy, P. and Dunn, L. 2010, *Reconciliation and Architectures of Commitment: Sequencing Peace in Bougainville*, ANU E-Press, Canberra, A.C.T.

Braithwaite, J., Charlesworth, H. and Soares, A. 2012, *Networked Governance of Freedom and Tyranny: Peace in Timor-Leste*, ANU E-Press, Canberra.

Braithwaite, J., Dinnen, S., Allen, M., Braithwaite, V. and Charlesworth, H. 2010, *Pillars and Shadows: Statebuilding as Peacebuilding in Solomon Islands*, ANU E-Press, Canberra.

Braithwaite, J. and Nickson, R. 2012, 'Timing Truth, Reconciliation, and Justice after War', *Ohio State Journal of Dispute Resolution*, vol. 27, no. 3, pp. 443–76.

Braithwaite, V. 1998, 'Communal and Exchange Trust Norms: Their Value Base and Relevance to Institutional Trust', in V. Braithwaite and M. Levi (eds), *Trust and Governance*, Russell Sage Foundation, New York.

Cassese, A. 1998, 'Reflections on International Criminal Justice', *The Modern Law Review*, vol. 61, no. 1, pp. 1–10.

Chenoweth, E. and Stephan, M.J. 2011, *Why Civil Resistance Works: The Strategic Logic of Nonviolent Conflict*, Columbia University Press, New York.

Cookson, M.B. 2008, 'Batik Irian: Imprints of Indonesia Papua', PhD thesis, Australian National University.

Deal, T.E. and Kennedy, A.A. 1988, *Corporate Culture*, Penguin Business, London and Ringwood, Vic.

Echeverria, G. 2012, 'Do Victims of Torture and Other Serious Human Rights Violations have an Independent and Enforceable Right to Reparation?', *The International Journal of Human Rights*, vol. 16, no. 5, pp. 698–716.

Elisabeth, A., Budiarti, A.P., Wiratri, A., Pamungkas, C. and Wilson, B. 2016, *Proses Perdamaian, Politik Kaum Muda, dan Diaspora Papua: Updating Papua Road Map*, Lembaga Ilmu Pengetahuan Indonesia, Jakarta.

ELSAM 2007, *Ekspose Hasil Eksaminasi Putusan Pengadilan Abepura dan Timor Timur*, Lembaga Studi dan Advokasi Masyarakat (ELSAM), Jakarta.

Fisse, B. and Braithwaite, J. 1993, *Corporations, Crime and Accountability*, Cambridge University Press, Cambridge.

Freeman, M. 2006, *Truth Commissions and Procedural Fairness*, Cambridge University Press, Cambridge.

Gerlach, C. 2010, *Extreme Violent Societies: Mass Violence in the Twentieth-Century World*, Cambridge University Press, Cambridge.

Giay, B. 2000, *Menuju Papua Baru: Beberapa Pokok Pikiran Sekitar Emansipasi Orang Papua*, Deiyai/Elsham Papua, Jayapura.

Giay, B. 2008, *Mari Mengambil Alih Kendali Kehidupan, Memperjuangkan Pemulihan Negeri Ini*, Deiyai, Jayapura.

Hayner, P.B. 2011, *Unspeakable Truths: Transitional Justice and the Challenge of Truth Commissions*, 2nd edn, Routledge, New York.

212 Theatre of peace

Hernawan, B. 2012, 'Jakarta-Papua Dialogue: Between a Rock and a Hard Place', *The Jakarta Post*, 11 June 2012, www.thejakartapost.com/news/2012/06/11/jakarta-papua-dialogue-between-a-rock-and-a-hard-place.html.

Hernawan, B. 2015, 'Contesting Melanesia: The Summit and Dialogue', *The Jakarta Post*, www.thejakartapost.com/news/2015/07/08/contesting-melanesia-the-summit-and-dialogue.html.

Hernawan, B. 2016, 'ULMWP and the Insurgent Papua', *Live Encounter*, 1 November 2016.

Human Security Research Group 2012, *Human Security Report 2012: Sexual Violence, Education, and War Beyond the Mainstream Narrative*, Simon Fraser University, Vancouver.

Humphrey, M. 2002, *The Politics of Atrocity and Reconciliation, From Terror to Trauma*, Routledge, London and New York.

Ignatieff, M. 1996, 'Articles of Faith', *Index on Censorship*, vol. 25, no. 10, pp. 110–22.

International Crisis Group 2012, *Dynamics of Violence in Papua*, International Crisis Group, Brussels/Jakarta.

Kaisiepo, V. 2012, *Satu Perspektif untuk Papua: Cerita Kehidupan dan Perjuanganku*, Kanisius, Yogyakarta.

Kaldor, M. 2003, *Global Civil Society: An Answer to War*, Polity, Oxford.

Kaldor, M. 2006, *New and Old Wars: Organized Violence in a Global Era*, Polity, Cambridge.

Karstedt, S. 2011, *Exploration into 'Extremely Violent Societies' and the Dynamics of Violence and Peace*, Regulatory Institutions Network, Canberra, Unpublished Work.

Karstedt, S. 2012, 'Contextualizing Mass Atrocity: The Dynamics of "Extremely Violent Societies"', *European Journal of Criminology*, vol. 9, no. 5, pp. 499–513.

Kiss, E. 2000, 'Moral Ambition Within and Beyond Political Constraints: Reflections on Restorative Justice', in R.I. Rotberg and D. Thompson (eds), *Truth v. Justice: The Morality of Truth Commissions*, Princeton University Press, Princeton, NJ and Oxford, pp. 68–98.

Komisi Kebenaran dan Persahabatan 2008, *Laporan Akhir Komisi Kebenaran dan Persahabatan (KKP) Indonesia-Timor-Leste*, Komisi Kebenaran dan Persahabatan Indonesia-Timor-Leste, Jakarta.

Kurniasari, A.S. 2012, 'Kriminalisasi Penyiksaan Oleh Pejabat Publik sebagai Konsekuensi Ratifikasi Konvensi Menentang Penyiksaan di Indonesia', PhD thesis, Universitas Indonesia.

Lederach, J.P. 1997, *Building Peace: Sustainable Reconciliation in Divided Societies*, United States Institute of Peace, Washington, DC.

Lederach, J.P. 2001, 'Five Qualities of Practice in Support of Reconciliation Process', in R.G. Helmick and R.L. Peterson (eds), *Forgiveness and Reconciliation*, Templeton Foundation Press, Philadelphia, PA and London, pp. 193–203.

McLeod, J. 2015, *Merdeka and The Morning Star: Civil Resistance in West Papua*, New Approaches to Peace and Conflict, University of Queensland, St Lucia, Brisbane.

Minow, M. 1998, *Between Vengeance and Forgiveness*, Beacon Press, Boston, MA.

Minow, M. 2000, 'The Hope for Healing: What Can Truth Commissions Do?', in R.I. Rotberg and D. Thompson (eds), *Truth v. Justice: The Morality of Truth Commission*, Princeton University Press, Princeton, NJ and Oxford.

Morgan, G. 1986, *Images of Organization*, Sage Publications, and Beverly Hills, CA.

Morgan, G. 2003, *Questioning the Unquestionable: An Overview of the Restoration of Papua into the Republic of Indonesia*, by Permanent Mission of the Republic of

Indonesia to the United Nations, Permanent Mission of the Republic of Indonesia to the United Nations.

Scharf, M.P. 1997, 'The Case for a Permanent International Truth Commission', *Duke Journal of Comparative and International Law*, vol. 7, pp. 375–410.

Schein, E.H. 1985, *Organizational Culture and Leadership*, Jossey-Bass, San Francisco, CA.

Shearing, C. and Ericson, R. 1991, 'Culture as Figurative Action', *British Journal of Sociology*, vol. 42, no. 4, pp. 481–506.

Smyth, M.B. 2007, *Truth, Recovery and Justice after Conflict: Managing Violent Pasts*, Routledge, London and New York.

Staub, E. 1998, 'Breaking the Cycle of Genocidal Violence: Healing and Reconciliation', in J.H. Harvey (ed.), *Perspectives on Loss: A Sourcebook*, Mazel, Brunner.

Tebay, N. 2009, *Dialog Jakarta-Papua: Sebuah Perspektif Papua*, 1st edn, Sekretariat Keadilan dan Perdamaian, Keuskupan Jayapura, Jayapura.

Tebay, N. 2012, 'Reconciliation and Peace: Interfaith Endeavours for Peace in West Papua', *Point*, vol. 36.

van Boven, T. 2012, 'The Need to Repair', *The International Journal of Human Rights*, vol. 16, no. 5, pp. 694–7.

van den Broek, T., Korain, F. and Kambayong, R. 2005, 'Building a Culture of Peace Towards "Papua, a Land of Peace"', in B. Hernawan (ed.), *Papua Land of Peace: Addressing Conflict, Building Peace in West Papua*, Office for Justice and Peace of the Catholic Diocese of Jayapura (SKP), Jayapura.

Widjojo, M.S. (ed.) 2010, *Papua Road Map: Negotiating the Past, Improving the Present, and Securing the Future*, Cet. 1st edn, Kerja sama LIPI, Yayasan Tifa, dan Yayasan Obor Indonesia, Jakarta.

Wilson, R.A. 2001, *The Politics of Truth and Reconciliation in South Africa, Legitimizing the Post-Apartheid State*, Cambridge University Press, Cambridge.

7 Lenses on torture and peacebuilding

Introduction

Let us move towards a conclusion by returning to the verdicts of the Jayapura court martial on the Papuan torture video case (see Chapter 4). The reason to highlight the verdict is because it encapsulates in the most recent example of the nature and logic of torture in Papua. While the six soldiers were found guilty and sentenced to jail for five to ten months, the court did not find them guilty of torture. Rather, they were found guilty of 'not following orders' from their relevant superiors. Similarly, the court found the commandant of the group guilty and sentenced him for seven months but not because of torture. Rather, it was because he 'deliberately provided an opportunity to his subordinates to not follow his orders'. As the verdicts fix on the matter of 'following orders', the court martial fails to recognise torture as a form of state-sponsored brutality. Instead of punishing torture to pave the way to build peace in Papua, the court reinforced and perpetuated the spectacle of the sovereign of the Indonesian State. As a result, the issue remains how appropriately sovereignty is asserted rather than whether rights and bodies are respected.

This drama helps summarise the intention of this book, namely to provide the first full-length examination of the nature and logic of torture that serves as a basis for strengthening the Papua Land of Peace framework in Papua. The examination has answered the following research questions:

1 What is the *raison d'être* and structure of the politics of torture in Papua?
2 What is the underlying logic that underpins this politics?
3 What are the differences between the ways in which the politics of torture is understood by perpetrators, torture survivors and spectators?
4 What kind of peacebuilding will adequately come to grips with these logics and practices?

In recapitulating the key findings, the chapter also draws new theoretical and practical implications resulting from previous chapters before concluding with final considerations to open up further research.

Torture as a mode of governance

This study shows torture in Papua has resulted from the construction of asymmetric power relations, state policies and practices, and a history of five-decade impunity (see Chapter 3). Torture in Papua is not merely a technology of obtaining information but much more problematic and disturbing. It constitutes a spectacle of the sovereign power of the state that outcasts and at the same time colonises Papua and Papuans. Furthermore, the evidence reveals that torture has become a state crime, a policy of terror that has played a major role in the ways in which the Indonesian state governs Papua. In other words, torture constitutes a mode of governance or 'art of government'. This governance is deeply rooted in the web of power relations in Papua that manifests the sovereign power of the Indonesian state in its policy not only to eradicate Papuan aspirations for *merdeka* (independence) but to secure much deeper domination.

Rejali's phrase 'torture as a civic marker' (2010) is relevant here. Based on his investigation into the history of torture from the Ancient Greeks to twenty-first-century liberal democracies, he argues that torture serves to 'separat[e] gradations of citizenship'. In other words, torture has been used as a means to govern citizens and to discriminate against non-citizens throughout the history of humankind. What has changed, according to Rejali, is the technology. When states are more democratic, more hidden technologies of torture are employed. The implication is clear here that torture likely exists in any political regime. Another implication from the secretness of torture in many democracies is that incidence rates of torture are probably unknowable with any comparative reliability. Even so, my quantitative and qualitative data give good grounds for believing that Papua is one of the places where the incidence of torture is very high and not very secret. While it is true that torture has become more secret as Indonesia has become more democratic since 1998, this is far less true of Papua because liberalism and democracy in practical terms have not spread to Papua since 1998. Papua is the exception of spectacularity.

Torture as a spectacle

While Rejali's notion of torture as civic marker explains why torture exists in any political regime, it has limits in explaining the internal dynamics of the public nature of Papua's torture. This study has analysed ten major patterns of torture in Papua that lead to the conclusion that torture in Papua is a spectacle and constitutes a policy of the Indonesian state to govern Papua (see Chapter 4). First, most of the victims are Papuans, farmers, males, civilians and highlanders who live in rural areas. Only a few cases involve victims that were OPM members or OPM leaders. Second, rape features as a dominant method to torture Papuan women. Third, almost all torturers are members of the Indonesian state security apparatus: TNI and the police. Fourth, techniques of torture only require low cost and low skills. Fifth, torture in Papua is regularly based on unjustified and one-sided accusations by the Indonesian security services. Sixth,

216 *Lenses on torture and peacebuilding*

under conditions of lawlessness and political transition, the Indonesian state apparatus has heavily relied on torture as a technique to handle secession movements. Seventh, drawing on the ICTY and ICTR judgements, Papua's state-sponsored torture constitutes a crime against humanity. Eighth, torture is patterned to show the central element of a spectacle: public display of the injured body. Ninth, the colonisation of public space has led to virtually complete impunity for torture. The tenth pattern of the Papuan torture is that local actors play a much more dominant role in exposing torture than international actors. To make sense of these findings, Foucault's theory of power, Kristeva's theory of abjection as well as Metz's theory of *memoria passionis* were put in creative interaction to proffer a fresh and holistic way of seeing torture (see Chapter 2).

The findings question Rejali's argument on the binary opposition of public torture and democracy. Papuan experience demonstrates how highly public torture coexists with Indonesian democracy. On the other hand, while torture is an open secret within Papua, Papua itself is a secret place. The militarisation of Papuan politics is concealed from the media and from national and international publics. Provided Papua is less visible and largely misrepresented in Indonesian public discourse, Indonesian democracy is not hesitant to resort to public brutality to eradicate opposition. Within this context, the Indonesian public largely acts as bystanders rather than caregivers, leaving the minority Papuan in isolation. The widely publicised Papuan torture video exemplifies the continuity of the spectacle of brutality since the impunity of the Indonesian state assumes the monopoly of meaning that penetrates the boundaries of law and morality. However, the same footage signifies the way in which Papuan civil society has managed to turn the spectacle of the sovereign into a spectacle of immorality by exposing the brutal and illegal aspects of public torture to a wider audience. By doing this, they have maximised the existing worldwide network of caregivers and observers to amplify their message.

Torture as a crime against humanity

In the language of international human rights law, four chief elements of governmentality (purpose, technologies and strategies, identity, and rationality) of torture meet the required criteria of a crime against humanity. That is, torture has become a deliberate policy of the Indonesian state to govern Papuans as the abject. The Torture Dataset documents how this policy has inflicted excruciating pain on the bodies of at least 431 civilians.

This research found the elements of being a policy, targeting civilians, and being widespread and systematic fundamental to constituting crimes against humanity as defined by the statutes of the ICTY, ICTR and ICC. Hence, there is no question that the practice of torture in Papua has breached international human rights law. However, just as the US illegal imprisonment of terrorist suspects in Guantanamo Bay draws minimal public attention, so too for Papuan torture. Despite stark differences in many respects, both phenomena signify the nature of the abjected zones in which meaning has collapsed. In Rejali's

Lenses on torture and peacebuilding 217

language, the abject is a marker for those who inherently possess the incapacity to live with civility and morality as citizens of the so-called civilised world. Therefore, they are cast beyond protection of law and morality. For the mighty power of the US, the terrorist suspects have been considered non-combatants so they are not protected by Geneva Conventions. President Obama's promise to close the facility is yet to be fulfilled (Bruck 2016). Similarly, for the Indonesian state, Papuans have been treated as underdeveloped and stone-age people so they have been governed by torture. Therefore the court martial hearings to try the YouTube video case showed no interest in presenting witnesses and victims to testify.

This goes to the essence of international human rights law's description of a crime against humanity. A crime against humanity dehumanises and downgrades us all as a human species. It is an attack on our common human dignity as a whole, not only on individual victims. Hence, it constitutes *hostis humani generis*, the enemy of humankind. The gravity of the crime has posed formidable challenges to law, politics and morality to eradicate torture as it has been embedded in the psyches of both the US and Indonesia states. In the context of Papua, these challenges set the scene of transformation of the theatre of torture to the theatre of Papua Land of Peace below.

Theatre of torture

Having analysed the ten major patterns of torture, this research reveals the correlations and interdependencies of types of actors (perpetrators-survivors-spectators) and their internal dynamics that construct, maintain and reproduce torture (see Chapter 5). The model of the theatre of torture demonstrates that theoretically there is only a little space available to evade the theatre of torture. The triangulation of 'perpetrators-survivors-spectators' represents broader and multilayered narratives of 'domination-suffering-witnessing'. Every actor has a fluid identity that enables them to construct and reconstruct new identities and boundaries in relation to other actors depending on their power relations. The theatre has identified at least eighteen possible sub-narratives which allow the same possibilities of interactions among them even though their intensity and influence are not always equal. Nevertheless, there are exceptions which do not match any of the identified sub-narratives, such as the narratives of wandering and forgetting. This finding indicates that the possibility of escaping the theatre of torture is real.

The verdicts of Indonesian court martials only illustrate the first two of four sub-narratives of perpetrators (see Chapter 5) within the theatre of torture that underpin the narrative of domination, namely 'denial' and 'procedure'. While the court sentenced the soldiers, its verdicts failed to recognise that torture existed. The verdicts also failed to use the word 'torture' and thus exemplify the form of denial practised by the Indonesian state in its brutality against Papuans (see Cohen 2001). Moreover, by solely referring to 'following orders', the court reinforces the justification of torture as a matter of 'procedure'. The practical

218 *Lenses on torture and peacebuilding*

implications have gone beyond the court room. The Jayapura court martials have effectively reduced torture from a crime against humanity, as defined by international law, to merely an administrative issue, a procedure that the state wants citizens to know exists, yet also wants to be able to regulate with show trials when there is international pressure. Conventions can be reversed later. In such ways, show trials reinforce the other justification of committing torture embedded in the Indonesian military and police force, namely the *habitus* of impunity. By not punishing the soldiers who committed torture, the court does little to eradicate the *habitus* of impunity because the existing militarised culture and systems of values have not been questioned or corrected by a judicial branch that is independent of the security apparatus. Similarly, the court remains far from being able even to name and criminalise torture, let alone to uproot the culture of pleasure that underlies the ways in which the soldiers recorded the footage of men in pain for entertainment and institution (see Hutchings 2013).

Theoretical implications

While the analysis of power relations is common in the literature of torture and state crimes in general, the Papua phenomenon draws broader theoretical and practical implications. Four theoretical implications can be drawn. First, this study demonstrates the fluidity of power relations that construct and constrain subjectivity and agency in a torture setting. The dynamics of domination and resistance not only demonstrates the unresolved tension between law, morality and politics, which has been the major theme in the literature of torture and counter-terrorism, but also confirms the applicability of Foucault's theory of power as a network. Asymmetric power relations likely converge into an oppressive regime although in this context, resistance continues to flourish as a proportionate response to the domination of the oppressive regime. In this sense, an oppressive regime will not likely entirely conquer and eradicate resistance. Moreover, the study found key elements of symbolic torture, such as 'governmentality, spectacle, marking the body, communicating power over the body', which very much resonate with the Foucauldian concept of symbolic power.

However, Foucault's conviction of his ability 'to kill the King' (Foucault 1980) and liberate law, ethics and politics from his majesty confronts a contrary reality in Papua. The Papua case study shows that state sovereignty continues to occupy the *sacrosanctum* of politics and law; determined opposition is charged with treason and terrorised. This pattern is not limited to transition to democracy in Papua. In liberal democracies, such as Western Europe and the US, we have seen 'extraordinary rendition transfer' of terrorist suspects in which the CIA and its European counterparts continuously transported suspects from one hidden place to another for torture to avoid legal consequences (Marty 2007), or indefinite detention in a territory that lies beyond any legal jurisdiction like Guantanamo Bay (ICRC 2007), or applying the latest technologies of torture in Abu Ghraib. Here torture is a private spectacle for the edification of other prisoners within the walls of secret prisons, but it is a project of awesome, unaccountable

Lenses on torture and peacebuilding 219

power of the most powerful of state sovereigns. The spectacle here is not broadcast (intentionally); the intent is that the spectacle is only narrow within that prison with the screams, whispers and glimpses of contorted bodies. Rendition and torture was indeed a sovereignty shuffle coordinated by the greatest state power.

Second, in line with various scholars' critiques (see Chapter 2), Foucault's prognosis of the diminution of public execution, replaced by hidden punishment in the form of prison, has confronted a challenge from Papuan experience. Instead of following a linear and teleological development towards abolition, this study shows the ways in which public torture, as a form of public execution, can coexist with a prison system as part of a criminal justice system.

Third, the fluid identity of the abject resonates with Kristeva's philosophy of 'subject in process'. It contains the notion of ambivalence, progress and dynamics. However, she never resolves the puzzle of whether the abject is able to cross boundaries that confine its non-identity to become an identity and a subject. The notion of abject emphasises the sense of incompleteness. This study reveals that Kristeva's theory of abjection provides an adequate theoretical framework to measure torture as one of the most extreme forms of dehumanisation.

Fourth, in contrast to Foucault's pessimistic view of agency's ability to confront domination, Papua's experience illustrates the effective work of the politics of hope in crafting a better future. Informed by Metz's theory of *memoria passionis*, abjected Papuans not only manage to cross the rigid boundaries between the abject and the subject to reclaim their agency but to reach towards revolt and healing. They are able to integrate themselves into the subject through collective memory, belief systems and social networks. These three components overcome the gap that lies between the abject and the subject. This finding may answer Kristeva's puzzle of the abject as well as Foucault's pessimism.

Practical implications

What is the practical implication of the model of theatre? This model provides an alternative strategy for practitioners, such as caregivers and law-makers, to revisit their strategies in combating torture. First, this study shows how the model of theatre may revisit the conceptualisation of victims and perpetrators as a binary opposition. Victims have been characterised as the voiceless and powerless whereas perpetrators have been depicted as the powerful. In the model of theatre, victims are only one sub-category of survivors among three other categories: agents, warriors and secondary victims. Although victims tend to opt for silence, Papuan experience demonstrates that not every survivor becomes a victim who disengages from public life permanently. Some are silenced, but many raise their voice advocating for justice based on the *memoria passionis*, belief systems and social network (see Chapter 5). Often a strategy of combating torture misunderstands this reality and assumes the role of caregivers as the only actor that can address the problem of torture. Papuan experience demonstrates that torture survivors can become agents for themselves. A new strategy should

220 Lenses on torture and peacebuilding

take into account this potential and translate it into a programme of participatory action.

Second, the model of theatre explains different, and often overlapping, layers of argument that construct perpetrators. The same principle of fluidity applies here and allows perpetrators to cross their boundaries and share the narrative of suffering and witnessing. This process results from constant interactions between perpetrators and survivors and spectators mediated by *memoria passionis*. Therefore there is a real potential to engage with 'whistleblowers' among perpetrators not only to better understand the mindset of perpetrators but more importantly to recruit them to be an agent of change for their *habitus*. This transformation will generate a more fundamental structural reform by employing non-violent methods.

Within the Papua context heavily coloured by the polarisation between 'us and them', this potential poses a great challenge for survivors and spectators to engage with Indonesian state actors because such an approach is often characterised as that of a collaborator or even a traitor (see Kirksey 2012). This model, however, offers a window of opportunity to build allies among enemies.

Third, in a similar way, identifying potential allies among spectators can go beyond 'caregivers', 'beneficiaries' and 'observers'. 'Bystanders' have often been underestimated as potential allies while Rejali's concept of 'civic marker' clearly identifies the complicity of bystanders in torture because the State portrays torture as a duty to protect the public interest. Practitioners may need to put more effort into engaging with bystanders to win more support for survivors in their advocacy for justice. By winning more support from bystanders, practitioners will minimise the space of justification in the name of public interests by which the State can claim legitimacy since fewer people will support violent methods.

Finally, the theatre of torture has disclosed the practice of torture in Papua as a crime against humanity punishable under both Indonesian and international law. Caregivers, law-makers and practitioners can use this study not only to advocate for the rights of the torture survivors but more broadly. They would be able to invoke the spirit of *reformasi* to interrogate the security and public sectors which have been acquiescent to the multilayered narratives of domination.

This approach may provide an alternative strategy for a resistance movement in Papua that begins to break the silence of national and international audience and thus engage bystanders at the national and international level with the birth of the ULMWP in 2014. Similarly, this perspective will help revisit the notion of nation-building for Indonesian society by sharing the *memoria passionis* with survivors as a form of solidarity and collaborating with whistleblowers. This strategy may become an alternative vehicle to strengthen the social cohesion of Indonesia which is more dominated by the state-centric notion of nation-building imposed by the Indonesian central state apparatus. By increasing inclusiveness among citizens, there is more of a chance to address a racial element in attitudes of civic disrespect and to promote equality for Papuans.

Theatre of peacebuilding

To address the problem of torture as networked governance of spectacle, this study has proposed a model of theatre of peacebuilding as a path to the metamorphosis of the theatre of torture. The model helps transform the multilayered narratives of 'domination-suffering-witnessing' as the themes of the theatre of torture into narratives of 'revolt-healing-solidarity' (see Chapter 6). The theatre of peacebuilding is founded on the central role of *memoria passionis*, which has laid the foundation not only to regain agency for survivors but also to rebuild the shattered community post-torture. Institutionalising *memoria passionis*, belief systems and social networks can be conceptualised as TRCP (Truth and Reconciliation Commission for Papua) which in conjunction with human rights commissions and human rights courts can hopefully play an instrumental role in strengthening and transforming local peacebuilding initiatives, as well as maintaining and institutionalising the initiatives in the long run. The idea of transformation and institutionalisation peace initiatives sets out the implications below.

Theoretical implications

The 'theatre of peacebuilding' model has theoretical and practical implications. At the theoretical level, first, Papua's experience provides evidence that institutionalising peacebuilding does not have to wait until conflict is over. Rather, the three key narratives (revolt-healing-solidarity) can be an entry point for institutionalising peace at a stage where state institutions are incapable of establishing truth and justice.

Mary Kaldor's (2006) concept of 'islands of peace' is relevant here. She argues that peace can start with a small network of people in a conflict zone that create a space of peace as a start and broadens the space when more people are involved. This concept resonates with Braithwaite and colleagues' concept of 'redundancy in peacebuilding strategy', which argues that imagined as a network, the weaknesses of a peacebuilding strategy can be compensated for by the strengths of other strategies (Braithwaite *et al.* 2010: 36). Furthermore, the 'theatre of peacebuilding' model may contribute to strengthening the existing 'Papua Land of Peace' model by incorporating new evidence from new empirical studies: violence never escapes our reality but at the same time, peaceful struggle largely paves the way to freedom and emancipation.

Second, restoring broken relationships between perpetrators and survivors with the mediation of spectators resonates with the core principles of restorative justice, which empirically works better than Western criminal justice because it is about 'granting justice, closure, restoration of dignity, transcendence of shame, and healing for victims' (Braithwaite 2002: 45). This restorative justice literature provides a now extensive evidence base from domestic criminal justice in the West that restoring broken relationships can lay a foundation for non-violence. Restorative justice principles relate to the theatre of peacebuilding model in the

222 *Lenses on torture and peacebuilding*

sense that this model connects all actors as a network that works together to transform narratives of 'domination-suffering-witnessing' into a narrative of 'revolt-healing-solidarity'. The emphasis on interdependence of actors who share common humanity characterises the internal dynamics of the theatre of peacebuilding. This element resembles restorative justice principles which seek to repair social connections and enhance communications between offenders and victims (Minow 1998: 92). Thus, justice can be restored through the willingness and genuine commitment of victims and offenders to come to terms with each other mediated by spectators. Peace can be institutionalised through the theatre of peacebuilding by which survivors, perpetrators and spectators genuinely work together and share *memoria passionis*. All of these processes will be best facilitated by a permanent TRC which is patient with truth, justice and reconciliation.

Third, a 'reimagined Papua Land of Peace' that governs the metamorphosis of the theatre of torture to the theatre of peacebuilding not only informs the peacebuilding literature which believes that peace is a process. More importantly, it sheds new light on the torture eradication debate. Instead of focusing on torture merely as a crime against humanity or a legal issue, cascades of peace offer a holistic approach of building peace in that this framework treats torture as a governmentality which needs a different analytical framework. Papua Land of Peace addresses the question of torture in three distinct but inseparable layers: macro-structural, micro-individual and communal. Informed by the Kristevan notion of 'revolt', Papua Land of Peace renews and rehabilitates these three layers of society, culture and polity which have been colonised by the governance of torture. Therefore, drawing on Metz's concept of *memoria passionis*, instead of going through a linear and teleological pathway, the process of metamorphosis from the theatre of torture to the theatre of peacebuilding is characterised by interruption, revolt and networking. The process undertakes an open-ended journey in the *longue durée* which might be crystallised into a TRCP.

Fourth, the spectrum of pyramidal enforcement laid the ground for a model to integrate restorative justice (TRCP) and punitive criminal law (human rights commission and human rights court). This integrative model may contribute to a theoretical answer to the ongoing debate between the restorative and retributive justice camps. The revised Papua Land of Peace framework illustrates that both forms of justice are deemed necessary and complementary to dismantle the governmentality of torture in the long run. The emphasis of the limitless timeframe is crucial. It allows the process of unravelling the web of power relations of domination without being subject to any time constraints. Further, the limitless timeframe will confront arguments to have immediate reconciliation and even forgiveness from victims to perpetrators. In the broader context of peacebuilding in Papua, the *longue durée* might allow the Papua Land of Peace framework to anticipate multi-polar violence which most likely will confront the peacebuilding trajectory.

Practical implications

For peacebuilders, the 'theatre of peacebuilding' model provides an alternative strategy for the existing peacebuilding movements in Papua that are largely characterised by two major elements: (1) focusing on engagement with state institutions and (2) preoccupation with the present. First, this study shows that creating 'islands of peace' or 'peace zones' is an alternative strategy for peacebuilders in Papua to explore further the three existing fundamental elements to build peace in Papua. These all belong to non-state institutions: *memoria passionis*, belief systems and social networks. This approach may complement the strategy of engaging state institutions responsible for truth-seeking and justice since it puts the emphasis on the capacity of non-state institutions to maximise their own resources. Creating 'islands of peace' may allow peacebuilders to use empirical evidence of the ways in which peace sometimes begins at a micro level. This approach is challenging for a society in a conflict situation because they may have exhausted most of their energy to stop conflicts. Therefore, they may not have sufficient energy left. On the other hand, the strategy of crafting 'islands of peace' may allocate limited energy more effectively.

TRCP may help facilitate the creation of islands of peace by crafting peace at different localities starting from grassroots communities and up to state institutions as we have seen in Aceh, Maluku, Poso, Bougainville and Timor-Leste. In this respect, TRCP can be a promising path in implementing the Papua Land of Peace framework. TRCP would have to take into account and address the reality of multi-polar violence and domination, while implementing the nine pillars and cascades of peace. In other words, TRCP will help create islands of peace until they are firmly established, owned and maintained by local communities. This process also has the ambition of progressive dismantling of the theatre of torture.

Second, informed by Chenoweth and Stephan's (2011) quantitative study of the high success rate of non-violent resistance compared to armed struggle, this study has identified competing and sometimes overlapping movements between non-violent and armed struggle in Papua. Therefore, peacebuilders need to ensure key elements that guarantee non-violent campaigns lead to genuine emancipation: (1) broad participation beyond Papuans, (2) Papuan leadership, which is now united under ULMWP, maintains strict discipline in employing non-violent strategies throughout the struggle and transition period, and (3) mobilising and consolidating national and international solidarity.

Third, the model allows peacebuilders to anticipate a post-conflict scenario in the future in which they may have to confront issues of eradicating authoritarian legacies, holding perpetrators accountable for past human rights abuses and redress to survivors. The model may allow non-state actors to learn from their own experiences of creating 'peace zones' at the micro level that can be generalised to a more structural level. Based on their own experiences of creating 'peace zones', they may be able to transform and institutionalise peacebuilding in a post-conflict situation. *Memoria passionis* may help to establish truth-telling processes that accommodate genuine apologies and remorse offered by perpetrators.

224 *Lenses on torture and peacebuilding*

Belief systems may lay the ground for forgiveness by which peacebuilders may be able to deal with the issue of retribution when the weak become the powerful that seek vendettas. Exploring social cohesion may contribute to broadening solidarity and healing fractures among the winners, the losers and the bystanders.

Final reflections

Torture is theatre in Papua. That is our conclusion. But in a militarised Papua, a militarised state shapes, sorts and regulates the audience of torture. The audience is confined to the oppressed people of Papua. This is an audience of millions compared to a regulated audience of hundreds inside prisons like Abu Ghraib. But the principle is the same in that the target audience of the spectacle is regulated by militarised state power. This decidedly statist part of the central conclusions is where the book departs from the otherwise useful Foucauldian analysis of capillaries of largely non-state power. Both cases – when the military regulation of the narrowed audience of state torture broke down in Abu Ghraib and the video of torture in Papua – illustrate the potential for peace advocates to flip the theatre of torture to a theatre of abhorrence for violence. Just as in Foucault's *Discipline and Punish* torture is the theatre of the king, in Papua torture is the theatre of the military. Therefore, torture is a structural product of militarisation of Papua by the Indonesian state. That structural phenomenon can be exposed by a movement like Papua Land of Peace that reveals the illegality and immorality of the phenomenon.

The militarised state produces, constructs and regulates Papua as a 'state of exception' (see Agamben 2005; Cribb 2011); a site in which law, human rights and morality collapse as in Abu Ghraib or Guantanamo Bay. While the powers of the Indonesian state and the United States are remarkably different in many respects, they deploy the same principle in that they construct and regulate their enemies as the abject, a non-identity, deprived of all legal and human rights and moral protections. As a result, not only very limited parties show inclinations to engage with Papua but also those who dare to engage would be treated as a non-identity and would suffer the same consequences as the abject. Just as in Kristeva's *Powers of Horror* where the abject is considered threatening to the stability of subjects, in Indonesia's state policy and in any foreign relations with Indonesia, Papua is considered threatening their stability.

Although the militarised state constructs the abject as an incomplete identity, the state has never been able to completely deconstruct the abject. On the contrary, an element of resistance embedded in the abject proportionally grows in parallel to the escalation of militarisation. Therefore, the more militarisation there is in Papua, the more resistance grows. Likewise, the more US aggression there is, the more there will be terrorist attacks against the US presence worldwide. As a result, a vicious cycle of either violence or peaceful revolt is created and nurtured.

As many elements within civil society inside and outside Papua have called for, demilitarisation would be a stepping-stone to break the cycle of violence and to institutionalise peace. There are two reasons why demilitarisation is a *conditio sine qua non*. First, demilitarisation in quantity would reduce numeric figures of military presence as a structural factor that produces torture. This step may contribute to broadening 'peace zones' as we have seen in many experiences of post-conflict situations, such as in the Aceh context after the Helsinki agreement, Bougainville and Timor-Leste. Second, demilitarisation in quality would address structural problems, including the legacies of the *habitus* of impunity embedded in the Indonesian security forces as well as Brimob; the overall security and defence policy in Papua to comply with the rule of law, human rights and respect for local cultures; investing large resources in community policing in Papua to protect public order, the rule of law and civic respect among all inhabitants of Papua; and engaging with the local military commanders, who are left as the minimal reserve to protect the international borders, to contribute to broadening peace zones. By institutionalising peace facilitated by a permanent TRC, a new theatre of peacebuilding is a fragile possibility.

This study is just the beginning of our understanding of the nature, the logic, the technologies and the implications of state oppression upon one of the most neglected indigenous communities in the world. This is just like a piece of a big mosaic that needs many more pieces to eventually capture a full picture. Therefore, further research needs to be done to explore the broader aspects of oppression that constitute crimes against humanity under international law, notably killings and disappearances, to reconstruct the architecture of Indonesian state oppression in Papua. Furthermore, a comparative analysis of Papua's experience and equivalent experiences from Aceh and East Timor may contribute to further assessing broader patterns of Indonesian state oppression against rebel regions. Such research may also delve into the impacts of long-term militarisation on the production of meanings and values, the questions of identity politics, public consciousness and a sense of morality, which go beyond the legal and political spheres. Together, these various elements would strengthen existing peacebuilding scholarship and practice.

References

Agamben, G. 2005, 'The State of Exception', in A. Norris (ed.), *Politics, Metaphysics and Death: Essays on Giorgio Agamben's Homo Sacer*, Duke University Press, Durham, NC and London, pp. 284–97.

Braithwaite, J. 2002, *Restorative Justice and Responsive Regulation*, Oxford University Press, Oxford and New York.

Braithwaite, J., Braithwaite, V., Cookson, M. and Dunn, L. 2010, *Anomie and Violence: Non-Truth and Reconciliation in Indonesian Peacebuilding*, ANU Press, Canberra.

Bruck, C. 2016, 'The Guantanamo Failure: Who's Really to Blame?', *The New Yorker*, August 1.

Chenoweth, E. and Stephan, M.J. 2011, *Why Civil Resistance Works: The Strategic Logic of Nonviolent Conflict*, Columbia University Press, New York.

Cohen, S. 2001, *States of Denial: Knowing about Atrocities and Suffering*, Polity Press, Cambridge.

226 *Lenses on torture and peacebuilding*

Cribb, R. 2011, 'A System of Exemptions: Historicizing State Illegality in Indonesia', in E. Aspinal and G.V. Klinken (eds), *The State and Illegality in Indonesia*, KITLV Press, Leiden, pp. 31–44.

Foucault, M. 1980, *Power/Knowledge Selected Interviews and Other Writings 1972–1977*, The Harvester Press, Sussex.

Hutchings, P.J. 2013, 'Entertaining Torture, Embodying Law', *Cultural Studies*, vol. 27, no. 1, pp. 49–71.

ICRC 2007, *ICRC Report on the Treatment of Fourteen 'High Value Detainees' in CIA Custody*, The International Committee of the Red Cross Regional Delegation for United States and Canada, Washington, DC.

Kaldor, M. 2006, *New and Old Wars: Organized Violence in a Global Era*, Polity, Cambridge.

Kirksey, S.E. 2012, *Freedom in Entangled Worlds: West Papua and the Architecture of Global Power*, Duke University Press, Durham, NC and London.

Marty, D. 2007, *Secret Detentions and Illegal Transfers of Detainees Involving Council of Europe Member States: Second Report*, Parliamentary Assembly of Council of Europe, Brussels.

Minow, M. 1998, *Between Vengeance and Forgiveness*, Beacon Press, Boston, MA.

Rejali, D. 2010, 'Modern Torture as a Civic Marker: Solving a Global Anxiety with a New Political Technology', *Journal of Human Rights*, vol. 2, pp. 153–71.

Index

Page numbers in *italics* denote tables, those in **bold** denote figures.

100 team 68–9, 77, 83, 183, 100 Papuan leaders 41
141st meridian 50

abduction method 137; induction 137; deduction 137
Abepura case 83, 123, 156, 198
abject: abjected Papuans 36, 56, 69, 72–3, 78–9, 99, 102, 121, 126, 180, 191, 200, 202, 219; abjected zone 34, 99, 199, 120, 154, 216; abjection 9, 16–17, 17, 22–3, 31–6, 41–3, 49, 51–2, 56, 63, 65–6, 68–9, 72–3, 76–9, 82, 91, 94, 102, 104, 106, 112, 119–21, 124, 126, 130, 134, 139, 147, 154–5, 168, 170, 180, 183, 186, 191, 200–3, 207, 216, 217, 219, 224; defilement 104; disavowed Papuans 49; disgust, impurity 99, 102, 104, 170; non-existence 32, 36; nonperson 32
Abu Ghraib 20, 90, 111, 124, 125n1, 218, 224
accountability 3, 129, 188, 190, 201, 203, 205, 205–6; civil monetary penalties 126n9, 205, 205–6; imprisonment 64, 97, 124, 126n9, 129n32, 187, 206, 216; pyramid of accountability 205, 205; pyramidal enforcement 205, 222; remedial investigation 205, 205–6; subpoena investigation 123, 198, 206
Act of Free Choice 2, 55, 57–60, 79, 81n15, 150, 159; internment 58, 60
Afghanistan 61, 84n45, 170n17
Akhavan, Payam 194, 210
ALDP (*Aliansi Demokrasi untuk Papua*) 8, 70
Algeria 170n17, 12, 20

Alleg, Henri 170n17, 174
Ambon 68, 103, 153
America 14, 45n17, 14, 52, 76, 79, 125n5, 133, 174, 176
Améry, Jean 127n20, 130, 147, 174
AMP (*Aliansi Mahasiswa Papua*) 78, 190
ANC political party: apartheid 194, 196
Ancient Greek 10, 12, 215
Anderson, Ben 18n1, 18, 130
Angkasa 63
anomie 16
Arendt, Hannah 18n4, 92, 171n22
Argentina's Dirty War 43n7, 59, 93
armed struggle 16, 163, 191, 223
art of governance 215
Ashley, Matthew J. 36
audience 2, 14, 44n7, 59, 68, 71, 73, 75, 90, 93, 124, 141–2, 158, 161, 163, 165, 167–8, 183, 190, 200–3, 216, 220, 224; '*implied audience*' 44
Aukerman, Miriam 195
Auschwitz 23–4, 37, 39, 40–1, 91, 130, 174
Australia x, xiv, 4, 7, 19, 75, 76, 81n12, 82n27–82n28, 82n31, 83n33, 82n45, 82n46, 85, 86, 127n15, 128n129, 129n36, 129n7, 160, 170n17, 173n39, 173n40, 211
Awom, Ferry 55

Ballard, Chris 8, 50, 66, 73, 81n10, 85
Barisan Merah Putih 167
Batam 76
Beanal, Tom 68
belief systems 17, 170n11, 219, 221–4
Benjamin, Walter 37–8
Bentham, Jeremy 12
Berlin 122

228 *Index*

Bewani 58
BIA (*Badan Intelijen ABRI*) 122, 130n40
Biak 15, 19, 51, 58, 63, 68, 72, 82n22,
   83n37, 88, *98*, 143, 144
BIN (*Badan Intelijen Nasional*) 157
Bintuni *98*
Bisset, Alison 195
Blaskić judgement 166
Bloch, Ernst 37
bombing 57, 61, **62**, 81n11
Bonhoeffer, Dietrich 24, 44n13
Boot, Machteld 116
border crosser 65
Borowai 153
Bosnia Hersegovina 102
Bougainville 19, 188, 198, 211, 223, 225
Boutros-Ghali, Boutros 14
BPUPKI xii, 85
Braithwaite, John x, 14–16, 18–19, 116,
   130, 134, 162, 173n40, 174, 177, 183,
   187–9, 195–8, 202, 205–6, 208n17,
   209n26, 211, 221, 225
Braithwaite, Valerie 130, 134, 162,
   173n44, 174, 210n32
Brimob 2, 70–1, 74–5, 83n36, 148–9, 206,
   209n24, 225
Brussels 122, 212, 226
brutality 9, 17, 25, 53, 74–5, 80, 90–1,
   104, 107, 119, 123, 143–5, 160, 166,
   168, 173n41, 214, 216–17
Budiarjo, Ali 53, 85
Bülent Diken 104
bystander effect 160

Cambodia 194
Canberra 18, 19, 46, 84n45, 85, 86, 87,
   126n6, 130–1, 174, 211, 212, 225
caregivers 3, 17, 138, 163–4, 166–7,
   170n14, 172n33, 202–3, 216, 219–20
Cassese, Antonio 194, 211
CAT 11, 18n5, 92, 110, 128n26
Catholic Church 5, 43n1, 66–7, 82n30,
   148, 169n5, 170n14
CAVR 102, 109, 119, 129n38, 167, 188
CDA 135
Chauvel, Richard xi, 18n1, 19, 54, 68, 85
Chenoweth, Erica 177, 187
Chile 105, 116, 197
Cholil, Muhamad 5, 19, 80n5, 85
Christianity 38, 40, 45n16, 45n17, 51;
   Christian faith 24, 36–8; Christian
   theology 41; political theology,
   Christians 30n2, 36–8, 40, 41–2, 44n24;
   theology of revolt 41–2, 177

CIDT 109–10, 128n27
citizens: non-citizens 10, 12, 65, 141–2,
   148, 160, 170n7, 170n14, 173n41, 215,
   217–18, 220
Cohen, Stanley 93, 130, 152, 165, 174,
   217, 225
Colombo 37, 39, 41, 44n12, 44n14, 45n16,
   45
colonising public space 60
conflict: post-conflict 5, 6, 14, 17, 27, 59,
   77, 79, 94, 105, 126n6, 127n21, 157,
   162, 167, 171n30, 177, 182, 183, 186–8,
   190–1, 194, 197–8, 207, 208n11, 221,
   223, 225
Cookson, Michael x, 18n1, 19, 83n35, 85,
   130, 174, 208n4, 211, 225
Crawfurd, John 50
Cribb, Robert 81n9, 85, 173n41, 174, 224,
   226
crimes against humanity 70, 74, 83n35,
   92, 93, 95, 116–17, 127n17, 127n22,
   129n33, 129n38, 216, 225; enemy of
   humankind 217; extrajudicial killing
   70, 119, 123; systematic 12, 25, 83n35,
   105, 116–17, 129n38, 150, 155,
   171n26, 216
crimes of obedience: *authorisation* 84n45,
   155; *dehumanisation* 104, 140, 155,
   219; policy formation 151, 154–6;
   policy implementation 154, 156;
   routinisation 155, 172n31
criminalisation 114
CTF (Commission for Truth and
   Friendship) 129n38
culture change 184, 204, 208n15
culture of violence 75, 120, 182

Damiens, Robert 13, 29, 109
Darley, John M. 125n5
Darmono, Bambang 77
Davis, Tracy 134
Deal, Terrence 208n15
degrading and inhumane treatment 11,
   18–19, 87, 109, 111, 128n27, 132
demilitarisation 181, 204, 207, 207n3, 224,
   225
democratic reform 194; democratisation
   112
Democratic Republic of Congo 120
Dershowitz, Alan 13
Dewulf, Steven 92
dialogue 15, 38, 68–9, 77, 121, 157,
   179n5, 182–5, 187–9, 191, 199–201,
   207, 208n11; comprehensiveness 183,

158; concreteness 183; conditions of dialogue 183; peacefulness 183; respect 6, 8–9, 16
DMP (*Dewan Musyawarah Penentuan Pendapat Rakyat*) 58, **59**
Dok VIII Atas 63
domination 17, 25–9, 31, 43–3, 60, 65, 78–80, 81n8, 91, 103, 105, 111, 117–18, 122–3, 129n35, 134–6, **137**, 138–9, 148, 149–52, 154, 161–2, 165–9, 173n43, 181–6, 192, **192–3**, 194, 199–200, 203–5, 207, 215, 217–23; rationality of 56, 168, 181, 216; technology 9–10, 12, 17, 27, 38, 56, 59–61, 63–4, 68, 70, 73, 91, 95, 99–110, 124, 126n13, 208n15, 215
Doreri 98
Drooglever, Pieter 50
Dutch colonial power 49, 51, 54

Earl, George Windsor 50
East Timor 3, 76, 81n10, 87, 89, 119, 120, 167, 173, 225; *see also* Timor Leste
Echeverria, Gabriella 201, 211
Eichmann, Adolf 92, 171n22, 171n24
electric shocks 58, 63
elements of torture 168
Elizabeth Stanley 105
ELSHAM (*Lembaga Studi dan Advokasi HAM*) 8, 15, 70, 114–15
Elsham Irian Jaya 15; *see also* ELSHAM
Eluay, Theys 72, 88
emancipation 25–3, 37, 39, 114, 149, 164, 165, 168, 180, 184–5, 208n7, 221, 223
Enarotali 1
enemies of the state 155
England 20, 50
Ericson, Richard V. 186, 204, 213
Evangelical Christian Church in Tanah Papua 15, 66–7, 87, 169n45; *see also* GKI
extraordinary rendition transfer 218

Fak-Fak 52, 58, 78, 83n33, 87, *98*, 132
Faleomavaega, Eni 76
Flyvbjerg, Bent 4, 19
Foucault, Michel 3–4, 10–11, 13, 16, 19, 22–30, 35, 40, 42–3, 43n4, 46–9, 59, 65, 79, 86, 90, 94, 96, 109, 119, 122, 134, 148, 169n1, 173n41, 174
fragility 25, 40, 178, 186
Frankfurt School 26, 38, 43n4
Fraser, Nancy 34
freedom 26, 27, 39, 56–7, 60–1, 65, 69,

81n11, 112, 116, 122, 129n30, 139, 146, 148, 168, 178–81, 184–5, 221
Freeman, Mark 174, 176, 194–5, 197, 199, 211
Freeport mine 74, 112, 115
Front Pembela Islam 173n41

Galtung, Johan 14, 19
Geertz, Clifford 4
Geissler, Johan 169n6
genealogy 15, 17, 43, 182; definition 49
Geneva 87, 122, 129n33, 217
genocide 10, 18n4, 33, 127n17, 154, 172n36
Genovese, Kitty 125n5
Genyem 153
Gerlach, Christian 187, 211
Giay, Benny 8, 42, 179n8
GKI (Gereja Kristen Injili) in Tanah Papua 1, 8, 45, 66, 169n6
Glazebrook, Diana 23, 46, 66, 86, 147, 174
Goffmann, Erving 135, 174
governmentality 17, 24, 27–8, 31, 42–3, 44n8, 49, 52, 60, 65, 79, 105–6, 110, 120, 148, 177–8, 182, 184, 201–3, 206, 207, 216, 218, 222; mode of governance 17, 25, 28, 31, 42, 49, 55, 79, 107, 126n6, 134, 161, 165, 166, 168, 177, 215
GPK (*Gerombolan Pengacau Keamanan*) 82n29
Grassberg 52
Graziano, Frank 43n7, 59
Greenberg, Karen J
Guantanamo Bay 170n17, 216, 219, 224
Gutierrez, Gustavo 36, 45n17

Habibie, Baharuddin J. 3, 41, 67–8, 77, 83n35–83n36, 183
Hague 8, 53, 83n40, 89, 122
Hamilton, Lee 154
Hatta, Mohammad 52–3
Hayner, Priscilla 196
Herman, Judith 144, 146
Hernawan, Budi i, ii, iii, iv, 2, 8, 15, 20, 23, 45n18, 46, **59**, **62**, 68, **69**, 73, **74**, 76–8, 86, 91, 94, **95–6**, *97*, **98**, **101–2**, **107**, *108*, **112**, **115**, **118–19**, **121**, 131, 190–1, 212–13
Hicks, David 170n17
Hindess, Barry 25–7, 46
holistic 7, 22–4, 42, 177, 183, 204
Holocaust 18n4, 24, 36, 92, 160; Nazi concentration camp 160, 173n43

230 *Index*

Howard, John 75–6
human rights 1, 2, 3, 5, 7–8, 11, 12, 16, 43n1, 65–7, 71–3, 75–6, 78, 80, 83n37, 91, 92, 110, 112, 121–3, 130n43, 142, 152, 156–7, 160–1, 163, 166, 181, 189, 191, 194–5, 197–9, 201, **205**, 206–7, 207, 208n11, 209n21–209n22, 210n33, 216–17, 221–5; violation 67, 75, 102, 128n27, 129n33, 152
Humphrey, Michael 163, 199
Hussein, Farid 77
Hutchings, Peter J. 218, 226

ICC (International Criminal Court) 92, 209n19, 216; ad hoc tribunal 130n43, 194, 198; hybrid tribunal 194
ICRC (International Committee of Red Cross) 67, 218
ICTR (International Criminal Tribunal for Rwanda) 92, 116, 117, 124, 127n18, 216
ICTY (International Criminal Tribunal for Yugoslavia) 92, 95, 116, 117, 124, 127n17, 129n32–129n33, 216
ideal type 135–7, 144, 147, 150, 169n2
Ifar Gunung 60, 82n19
Ignatieff, Michael 196
impunity 3, 9, 13, 66, 83n37, 112, 119–20, 122–4, 129n35, 129n38, 130n43, 161, 194, 198, 202–3, 210n33, 210n35, 215–16, 218, 225
incarceration 64, 71; *see also* prison
Indonesianisasi 208n9
intel 7, 185; *see also* intelligence
intelligence 10, 13, 17, 55–6, 84n47, 107, 122, 130n40, 150, 157–8, 166–7, 171n23, 201
international human rights law 92, 112, 210n33, 216–17
Iowara camp 148
IPWP (International Parliamentarians for West Papua) 2
Irian Barat 19, 54, 81n6, 82n16, 85, 88; *see also* Papua
Irian Jaya 1, 15, 19, 69, 85, 87–9, 132; *see also* Papua
island of civility 203
islands of peace 221, 223

Jakarta 1, 7–8, 18–19, 20–1, 57, 58, 67–8, 73–5, 77–8, 81n9, 82n30, 83n37, 83n41, 84n48, 84n50, 859, 97, 130–2, 156, 159, 172n35, 173n41, 175, 182, 183, 191, 199, 207, 208n11, 208n14, 210n19, 211–13

Janis, Irving L. 171n30
Java 51, 63, 74, 80n4, 81n9, 85, 100, 143, 151, 153, 157, 172n32
Jaringan Damai Papua 15, 77, 184
Jayapura viii, 1,-2, 9, 15, 19, 20–1, 43, 46, 55, 58, 60, 63, 66–9, **69**, 70, 72–3, 78, 82n17–82n19, 83n37, 84n49, 85–8, 98, 114, 130n39, 131–2, 142, 148, 153, 172n37, 178, 191, 208n7, 209n24, 211, 213–14, 218
JDP (*Jaringan Damai Papua*) 184
Jilani, Hina 76
justice: delivery of justice 194; prosecutorial justice, punitive justice 189, 194; restorative justice 188, 195–5, 206, 209, 221–2; transitional justice 3, 5, 8–9, 11, 13, 15, 16, 29, 37, 43n1, 45n15, 71, 73–4, 95, 97, 119, 121, 139, 141, 142, 144, 156, 157, 163, 172n33, 173n41, **178**, 179, 182, 185, 188, 189, 190, 192, **192**, 194–9, 201, 206, 207n1, 209n26, 219–23

Kaisiepo, Frans 52
Kaisiepo, Viktor 191
Kaldor, Mary 221
Kalisosok 63–4
Karstedt, Susanne 177, 186
Kelman, Herbert C. 154
Kennedy, Allen 208n15
Kennedy, John F. 54, 81n7, 186, 208n15, 211
Khmer Rouge regime 194
Kimbim 61
KINGMI 1
Kirksey, Eben 18n1, 20, 66, 68, 70–1, 73, 87, 220, 226
Kirsch, Stuart 63, 82n24, 87, 99, 102–3, 106, 131, 147, 173n40, 175
Kiunga 7, 89
KNPB (Komite Nasional Papua Barat) 2, 78, 190
Kobakma 61
Kodam (Komando Daerah Militer) 54, 55, 58, 63, 80n5, 81n16, 141, 150
kodim (*Komando Distrik Militer*) 58, 73, 106, 120, 142
Komnas HAM (Komisi Nasional Hak Asasi Manusia) 6, 8, 66, 70, 72, 74–5, 80, 83n35, 115, 122–3, 156, 198–200
KontraS (*Komisi untuk Orang Hilang dan Tindak Kekerasan*) xiii, 87, 89
kopassus (*Komando Pasukan Khusus*) 63, 72, 82n25, 83n40, 185, 206

Index 231

Kopkamtib 56–7, 65
korban 169n3, 173n41, 210n28, 131; *see also* victim
koreri 52; *see also* messianic movements
Korowai 126n14
Kotaraja 2
Kristeva, Julia 22–5, 31–5, 40, 42–3, 44n11, 46–7, 49, 79, 87, 91, 94, 104, 121, 131, 148, 169n1, 175, 180
Kwalik, Kelly 66

Langbein, John 11–12, 20
Larson-Stoa, Deborah 146
Latané, Bibb 125n5
Lausten, Carsten 104
Lederach, John P
Levi, Primo 160, 173n43
Linfield, Susan 165, 175
LIPI (Lembaga Ilmu Pengetahuan Indonesia) 77, 184–5, 208n11
London 2, 18–19, 20–1, 45–7, 85–8, 102, 130–3, 174–6, 211–13, 225–6
longue durée 187–9, 197, 222
LP3BH Manokwari 8, 70, 87, 115, 132

Makassar 2, 54, 78, 83n37, 123, 153
Makki 61
Malkki, Liisa 147, 175
Maluku 51, 89, 198, 223
Mambesak 66, 80
Mandatjan, Barend 55; Arfak leaders 55
Manokwari 2, 8, 52, 55, 58, 70–1, 78, 81n15, 86–7, 132, 169n6
Marxism 25
Masoka, Aristoteles 72
mass atrocities 186, 195; mass violence 187
Matza, David 172n31
McAfee, Nöelle 32
McArthur, Elizabeth 109
McClintock, Anne 31–4, 47
McLeod, Jason 185
Meister, Robert 158
Melanesian Spearhead Group 78, 80, 191
Melbourne 86, 88, 174
memoria passionis 22, 37–9, 41–2, 144, 146–7, 165
memory 17, 18n1, 22, 24, 35, 37, 38, 39, 41–2, 44n15, 45n16, 60, 110, 144, 145–7, 149, 159, 162, 165, 170n15, 193, 219; memory of freedom 39; memory of suffering *see* memoria passionis
Méndez, Juan 110, 128n27
merdeka 41, 53, 61, 68, 78, 81n6, 141–2, 157–9, 161, 167, 180–4, 186, 204, 215

methods of torture: deprivation of basic needs 107, *108*, 110, 128n24; electric shock 9, 101, 107, *108*, 110; electrocution 103, 106, 142–3; mock execution *108*; parading 109–10; psychological torture 58, 109, 128n24; public humiliation *108*, 109, 110, 114; pulling out fingernails *108*, 109; solitary confinement 64, *108*, 110, 128n27; starvation *108*, 110; stripping 101, **102**, 105, *108*, 109; waterboarding 109, 111, 128n26
Metz, Johann Baptist 22–5, 35–43, 43n3, 44n12, 44n14, 44n15, 45n16, 45n17, 45–7, 94, 159, 165, 169n1, 174–5, 186
Milgram, Stanley 171n24
military operation 5, 57, 60, 63, 67, 82n21, 82n31, 159
militia 79, 83n36, 107, **107**, 167; recruiting proxies 79
Minow, Martha 197, 212, 222, 226
Morning Star flag 15, 68, **69**, 116
motivational postures: capitulation 16, 162–3, 173n43, 209n25; commitment 11, 12, 15–16, 57, 65, 77, 134, 156, 161–4, 179n6, 191, 194, 203, 209n25, 222; disengagement 147, 162, 164–6, 173n43, 209n25; game playing 162, 164; resistance 3, 15–17, 23–7, 35–6, 40–2, 44n13, 45n17, 49, 55, 57, 65–6, 77, 80, 82n28–82n29, 95, 123, 126n8, 140, 144–5, 149, 160, 162–5, 170n17, 177, 183–4, 187, 190–3, 202, 218, 220, 223–4
MOU Helsinki 3
MPR (Majelis Permusyawaratan Rakyat) 56, 67
MRP (Majelis Rakyat Papua) 73, 103
MSG (Melanesian Spearhead Group) 78–9, 191, 202
multi-polar violence 183, 187, 189, 192, **192**, 195, 199, 204, 207, 222–3
Münninghoff, Herman 66
musyawarah 57–8, 69; *Musyawarah Besar (Mubes)* 69

Nabire 58, 70, 97
narrative of domination 136, 138, 154, 162, 165–8, 186, **193**, 194, 203, 217; denial 76, 79, 93, 136, **137**, 150, 152–4, 156, 160–3, 165–6, 168, 171n26, 171n28, 172n31, 173n41, 198, 202, 217; *habitus* 5, 80n2, 100, 105, 109, 129n35, 136, **137**, 138, 150–4, 156, 162–3,

232 *Index*

narrative of domination *continued*
165–6, 168, 171n26–171n27, 218, 220,
225; pleasure 136, **137**, 138, 150, 153–4,
156, 162–3, 165–8, 218; proceduralism
81n8, 136, **137**, 138, 150, 154–6, 162–3,
165–6, 168, 171n22, 172n35
narrative of suffering 136, 138–9, 161,
163–5, **193**, 194, 220; agent 17, 26,
33–4, 84n47, 91–2, 104, 107, 122,
129n34, 136, **137**, 137–9, 142–7,
149–50, 155, 161, 163–4, 166–8,
171n23–171n24, 177, 179, 200, 203–4,
219–20; secondary victim 17, 136, **137**,
138, 147, 149, 161, 164, 168, 219;
victim 1, 3, 5–7, 15, 17, 36, 38, 73–4,
81n15, 82n17, 83n37–83n38, 91, 95, 96,
102, 105, 110, 117, 123–4, 125n3,
126n8, 136, **137**, 137–9, 141, 143,
145–7, 149, 153, 155, 156, 157, 159,
161, 163, 164, 166, 168–9, 172n31,
173n41, 182, 187, 194–5, 198–9,
209n19, 210n33, 215, 217, 219, 221–2;
warrior 17, 136, **137**, 138–9, 141–2,
146–7, 149, 159, 161, 164, 168, 170n7,
177, 219
narrative of wandering **137**; narrative of
forgetting **137**; script 60, 135–42,
144–68, 170n7, 170n16, 171n26,
172n35, 173n43
narrative of witnessing: beneficiary 136,
137, 138, 142, 156, 158–61, 164–5,
167–8, 173n43; bystander 17, 93, 123,
125n5, 136, **137**, 138, 156, 160–1,
164–6, 168, 173n40, 173n43, 202–3,
216, 220, 224; caregiver 3, 17, 136, 148,
138, 156, 157, 161, 163–8, 170n14,
171n19, 172n32–172n34, 177, **193**, 194,
200, 202–3, 216, 219–20; observer 17,
77–8, 83n41, 84n48, 96, 136, **137**, 138,
156–8, 161, 164–8, 172n35, 177, 191,
199, 202–3, 216, 220
nation-building 220
Netherlands 4, 7, 50–3, 79, 89, 130n41,
169n4, 170n16, 172n32, 172n35, 180
Netherlands East Indies 51–3
Netherlands New Guinea *see* Papua
New Guinea 50, 180; *see also* Papua
New York Agreement 54, 57–8
New York City 125n5
Nightingale, Elena 146, 174, 176
NKRI (Negara Kesatuan Republik
Indonesia): nonnegotiable price 182
non-violent resistance 16, 66, 80, 177, 183,
187, 190–1, 223

Nowak, Manfred 76, 109

Obama, Barrack 217
Obano 52
Oceanic Negro 50
Office for Justice and Peace of the Catholic
Diocese of Jayapura 43n1; *see also* SKP
Jayapura
Ondawame, John 55, 61, 64, 82n28, 87
OPM (Organisasi Papua Merdeka)
(Organisasi Papua Merdeka) 1, 8, 55,
57–8, 61, 63–4, 66–7, 70, 75, 80,
82n26, 82n28, 82n31, 83n40, 84n52,
94, 95, 99, 106, 111, 112, 124, 141,
142, 150, 155, 157, 163–4, 171n23,
171n30, 182, 215
Osborne, Robin 5, 20, 52, 88
Otsus 49, 72, 73, **74**, 75, 79, 83n39, **115**,
116, 189, 191
Ottow, Carl 169n6

pain: inflicting pain 1, 9–11, 13, 15, 17, 29,
31, 65, 79, 103, 110, 118, 120, 127n17,
139, 146, 153, 168, 216, 218; inscription
of pain 15
Palu 78
panopticon 4, 14
Papua factionalism 172n32, 191
Papua i, ii, iii, vii, viii, ix, x, xii–iii, 1, 2, 3,
4, 5, 6, 7, 8, 9, 10–18, 18n1, 18n3, 19,
20–5, 27–8, 34–7, 39, 41–3, 43n6, 46,
49, 50–9, 60–9, 70–9, **74**, 80,
80n1–80n2, 80n5, 81n8, 81n11,
81n14–81n15, 82n20, 82n24,
82n27–82n28, 82n30, 80n32, 83n33,
83n35–83n37, 83n39, 84n44–84n45,
84n47, 84n49, 84n50, 84n52–84n53,
85–9, 90–1, 93–7, *97*, *98*, 99, 100–9,
110–12, **113**, 114–19, **114**, 120–5, **121**,
126n6, 126n7, 126n10–126n14,
127n14–127n16, 127n18, 128n23,
130n42, 130–2, 134–9, 140–2, 144–9,
150–9, 160–9, 169n4, 169n6,
170n7–170n8, 170n10, 170n12–170n16,
171n20, 171n23, 171n25–171n26,
171n28, 172n32–172n35,
172n37–172n38, 173n40, 174–5, 177–9,
178, 180–9, 190–5, 197–9, 200–7, **205**,
207n2–207n3, 208n4–208n5, 208n7,
208n9, 208n11–208n13,
209n20–209n24, 210n32, 211–19,
220–7
Papua Land of Peace 4, 15–17, 43, 49, 77,
80, 121, 125, 169, 177–8, **178**, 180,

182–92, 195, 202–3, 207, 214, 217, 221–4
Papua New Guinea xiii, 7, 46, 57, 65, 82n22, 85–6, 89, 126n10, 141, 154, 158, 174, 188
Papua Peace Network *see* Jaringan Damai Papua
Papua Road Map 208n11
Papuan Church leaders 2, 70, 77, 184, 190
Papuan Congress 69, 81n15, 114, **114**, 159
Papuan refugees 4, 7, 57, 65–6, 145–8, 164, 169n4, 170n14
Papuan resistance movements 55
Papuan Spring 69
Papuan torture video 214, 216
Papuanisasi 181, 208n7, 208n9
paradigm of evil: banality of evil 10, 92
PDP (Presidium Dewan Papua) 69, 72
peace 3–4, 8–9, 14–17, 24, 43, 43n1, 49, 68, 77, 80, 121, 125, 162, 169, 177–8, **178**, 179–80, 182–92, **192**, 193, **193**, 194–6, 202–3, 207, 208n11, 206n16, 209n24, 210n34, 214, 217, 221–5; definition 5, 6, 9, 14, 29, 177, 127n17, 128n27, 157–8
peace agreement 77, 162, 184
peace zone 223, 225
peacebuilding: cascades of peace 192, 193, **193**, 202, 207, 222–3; definition 14–6; pyramid of peacebuilding 4, 9, 14–18, 43, 165, 167, 173n40, 177, 183–4, 186–8, 190, 192, **192**, 193, **193**, 194, 195–6, 199–200, 202–3, 205, 207, 208n16, 210n34, 214, 221–4, 225
peacebuilding processes: communal level (narrative of solidarity) 3, 144, 177, 190, 193, **193**, 198, 201, 203; individual level (narrative of healing) 23, 42, 168, 170n17, 193, **193**, 197, 201, 204; macro-structural level (narrative of revolt) 25, 26, 42, 186, 190, 193, **193**, 204, 207
pemekaran 79, 95
Pepera 81n15, 81n16; *see also* Act of Free Choice
PGGP (Persekutuan Gereja-Gereja di Papua) 75, 112, 114
PIF (Pacific Island Forum) 191
PNG (Papua New Guinea) 4, 57–8, 63–5, 95, 98–9, 141, 145–8, 153, 158, 162, 164, 165, 165n4, 170n7, 170n14, 170n16, 171n18–171n19, 171n29
political prisoners 57, 64, 77, 81n11, 84n52, 122, 156–7

politics of torture: logic of torture 4, 17, 125, 134, 214
Poso 198, 223
Poster, Mark 25
Postlewait, Thomas 134
power 4, 8–10, 12–14, 16–17, 22–32, 34–5, 37, 42, 43, 43n5–43n7, 49–56, 59, 61, 65–9, 71–3, 75–6, 80n3, 80n5, 90–1, 94, 96–7, 102, 105, 107, 109, 111, 115–16, 118–20, 122, 123–5, 129n38, 135, 138–9, 146–8, 152–4, 157, 160, 164–5, 167–8, 170n17, 173n40–173n41, 177, 180–7, 189–90, 198, 204, 207, 215–19, 222, 224; asymmetric power relations 10, 123–4, 160, 168, 177, 181, 183, 186, 207, 215, 118; bio-politics 28; bio-power 28–9; to exercise power 27; power relations 10, 11, 17, 22–9, 31, 34–5, 43n6, 48, 54–5, 67, 80n3, 94, 123–4, 129n38, 135, 148, 160, 168, 177, 181, 183, 185–6, 198, 204, 207, 215, 217–18, 222; ubiquity of power 27
power of gaze: footage of torture 14, 90; gazing at the spectacle 121; logic of spectacularity 31, 123, 125, 134; politics of looking 44n7; spectorial gaze 93
prison 4, 14, 25, 28, 33, 60, 63–5, 79, 90, 97, 110–11, 125n1, 218–19, 224; secret prison 218
prisoner 14, 57, 64, 77, 81n11, 84n52, 110, 122, 156–7, 218
PTSD (Post-Traumatic Stress Disorder) 143, 146–7; contrition 147; disconnection 147, 149, 152; hyperarousal 146, 197; intrusion 146–7, 193
public official: definition 5, 6, 9, 11, 14, 92, 110, 117, 127n17, 128n27, 157–8
punishment 9, 11, 18n5, 28–9, 30n3, 30, 51, 52, 61, 71, 96, 110, 125n5, 126n9, 128n27, 153, 158, 205, 206; shock on-the-spot punishment 9
Pyramid valley 60

rape 67, 101, **101**, 102–5, 105, *108*, 119, 124, 127n17–127n18, 127n20–127n21, 170n17, 215; desubjectivication 104; rape as a weapon of war 102, 127n21; sexual violence 105, 117, 127n17; total passivity 104; *see also* abject
reasons of torture: accusation of killing military personnel 9, 106; demonstration

234 *Index*

reasons of torture *continued*
2, 68, 73, **74**, 78, 83n33, 111, **112**, 112,
173n41, 179
reconciliation 3, 15–17, 68, 177, 179, 181,
188–90, 194–204, **205**, 208n11, 209n19,
209n21, 210n27, 221–2; truth
commission 129n38, 186, 196–7, 199
reformasi 1, 3, 49, 64, 67–8, 72–3, 106,
115, **115**, 116, 158–9, 165, 198, 204,
208n7, 220
Rejali, Darius 9, 10, 12, 20, 110–11, 116,
128n24, 132, 151, 175, 215–16, 220, 226
revolt 17, 23, 26, 31, 35–6, 40–3, 44n11,
49, 67, 121, 125, 177, 186, 192–4,
199–200, 203–4, 207, 209, 219, 221,
222, 224; rebellion 35, 141–2; renewal
23, 42, 193; social protest 35
right to justice 201
right to know 201
right to reparation 201
right to self-determination 3, 78, 81n15;
separatism 3, 157
ritual of torture: *inscribing a crime scene*
30; *producing agonising death* 30; *self-
confession of truth* 30; *self-proclamation
of guilt* 29, 30n4, 71
Roman Empire 10, 44n12
Roman philosopher 10; Aristotle 10;
Cicero 10; Seneca 10; Tertullian 10
Rome Statue 92
Round Table Conference 53
RPKAD (Resimen Para Komando
Angkatan Darat) 58
rule of law 12, 16, 55, 64, 67, 71–2, 75,
112, 119, 129n30, 194, 203, 225
Rwanda xii, 92, 102, 127n21, 133

Samsudin 64–6
Sanz, Ortiz 57, 59
Satgas Papua 70
Scarry, Elaine 110, 146, 169n4
Schabas, William 95
Scharf, Michael 209n19
Scheff, Thomas 137
Schein, Edgar 208n15
Schmitt, Carl 36, 44n12
Scott, George R. 10–12, 21, 45, 94, 133
self 26–7, 32–4, 147; care of the self 27
Semarang 2
Sentani 60, 69, 78, 82n22, *98*, 159, 172n37
Serui *98*
Shearing, Clifford D. 186, 204–5, 213
shock and awe: visibility 14, 29, 15, 60,
64, 72, 75, 90, 105, 118–19, 163

Sierra Leone 102, 133, 197
signature of terror 73; message of terror
73, 118, 120, 124, 163, 165
Skjelbæk, Inger 105
SKP Jayapura 9, 87, 89, 213
SKP Merauke 9
SKP Timika 9, 169n5, 176
slave 10, 51–3; *hongi* expedition 51; piracy
51; slavery 51, 108
Smith, Linda T.
Smyth, Marie B.
Soasiu 54
social body 13, 28, 30, 31, 54, 60–1, 72
solidarity: international solidarity 17, 23,
36–8, 40–2, 68–9, 75–6, 79–80, 83n37,
105, 121, 125, 127n14, 127n21, 144,
156–7, 163–4, 166–7, 172n32, 177, **178**,
179, 186, 192, **192**, 193, **193**, 194–5,
199–200, 202–3, 207, 207n1, 209n25,
220–4
Sontag, Susan 166
Sorong 2, 58, *98*
South Africa 116, 194, 196, 213
sovereignty 3, 28, 29, 49–50, 53, 59, 72–3,
76, 79, 80n5, 214, 218–19
Special Autonomy Law for Papua 115; *see
also Otsus*
spectators: act of witnessing 161;
definition 5, 6, 9, 14, 29, 117, 127n17,
128n27, 157, 158
Spierenburg, Petrus C. 11, 21
Sri Lanka 87, 188
Stasch, Rupert 126n14
state of exception 75, 224–5
state violence 3, 103, 166, 182, 187–8,
208n11
states of denial: *implicatory denial* 152;
interpretive denial 152; *literal denial*
152, 161
Staub, Ervin 201, 213
Stephan, Maria 177, 187
stereotyping: racial stereotyping 99, 100,
114–15, 126n13, 158
storytelling 139, 144, 186, 196, 203–6,
209n19
Stover, Eric 146, 174, 176
Subianto, Prabowo 67
Suharto 4, 49, 54, 56–7, 60, 67,
81n8–81n11, 82n29, 115–16
Suharto's New Order 49, 67, 81n10,
82n29, 115
Sukarno 3, 4, 49, 52–7, 80n5, 81n7,
115–16
Sukarnoputri, Megawati 69, 72–3

Index 235

Sultan of Tidore 51
Surabaya 63–4
Suripatty, Steven 68, 83n33
surveillance 7, 56, 66, 72, 79, 81n10,
    84n47, 109, 119–20, 134, 185
survivor: agency 17, 24, 26–7, 36, 40, 42,
    50, 56, 66–7, 69, 77, 91, 104–5, 122,
    134, 147–9, 168, 170n8, 170n17, 180–1,
    185, 193, 200, 203–4, 208n7, 218–19,
    221; based on class, geography, gender
    101; definition 9, 17, 24, 35, 55, 58,
    60–1, 70, 82n23, 91, 94, **94**, 95, **95**, 96,
    96, *97–8*, **98**, 98, 100–7, 109–10, 116,
    118, 121, 123–5, 125n2, 127n19,
    128n23, 128n26, 134–6, **137**, 137, 138,
    139, 142–7, 149, 154, 156–7, 159–66,
    168–9, 169n2, 169n4, 170n8,
    170n12–170n13, 170n17, 171n20,
    172n32, 172n34–172n35, 177, 189, 190,
    198–204, 206, 214, 217, 219–23;
    secondary victim 17, 136, **137**, 138,
    147, 149, 161, 164, 168, 219;
    subjectivity 17, 24–5, 31, 36, 39–41,
    44n10, 75–6, 104, 155, 202, 218;
    warrior 17, 136, **137**, 138–9, 141–2,
    146–7, 149, 159, 161, 164, 168, 170n7,
    177, 219
Sykes, Gresham M. 172n31
Szalay, Alexandra 68, 83n36, 89, 129n31,
    133

Tabu, Martin 64
Tadić judgment 117
Tanah Papua 169n6; *see also* Papua
Tanggerang 63
Taylor, Diana 43n7, 93
Tebay, Neles 15, 77, 179n8, 182–4, 207n1
technology of war: war strategy 60, 61, 68,
    70, 95, 99
Tembagapura 52
Ternate 51, 78–9
territorial commander of the army:
    Kodam 54–5, 58, 63, 80n5, 81n16, 141,
    150; TNI 1, 2, 5, 16, 54, 55, 57, 58, 63,
    74, 80n5, 99, 107, **107**, 109–11,
    114–16, 118–20, 122, 123–4, 149,
    153–5, 157–8, 163, 167, 198, 215;
    Koramil, Kodim 58, 73, 106, 120, 142;
    militarisation of Papua 155, 161,
    181–2, 204, 216, 224
territorial integrity 63, 76, 79, 120, 134
theatre of peace building 4, 17, 177, 184,
    192–3, 195, 200, 202, 207, 221–3, 225
theatre of torture 4, 17, 134–5, 136, **137**,

137, 13–19, 146, 161, 165, 168–9,
    169n1, 177, 179, 186, 193, **193**, 200,
    204, 207, 217, 220–4; display of
    sovereign power 75, 91; illegality and
    immorality 90, 122, 124–5, 163–4, 224;
    policy of terror 13, 29–31, 44n7, 168,
    215; public display 11, 13–14, 72, 75,
    81n9, 90–1, 109, 118–19, 216; public
    display of expiring body 11; theatricality
    134, 139, 165, 169n1, 174–5; visibility
    14, 29, 64, 72, 90, 119, 163
theatrum mundi 38, 169n1
theatrum philosophicum 169n1
Third Papuan Congress 114
Thompson, Kevin 26
Tidore 51, 53–4, 79
Tigi 1
Timika 9, 87, 132, 140, 169n5, 176, 191
Timmer, Jaap 18n1, 21, 73, 82n32, 89
Timor Leste ii, 3, 21, 64, 88, 102, 105,
    109, 119, 129n38, 130n43, 131, 133,
    159, 167, 173n40, 174, 188, 196, 197–9,
    201–2, 211–13, 225
Tjondronegoro, Sujarwo 57
torture 10, 14, 26–9, 32, 39, 43n2, 43n4,
    54, 56, 60, 63, 66, 71, 72–3, 79, 81n12,
    90–2, 95, 102, 107, 116, 120, 147, 152,
    158, 182, 185, 191, 208n6; definition
    9–14; elements of torture
    (instrumentality 10; intensity 4, 9, 110,
    161, 168, 217; intentionality 1, 10, 168);
    penyiksaan 6, 131, 212; physical torture
    107, 109; symbolic torture 3, 30, 31, 43,
    218
torture and democracy: Civil Discipline
    model 12; Juridical model 12; National
    Security model 12, 110, 216; ticking
    bomb argument 13
torture as a civic marker 215
Torture Dataset 3–5, 7–8, 13, 17, 94, 99,
    105–6, 109–11, 114, 117, 125, 126n9,
    130n39, 135, 150, 162, 168, 216
torture phenomenon 9, 13; torture practice
    9, 117–18, 124, 135, 151
torture ritual 13–14, 29, 90, 120
torturers: perpetrators 2–6, 9, 17, 73–4, 92,
    117, 125n4, 127n21, 129n38, 130n43,
    135, 137–9, 150, 155, 160–5, 167–9,
    177, 189, 190, 194, 198, 199, 201, 202,
    204–6, 214, 217, 219–23
TPN (*Tentara Pembebasan Nasional*) 1,
    82, 82n31, 111
TPNG (Territory of Papua New Guinea)
    57–8, 81n12–81n13

236 *Index*

TRCP (Truth and Reconciliation Commission for Papua) 17, 177, 189, 190, 192–5, 197–207, 221–3
Treaty of London 50
triangulation method 7
Trikora 3, 55, 80n5, 81n6
Triton Bay 50, 52
types of violence: battle deaths in state-based internal armed conflicts 187; interpersonal violence 103, 187; state violence 3, 103, 166, 182, 187–8, 208n11; terrorist attacks 12, 187, 224

Ujung Pandang 63
ULMWP (United Liberation Movement for West Papua) 78–80, 191, 202, 220, 223
UN Human Rights Council 76, 122
UN Special Rapporteur 76, 109, 110, 128n27
UNHCR (United Nations High Commission for Refugees) 65, 170n14
United Kingdom 7
United Nations 2, 14, 54, 59, 65, 80n4, 121, 130n42, 208n4
United States of America 7, 13, 20, 81n7, 83n34, 212, 224, 226
UNTEA (United Nations Temporary Executive Administration) 54
UP4B (Unit Percepatan Pembangunan Papua dan Papua Barat) 77, 185
US Congress 76

van Boven, Theo 201, 213
van den Broek, Theo 23, 41, 45n18, 46,

68, 83n36, 86, 89, 129n31, 133, 178, 179n5, 179n6, 179n8, 180, 207n1, 213
Vanimo 58
victims of torture 6, 102, 163–4
Vlasblom, Dirk 8, 9, 55
VSI (Violent Society Index) 186–7

Wahid, Abdurahman 68–9, 72–3
Wallace, Alfred R. 50
Wamena viii, 2, 58, 60, 61, **62**, 68, 70, 72–5, 78, 82n21–82n22, 87, 89, 119, 126, 156
Wanggai, Herman 76
Wasior 70, 72, 75, 83n38, 85, 86–7, 119, 131–2, 156
Weber, Max 169n2
Wenda, Matias 58, 60–1
West Papua xii–iii, 2, 18n1–18n2, 19, 20–1, 54, 73, 78, 83n33, 85–9, *97*, *98*, 130n42, 131, 169n6, 170n16, 174–5, 180, 212–13, 226; *see also* Papua
Widjojo, Muridan 77
Widodo, Joko 77, 173n41
Wiesel, Elie 24
Windsor, George 50
Wondama 70, 98
World War II 11, 51–2, 61

Yapen-Waropen 98
Yogi, Tadeus 1
Yogyakarta 53–4, 78, 80n5, 212
Yudhoyono, Susilo B. 24

Zocca, Franco 66, 89